Paul Robeson's Voices

Paul Robeson's Voices

GRANT OLWAGE

Oxford University Press is a department of the University of Oxford. It furthers
the University's objective of excellence in research, scholarship, and education
by publishing worldwide. Oxford is a registered trade mark of Oxford University
Press in the UK and certain other countries.

Published in the United States of America by Oxford University Press
198 Madison Avenue, New York, NY 10016, United States of America.

© Oxford University Press 2024

All rights reserved. No part of this publication may be reproduced, stored in
a retrieval system, or transmitted, in any form or by any means, without the
prior permission in writing of Oxford University Press, or as expressly permitted
by law, by license, or under terms agreed with the appropriate reproduction
rights organization. Inquiries concerning reproduction outside the scope of the
above should be sent to the Rights Department, Oxford University Press, at the
address above.

You must not circulate this work in any other form
and you must impose this same condition on any acquirer.

Library of Congress Control Number: 2023944946

ISBN 978–0–19–763748–7 (pbk.)
ISBN 978–0–19–763747–0 (hbk.)

DOI: 10.1093/oso/9780197637470.001.0001

Contents

Acknowledgments	vii
About the Companion Website	xi
Introduction: Voice-Thinking	1
1. Becoming Paul Robeson's Voice	18
2. "Negro Spiritual": Voicing Desire	54
3. Natural Acts, or To Sing Simply	95
4. A Voice for the People	132
5. Voices Politic	179
6. A Microphone Voice	209
Afterword: In-between and Against: A Voice for the Times	261
Notes	267
Works Cited	337
Index	353

Acknowledgments

I first encountered Paul Robeson's name through other peoples' ears; or rather in the textual remembrances of their hearing of his voice. Specifically, Robeson made not infrequent appearances in the writings of Black South Africans from the 1930s on. His name pops up often enough in the pages of the *Bantu World*, a Black daily published in Johannesburg. News of Robeson's planned visit to the country—which did not materialize—was reported with feverish excitement: it "undoubtedly thrilled the whole of Bantudom."[1] As with most listeners, it was Robeson's voice that entranced. The South African author Peter Abrahams, recalling his visits to the Bantu Men's Social Centre in downtown Johannesburg in the 1930s, heard Robeson's "deep voice touched with the velvet quality of organ notes" as it resounded through the Centre's hallways from a gramophone record.

> That was a black man, one of us! I knew it. I needed no proof. The men about me, their faces, their bearing, carried all the proof. That was a black man! The voice of a black man!
>
> The glorious voice stopped. . . . The moment that had given us a common identity was over. Robeson the man had called him. A name to remember, that.[2]

It was a name that I remembered. At the time I was working on the early history of Black choral singing in South Africa, and in search of the vocal progenitors of that tradition I found my way to the Sound Archive of the British Library listening to gramophone records—brittle shellac 78s—that Robeson had recorded for His Master's Voice, and to which Abrahams and other members of the Bantu Men's Social Centre had listened. That period of sustained close listening was made possible by an Edison Fellowship at the British Library, and by the interest in my project of Timothy Day, then curator of classical music at the Sound Archive, and his successor Jonathan Summers. I also spent some time at the EMI Archive Trust, in Hayes, London, where Robeson recorded at HMV's facilities, with orchestra in Hayes's A Studio and with piano accompaniment in the B Studio. There my

viii ACKNOWLEDGMENTS

requests for arcane information—recording log books, contracts, and the like—were met with interest but also suspicion; and some were denied. (In general, commercial music companies were not receptive to my requests for information about Robeson's recording activities; most likely because of the unequal terms of engagement.)

Listening to gramophone records from the early years of electrical sound recording for many hours a day for several months was both challenging and rewarding. The obsolete sound technology of 78s revealed unfamiliar vocal styles and sounds, many foreign to twenty-first-century sensibilities. I was introduced to another Robeson, to the singer's early voice, which is much less heard than his later work reissued on countless digitally remastered compilations. And I also encountered the extent of his repertory; he sang far more than "Ol' Man River" and spirituals. EMI's seven-CD box set of Robeson's recording work for HMV in the 1920s and 1930s contains no fewer than 170 tracks. But for all this wealth of sonic material, too little has been written about Robeson the vocal artist. *Paul Robeson's Voices* is thus timely, and more so because it celebrates the 125th anniversary of the singer's birth in 2023. The book is a tribute, foremost, to Paul Robeson, a paean to his art of song, a hymn to a life in song. It acknowledges more than that which is well known about the man—the humanist, activist, and radical thinker—for it celebrates also Robeson the scholar-singer: the comparative musicologist and student of world song cultures and languages. It honors his aesthetic experimentations and technological innovations.

I also want to pay tribute to someone else: to Joellen ElBashir, the long-serving curator (until 2021 when she retired) of the Moorland-Spingarn Research Center (MSRC) at Howard University, Washington, DC, and preparer-in-chief of the 387-page finding aid to Robeson's papers. Joellen's intimate knowledge of the material helped me navigate the intimidating expanse of its terrain. Without her preparatory archival work, generous help, and geniality, my work at MSRC, which began in 2012, would have been much more complicated and far less pleasurable. I am indebted to you, Joellen.

The many research visits I made to the United States, between 2011 and 2018, were made possible by the financial support of the National Research Foundation of South Africa. Work at the MSRC was complemented by visits to the other major repository of material on Robeson, the Schomburg Center for Research in Black Culture; and other research libraries of the New York Public Library system house additional material. The staff at the Schomburg were, by turns, officious, indifferent, or pleasant but not especially knowl-edgeable about the collection, common enough traits of monolithic institutions. There are many other archivists, librarians, amateur collectors, and enthusiasts on varied subjects who facilitated my research, answered questions, and supplied me with material, and to whom I am grateful. Of particular help was Rob Hudson, the manager of archives at Carnegie Hall. Among others, I thank the Carnegie Hall Rose Archives and Carl Van Vechten Trust for permission to reprint images that appear in the book. It was a lengthy—yearlong—process to secure permission for the archival ma-terial that appears in the book. Susan Robeson, Paul's granddaughter and trustee of the Robeson estate, read through the manuscript in some detail, and I acknowledge her generosity, interest in the book, and commitment to Robeson's legacy. By and large, my use of much of the source material was approved. But I was not permitted to draw on material from diaries, family correspondence, and some of Robeson's unpublished writings, nor to reprint unpublished photographs, and the book is perhaps a little less interesting, rich, and complex for that embargo.

The book's appearance at Oxford University Press was due to editor-in-chief Suzanne Ryan's initial interest in Robeson. Executive Editor Norm Hirschy shepherded the manuscript through the review process, and Project Editors Sean Decker and Madison Zickgraf who managed the book's produc-tion were always on call to answer my (hopefully not too) many and diverse questions. I am indebted to this quartet, and others involved in the produc-tion of the book, for making it a happy enough enterprise; as well as to the Faculty of Humanities, University of the Witwatersrand, for a book grant that covered miscellaneous expenses.

It would be remiss if I did not thank the book's trio of reviewers for their generous engagement with the draft manuscript. Their astute insights and suggestions (most of which I took on board) improved the work tre-mendously. Intellectual debts are of course legion, and extend to other scholars' work and to the interlocutors of my other writings and conference presentations on the singer. Sections of the book have previously appeared in other guises, and I thank the publishers for permission to reuse that writing here: "Paul Robeson's Microphone Voice and the Technologies of Easy Singing," *Technology and Culture* 59, no. 4 (2018): 823–849 (Johns Hopkins University Press); " 'Warbling Wood-Notes Wild': Nature, Art, and Race in Paul Robeson's Early Singing," *Musical Quarterly* 98, no. 3 (2015): 262–302 (Oxford University Press); "Listening B(l)ack: Paul Robeson after Roland

X ACKNOWLEDGMENTS

Hayes," *Journal of Musicology* 32, no. 4 (2015): 524–557 (University of California Press); "'The World Is His Song': Paul Robeson's 1958 Carnegie Hall Concerts and the Cosmopolitan Imagination," *Journal of the Society for American Music* 7, no. 2 (2013): 165–195 (Cambridge University Press).

For the early stages of my research the Robeson Estate was under the firm hand of Paul Robeson Jr., who, as Joellen ElBashir told it, used to pop into the MSRC to check up on and borrow items from the collection. His visits never coincided with mine, and I did not have the opportunity to meet him. The *Washington Post*'s obituary for Robeson Jr. observed that he "devoted much of his life to protecting and preserving his father's legacy and keeping alive his voice—both as a singer and as an activist."[3] I'd like to think that *Paul Robeson's Voices* was written in the same spirit. And that it does more. While it encourages the reader to think about a particular voice, and the vocal identities that sound forth from that voice, it challenges us to listen to voices in their complexity, to question what we hear when we listen to a voice, to interrogate what and how a voice means.

About the Companion Website

http://www.oup.com/us/PaulRobesonsVoices

This book features a companion website that provides material that cannot be made available in the book. This includes color images of the spectrum graphs, and short excerpts of sound recordings. The reader is encouraged to consult this resource in conjunction with the book. Examples available online are indicated in the text with Oxford's symbol ⏵.

Introduction

Voice-Thinking

Once he did not exist.
But his voice was there, waiting.

Light parted from darkness,
day from night,
earth from the primal waters.

And the voice of Paul Robeson
was divided from the silence.[1]

Thus begins Chilean poet Pablo Neruda's "Ode to Paul Robeson." It is a reworking of the creation myth, writing Robeson's voice into the genesis story. As "the voice of man," as Neruda christens Robeson's voice, it prefigures the singer's own—and humanity's—existence. The power of Robeson's voice would make it the subject of many literary endeavors. In these, as in Neruda's "Ode," the voice is superabundant, functioning as a surplus; it is more than its mere soundings, "bigger" than the man. Pulitzer Prize–winning African American poet Gwendolyn Brooks's own ode to the singer makes this clear:

That time
we all heard it,
cool and clear,
cutting across the hot grit of the day.
The major Voice.
The adult Voice

. . .

Warning, in music-words
devout and large,
that we are each other's

Paul Robeson's Voices. Grant Olwage, Oxford University Press. © Oxford University Press 2024.
DOI: 10.1093/oso/9780197637470.003.0001

2 INTRODUCTION

> harvest:
> we are each other's
> business:
> we are each other's
> magnitude and bond.[2]

Here, as elsewhere, the voice indexes what Robeson as political subject came to stand for in the global ideoscape: it is humankind's conscience—and its rebuke. Trinidadian writer C. L. R. James provides a more concrete instance of this, recalled in his collaboration with Robeson when the young star played the protagonist in James's play *Toussaint L'Ouverture*, on the Haitian revolutionary leader, in London in 1936. During a rehearsal, remembered James, "Paul was reading his part in the scene and suddenly his voice opened up and the transition from his usual quiet undertone to the tremendous roar of which he was capable was something to hear. . . . When he was reading 'Those lightnings announce the thunder. A courageous chief only is wanted,' he stopped. I and everyone looked to him to go on. He turned to me. 'James,' he said, 'I don't want to go any further. I think it should stop here.' It was the first and last time that he made any changes in the script."[3] For all involved, the thunder of Robeson's voice sufficed, substituting for the words omitted from James's script, and symbolizing the "hero who shall have re-established the rights of the human race." At this point in the singer's career and life, in the mid-1930s, Robeson had only just begun to emerge as a political activist. His voice assumed a subject position its bearer had yet to fully enact. It was prophetic.

The poetic musings on Robeson's (political) voice endow it with agency, energy, and an excess of meaning. They invite us to think of the voice as a life force; indeed, as a social force. But this status accorded the voice, lest we forget, is a result of the voice's material soundings. Put another way, the largesse of Robeson's voice—Brooks's "major Voice"—which rendered his voice a subject fit for eulogizing, is possible because of the "largeness" of his voice—"the big Voice," one biographer called it—which impressed its sonic presence on listeners.[4] In Robeson's appearances on the public stage, in theater, film, and concert, his sonic voice thus always took center stage. *Pace* Neruda's gambit, which announces a primordial voice—always "there, waiting"—Robeson's singing voice did not always exist. It has a history, borne of family, culture, the professions of performance, and institutions of concert singing, habits of listening to, and practices of writing about, the voice.

INTRODUCTION   3

Paul Robeson's Voices thus traces the formation of Robeson's voice as sound, listening to the forms in which it sings forth, and interrogates the discursive formulations by which the voice is represented.

Paul Robeson's Voices reflects on Robeson's sounding voice. It is interested in Robeson's voice as it exists in two broad, and intersecting, domains: as sound object and sounding gesture, specifically how it was fashioned in the contexts of singing practices, in recital, concert, and recorded performance; and as subject of identification, that is, how the voice envoices modes of subjectivity, of being. As such, the book is a study of Robeson's "vocality," which Katherine Meizel describes "as a site where the making of sounds and making of identity intersect."[5] Her recent work on multivocality affirms this—"Vocalities are sonic subjectivities" (215)—but introduces the idea that singing subjects may perform plurally, articulating "multiple vocal subjectivities."[6] In my own exploration of Robeson's sonic subjectivities, I pursue the latter term in the equation in terms of, and to put it more strongly yet, *on the terms of*, the former; that is, I uphold matters of the aesthetic such that not only do they constitute the focus of the book but, as I argue, it is through the aesthetic that the subject and its politics are formed. Put simply, Robeson shaped his sense of self and politics through song. And so I turn to his singing above all.

Because of the centrality of the voice to Robeson's sense of self and its importance in his life and professional artistic practice, it is surprising that no book-length account of his singing exists despite the burgeoning of scholarship on Robeson that proceeds apace: there are several monographs on his stage and film work, many more on his "philosophy" and politics, and yet still more biographical studies; there is even a *Paul Robeson for Beginners.*[7] The reasons for this are several, and turn on the relationship of music and the political, as well as disciplinary practices and prejudices against many of the types of music Robeson sang.

At the centennial celebrations of the singer's birth in 1998, Henry Foner itemized Robeson's "incredible record of accomplishments." Surprisingly, most of those Foner lists have nothing to do with music.[8] Similarly, Robeson's plaque (see Figure I.1) on the little-known, and neglected, Harlem Walk of Fame, on 135th Street just off Frederick Douglass Boulevard in uptown Manhattan, identifies him by inscription as activist, humanitarian, actor, and scholar athlete, but not as a singer, although Robeson-the-singer is gestured at in pictorial form. (Similarly, Robeson's star on the Hollywood Walk of Fame, installed in 1979, is marked by its absence of the symbol of

Figure I.1. The Robeson plaque on the Harlem Walk of Fame, New York City. Photograph by author.

the phonograph record, representing excellence in sound recording and music; the star acknowledges only his contribution to the motion picture industry.)[9]

In this narrative, Robeson-the-singer is not given undue importance. It recalls the Cinderella status that music has sometimes held, within both the hierarchy of the arts and cultural life at large, and which has long been laid bare by philosophers and historians of music. Robeson himself contributed to this narrative on several occasions, although we should be mindful of the singer's often shifting positions and ambiguous utterances. Toward the end of the 1940s, Robeson announced that he would cease concert singing in order to focus on what, at the time, he considered to be his more important political work: as an advocate of civil rights, critic of imperialism and global capital, and activist for the causes of international labor, among others. Writing to the singer about this "change in vocation," the dean of the Graduate School of Religion at the University of California, Los Angeles, pointed out, however, that the premise for Robeson's decision was a fallacy. He argued that Robeson's singing perforce entailed activism:

INTRODUCTION 5

Your art was powerful as well as magnificent. You seemed to be singing for a great cause. . . . I fell to wondering if your concert work is so far removed from your deep sense of obligation to foster better race relations. Personally I do not see how you could be accomplishing more for your purpose.[10]

The yoking of Robeson's song and politics in the late 1940s was nothing new, nor was his reluctance to sing. A decade earlier, the *Yorkshire Observer* gave its readers "behind-the-scenes" insight into the "political difficulties" experienced by concert promoter Harold Holt, who represented Robeson in Britain, in getting the world's great singers to appear for a prewar British public. While Mussolini pressured the tenor Beniamino Gigli to abandon his London concerts, Holt was faced with the unenviable task of "persuading Paul Robeson, who has given up bourgeois concerts, to leave the Left Wing for a time to become a touring international celebrity again."[11] Holt succeeded, at least for a time.

This politicizing of the subject, through Robeson's own concert practice and extra-musical acts, his popular reception, and posthumous scholarship, has had implications for considering his voice as a subject of inquiry. In 1945 the Fort Wayne *News-Sentinel* reviewed a Robeson concert in the Midwest city under the title "Robeson, the Red," excoriating the singer for his "bad taste" in "attempting political propaganda from the concert stage": "it is extremely unfortunate that a man with so noble a voice should use it to the detriment of his own people, and to the detriment of America, in such a political harangue."[12] Although the Fort Wayne newspaper was slightly early in the vehemence of its critique, only two years later local judicial action often interdicted the singer from making his concerts political events, and by the final year of the decade concert organizers and local authorities were routinely intimidated by state security agencies to cancel performances and deny their venues to the singer. Pete Seeger encapsulated what has often been said of the extent of Robeson's persecution: "You are the most blacklisted performer in the history of America."[13] On the one hand, then, we have Robeson's own sometimes ambivalent stance on concertizing, and on the other hand the state's and broader public's antagonism toward his politicized (singing) voice. Both scenarios, perhaps, have had consequences for writing about the singer's voice.[14]

The story of Robeson's fall from celebrated global star and American hero in the 1930s and early 1940s is well known: the artist cum activist was persecuted for his socialist (his accusers would say communist), civil rights,

6 INTRODUCTION

and anticolonial politics, and denounced by the US state and by the public at large as "un-American" during the McCarthy era. Only with the end of the Cold War, suggested one commentator, could Robeson's name be uttered in the United States without a "sting."[15] A complex exercise in Robeson's redemption, of which the centennial celebrations were the first culmination, was initiated following the Cold War's end, and had implications for how Robeson was presented anew. Kate Baldwin argues that as a consequence of the restorative acts of the 1990s, "Robeson the artist becomes detached from Robeson the activist in the creation of a new *American* 'genius.'"[16] But Baldwin overstates the case; indeed, of late the pendulum has swung decisively in the opposite direction.

The two collections of scholarly essays that memorialized Robeson on the centenary of his birth in 1998 display a judicious selection of writings that traverse the biographical, political (on topics of citizenship, labor, and race, for instance), and artistic (the visual arts, film, theater, and music). More than this, the essays on his art more often than not read his artistic practice in terms of the political. Contrary to Baldwin's assertion, what has become an a priori attachment of Robeson's singing to his politics has the effect, one might argue, of limiting our understanding of his singing and voice. If we perforce hear Robeson's singing as always political, what do we not hear, and what do we neglect to listen for? For one, we limit the discussion to a small set of repertoire, that which articulates not only Robeson's politics more explicitly but our politics of scholarly production too. The spirituals, the *Show Boat* tune "Ol' Man River" (in Robeson's famous revisions to the lyrics, which "made the song the central etude within his program for social justice"),[17] and the populist cantata *Ballad for Americans* have received considerable attention, whereas only passing reference is made to, among others, Western (as well as East European) art song and "bad music," to use Simon Frith's term for the many popular sentimental, dialect, and film songs Robeson sang.[18] A hermeneutics of singing-as-politicking, as in the popular music studies tradition of lyrical analysis, also tends to privilege a discussion of lyrical content over vocal practice and sound: to read the verbocentric rather than listen to the vococentric, to borrow Michel Chion's terminology.[19]

To claim that Robeson scholarship has only focused on his songs' verbal texts would however be to caricature it, because the power of Robeson's voice seems to compel us to engage with it even if briefly, casually, or decontextualized (from the several performance, if not political, contexts in which he sang). Hazel Carby's otherwise compelling account of Robeson's early art, in the 1920s, is less convincing when she turns to song because she is silent about aspects of the art world in which Robeson sang. She concludes that the "formal qualities of control and discipline over voice and body gain political resonance precisely because Robeson is presented as a controlled and disciplined Negro."[20] Perhaps. But without acknowledging the form of the art song recital, within which Robeson presented spirituals in concert at the time, or the classical voice training, for which an aesthetics of vocal control and interpretive discipline is paramount, and to which Robeson subjected himself in the second half of the 1920s, Carby's argument loses its force. The imperative to politicize Robeson's voice, I suggest, has not always been at the service of our understanding of the singer's vocal art itself. It is for this reason that my own accounts of Robeson's voice proceed from the traditions of singing, the practices of the song recital, and mediation of sound technologies, all of which combined to shape Robeson's voice, as much as the more fashionable narratives of race, nation, and others.

These contexts of performance culture are uppermost on the agenda of performance musicology. That they have not been so for Robeson scholarship is an effect of disciplinary conditions. Tellingly, the revival in Robeson scholarship has not, for the most (and not at first), been populated by music scholars. Coinciding with the cultural turn, the Robeson revival resulted in several interpretively rich writings on his art, foremost of which are Carby's work in *Race Men* and film scholar Richard Dyer's 1986 essay in *Heavenly Bodies*, probably the first critical writing on Robeson under the impress of the cultural studies movement.[21] This early work, like the varied forms of Robeson's practice, was thoroughly interdisciplinary, endeavoring to give account of the gamut of Robeson's art, and inevitably entailed interpretative forays into Robeson's singing too. But a musicological reading reveals its shortcomings when dealing with musical texts, practices, and sounds. More recent work, by contrast, has been less expansive, more disciplinarily bound, focusing on film, or theater, or a single musical work.[22] Why musicologists in particular have not been that interested in Robeson is a more complex story and involves the discipline's own history and preoccupations, and its difficulty in placing Robeson's music-making.

The recent history of the discipline of musicology has been often rehearsed. In *Music as Performance*, Nicholas Cook attributes musicology's failure, until quite recently, "to engage fully with music as performance to habits of thought that are deeply entrenched in the discipline." On the one hand, the study of music has been "skewed" by its "orientation towards music

8   INTRODUCTION

as writing," such that histories of music are those of composition. The consequence of this for thinking about performance, on the other hand, is that "the
idea of music as sounded writing" privileges a "paradigm of reproduction,"
whereby performance is seen as reproducing the work. Fred Moten calls out
"the discourse of classical musicology" for its "denigration of performance."[23]
And then of course the type of music that musicology has traditionally been
interested in is Western art music.[24] As a subject of musicological inquiry,
Robeson's musical art did not measure up: he was an interpretive performer
of often non-canonical texts; even the art music he included in his recitals for
an extended period was from musicology's peripheries: English and Russian
art song. It is little surprise then that the first scholars to engage critically with
Robeson's singing came from outside musicology. Nor is it surprising that
musicologists have become interested in Robeson only recently. Matthew
D. Morrison has called attention to "practices of exclusion embedded in
musicology—especially in relation to race, racialized people, and race relations."[25] The discipline has opened up, both methodologically—and so Cook
speaks of the "explosion of research in musical performance" nowadays[26]—
and topically: the subjects of race and gender that animated Dyer and Carby
in the 1980s and 1990s are more central to musicological practice in the new
millennium.[27] Morrison's "race-based epistemology" termed Blacksound,
which places "race—its construction, performance, and material relations—
at the center of musicological analysis," is one of the more recent theoretical
interventions in the field.[28]

There is also a more specific reason for the passing over of Robeson as a
musicological subject. Robeson's own occasional, and again ambivalent,
statements against high art, an implicit critique also of the racialized class
power structures within which classical music operated, positioned his
singing equivocally. In early 1934 the provincial British press reported extensively on one of the singer's many provocative announcements: "the great
Negro singer has decided that classical music shall play no further part in his
programmes," reported the *Cambridge Daily News*. "This is a permanent departure."[29] In fact, there was no such departure from art music per se, then or
thereafter; and what Robeson referred to was specifically the repertoire of the
Austro-German *Lieder* tradition, which he had assayed in the early 1930s to
lukewarm reception. What did increasingly occupy the singer's interest and
drive his song choice from then on was an aesthetics of the folk, such that
he would, by the end of the decade, gain the moniker "people's artist." The
implications of this for the repertoire he sang, and the audiences he wished

INTRODUCTION   9

to court, was that labor songs, protest music, and folk song formed the mainstay of his repertory. In other words, Robeson sang the musics of not one but of many "low-others," to use Richard Middleton's phrase. Indeed, a typical Robeson recital program from the mid-1930s presents different song types "within a structure of family resemblance" voicing for his listeners "an interchangeable cast of others."[30] Middleton has outlined how "popular music," in its broadest conceptualization the music of vernacular traditions, has functioned as musicology's other, goadingly suggesting that "popular music only exists when it knows its place."[31] But Robeson's vernacular musics are not so easily placed.

For a complex of reasons related to patronage, institutions (of broadcasting, recording, and the concert business, among others), recital practice, and his vocal history, Robeson endeavored to steer what he called "a middle course" rather than sing only for assorted low-others: "I am appealing not to the highbrow and not to the lowbrow, but I am singing for all."[32] A review of a concert Robeson gave in the Scottish town of Perth in 1934 noted thus that both the "most humble listener and what has now become known as the 'high-brow' must have left the hall at the conclusion of the concert feeling that a profitable evening had been spent."[33] Robeson's singing was decidedly "middlebrow," that loose category for the placement of cultural practices, commodities, and sensibilities that constituted the mainstay of interwar Western societies. Midcentury middlebrow culture is, however, as Kate Guthrie notes, not something that people care about now, and has proved "particularly problematic for musicologists" because its "very existence challenges established notions of 'art.' "[34] All the better to focus on Robeson's politics than get too close to his art. Middlebrow culture also challenges racial, ethnic, and class notions of folk authenticity; hence, as Michael Denning has documented for Robeson's performance of *Ballad for Americans* in the early 1940s, a generation of postwar critics charged Robeson's singing for being easy-listening, sentimental, and middle-class.[35] The aesthetic sting of middlebrow-ness, as much as the political taint of the Cold War, made Robeson an unfashionable musicological subject. Indeed, the bourgeois populism of Robeson's singing had already challenged critics of his time. One reviewer, who took the nom de plume Counterpoint, complained that it was "awfully difficult to reconcile serious musical criticism with such an admixture" of music as presented in a Robeson concert.[36]

Recent scholarship, including the quickening of musicological interest in Robeson, seems to have answered the question of where to place

10   INTRODUCTION

his voice: where art intersects with the political, enacted through the voice and song. Shana L. Redmond's *Everything Man* is the most recent contribution. It places Robeson's voice—or Voice in Redmond's typography and typology—front and center, and its intent is clearly announced: "Robeson's continued vibration within global political imaginaries is the impetus and guide for the adventure undertaken."[37] *Paul Robeson's Voices* shifts the focus. I too am captivated by and captive to Robeson's voice, but I am attentive first and foremost to the acoustic vibrations of his voice. I am less concerned with the metaphorical cachet of the voice, or with the re-soundings of the afterlife of Robeson's voice. I do not suggest that we detach Robeson's art from (his) politics, that we engage in a scholarship of disengagement. To do so would seem perverse for a life so richly political considered in a moment—now—in which the idea of the musical as always already political holds sway. What I do propose, and it is the strategy that I follow in my ruminations on Robeson's voice, is that we proceed from the sounding voice and the performance contexts in which it sounds.

In this task, I am mindful that I am something of an outsider. I am set apart from Robeson by more than the usual distance—of time and culture, among others—that separates the historian from their subject. As a white, non-American, non-professional singer, I write about a famed Black American singer's vocal art, and my perspective on Robeson is of course colored by the terms of my relationship with him; and others "nearer" to him will perhaps hear his voice and interpret his songworld differently, and claim him in other ways. Robeson himself, as this book makes clear, is a complex subject who occupied many (vocal) positions. I am reminded of the Black composer-scholar George E. Lewis's cautionary tale, about the "propriety of limiting 'Americanist' musical research to the United States." He proposes rather the value of "seeing U.S. history from the *other* side," advocating that Americanist musicology might "profitably begin from a global perspective . . . one that implicitly recognizes the permanence of permeability, the transience of borders," and hybridity.[38] I hope I offer some of that perspective.

Lewis draws on the trope of the "noisy, nomadic dimension in American identity" which animates his call for a nomadic musicology to challenge restrictive tendencies towards " 'fixed paths in well-defined directions.' "[39] This recognizes the multiethnic, multilingual, globalized nature of American musics, and seems a particularly apt way to listen to Robeson's sometimes messy, mobile multivocality. Voice-thinking requires us to take stock of the

INTRODUCTION   11

complexity of Robeson's voice—as Blacksound—acknowledging the diverse grounds of the voice's production.

Chapter 1 documents the early formation of Robeson's voice, a dollop of biography amid the book's interpretive pursuits. More precisely, it is an account of the genesis and development of the singing voice in formation—of the voice's early life, if you will. This follows a conventional approach to historical biography and its sources, except that I am interested in the total life only insofar as it contributes to the story of the voice. My interest in biography is thus for the purpose of reframing the object of inquiry as the voice. I am also interested in the professional discourse and practices—marketing categories and vocal typologies—through which Robeson's voice was classified and circulated. These too were shapers of his vocal identity. And in chapter 6 I document how Robeson's use of a variety of sound technologies— some established, others emergent and experimental—further shaped the sound of his voice and his practices of singing. If we are more attentive to the domain of the sonic, we may learn more about Robeson the singer and, in some instances, also problematize how we read the political.

For example, in chapters 2 and 3 (and to some extent in chapters 4 and 5) I situate Robeson's singing in a network of voices, Black and others. Our objects of interpretation, as Middleton puts it, give up "more meaning when placed within [a] broader network of voices."[40] And so in chapter 2 I interrogate the dominant discursive formation of Robeson as Black subject in the 1920s, tackling that vexed musicological topic of authenticity and in turn reconsidering the identity politics of criticism. My discussion is rooted in sound practices: in Robeson's, but also in those of Robeson's self-acknowledged model the tenor Roland Hayes and his longtime accompanist Lawrence Brown, who also performed with Hayes for a brief time. Here I consider recital programming, singing voices, and the practices of written and performative arranging of Black folk song into and as recital music; and I do not forget how the piano and its relationship to the voice function in this process (for the piano is vital to the art song tradition, even as it remains all but unheard in Robeson scholarship). Similarly, while my intention in chapter 3 is to "dissect" Robeson's voice, to present what I call an anatomy of his singing, and I undertake this operation by close listening and computational analysis of the sonic matter of his voice, I do so in critique of another, also racialized, dominant discursive construction: Robeson as a "natural" singer. This foregrounds the aesthetic contexts in detail in which Robeson sang, and in which his voice was fashioned, enabling us to see more

12 INTRODUCTION

clearly how the subject of criticism—Paul Robeson—is politicized at the same time that the subject's voice is political. Pursuing the latter is the task of chapters 4 and 5.

Chapters 2 and 3 focus largely on Anglo-American critical discourse on Robeson; and there is much interesting work to be done, by those with the appropriate linguistic chops, on Robeson's reception in many other parts of the globe. Similarly the epistolatory evidence I draw on in chapter 4 was penned primarily from subjects of the British Commonwealth. It is the voluminous writings of Robeson's fans, an entirely untapped source, that I draw on in offering another interpretation of Robeson's political voice in chapter 4. This offers a more global, albeit English-language, perspective on Robeson's voice, and also a plebeian one. Tracing the genealogy of the singer's internationalism, I suggest that it was through the ethics and aesthetics of a musical cosmopolitanism that Robeson, celebrated as the People's Artist, performed for the people. Here I pursue my central argument more forcefully, that affordances of the aesthetic should be considered a stronger determinant of Robeson's politics, a reversal of accounts that detail how the singer's politics suffused his song practice. In this my work chimes with varied endeavors that conceptualize his voice as political. But I do so cautiously, and ask in chapter 5, through listening to the material sounds of Robeson's voice—accent, tone, and intonation—what the limits and possibilities of the voice are vis-à-vis the domain of the political? In this task, I explore different, sometimes contradictory, readings of the voice—official voices, heroic ones, protesting enunciations. Robeson's political voices operate diversely.

The chapters assume a rough chronology. The first two chapters focus on the formation of the voice and the early years of Robeson's concert career. By the end of chapter 3 the singer's mature voice makes an appearance. Chapters 4 and 5 consider the mid- and late career, and the final chapter, by and large, tackles the final decade of Robeson's public singing life. While the chapters home in on distinct interpretative topoi, this broad chronological narrative brings to the fore some of the traditional concerns of diachronic style history: influence, comparison, trajectories, development, and idiom. It gives us a view of something of the totality of Robeson's singing career, although it does so through close reading and listening to select texts, and does not pretend to be exhaustive. This schema also provides a corrective to some of the recent scholarship on Robeson, which is often focused on particular moments of Robeson's life with the perhaps unintended consequence that the vocal subject is presented already formed, uniform (even one-dimensional),

INTRODUCTION   13

and single-minded in its furtherance of political ideals. To belabor the point, if we attend to Robeson's vocal art as our starting point, we gain a more holistic view of the subject that is less certain and complete.

I am also slightly uneasy with some of hermeneutic scholarship on Robeson's thought and art for another reason. These concerns too are historiographic: as more material has become (easily) available on Robeson, so scholarly writing has relied increasingly on a limited library of secondary sources. Long before the centenary celebrations, which marked his birth, a Robeson revival was well underway on account of his death in 1976. Among numerous public events, the United Nations Special Committee Against Apartheid held a Robeson tribute in 1978. In that same year, Philip S. Foner's compendious source book, *Paul Robeson Speaks: Writings, Speeches, Interviews*, appeared. An annotated collection of Robeson's utterances, it "endeavored to provide a selection representative of the many aspects of Robeson's thoughts and activities and of the broad range of causes and issues to which he dedicated his life." "To understand Paul Robeson," Foner instructs us, "one must read what he himself said and wrote."[41] Lenwood Davis's *Paul Robeson Research Guide* upped the bibliographic ante a few years later; although at almost 900 pages it remains a very select bibliography.[42] With this bounty of material readily at hand, Robeson's first postmodern interpreters, like Dyer and Carby, had no need to venture into the archive. Not so the biographers of old—first Martin Duberman, later Sheila Boyle and Andrew Bunie, and Paul Robeson Jr.— whose archivally rich work added more than 2,000 pages to the Robeson biography.[43] Foner concluded his prefatory remarks with the directive: "Now it is time to let [Robeson] speak again for himself."[44] But Robeson's speech in these source works is of course marked by their compilers' and authors' own voices and scholarly practices, and is bound by their curatorial choices. The effect then of what appears to be a surfeit of Robeson material is that a relatively small selection of the Robeson archive continues to inform much recent scholarship; and that it has sustained such varied interpretations is of course another historiographic lesson.

Limiting our attention to recycled sources also narrows our purview of the subject, and we are less likely to open our reading of Robeson to other ways of hearing him. Because the published source material has not, by and large, focused on the performance contexts of Robeson's singing, it has not facilitated inquiry into such. For this reason, rather than turn to the well-mined source books I have returned to the archive, specifically to the two primary sites of material, which in themselves could sustain a lifetime of scholarship: the

14 INTRODUCTION

Paul Robeson Collection housed in the Schomburg Center for Research in Black Culture, New York Public Library, and the Paul Robeson Papers preserved at the Moorland-Spingarn Research Center, Howard University, Washington, DC.

My turn to the archive has of course been circumscribed by many of the mundane practices of doing archival research but also by my interest in Robeson's singing voice, a voice that sounds through the archive in traces manifold: in the mass of journalistic criticism on his concert life and only slightly less voluminous reviews of his phonographic work, in diaries and letters, in recording sheets and legal contracts, recital programs and ephemera, in an accompanist's annotations of a score, in a photographic still of the singer in concert, and in an inscription in a book from the singer's personal library, and, still more, in a prisoner's poem and a child's supplication.[45] And then there are Robeson's own voices, which appear to us in writing and sound, in studio, broadcast, and live recordings; a visiting Edison fellowship to the British Library Sound Archive gave me access to the original HMV gramophone recordings the singer made. Robeson's circle frequently complained that he was an unreliable and reluctant correspondent. No doubt he invested his writing energies elsewhere. In addition to the published source book material—the *Writings, Speeches, Interviews*—there exists a vast collection of fragmentary notes, rough drafts, and complete texts, mostly unpublished, and expansive in its subject matter. In some of this Robeson recounts and reflects on his own artistic practice. My archival digging therefore was very much directed toward searching for Robeson's voice. In turn my interpretive practice in this book has been directed *by* his voice. I practice voice-thinking.

In *Boccherini's Body*, Elizabeth Le Guin introduces the idea of "cello-and-bow thinking" to account for the type of carnal knowledge, grounded in a performer's physical relationship with an instrument, that informs performance. It involves an "extensively explored bodily element" that is kinesthetic, sub-verbal, sub-intellectual.[46] I do not pursue the rendering of this knowledge in the "extremely fine grain of detail" that Le Guin does; for one, while Le Guin the cellist can execute Boccherini's music and thereby, in the guise of Le Guin the musicologist, articulate the performer's carnal knowledge, I cannot sing Robeson's voice.[47] But I do take her injunction, in a broad sense, seriously: I want to re-hear Robeson's singing as an embodied activity, proceeding in the first instance from the bodily production of his voice and its sonic manifestations as informed by specific song practices. Listening to how Robeson performed his voice in the contexts of recital and recording

INTRODUCTION 15

practices yields a certain knowledge of the subject. As Bonnie Gordon has noted, the experience of song is "ontologically and phenomenologically determined . . . conditioned by the always-constructed experience of inhabiting a body" that has materialized in a specific time and place.[48] Proceeding from the vocal subject in this way, which might be considered a sort of primary, even primal, knowledge, places the subject in new ways in relation to another type of voice-thinking: the many, varied discursive accounts by which Robeson's voice was represented, and which appear to us in the assorted historical materials contained in the archive and in scholarly writings.

Voice-thinking, in this regard/audition, is involved in what Nina Sun Eidsheim calls "listening to listening," so as to trace voice to ideas, and meaning to sounds. Research on the voice, Eidsheim observes, may be divided into two camps, one pursuing what's "measurable" in sound, and the other interested in the symbolic. But each of these orientations reveals a lacuna, and Eidsheim forwards instead a "critical performance practice methodology" in which research of the "thick vocal event" connects the study of sonic materiality to the symbolic world because a critique of the symbol is at once a critique of systems of thinking.[49] Voice-thinking aligns with this agenda, and is practiced in the pages of *Paul Robeson's Voices*. Different chapters analyze different features of what is measurable in Robeson's singing. Listening to these sound measurables opens up a pathway to hear something of the gamut of Robeson's art, and presents a picture of the complexity of the thick voice, illuminating how it articulated with and indeed challenged the song worlds out of which, in which, and against which it performed. Different chapters also grapple with some of the varied symbolic work that Robeson's voice has been put to. Professional critics, fans, and scholars have all had a go at interpreting Robeson's voice. The book endeavors to make sense of this hearing/understanding, and in the process it critiques the soundness of some of this thought.

In these twin pursuits—accounting for the voice's materiality and its symbolization—readers will note my indebtedness to the tradition of scholarship on vocality, another endeavor in voice-thinking. The concept of vocality, for Meizel, encompasses more than sound qualities and vocal practices, it "encapsulates the entire experience of the speaker or singer and of the listener, all of the physiological, psychoacoustic, and sociopolitical dynamics."[50] In her most recent work Meizel interprets vocality as "an embodied act and as a constructive process . . . as a way of singing inscribed and reinscribed with the lived experience of vocal sounds (linguistic and extralinguistic),

16 INTRODUCTION

practices, techniques, and meanings that factor into the making of culture and identity, and in the negotiation of power."[51] These too are the concerns of *Paul Robeson's Voices*. But in thinking about Robeson's voice "as technology of the self and of culture,"[52] I also distinguish my enterprise—and voice-thinking—from one direction that vocality studies has taken, which is perhaps exemplified in Redmond's reading of Robeson in *Everything Man*. Vocality, she notes, "is a reading practice as much as one of performance," and it attracts the placeholder "Voice" in her writing. Conflating vocality and voice thus reveals possibilities and limitations. As Redmond puts it, Robeson is "less subject than opportunity" to examine "the multitextual, technological, and international afterlife of Black political cultures." His Voice is metaphorically enacted—as vibration, hologram, play, and more. These are the "forms" that Robeson assumes in Redmond's self-described undisciplined project.[53] Voice-thinking is interested rather in musical forms and practice: song genres, melody, piano parts, voice relationships, singing, songfulness, expressivity, and not least the sounds of the voice. It may be described as a formalist enterprise, and is quite disciplined in its historical-archival practice and musicological analytical and interpretive moves. The voice-thinking I practice in *Paul Robeson's Voices* prioritizes the sonic voice.

I want to emphasize that voice-thinking is not a new methodology or another theory of the voice. There are enough of these, and this book is not concerned with theorizing the voice and vocality per se. As Meizel notes, there is no one way of doing voice studies, "of asking or answering the flood of questions raised when we wonder what voice is."[54] Naming my practice voice-thinking gestures at my specific orientation of the study of vocality: it proceeds from and heads toward the sonic voice; it is about voice (rather than Voice), and for it. But as much as the voice's acoustic matter is not simple, voice-thinking is no simple matter. This much is clear from the insights of the philosophy of the voice: another modality of voice-thinking, select instances of which make intermittent appearances in the book. The voice is a complex object, and bears a complex relationship to the subject and subjectivity. By no means confined to a sounding object, yet alone the singing voice, the voice, in Mladen Dolar's typology, is manifest in linguistics, metaphysics, ethics, physics, and yes, politics.[55] The voice, moreover, is slippery because it always stands in between; and much of the philosophy of voice might be understood as an extended essay on in-betweenness. The voice is in between body and language, being and meaning, it intersects biology and culture (or nature and art, a delineation I pursue), and subject and Other (and is thereby entangled

INTRODUCTION 17

in understanding, desire, fantasy, and resistance, topics I take up in my musings on the voice). This places the voice "in a most peculiar and paradoxical position: the topology of *extimacy*, the simultaneous inclusion/exclusion": it both links the opposed categories, is common to both, but belongs to neither.[56] Meizel's conceptualization of the voice as a "borderscape," an idea I return to in the Afterword, is a continuation of this posture, of the voice's in-betweenness, its ability to mark and separate, to cross and transgress.[57] The voice's complexity is affirmed in Eidsheim's critique of the certainty of knowledge about sound that conventionally results from the acousmatic question. But, she counters, we ask the acousmatic question—what is the source of a voice?—precisely because of "the voice's inability to be unique and yield precise answers": "it is not possible to know voice, vocal identity, and meaning as such; we can know them only in their multidimensional, always unfolding processes and practices, indeed in their multiplicities. This fundamental instability is why we keep asking the acousmatic question." It is for this reason that Eidsheim proclaims that "voice is not singular; it is collective."[58] *Paul Robeson's Voices* acknowledges the singularity of Robeson's voice. But it is a quest, undertaken through voice-thinking, to understand Robeson's voice as collectively produced and heard multiply in its many soundings.

1

Becoming Paul Robeson's Voice

Raising a Voice

Robeson spoke a lot about his voice. Such was the centrality of his voice to his métier and to his sense of self-identity that it could be no other way. During the US tour of *Othello* in the early 1940s, for which Robeson revived the role of the Moor he first played in England in 1930, he reflected on his voice's history, telling an interviewer that he was raised in a vocal household, and that throughout his childhood the family orated, recited, debated, and even just spoke for fun. He recalled often that his father "had the greatest speaking voice I have ever heard . . . it was a deep, sonorous basso."[1] This catalog of different modes of vocality, including the more obviously rhetorical verbal practices such as oration, recitation, and debate, makes the most ordinary of verbal communications—speech—less plain, into speaking *with a voice* (and we might imagine the Robesons on occasion speaking for sheer sonorous vocality). The meaning of the voice is thus expansive—by no means limited to the singing or theatrical voices—and the context of Robeson's vocal "bringing up" provides a family and social genealogy for the making of Robeson's singing voice. It is an instance, as Nina Sun Eidsheim has said, of the voice being "always already a continuous formal *and informal* pedagogical enterprise." The voice is trained—entrained, to use Eidsheim's term—in the everyday, corporeally and vocally, and in so doing "manifests cultural and societal values."[2]

Robeson continued to orate, recite, and debate into adulthood, sometimes professionally: he recorded and broadcast recitations of poetry, and his theatrical performances, as in the three productions of *Othello* in which he starred over several decades, were often criticized for a want of acting ability for which oration compensated. A young Ute Hagen, who played Desdemona opposite Robeson, recalled that his Broadway Othello was "a rather vocal, verbal, conventional, ordinary shape of a performance," and the acting coach for the production Sanford Meisner observed that he "couldn't act the demands of the part, only recite them."[3] Indeed it was a critical commonplace to note the

Paul Robeson's Voices. Grant Olwage, Oxford University Press. © Oxford University Press 2024.
DOI: 10.1093/oso/9780197637470.003.0002

BECOMING PAUL ROBESON'S VOICE   19

dominance of Robeson's voice in his acting roles: "his voice booms musically in startling contrast to those of his fellow actors," observed *Billboard* of the production's Broadway premiere; "he seems to concentrate more on vocal tones than on acting. He recites the musical lines as a musician rather than as an actor."[4] By the time of Robeson's final appearance in the theater, for the Shakespeare Memorial Theatre production of *Othello* in 1959 in Stratford, England, he still conceived of his performance of Othello as a primarily vocal one. His health in decline, he convinced doctors at the Kremlin Hospital to release him for the production only because his performance would involve more voice work than physical acting.[5]

The voice marked also Black cultural practices more broadly. Robeson's father, William D. Robeson (named for the Roberson plantation in North Carolina on which he was born a slave), became a pastor as a freed man. In the (auto)biographic record, the lineage of Robeson's father's, and then his son's, voice is one of impeccable African American credentials: it begins in the South, in slavery; proceeds with the freedom train north; and ends (or starts anew) with an education for and career in the church, a profession the father had wished for his son but which Paul Robeson had declined to pursue. At each turn in this story the singing voice is to be heard. Robeson's recollections of the "close-knit" Black community in Princeton, New Jersey, where he spent his early childhood, is shot through with song:

> Here in this hemmed-in world where home must be theatre and concert hall and social center, there was a warmth of song. Songs of love and longing, songs of trials and triumph . . . the healing comfort to be found in the illimitable sorrow of the spirituals.
>
> Yes, I heard my people singing!—in the glow of [the] parlor coal-stove and on summer porches sweet with lilac air, from choir loft and Sunday morning pews. . . . Then, too, I heard these songs in the very sermons of my father.[6]

The worlds of the family and community necessarily intersected closely for Princeton's Black population, no doubt fostered by the town's civic and cultural strictures on Black participation; "the decaying smell of the plantation Big House" lingered in the northern town, Robeson reflected, charging it with being "spiritually located in Dixie." In this we are reminded that Robeson's experience of Black music was shaped by the trauma of slavery and its legacies.

20 PAUL ROBESON'S VOICES

For Princeton's Black community the home was thus the concert hall, and with a pastor-father the church was an extension of the Robeson home.

The Black church was thus a formative musical learning ground. Wrote the singer's wife and first biographer, Eslanda Robeson, of his youth: "He led the singing in church with his big, unmanageable, but beautifully moving bass voice, and was often carried away by the religious emotion which swept the congregation with the music. He became an essential part of the church, and, in turn, the church, the music, and the people became an essential part of him."[7] The church, in its broadest sense, was the singer's most productive well for song material, for spirituals and hymns, and would become an important place of concertizing in the latter stages of Robeson's career when his radical politics led conventional concert venues to close their doors to him. The alliance between the singer and the Black church, conceived through the father-pastor, led Robeson to style himself as "a son of Zion," that is, of the Church itself,[8] and critics in turn would draw the comparison frequently: his concerts were a "preachment"; he "was unabashedly a preacher, in the tradition of his Methodist minister father."[9] By all accounts, including Robeson's, the father too was endowed with a remarkable voice. From the earliest presentations of his self to the public Robeson identified the source of his voice in the father's voice: "When people talk about my voice . . . I wish they could have heard my father preach." Robeson's vocal inheritance from "the grizzled burly evangelist with the magnificent bass voice" was a tale the singer told throughout his life.[10] Near the end of his career he recalled of his father's voice: "He had the greatest speaking voice I have ever heard. It was a deep, sonorous basso, richly melodic and refined, vibrant with the love and compassion which filled him." An obituary that appeared in the Somerville town newspaper, where William Robeson had a pastorate at the St. Thomas AME Zion Church, made special mention of "the temperament" the reverend possessed, and which had "produced so many orators in the South."[11] For one historian, that "distinct Robeson voice" must be traced directly to "the roots of the Negro preacher" and his milieu.[12]

More particularly, then, the father's and son's voices are grounded in a broader cultural vernacular practice, one in which the distinction between speech and song is partially collapsed. The singer identified what he called "melodic speech" as a characteristic of African American orality, a mode that was particularly true of Black preaching, exemplified by his father and older brother who became the pastor of the AME Zion Mother Church in Harlem.[13] The tenor Roland Hayes would christen this practice "song

BECOMING PAUL ROBESON'S VOICE 21

sermons," a tradition of performance that guided his own arrangements and singing of spirituals: "Just as the late James Weldon Johnson, the Aframerican poet, heard some of the mastersinging ministers of my people in his childhood Florida, so it was my childhood experience in my 'Angel Mo' community in Georgia to hear the same sermons sung-preached by Charles Foster and others."[14] In the following chapter I detail Robeson's artist debt to Hayes, and elsewhere the book explores some of the connections between the Robeson voice and the sounds of the Black church and preaching tradition.

The young Robeson used his voice consciously at home and church, where he sang in the choir, and also at school and college where he debated, orated—and sang.[15] Unsurprisingly his first forays into professional acting were the result of his voice's allure. His "magnificent bass speaking voice" caught the ear of a theater producer and led to his first stage role: the roundly panned play *Taboo* of 1922 nonetheless drew favorable reviews of Robeson's speaking voice. In the same year he was co-opted by a vocal quartet appearing in the first all-Black Broadway revue *Shuffle Along* because he could "sing quite clearly three tones lower and many notes higher" than the bass singer he replaced. The English actress Mrs. Patrick Campbell, his co-star in *Voodoo* (titillatingly renamed for *Taboo*'s British tour), advised Robeson to " 'sing a lot and long—more—more.' " "It is the consensus of opinion," reported Robeson, "that the most enjoyable feature of the show is my singing."[16] As suggested by Campbell, the objectification of Robeson's voice would lead to his singing voice being increasingly insinuated into otherwise spoken theater, a practice that would continue in the commercial films he made later. Even "serious" theater accommodated his voice in this way. Where the original Brutus Jones, brought to stage by Charles Gilpin, did not sing in Eugene O'Neill's *The Emperor Jones*, Robeson's Jones would sing for the 1924 revival (and in the 1933 film version); and as became habit, the critics "especially praised [his] speaking and singing voice."[17] His voice was, in large part, his entry point into the production—of Robeson's audition, the director's assistant Bess Rockmore recalled his "marvellous, incredible voice"—and what listeners, general and professional, came away from the theater commenting on.[18]

This more marked—because singing—entry of the voice into predominantly verbocentric genres is one sign of the status that Robeson's voice had begun to assume, already in the early 1920s before he considered pursuing a career in music. (More prosaically, it is also an instance of a performer capitalizing on his "perfect equipment," as one letter-writer referred to his voice.[19]) It was also the beginning of the public fashioning and reception of

22 PAUL ROBESON'S VOICES

Robeson as a voice. The voice thus became the primary sign of the artist, and of the subject, as I explore in this book: "his voice is recognized immediately wherever in the world it is heard."[20] But this recognition demands a reckoning. We should not, as Eidsheim cautions, mistake the voice for essence, and rather seek to untangle "notions of voice as innate, essential, singular, defined statically, and a priori." Instead we should conceive of the voice as performed through processes of entrainment, style, and technique.[21] In this chapter, I am interested in how Robeson's singing voice came into being; how he "found his voice." In the story thus far, we have encountered several strands of his vocal makeup: genetic (the father's voice), family practices (in the vocal household), and institutional culture (of the Black church and preacher's arts). Next I trace the first, tentative steps Robeson took toward a singing career, and then document in some detail his encounters with the formal pedagogies of classical singing, about which most accounts of his voice remain silent. But in finding a voice, Katherine Meizel cautions that even "a classically trained singer may navigate multiple vocalities": "They may in some ways leave one vocality for another . . . or they may feel that they embody two or more vocalities. . . . They may rely on shifts in vocality to negotiate the boundaries and intersections of different geographical, social, and cultural spaces."[22] Even as I attend to Robeson's classical training in the pages that follow, we need to keep Robeson's multivocality in mind; and we will see later in the book how he sung plurally at different times and in different contexts.

Toward Song: First Steps

The move from theater to concert stage was not straightforward, nor ever complete; there was no linear career progression toward song, even if Lindsey Swindall suggests that we should conceive of Robeson first as an orator who later sang and performed in dramatic theater.[23] Robeson's performance career was a composite one, working in different media and genres at different stages of his life, sometimes in more than one medium during a particular period, other times focusing on a specific medium. If Robeson ever wished to privilege one medium, it was a desire often thwarted by unexpected opportunity, financial considerations, and his body's (and voice's) temporary but regular failings. These realities caution us from attempting to present his career in terms as grand as "destiny," as Robeson's biographer-son would have it.[24] But there are moments in his career at which one can chart a movement toward—and, at other points, a withdrawal from—the concert stage.

BECOMING PAUL ROBESON'S VOICE   23

For better or worse, Robeson is enduringly associated with the musical *Show Boat*. The part of the Mississippi stevedore Joe, who sings just one song, the famous "Ol' Man River," was in fact written for him. Several ironic turns of events transpired. In the end Robeson did not take up the role for the original Broadway production in 1927, choosing instead to pursue a recently launched concert career, and more to the point a tour of Europe. But it was because of Robeson's initial successes on the concert stage that he was considered for the part in the first place. To this end Jerome Kern and Oscar Hammerstein II had sketched a scene in the musical in which Robeson stepped out of character as Joe and appeared as himself: Robeson the concert singer. As Joe he would sing "Ol' Man River," plantation songs, and Stephen Foster numbers, after which he would re-emerge in a tuxedo and sing, as if in concert rather than musical theater, the spirituals for which he had become known. Of this early scenario, which was necessarily cut when Robeson quit the show, Scott McMillin has suggested that "one of the music-history lessons running through the original *Show Boat* would have been complete: the day of Stephen Foster's popularity has given way to a new day, when the genuine music of the black people, the spiritual, has attained concert-hall status."[25] This music history lesson chimed with the position advocated by the Harlem Renaissance, and which Robeson had adopted: the spirituals were considered art (and the following chapter has much more to say on this).

That Robeson had determined to venture on a concert tour of Europe rather than star in a lucrative Broadway musical speaks of a shift in his artistic focus, one that had recently begun to take shape. It was only in 1925 that Robeson seriously contemplated a career in music, a consideration possibly borne from critics' praise of his voice in the theater. Prior to this he had dabbled in song, performing at church fundraisers, YMCA and fraternity events, dinners of the National Association for the Advancement of Colored People (NAACP), and private parties of the Harlem elite. Toward the end of 1924 he received a break, one that would also signal the start of an increasing refocus of his artistic energies away from (albeit temporarily) the theater. After hearing Robeson in *The Emperor Jones*, the Boston socialite Mrs. Guy Currier proposed presenting him in concert at the Copley Plaza Hotel in Boston. The ensuing recital of November 2 was his "first appearance as a professional concert-hall soloist," and it was the planting of the seed of a concert career (see Box 1.1).[26] The very first overtures made by a recording company to capture the singer's voice on disc also stemmed from his theatrical successes. Earlier in 1924 the Chicago Music Publishing Company approached the performer to record a selection of the latest music from

24 PAUL ROBESON'S VOICES

Box 1.1. Program, Copley Plaza Hotel Concert, November 2, 1924. Paul Robeson Collection, microfilm 2. The Schomburg Center for Research in Black Culture, New York Public Library.

PROGRAMME

I.
a. Swing Low, Sweet Chariot . . . . Arr. by Lawrence Brown
b. The Gospel Train . . . . Harry T. Burleigh
c. Couldn't Hear Nobody Pray . . . . Arr. by Mr. Hooper

II.
a. Somebody's Knocking at Your Door . . . . .Nathaniel Dett
b. Every Time I Feel the Spirit . . . . Arr. by Lawrence Brown
c. Deep River . . . . Arr. by William Arms Fisher

III.
a. Peter, Go Ring Dem Bells ⎫
                             ⎬ . . . . Harry T. Burleigh
b. Didn't It Rain? ⎭

INTERMISSION

IV.
"In the Bottoms" (Suite for Piano) . . . . Nathaniel Dett

Mr. Hooper

V.
a. Li'l Gal . . . . J. Rosamond Johnson
b. Mammy's Angel Chile . . . . C. White

VI.
a. Nobody Knows the Trouble I See . . . . Harry T. Burleigh
b. All God's Chillun Got Shoes . . . . .Arr. by Mr. Hooper
c. Go Down, Moses . . . . Harry T. Burleigh

popular shows going on in New York at the time, which would include songs featured in Robeson's own theater work.[27] Nothing came of this. But the half year following the Copley Plaza recital would involve Robeson in a more intense engagement with his singing voice: he met and commenced work with Lawrence Brown, who would become his long-term accompanist, they gave their first New York recital (on April 19) and made their first recordings for Victor in the Camden studio in July. "It seems we are really launched at last," noted Robeson's wife Eslanda.[28]

Robeson thus entered the professional concert field from the theater stage. He also, significantly, approached singing from the perspective of speech and language. Eslanda suggested that Robeson "sings the way he talks . . . he's always believed singing originated from the spoken language. . . . He came to music, in fact, through languages."[29] We have seen in brief how, grounded in his experience of African American preaching, Robeson conceptualized modes of vocality as existing in a fluid continuum, and how his own vocal work—his musical speech—put this into practice. I discuss more fully later in the book how other elements of his performance practice point to an elaboration of the interrelatedness of song and speech: he would learn new song repertoire through the recitation of song texts; his lifelong study of languages—and he preferred to learn a language before singing in it— informed his singing in many ways; and he would insert spoken-word performances, of poems and dramatic scenes, into his concert programs and broadcasts. The genesis of song from speech would even inform Robeson's theory of a universal body of folk music that had its genesis in the mid-1930s and found complete expression in the latter stages of his life.[30] I mention this here to point out that while I am primarily interested in Robeson's singing voice, it was a voice formed in its interactions with different artistic fields and modes of vocalizing.[31]

At a point in the mid-1920s when Robeson could have pursued a career in the theater, we might ask why he decided to turn to the concert stage? A banal explanation is that concert singing provided another artistic endeavor and source of income to complement the theater and musical revue work. Given the reception of his voice and the opportunities presented there was, so it may seem, a certain inevitability about Robeson's appearance in concert. But the path to song was not easy. For one, Robeson was not a trained musician. Following his initial successes on the concert stage he would receive vocal coaching, on and off, with several teachers in different parts of the world for the better part of the 1920s and into the 1930s. For the first

26 PAUL ROBESON'S VOICES

few concerts he received succor from the professional Black musicians with whom he worked: Harry T. Burleigh coached him for the Copley Plaza concert in Boston, and thereafter Brown, who had accompanied Roland Hayes and Marian Anderson, performed the dual role of coach-accompanist. His lack of training (and later his ambivalent attitude toward some of the training he received), however, underlay an anxiety about his voice and its fitness for concertizing. Appearing on the concert stage was thus hardly inevitable. Rather it was a bold move that once taken stuttered along at first less assuredly than the consolidated biographic record would have us believe.

What made the concert stage attractive was the relative degree of artistic control it afforded Robeson.[32] Already in the early 1920s, when establishing himself as an actor, he balked at the dominant representations of Blackness in the theater. He was a reluctant participant in *Plantation Revue*, informing his wife-manager that he intended to focus on serious theater, and by the time his nascent concert career had taken off he refused the offer to star in *Lulu Belle*, "full of the conventional black stereotypes."[33] To return to the "coon songs" of *Lulu Belle* after the song recital successes would have been a reversal of the "progress" enacted in the *Show Boat* scene noted earlier. *Show Boat's* own performance of race, however, was in part the reason for Robeson's withdrawal from the original production. But with only a trickle of regular serious theater and concert work for a Black performer coming in Robeson climbed down from his artistic high horse: to much fanfare he appeared in the London production of *Show Boat* in 1928, and the series of commercial films he made throughout the 1930s often required him to play atavistic racial clichés. And some of the bad music I mentioned in the Introduction, and which Robeson recorded extensively in the 1930s, was no less caught up in the representations of American commodity racism.

But at first the concert world appeared to give him the authority—an authoring of an artistic (and later political) self—that he did not possess in mainstream theater and in film. A telling instance of this is Robeson's recital programs, which he and his accompanists and coaches compiled. For roughly the first five years of his concert career the programs were made up almost entirely of African American spiritual and secular songs: "we staked our careers-to-be on the concept that the songs of the Negro slaves were concert material, ranking in musical stature with the acknowledged classics. It was a revolutionary idea; and it was a success."[34] The "revolution" in concert programming entailed, for Robeson, both the presentation of family history and an engagement with African American cultural politics, a multiple (self-)authoring that exceeded the limiting representations imposed on him in the theater. Robeson's voices, even in the early stage of his career, thereby performed plurally, both as a commodity in support of a repressive market system and as an agent to "create otherwise-denied spaces where [his] self-narrations ... sound[ed]."[35] Thus later, it was in large part through song that Robeson would express a more explicit politicized voice; one which I consider more fully elsewhere in the book. The allure of the concert stage was in part an attraction to the freedoms it promised, and Robeson would repeatedly, if temporarily, withdraw from the theater (and film) in pursuit of such freedom.

After the success of his appearance in the London *Show Boat*, his record company noted that Robeson "has for the time being abandoned his career as a Musical Comedy star and devoted his thrilling voice and fine artistic intelligence to the Concert platform."[36] When Robeson wrote to Brown about his decision to take part in the London *Show Boat* it was, he clarified, for financial reasons (it "will give us something to live on while things are taking shape"), for publicity ("it might make London concerts easy"), and it was easy work, involving little speaking, which tired his voice, and only one song sung thrice.[37] In other words, *Show Boat* was a placeholder and launch pad for concert work. It proved to be so in the most direct way: in July 1928 the Robeson-Brown duo performed a series of critically successful and financially lucrative matinee concerts in the same theater, the Drury Lane, in which *Show Boat* played in the evenings. Those who had glimpsed his voice in the theater could hear more of it in concert.

Voice-Help

By most accounts Robeson's debut recital at Carnegie Hall in 1929 was a triumph. No less than the "dean of American music critics," W. J. Henderson, declared that Robeson was "a master of the art of singing."[38] In the time of the half decade since his first formal recitals he had become a celebrated concert singer, performing in the world's great concert venues, praised by the most eminent critics on both sides of the Atlantic. Working in these performance spaces and for the professional listeners who took the concert hall as their beat situated Robeson's singing within the tradition of the song recital, which he acknowledged as a specialized field.[39] Robeson's awareness of and engagement with the specific practices that constituted the concert

28 PAUL ROBESON'S VOICES

field played out dialectically: the desire to take on an aspect of the practice often led to partial failure and revelation, yielding to the recognition that the practice—imperfectly and or partially attained, and sometimes reinvented— could nonetheless still fit within the tradition; in turn broadening the field. Tensions in Robeson's thinking on repertoire and about his own singing voice exemplify this process in different ways.

Robeson had of course focused on African American spirituals and secular songs for the first half decade of his concert career. By this time spirituals had already been presented in art song recitals, and would soon become a staple of the art song repertoire. Roland Hayes's concert at Chicago's Orchestra Hall at the start of 1924, that is before Robeson began professional concertizing, concluded with four spirituals arranged by Burleigh;[40] and the singing of spirituals even at this time was not limited to Black artists—even if the musical press sometimes preferred it that way: "Edna Thomas is an old favourite in Negro Spirituals," opined the magazine *Gramophone*, "but, as with most white singers, they sound with her at worst, like music-hall songs, at best flippant, or insincerely exaggerated, or just weak."[41] There was, in other words, a nascent tradition of the art singing of spirituals, one in which Robeson would participate. A writer for the *British Musician and Musical News* put it thus: "He sings spirituals primarily as an artist,—as a person who wishes to display a form of art."[42] Robeson's "revolution," we have seen, was that his entire program was devoted to spirituals and Black secular folk song. But while the mode of the spirituals' presentation—arranged for solo voice and pianoforte accompaniment, and part classically sung—conformed to the practices of concert music, they did not, Robeson realized, make a standard concert program. An all-spiritual program held the attention of the world for only so long, and by the late 1920s listeners and critics alike agitated to hear the singer in other repertoire.[43] Finding the right new material would be a process of vocal self-discovery taking several years.

In the first years of his singing career Robeson periodically expressed misgivings about his vocal art and the direction his singing should take, wondering whether he should sing opera, or just spirituals, musical theater, or art song. The hope of doing opera, for example, never materialized: in due course Robeson would program the occasional operatic excerpt, but despite several offers he would never perform on the operatic stage.[44] His early questioning of his (vocal) identity was an ontological questioning occasioned by his entry into the concert field. Meizel has written that in a singer's quest for "finding a voice," "singers *will* their voices in the search for self," a process that more often than not situates the voice/self in the "neoliberal music market."[45] This is no less the case for Robeson's vocal self-development.

At the outset of his singing career Robeson was an untrained singer, of "simple music" done "simply" in his own estimation. His was a voice, we have seen, formed in its encounters with Black cultural and family practices. Sterling Stuckey offers a condensed account: "Though Robeson's success with spirituals seemed sudden, he had gone through a long period of preparation, without planning to sing professionally. He had been to music school in the Black church, and that training prepared him for a concert career before audiences, no matter how sophisticated."[46] But it wasn't as straightforward as Stuckey makes out. Stepping onto the concert stage challenged Robeson's sense of vocal self, and how he responded to that challenge led to the making of his singer's voice. When Robeson returned to Carnegie Hall in January 1931, just over a year after his debut, only half the program consisted of spirituals. Making up the rest of the program was standard repertoire, with Beethoven, Mozart, Purcell, Schumann, Tchaikovsky, Borodin, and Sinding on offer.[47] Working on this repertoire brought with it a dual realization, one mechanical, another aesthetic. The songs of the concert field required, Robeson came to understand, specific vocal techniques and some seemed to be merely vehicles for vocal display. Neither these techniques nor an aesthetics of virtuosity appealed to Robeson, and in various utterances at several points in his career he claimed to reject the art song repertoire.[48] But the rejection was only ever partial and works of the art song repertoire appeared on Robeson's programs for the remainder of his career; although their inclusion was not for their canonical status, and I consider the politics of Robeson's engagement with this repertoire in a later chapter. Thinking through matters of repertoire choice helps us to account for the place and nature of Robeson's singing voice, one located within the art song field but which resisted some of its vocal calling cards.

The dominant image of Robeson, perpetuated by the singer and in the numerous biographies, is of an untutored, a "natural," singer.[49] The first recordings for Victor and the first important solo recital in New York (at the Greenwich Village Theater) are marked as seminal events in a watershed year in which the singer's voice is as yet untouched by the concert field. But already by this time there are indications that Robeson's voice was in training. His biographer-son records that in the several years directly preceding 1925, when Robeson sang routinely at occasional events, his accompanists

30 PAUL ROBESON'S VOICES

were Harlem's skilled music teachers and choir directors, and that between engagements he "scheduled fairly regular rehearsals and continuous voice study."[50] Details are sketchy until the approach to 1925.

The Copley Plaza recital (of late 1924), for instance, was prepared under the tutelage of Harry T. Burleigh, several of whose works were included on the program. Burleigh was a professional baritone, in the classical tradition, and voice teacher who taught at William Marion Cook's music school in New York. If the goal was for Robeson to perform Burleigh's art song arrangements of the spirituals in the appropriate voice, we can imagine the technical and interpretative pointers the elder musician might have offered the young singer. Robeson was, by 1924, also working with a regular accompanist suggested by Burleigh, Louis Hooper, someone he continued to work with "diligently" even after he withdrew from Burleigh's influence, feeling not quite at ease with the latter's "decidedly classical European concert style."[51] The tension between the dictates of "the classical style" and Robeson's singing voice and aesthetic ideals was thus present at the outset of his engagement with the concert field. As we will see, it was in working through those tensions that Robeson's voice would be formed in the coming decade.

More so than during the time of Robeson's singing at occasional events and in the theater, facing the concert field's practices in the formal recitals of late 1924 brought with it the realization that his voice required training. Eslanda hoped the Copley Plaza concert would be an opportunity for her husband to work with a vocal instructor; whether this was Burleigh is unclear. But the short-lived partnership with Burleigh did not result in a withdrawal from the idea of voice training; rather it encouraged the search for a compatible coach.[52] Archival sources indicate that in addition to rehearsing with Burleigh at this time, Robeson met with the vocal coach Mrs. Flora Arnold in New York, and then, in preparation for the Rutgers concert in December of that year, the tenor Paul Draper was engaged. Draper had studied with the noted *Lieder* singer and teacher Raimund von zur-Mühlen in London (as had Brown, Robeson's accompanist to be).[53] It seems that Robeson worked briefly with Draper until the tenor's untimely death from a heart attack in February 1925. The abrupt end to Draper's coaching opened another door.

During the winter of 1924 and 1925 the Robesons were regular concertgoers; they seemed particularly keen to hear the leading male voices of the day. On one day they heard Emilio de Gogorza at Town Hall in the afternoon, and Hayes at Carnegie Hall in the evening. Within a two-week period Robeson heard Hayes in recital on three occasions, even traveling to

Philadelphia to attend the tenor's Academy of Music concert as a guest of the African American musician Carl Diton. Part of the attraction must have been Hayes's accompanist, Brown, because in March Brown relocated to New York to begin work with Robeson. If Robeson had not connected with Burleigh, he found a kindred spirit in Brown with whom he would develop an enduring partnership. Brown's own work as an arranger and performer of spirituals made him a likeminded collaborator, someone with significant experience of the concert field, both in the United States and Europe, and at the same time, perhaps unlike Burleigh, receptive to a more open conception of the field. Given Brown's classical training, in Boston and London at the New England Conservatory and Trinity College of Music respectively, and his concert work with Hayes among many other art song performers in England and the United States, we can imagine the coaching role he performed for the young Robeson. In the mid-1950s, after Brown had quit as Robeson's permanent accompanist, he continued to teach in New York. But despite Brown's extensive work with art singers, the countenance of a specialist voice coach was still sought.

And so late in the summer of 1925, when Robeson appeared in a brief run of *The Emperor Jones* in London, he renewed his acquaintance with Flora Arnold and resumed voice training. The biographic record does not indicate what necessitated the lessons. They may have involved preparatory work for the upcoming concert tour—Robeson's very first tour—of the United States planned for the first few months of 1926. Or they may have been a corrective measure for vocal fatigue from *Jones*, in which he also sang. Whatever the reason for vocal instruction, by the time of the American tour of 1926 Robeson's voice was beginning to be heard as (partially) trained: "Training has obviously been given the voice, but it was not made clear by the recital just how extensively and thoroughly" commented the *Milwaukee Journal*.[54]

Another voice consultant was the singer and pedagogue Amanda Aldridge, daughter of the Black Shakespearean actor Ira Aldridge, to whom the Robesons were introduced on the same trip to England. Aldridge had heard Robeson on radio, enthusing about his "*most beautiful* voice . . . his renderings are so artistic!"[55] He became, according to Aldridge, one of the "most famous of the coloured race who have spent many months of study with me"; and her obituary also made mention that she "helped train" him. It is unclear for how long Robeson studied with her and what the lessons involved, although he paid for coaching during the latter part of 1925 and worked on repertoire for recital performance, no doubt for the forthcoming

32   PAUL ROBESON'S VOICES

concert tour of America. Robeson may also have worked with her on and off during later visits to London.[56] Their meeting was facilitated by Brown, who had known Aldridge since the early 1920s when he accompanied Hayes (who had also received coaching from Aldridge), and who remained friendly with the pedagogue until her death in 1956. Robeson thus entered into the small circle of Black artists in London (another was Johnny Payne) who congregated around Aldridge and the traditions of high art of which she and her father were the inheritors. After his own debut in *Othello* in London in 1930, Robeson imagined himself as continuing in the "tradition of Aldridge."[57]

Amanda Aldridge's vocal credentials were impeccable. She had entered the Royal College of Music, London, soon after the institution opened its doors in 1883, where her teachers were Jenny Lind and then George Henschel, the latter engaged by Robeson a few years later. Aldridge made much of this illustrious training in promoting herself, prominently featuring a testimonial by Lind in her advertising: "I feel convinced that she has attained a real insight into the Art of Singing and a correct judgement as to the formation and healthy development of the Voice. . . . I have therefore no hesitation in recommending her as a Master of Singing." Aldridge was quite properly a "Certified Pupil of the late Mme. Jenny Lind,"[58] and with the Swedish singer's myth lasting well into the first decades of the twentieth century this was no small drawing card. Lind had long given up the stage for a concert career by the time she was co-opted on to the Royal College teaching staff, and Henschel preferred a concert career from the start. It was this preference for the song tradition, rather than opera, that informed Aldridge's own singing career; and it was an affinity she (and Henschel) shared with Robeson.

The Robesons' developing aesthetic outlook at this time is evident from, and likely formed by, the artistic company they kept, and the events they frequented. Socializing with London's art elites became routine. They visited the composer Roger Quilter, a leading figure in the promotion of English art song, and for a brief time were part of Quilter's circle; indeed Brown was one of Quilter's acolytes. In addition to meeting Quilter and Aldridge, they heard the baritone John Goss, and listened to Quilter's favorite baritone, Mark Raphael. Hearing the best English art singers while Robeson's own voice was in training led perhaps inevitably to a sharpening of the Robesons' aesthetic judgment and informed his song selection: Robeson would sing from the English art song repertoire for much of his life.

Early in his concert career Robeson's voice was not always performance fit, revealing "the misusages of too frequent performance."[59] The US tour of early 1926 culminated in a post-tour concert in Boston's Symphony Hall in March, and was another not entirely successful outing for Robeson, owing largely to the singer being in poor health. Eslanda wrote about the event in some detail in her biography of her husband, presenting the concert as the nadir of Robeson's singing career to date: "Paul was so shocked at his performance that he declared that he would never sing again. He would return to the [theater] stage and remain there. Poor boy, his despair was pathetic." She also presents herself as the problem-solving manager. Reflecting on the vagaries of Robeson's voice's sound—"so gorgeous one day and so dead the next"—she wonders: "There must be some way to sing well, at least fairly well, over a cold; there must be a way to sing well even over nervousness; there must be some general fortification against these enemies of the voice." For Eslanda the answer to combating the "enemies of the voice" lay in training, and without telling her husband she began the search for "no ordinary" a teacher.[60] One of the boons of training, Robeson came to realize, was the provision of a technique that allowed for the repeatability of an artistic performance at any time, including during times of vocal stress.

In the wake of his first concert tour and the difficult Boston concert Eslanda's search for a voice teacher led her to an old friend, Theresa Armitage, an "authority on voice training."[61] Armitage could not take Robeson on at the time, referring him to Frantz Proschowsky, a noted pedagogue and author of *The Way to Sing* (1923), who ran a profitable studio in New York. Critics at the Boston concert had rung several bells of warning. One concern was Robeson's limited range, "a baritone of not large range . . . almost harsh at its lower edges," observed Boston's *Transcript*.[62] It was a specific area, among several more general problems such as breath control, that Robeson worked on during this time; Eslanda diarized that he was learning "to make the most of his low tones."[63] Work with Mr. Pro, as Eslanda nicknamed him, seems to have proceeded to plan at first, and lessons were sometimes scheduled as frequently as daily. The "well-known teacher," as the *Musical Leader* referred to the pedagogue, must have been sufficiently pleased with Robeson's progress to present the singer in recital at his prestigious Riverside Drive studio. Two leading trade magazines, *The Musical Courier* and *The Musical Leader*, reported that the "success of [the] program was in no small part due to [Proschowsky's] experienced advice," "the result of thorough study and careful coaching."[64] Eslanda recalled the "Concert at Pro's studio"

34 PAUL ROBESON'S VOICES

differently: "it was a dreadful failure, as Paul was at his worst."[65] Soon thereafter the relationship with Proschowsky ended—"there came a time when Paul seemed to make no further progress" is all the record reveals—and the singer commenced work with "a famous German voice-teacher who divided her time between New York and Berlin."[66]

It is likely this was Anna Schoen-René. Known as the Prussian General, and considered "one of the world's foremost vocal teachers" of the time, Schoen-René had studied with Pauline Viardot-García and later "specialized in the teaching of male voices with Manuel Garcia." By the time that Robeson came to work with her she was attached to the Juilliard Graduate School.[67] It is not clear whether Robeson studied at the Juilliard or privately with Schoen-René; although Walter White, later the leader of the NAACP, wrote a recommendation for Robeson on his "personal and musical qualifications" at the request of the Juilliard Music Foundation.[68] In one of the very few references Robeson made to a specific voice teacher, he recalled that "Mme. Schoen-Rene helped me a great deal."[69] When Schoen-René left "for her Berlin season" that arrangement too came to an end.

Within a month Robeson was working with Armitage who had settled in New York, and who would become the singer's "vocal adviser" until the end of the decade.[70] Robeson worked with her intensely in mid-1926, and periodically thereafter. In the latter part of 1927 he was presented in concert under the auspices of Armitage at the C. C. Birchard Hall, New York. The press, which observed that Robeson "has been coaching for some time with Miss Theresa Armitage," congratulated her "on the splendid results." And by the time of the 1929 Carnegie recital Robeson was still seeking her out for help with specific technical matters. Eslanda often accompanied her husband to lessons, and left a single extended account of one of Armitage's coaching sessions. It is instructive for what it tells us about the teacher's method and the singer's still limited awareness of technical matters despite his work with Proschowsky and Schoen-René:

Paul's "lessons" were usually great fun. "Isn't it too bad my range is so short" he said one day. "Oh, it's short, is it?" asked Miss Armitage, with a twinkle in her eye. They became engrossed in their work, and at the end of an hour she said: "Now, my dear child, that low note you just sang so beautifully was low D, and the last magnificent top note was middle E. You just think your range is short. It's all of two and a quarter octaves, which is long enough for any reasonable person." "You don't mean to tell me that high note was

E," Paul said incredulously. "It was so easy; if I'd known how high I was I'd have been scared to death." He grinned, and danced up and down in his delight. Miss Armitage smiled; she enjoyed working with this great over-grown boy. I'll never take you any higher than you can go easily, so don't be afraid," she said reassuringly. She would often tell him: "Now, Paul, don't dig for your low notes. Raise your chin and sing them freely; think them high, and they will be bright; if you keep reaching down for them they will be dark." Or, "You must not climb up and reach for that top note; think it low and bring your chin down on it, and it will come easily." And, sure enough, to his amazement, his low notes became clear and resonant, and his high notes easy and firm. Paul was elated. "It's all so simple" he said. "Don't cover up your voice so, child," Miss Armitage said; "just open your mouth and throat and let the tone come out freely. Don't set your throat that closes it. Relax it, and you'll see how the voice rolls out." Paul tried relaxing his throat, and his whole body as well. "Gee," he said delightedly, after an hour's work, "you know my throat doesn't feel tired at all; in fact, my voice actually feels rested." He strolled up and down the studio, amazed that this should be so. Miss Armitage laughed. "And now, my child, you will always know that you are singing right when you do not tire. When you set your throat and cover your tones, you tire the muscles. But when you relax your throat you will find the more you sing the more flexible your voice will be, because correct singing oils the chords naturally and rests the voice." Paul was tre-mendously interested, and worked long and faithfully.[71]

Near the end of his singing career, Robeson himself reflected on the time of his voice training years. He had been invited to write the preface for what would become the London-based pedagogue Georges Cunelli's *Voice No Mystery* (which finally saw publication in 1973). Robeson's accompanying notes on an early draft of Cunelli's primer, then with the working title "Sing or Not to Sing," are revealing of Robeson's position on voice training: a sort of post-career justification, and a comment on different types of voice coaches he worked with. He concurred with Cunelli that singing is an ex-tension of speech, highlighting the author's counsel that it is "extremely important to keep the line between speech and song continuous, harmo-nious and in balance." This in turn was underpinned by their agreement on a broader principle: that "the voice is beautiful by nature, not by teaching." The consequences of this for vocal training were made apparent in select quotations Robeson extracted from the book: "music must always be adapted

36   PAUL ROBESON'S VOICES

to the character of the voice, and not the voice to the character of the music," and "don't let anyone touch what is only yours." In Robeson's engagement with Cunelli's book, familiarity with the discourse of classical voice pedagogy is uttered in rejection of aspects of its standard practice. We can thus juxtapose critics' concerns and Proschowsky's work on extending Robeson's range with Robeson's experience of the sometime failed training to do so and his no doubt delight to read in Cunelli the following dictum that the singer highlighted: "Any attempt to produce an artificial range by stretching the speaking or singing voice badly affects the normal functioning of the vocal apparatus."[72] Not all Robeson's encounters with classical voice training were disappointing. His work with Armitage suggests an affinity of approach, and the singer's future vocal coaches were also chosen, at least in part, for their compatibility with Robeson's outlook on singing.

Thus Robeson also received instruction from one of the leading authorities on the voice in Britain, George Henschel. This was probably on the recommendation of Aldridge, who had herself counted the elder master of singing as her own teacher.[73] Henschel saw Robeson during the latter stages of 1929 until at least mid-1930 at the Red House Studio in Kensington, London, offering to "reserve as many lessons for him as he would like to have" prior to the singer's sailing for the US tour of late 1929. Henschel had given Robeson his book, *Fifty Songs by George Henschel* (1905), which he inscribed to the singer, and was pleased to hear from Eslanda that Robeson was "deriving pleasure and profit from my little book and the records."[74] The little that is known about Henschel's teaching practice suggests he was a good fit for Robeson. For one, Henschel seems to have been flexible in approach, not bound to one school of voice teaching, and rather taking his lead from a student's particular needs. "When we ask Mr. Henschel to say something about his method, he laughingly replies: 'If in the course of the season I have twenty-three or thirty pupils, I have twenty-three or thirty methods.' "[75] The Robesons would have concurred, for one thing they wanted to avoid in the instruction of Robeson's voice was "technique [that] seemed to level all the voices to one uninteresting mould."[76] There are also more specific features of Henschel's own singing practice that we can identify in Robeson's. The prefatory matter to *Fifty Songs* noted "the importance [Henschel] always attaches to the distinct enunciation of the words in his singing interpretations. In this respect he is a model to young vocalists." Throughout his career Robeson was similarly lauded for an ideal singer's enunciation. Of a 1929 Town Hall recital in New York, undertaken just after working with Henschel, one critic observed

BECOMING PAUL ROBESON'S VOICE   37

how Robeson made every word "intelligible . . . without any sacrifice of musical tone or shattering of the melodic line."[77] Another mark of Henschel's teaching was a focus on the expressive function of vowel sounds, to convey character by creating vocal color. In this light we may consider Robeson's satisfaction with his 1929 Carnegie Hall performance, particularly, as Robeson phrased it, the "great variety of mood-color etc. I [did] so because I sang the songs and forgot my voice."[78] That he should conceive of mood variety, in the first instance, as vocal color, is reminiscent of a central point of Henschel's teaching. There is a sense in Robeson's note to himself—penned in a diary— of a singing lesson well learned, of a technical means used for an expressive end. Daniel Leech-Wilkinson notes that Henschel's singing approach in general was "straightforward"; a contemporary critic wrote that there "is no show and no self-consciousness" about his singing.[79] It is an approach wholly in accord with Robeson's own ideas on singing, perhaps partly formed in his encounter with Henschel.

Even in Schoen-René, Robeson likely encountered a teacher whose method, or as she preferred to call it "a scientific education in vocal art," chimed with his own sentiments on singing. As a direct inheritor of Manuel Garcia's teaching, she emphasized above all the attainment of "purity of tone and evenness of line," the production of which depended on effective breathing, vocalization, and resonance. So paramount was tone that if "florid and flexible technic" was advisable "it must always remain secondary to the production of pure tone itself."[80] From its first public hearings Robeson's voice had been lauded for its tonal qualities. But after some training, and by the end of the 1920s, the hearing of Robeson as possessing a voice of sheer tone had become the norm. Critics' observations of his newly acquired vocal resonance and smoothness was thus routinely ornamented by a vocabulary that proclaimed the luxurious, velvety, richness of his voice's sound. Charles Isaacson's paean to Robeson's voice as tone is not unusually effusive: "From an ocean of tone, whose depth seems never to have been plumbed, the phrases rose like magnificent jungle animals, ripe and shining, monarchs in their domain, strong with unchallenged power. Effortless singing it was. . . . At moments the sheer loveliness of certain tones awakened a flood of sensuous delight: those tones are the most perfect uttered by living man."[81]

By the time of the first Carnegie Hall recital of 1929 then there is sufficient evidence to suggest that Robeson performed, at least in part, as a trained singer; and critics often noted his training and its effects on his singing.[82] Their observations indicate an awareness of songful ideals—smooth singing,

38   PAUL ROBESON'S VOICES

variety of vocal timbre—and the sublimation of vocal technique in achieving those ideals. The lessons offered by several voice experts over half a decade were cumulatively responsible for the sound of Robeson's voice by the late 1920s, something the singer well realized. It is a reminder of the "enormous impact that teachers' and institutions' tonal ideals and pedagogical practices have on the ultimate sound of a classical singer's voice." And in this is another teachable moment, on "the constructedness of vocal timbre in formally trained voices": "voices are not innate, but cultural . . . voices are not intrinsic, but are shaped by a pedagogical collective."[83]

Rather than embark on a sustained and systematic program of formal voice training, Robeson opted for ad hoc sessions with different teachers to resolve problems that cropped up during the early stages of his professional career. Learning to sing, for Robeson, involved a tentative and selective listening to vocal authority. Although his experience with the professional voice academy was not always a happy one, it was productive of his voice, allowing him over a period of half a decade and more to discover his concert voice. That he worked tirelessly on his voice throughout his career is well known, and the teachers I have mentioned were not the only ones he consulted.[84] Thus his accompanist, who probably knew Robeson's voice more intimately than anyone, could write in mid-1931, more than six years after Robeson had first begun voice coaching, that the singer had "improved tremendously in his singing [over the] last few weeks" while in London, and only a few weeks later, again: "Paul is improving all the time and I have high hopes for his work next year."[85]

I began this section by invoking contemporary critical authority as witness to Robeson's mastery of singing. In close I do similarly, pointing to critics' observations on the progression of Robeson's singing. In response to his end-of-1929 Carnegie Hall concerts, the *New Yorker* noted that since "his debut as a vocalist he has improved his production enormously and added several notes at both ends of the scale," and in similar vein the (New York) *American* enthused that his "management of tone, breath, phrase and coloring have improved remarkably since he first challenged attention as a serious candidate for recognition in concert."[86] But Robeson's troubles with his voice were by no means at their end. Despite critics' sometimes overly enthusiastic, perhaps uncritical, reception—one Hungarian critic who heard Robeson in concert in Budapest in April 1929 concluded that he was "technically beyond criticism"—Robeson's vocal art would remain unsettled into the mid-1930s. Martin Duberman summarized the situation as

BECOMING PAUL ROBESON'S VOICE   39

such: "Well aware of the technical limitations of his voice, he was yet being received, and by an ever-widening circle of admirers, as the embodiment of vocal perfection."[87]

(De)Classifying the Voice

To make sense of voices we classify them. Robeson's voice was no exception, even as it resists easy classification; one reason, I suggested in the Introduction, for his musicological neglect: his voice and singing do not fit into bounded categories. As a professional musician Robeson did not only sing on the concert stage. He appeared live on the musical theater stage, crooned popular music of the Tin Pan Alley tradition on record, and made the odd musical hall appearance. (He cultivated spoken voices for dramatic theater and concert recitation too.) But after establishing himself in the concert field, Robeson's concert voice became his dominant voice, and the vocal styles appropriate to other traditions he occasionally attempted were departures from the dominant voice and sometimes partial failures: bad music, if you will.[88] Singing in different traditions was common in the 1920s and 1930s, the time during which Robeson became a star. Laura Tunbridge reminds us of the "flexibility with which performers approached high- and lowbrow registers during the interwar period," and Allison McCracken of the "cultural normalcy of . . . vocal nonessentialism in the performing world of the 1920s": singers routinely switched between vocal codes and voices were socially fluid.[89] Many art singers in the Gramophone Company stable (popularly known as His Master's Voice or HMV), for which Robeson recorded for over a decade, performed non–art song repertoire. Peter Dawson and John McCormack, who like Robeson were singers with complicated national allegiances (and who, together with Robeson, headed the annual HMV Christmas list), moved easily between art, popular, folk, and film song.

The paratextual forms and discourses that accompanied Robeson's voice on record and in concert—labels, listing practices, reviews, and programs—instructed listeners how to receive his voice; and they provide contexts for understanding the identity of a voice still in formation. For example, the Gramophone Company classified its recordings in various ways, categorizing its discs by label and series. Robeson's HMV recordings appeared on the plum label and predominantly in Series B. An in-house advertisement for the "Plums" in 1928 promoted the label as offering "an unrivalled

40   PAUL ROBESON'S VOICES

repertoire of popular operatic, orchestral, organ, vocal, instrumental, and dance music."[90] For one historian the label presented a "mixed repertoire, tending towards the popular, or what we might now call light music or easy listening, but with a sprinkling of popular classics."[91] Appearing on the plums was a sign of Robeson's popularity as a recording artist, and perhaps of the crossover status of his in-between voice: his was certainly not the voice of a music hall performer nor was it the voice of a typical classical singer. HMV's listing categories in its monthly catalogs seem to point toward this. Typically his records are labeled "Vocal Records," a specific designation for "serious" music, such as opera and *Lieder*, and from which the category of "Light Vocal" was excised. Robeson's recordings of spirituals are listed under HMV's serious vocal records category. But so too are his recordings of the popular song tradition, perhaps because by then his voice bore the authority of a partly trained voice no matter the repertoire it sang.[92] It was in the company of Beniamino Gigli, Joseph Hislop, Lawrence Tibbett, Dawson, and Feodor Chaliapin, that Robeson thus appeared as one of HMV's "Great Men Singers of Our Day."[93]

The leading British magazine of recorded music *Gramophone* distinguished "singers of popular songs of the day" into "two classes": "those who have really good voices and use their art on these trifles, and those whose chief claim to popularity is their talent in putting these songs over without the same vocal abilities but with consummate artistry and effect." In the former camp were Tibbett, the lyric British tenor Frank Titterton, and Robeson, "who combines the technique of the trained singer."[94] Here, in *Gramophone*'s estimation, did Robeson display a mastery of technique that made him a concert singer. The aligning of the concert singing of spirituals with the idea of classical music marked, as I noted earlier, Robeson's own intentions for singing spirituals and the aesthetic agenda of the Harlem Renaissance. It is also evident in the programming decisions by which Robeson's singing was presented in concert, that is, by the repertoire that "accompanied" him, and which thus provided a context for hearing his own music-making. One of his first recitals, at Rutgers College in December 1924, makes this plain (see Box 1.2). It was a voice recital shared by two singers, the other a soprano Charlotte Murray. Typical of the time, the vocal portions were broken up by a solo contribution from the accompanist, Mr. Hooper, who performed a piano suite by the Black Canadian-American composer Nathaniel Dett at the start of the second half. Murray sang the original art songs, works by Burleigh ("Now Sleeps the Crimson Petal") and other Black classical composers, whereas

Box 1.2. Program, Rutgers Concert, December 17, 1924. Paul Robeson Collection, microfilm 2. The Schomburg Center for Research in Black Culture, New York Public Library.

PROGRAM

I.

By and By.. ....Arr. by Burleigh
I Want to be Ready...................................Arr. by Burleigh
Deep River..Arr. by Fisher

II.

Sometimes I Feel Like a Motherless Child..............Arr. by Burleigh
I Don't Feel Noways Tired.............................Arr. by Burleigh
Sinner Please Don't Let This Harvest Pass...........Arr. by Burleigh

CHARLOTTE MURRAY

III.

L'il [sic] Gal................................ ....J. Rosamond Johnson
Seems Lak to Me.............................. ....J. Rosamond Johnson
Nuthin.................................. ....Carpenter

INTERMISSION

"In the Bottoms" (Suite for Piano) ....Nathaniel Dett

LOUIS HOOPER

IV.

Every Time I Feel the Spirit....................Arr. by Lawrence Brown
Didn't It Rain?...................................Arr. by Burleigh
Go Down Moses.....................................Arr. by Burleigh

V.

Thou Hast Bewitched Me Beloved..................S. Coleridge Taylor
Now Sleeps the Crimson Petal.....................Harry T. Burleigh
Thou Art Risen...................................S. Coleridge Taylor

CHARLOTTE MURRAY

VI.

Swing Low, Sweet Chariot.....................Arr. by Lawrence Brown
Couldn't Hear Nobody Pray........................Arr. by F. Work
The Gospel Train.................................Arr. by Burleigh

42 PAUL ROBESON'S VOICES

Robeson sang only arrangements of spirituals, at once a move toward and remove from art music.[95]

In the decade following the Rutgers concert Robeson's voice was increasingly brought within the ambit of "serious" music, in its training, and even in the art song repertoire the singer attempted. The Rutgers plan of sharing the stage with identifiable classical musicians thus became the modus at various points throughout his singing career. While still singing only spirituals in the late 1920s he was joined in concert by solo classical instrumentalists, such as the young Black pianist Justin Sandridge for the US tour of 1929, or the British cellist Livio Mannucci for a Royal Albert Hall concert in the same year.[96] In the United Kingdom it was the norm, especially for the Holt International Celebrity Concert tours Robeson undertook for much of the 1930s, for the star singer to be "assisted" by second-tier, although often highly regarded, classical performers. Sharing the concert platform with other musicians at first served a practical purpose: to bulk up the program at the outset of the singer's professional career when he was short on repertoire. Sharing the stage specifically with classical musicians was more complex. It aligned with the class ideals of the striving Black elites of the Harlem Renaissance, but also served artistic ends, varying the music on offer at a time when Robeson's all-spiritual recitals often drew criticism for being monotonous, and for the first few years of the 1930s complementing Robeson's own singing of the art song repertoire in recital. The appearance of classical musicians on a Robeson program thus further secured the status of the singer as an artist to be taken seriously. But it also highlighted how Robeson's singing was different from, and partly rejected, the world of classical music. The singer's concert tour of the British provinces with the Léner String Quartet in 1935 brought this to the fore. Of the "two entertainments in one"—"a mixed musical grill"—one pundit concluded that "we have dissonances in modern music, and now, it seems, we must have them also in the construction of programmes."[97]

The singer made his own position explicit as his artistic vision and practice matured in the mid-1930s (and which I discuss further in chapter 4 as Robeson reinvented himself as the people's artist). In a series of statements to the press Robeson nailed his aesthetic colors to the mast: "I am convinced that I can not only retain the interest of the serious music-lover, but also entertain the man in the street." He put it another way: "I have endeavoured to steer a middle course. I believe that such a programme will appeal to all types of music-lovers," and thus: "I am appealing not to the highbrow and not to the lowbrow, but I am singing for all."[98] For this reason the *Manchester Guardian* pointed out that Robeson was "the only one who makes no concession to the highbrow public," whereas "Kreisler, McCormack, and Tauber, who share that power, begin their concerts at 3 p.m. with 'the classics,' and wend their ways down to the common denominator of popular taste by half-past four."[99] Robeson's joint appearances with classical musicians was precisely a concession of sorts, although it was also more than just a musical bone for the highbrow. It is indicative of the extent to which the singer had become imbricated in the concert field and formed by its practices, even as he sought to extricate his artistic self from aspects of the field. Hence the difficulty in placing Robeson's voice. Perhaps we would do best to follow the lead of the *Dublin Evening Mail*, which proclaimed that Robeson "is not a classifiable singer."[100] Indeed, endeavors to categorize Robeson's voice perhaps miss the point. The will to classification denies the voice a fluidity to sound across traditions of singing and vocal typologies. Even identifying Robeson's voice type proved complicated.

A "Dusky Chaliapin": Securing a Bass

One of the earliest pieces of extended writing on Robeson, Elizabeth Shepley Sergeant's *New Republic* feature of 1926, christened him the "Negro Chaliapin."[101] Invoking Feodor Chaliapin, the Russian operatic bass, as a point of comparison was a common enough move already at this very early point in Robeson's singing career, and it would become increasingly popular to do so: "He is the Chaliapin of the moment," proclaimed the *Chicago Herald-Examiner*; Robeson's voice "is believed by many to be the greatest voice of the present, now that Chaliapin sings no more."[102] Through comparison with the Russian singer, routinely claimed as the greatest bass of the first decades of the century in the contemporary musical press, Robeson's voice continued to gain status.

Chaliapin was prominent in the artistic and social life of New York City and London in the 1920s and 1930s when Robeson's star was on the rise, and the two singers held each other in high regard.[103] Robeson first heard the Russian in recital at a farewell event for the latter at the Metropolitan Opera House in 1925, although they had met socially prior to this. He would hear Chaliapin several times more in performance, in the world's great opera houses—Covent Garden and the Théâtre des Champs-Élysées—and owned many of the Russian singer's recordings, which he listened to "often and

44   PAUL ROBESON'S VOICES

avidly."[104] Chaliapin was not just one of Robeson's heroes but, as he explained in an interview late in his life, in the field of music Chaliapin was the artist who had made the greatest impression on the young singer.[105]

Their very origins afforded comparison. The Russian was born to a peasant family, Robeson had slave lineage; and Robeson would make frequent reference to the structural correspondences between the histories, lives, and experiences of Black Americans and the Russian peasantry. From this he extrapolated a relationship of empathy for all things Russian, including language and music, and Soviet politics.[106] For Robeson, Chaliapin was a standard-bearer of Russian culture. And for this reason the Russian singer made an unexpected appearance during Robeson's testimony to the House Un-American Activities Committee, in June 1956, when the American was interrogated on his connections to Soviet Russia; or what the committee called "promoting the Communist cause." (Robeson retorted: "I am here because I am opposing the neo-Fascist cause, which I see arising in these committees.") After sustained probing, to which Robeson more often than not either refused to answer the committee's questions or, as his interrogators said, made a speech instead, the following was put to him: "Did you write an article that was published in the *U.S.S.R. Information Bulletin*? Quote, I want to emphasize that only here in the Soviet Union did I feel that I was a real man with a capital M. Close quote." "I am quite willing to answer the question," responded Robeson: "When I was a singer . . . I am a bass singer. So for me it was Chaliapin," and at the mention of Chaliapin, Robeson turned to the mode of musical speech for which he was noted,

> the great Russian bass. . . . I learned the Russian language to sing their songs. . . . The great poet of Russia [Pushkin] is of African blood. . . . It is important to explain this. . . . When I first went to Russia in 1934. . . . In Russia I felt for the first time like a full human being. No color prejudice, like in Mississippi. No color prejudice, like in Washington. It was the first time I felt like a human being. Where I do not feel the pressure of color as I feel it in this committee today.[107]

The chain of identifications that Robeson sets up in response to the fundamental terms of his interrogation—and the proceedings that day were adjourned when Robeson soon thereafter accused the committee members "You . . . are the Un-Americans!"—are core to his identity, as an artist and person: singer, bass, Chaliapin, Russian, African, human. Chaliapin is the

BECOMING PAUL ROBESON'S VOICE   45

pivot in the progression from artist-identity to human subject. It says something of the importance of the Russian singer to Robeson's sense of being that he named Chaliapin at this highly politicized event at a key moment in his—and the nation's—life.[108]

To listen now to Chaliapin and Robeson on record, say to their interpretations of Mussorgsky or of Russian folk music, such as "Song of the Volga Boatmen" which both recorded several times, might elicit bafflement at the persistent comparison of Robeson with Chaliapin.[109] The difference between Robeson's first recording of "Volga Boatmen," laid down in March 1938 at Abbey Road, London, and Chaliapin's many recordings of the song he had made famous in the West is striking; and other than the basic outline of the arrangement used by Chaliapin that Robeson follows they have little in common. Produced just weeks before the Russian's death, in a symbolic passing of the baton as Robeson would become as associated with the song as Chaliapin had been, Robeson's first outing on record is often ponderous and not especially exciting. Chaliapin's performances exude dynamism and drama, qualities of expression for which he was renowned, and are enthralling for these. Far more so than Robeson's properly "Western," even "English," reading, Chaliapin's is an interpellation of the oriental other (for the Western listener). His idiomatic Russian and sureness of the song material and voice—he leads the orchestra—conjures an authenticity that Robeson's part English-language version and occasionally hesitant delivery—he lags behind the orchestra—does not approach. To drive home the Russianness, Chaliapin is supported by a dominant brass sound, whereas the HMV studio orchestra for Robeson is all sweet strings, with a harp added for good measure. Richard Taruskin has noted that the conventional viewpoint on Russian music has been as "the 'West's' most significant 'other.'"[110] In the Western press Chaliapin was seldom presented as just a great bass but specifically as "the great Russian bass," and Robeson was, similarly, "The Great Negro Singer" (at least during the 1920s and into the 1930s, whereafter the qualifier of race appeared less frequently). (White) America's most significant other, the argument could be made after Taruskin, was Black America, and these correspondences of alterity informed the comparative framework. The London *Evening Standard*, in a review titled "Dusky Chaliapin," noted in Robeson's voice "that indescribable richness of bass tone which, it seems, is possessed only by Russians and coloured people."[111] As a low male-voice singer it is an obvious point of comparison that Robeson was likened to the greatest living bass, facilitated no doubt by the dearth of celebrity basses.

46 PAUL ROBESON'S VOICES

But even such a core part of Robeson's singer's identity—being a bass—was not always uncontested, and it is to the vicissitudes in vocal typologies that I now turn.

A brief overview of the classifying of Robeson's voice type in the first few years of his concert career would look as follows. The few theater critics who drew on musical terminology identified his actor's voice as a bass. For his first two public recitals as a singer—at Copley-Plaza, Boston (November 2, 1924) and Rutgers College (December 17, 1924)—there is no mention of voice type, as if the singer, as yet unencumbered by the full range of classificatory requirements of the concert field, performed *au naturel*. By the time of the first major solo recital at the Greenwich Village Theater the following April, Robeson is presented in the program book as a "bass-baritone," an attempt to formalize the voice type as the singer appeared in formal evening dress. And by the concert tour of 1926 the dominant identification of the voice settled on baritone: a *Detroit News* headline ran "Robeson, Negro Baritone, an Artist in Spirituals"; his recital broadcasts on WRNY's Edison Hour in June and July 1927 advertised him as a baritone; and program books, when they did identify and advertise the voice type, followed suit: he was presented as "Paul Robeson, Baryton" for the Paris Salle Gaveau recital of October 29, 1927, and advertised as "The Great Negro Baritone" for the Carnegie Hall concerts of November 1929.[112] This preference for identifying Robeson as a baritone continued into the early 1930s. How might we account for the shift in Robeson's voice type, from (spoken) bass in theater criticism to (singing) baritone by the apparatus of the institution of the song recital?

Two technologies of the voice are implicated in this process of producing Robeson's baritone. One is sound recording, which I touch on in passing here because Robeson's recorded voice is the subject of chapter 6. In the most general sense, and as has been common comment in the literature on sound technology since Benjamin's and Adorno's early musings, the mechanical reproduction of sound involves at once a resignification and loss of the original—auratic and real—sound object. Specifically, bass voices still recorded poorly when Robeson first entered the studio in 1925 at the dawn of electrical recording. For this reason his voice was probably recorded higher than it might have been had the technology permitted otherwise. I pursue this argument in some detail at a later point, noting for now an observation of causal listening: multiple recordings of the same song are sung in increasingly lower keys as Robeson's career progressed, and as recording technology better reproduced bass voices. The convict song "Water Boy" of 1926 is sung in E major, the HMV recording of 1933 in D major, and a 1945 record lower yet in B major.[113]

The other technology of the voice that affected Robeson's voice type is art singing and its attendant pedagogy. Once he had decided to pursue a career as a concert singer he was set, as we have seen, on the path of voice training, the combined technologies of which would attempt to produce an ideal voice: Robeson as baritone. This perhaps masked his "real" voice. "Advertised as a baritone, but really a bass," mused the Chicago critic Edward Moore.[114] Prior to training the voice, in speech and song, is always narrated as a deep bass in the biographic record.[115] Robeson thus experienced the attempt to produce a classical baritone voice as something akin to a vocal trauma. For this reason the singer approvingly cited a core principle of Cunelli's natural method, that "music must always be adapted to the character of the voice, and not the voice to the character of the music."[116] Hence Robeson's ultimate rejection of the ends of the voice training project, that is, the production of a *Lieder* and or opera singer.

Commentators have dated the demands for the expansion of Robeson's repertoire beyond the arrangements of Black spirituals and secular songs to the late 1920s, in the runup to his first public performances of the Western art song repertoire in the early 1930s. But such demands were already being made very shortly after his professional concertizing commenced. Noting the "spiritual invasion of New York," the *Herald-Tribune* lamented the "oppressive atmosphere of monotony" of Robeson's programs, which by then New Yorkers had heard many times. While a program of all-Black music was a more "novel entertainment" for the provincial Philadelphia *Bulletin*, the paper drew on the same turn of phrase, asking whether the program "inclined to create an atmosphere of monotony"? Other critics shifted the focus to the singer's failings and promise: "Mr. Robeson's range of interpretations is limited," observed the *New York Sun*; he "could do bigger things if he chose," pronounced Richard Davis of the *Milwaukee Journal*.[117] Such sentiment would surface from time to time during the ensuing years—"It would be interesting to hear what the singer could do beyond the modest range of these Dixie-land ditties" wrote London's *Daily Mail*—and grew apace during 1929. The *New Yorker* summed up a dominant strain in Robeson criticism at this time, convinced that he had "outgrown the negro-spiritual stage," and concluded that it was "a pity for an artist of Mr. Robeson's gifts and intelligence to appear only as an intoner of racial airs."[118]

48 PAUL ROBESON'S VOICES

While the periods of vocal study Robeson undertook in the mid- and late 1920s served to shore up his concert voice—preparing it for the rigors of professional singing and sorting out technical problems—they also prepared the voice for singing Western art song repertoire; the technologies of the voice had of course been developed in service of the songs it was meant to properly sing. Presented with a young novice bass, some of his voice teachers sought to remake Robeson into a lyric baritone, no doubt in an attempt to open up his voice to a more extended repertoire than that on offer to a bass singer.[119] But if Robeson's avowed rejection of art song and its singing techniques was, as I documented earlier, partial, the remaking of his voice as a baritone was also never complete. Reflecting on his pre-concert years, the singer told the Washington, DC, magazine *The Easterner* that as "little as [he] thought of his acting [then], he thought even less of his voice, especially because it was a bass." He was moreover "erroneously billed as a baritone, and he has been a 'baritone' ever since."[120] Robeson was not alone in observing the error.

The debut concert tour of 1926 that initiated the intensive period of vocal training that I chronicled earlier had included Chicago's Orchestra Hall on the itinerary. A poor turnout for the February 10 recital seems to have galvanized Robeson's and Brown's performance, which drew uniform praise from the gathered critics. For Glenn Dillard Gunn of the *Chicago Herald and Examiner*, Robeson's voice was, even at this early time, "distinguished among the great voices of the present." And the Chicago critics, as with other thinking listeners at the time, questioned the presentation of Robeson as a baritone: "rather of the basso timbre," observed Karleton Hackett of the *Chicago Evening Post*.[121] What led these and other listeners to hear Robeson as a bass, rather than as the baritone the institution of the art song recital desired Robeson to be(come)? Perhaps it was the quality of the voice in a particular (low) register that enticed. Richard Miller has stated that the overriding determinant of voice type is tonal quality in a particular register.[122] Hackett made mention of the "especial richness in the middle lower notes," while footnoting that "at times the upper notes did not respond quite as he might have liked."[123] Robeson's tessitura, that range of comfort, thus seemed to be of a lower register. A year later, during the second American tour, a Kansas critic thought his voice "already remarkably fine, especially in the lower tones, which he uses with discrimination, not as a medium of roaring exhibition."[124] The attribution of good taste to Robeson's performances, a recurring feature of Robeson concert criticism, is here also the recognition that in the sparing use of the lower voice is the distinctiveness of the voice

Example 1.1. Avery Robinson, arr., "Water Boy. A Negro Convict Song" (London: Winthrop Rogers, 1922), mm. 1–4. With permission, Boosey & Hawkes.

to be discovered. We might listen to Robeson's singing following this line of thought.

One of Robeson's, and his audiences', favorite songs was the prison song "Water Boy," arranged by Avery Robinson (see Example 1.1). It was one of the first songs Robeson recorded, and was featured on the Chicago program.[125] We should, as I have cautioned, be wary of taking the early recordings as a representation of Robeson's bass.[126] But we can still listen to these recordings for how Robeson's voice sounds across registers. The unaccompanied introductory measures of "Water Boy" serve to display the lower voice in several ways (listen to Sound Recording 1.1a ▶). Each of the introduction's three vocal phrases, triadic outlines with the third phrase introducing the seventh, descends a fifth from its starting pitch. The lowest note for all three phrases is the same—E_3 in the printed sheet music, $C\sharp_3$ in the 1926 recording—its thrice repetition emphasizing the lowest points of the introduction. It is these low points that Robeson's performance reinforces. The first melodic phrase, set to the titular words "Water Boy," contains three accents of sorts: on the opening phoneme of "Wa-" and on the first and third notes that "boy" takes. Of these three marked notes it is the final one, also the lowest in pitch, on the "-oy" of

50 PAUL ROBESON'S VOICES

"boy" that is most marked, something Robeson achieves by effecting a microtonal glide from below on to the notated pitch (0:10–0:12). As it happens, this is also the note of longest duration in the phrase, and so once marked the lowest note is also heard longest, impressed doubly on the listener. The final note of the second phrase ("where are you hiding?") is given distinction through timbral differentiation. Where Robeson sings "where are you hi-" (0:13–0:17) with particular openness, delaying the articulation of the consonant to the last moment, he immediately closes the "-ding" of "hiding" (0:18–0:19) alighting on the velar nasal "ng" (or ⟨ŋ⟩ to use the phonetic alphabet symbol). In doing so, the lowest note in the phrase is timbrally marked in relation to those preceding it. And the final, low note of the third phrase (the "-my" of "Mammy") is, simply, the longest to this point. Given a fermata in the score Robeson's performance of the introduction as unmetered aids in according the paused note its due share of time.

I could proceed through the rest of the 1926 recording of the song in similar fashion, suggesting how Robeson's low register might be privileged in our hearing of his voice. For instance, in the song's many octave leaps—always down—we receive a glimpse, on the low note of the octave, of the vocal resonance by which critics routinely characterized his voice. But we have only to fast-forward to the final sounds of the song, those that remain most immediately in the listener's mind. The final iteration of "Water Boy" is the lowest phrase of the song, the final note the lowest yet—B_2 on the score, $G\sharp_2$ in the recording. The confidence and fullness of tone with which Robeson sings this final phrase stands in contrast to the decidedly "thin" voice of the immediately preceding much higher phrase, which ranges between $G\sharp_3$ and $C\sharp_4$ in the recording (listen to Sound Recording 1.1b ⏵). (A lyric baritone, though, would be quite comfortable here.) If we subscribe to the identificatory guidelines of vocal *Fach*, then Robeson's *primo passaggio*, that point at which the primary register terminates, is around $G\sharp_3$ in the early "Water Boy" recording. In Miller's scheme this would make Robeson's voice type a lyric bass.[127] Herman Devries, writing for the *Chicago American*, similarly identified Robeson as "a sonorous, healthy, full-toned basso-cantante." Designating in the first instance a lyrical rather than dramatic or buffo singer, and in the second instance a slightly higher bass than, for example, a basso profundo, the lyric bass—if we must categorize Robeson's voice—is probably more on the mark. Despite his promotion as a baritone, and subsequent training for a baritone *Fach*, then, Robeson's real bass voice seems to sing to us in those song moments it best fits. More astute critics noticed this. When music critic Karleton Hackett heard "Water

BECOMING PAUL ROBESON'S VOICE   51

Boy" at the Chicago recital of February 1926, he felt it was "one of those things that takes right hold of you." Hackett attributed Robeson's hold on his listeners to his voice's tone "and depth of feeling back of the tone," concluding that he "was not a tenor singing a love song, but a bass singing of convicts calling for the water boy."[128]

Robeson's voice continued to be represented as a baritone into the early 1930s, perhaps more from force of habit than anything else. Because by 1928, after the first few years of voice training and Robeson's growing awareness of his vocal self, there is also a greater recognition of his voice type as a bass. Certainly this is true of London critics reviewing the Drury Lane concerts between June and September 1928 that piggybacked on the singer's appearance in *Show Boat* in the same theater. Of interest are critics' comments on his impressive range, one of the boons no doubt of training: "a bass voice of wonderful compass," noted the *Morning Advertiser*; a bass of "wide range," reported the *Daily Sketch*.[129] Whereas in earlier years Robeson was criticized for his limited range, its extension—by "several notes at both ends of the scale" according to the *New Yorker*[130]—now permitted the voice to be heard more convincingly, perhaps, as a higher low-voice singer. Thus when John B. Miller, writing for the *Capitol Times* of Madison, hailed Robeson as the "brilliant Negro basso-baritone," he clarified that his voice "is both bass and baritone, having at different times the best qualities of both," the singing "characterized, even in the highest tones, by a velvety soft smoothness."[131] As Robeson produced an increasingly ideal tone throughout a now extended range, he could be heard, Miller seems to say, as a baritone at certain moments in certain songs, and as a bass at other times.

Finding a Voice

The final chapter of Eslanda Robeson's biography of her husband, published in 1930, bears the title "Finding Himself." The chapter turns on the device of the wife and husband in conversation, debating Robeson's character flaws, and what Eslanda deemed to be her husband's "shortcomings." The chief evidence Eslanda presents is from the fields of performance, both concert work and serious theater:

> Take your concerts for instance; you just won't learn a new song until you're convinced that you can't sing the same old programme any longer. . . . I think

52 PAUL ROBESON'S VOICES

that's half the reason for your feeling about singing other music. You realise that you will have to get down to brass tacks and study, learn how to sing them correctly, learn the languages so you can articulate the words clearly and easily, read about the composers, their lives and their countries, so you can understand the spirit of the songs. . . . so you settle back and say, "I'm a special interpreter of the Music of My People," and stop there, because you know *that* music.[132]

In Eslanda's account, this late-night chat, while taking "a turn along the Heath" in Hampstead where they lived in London, seemed to spur the singer to action. Robeson committed to "have a go at those German songs. . . . Larry is always after me to try," and to this end purchased study literature on Mussorgsky, Bach, Schubert, and Beethoven, together with an order of classical music recordings. Eslanda wrote that days, weeks, months "slipped by with Paul spending long hours shut up with his gramophone, playing the fine records over and over, soaking himself in good music; reading his books, buying new books and devouring them; working with Larry, learning new songs. He bought a metronome. . . . He worked hard with his teachers over the new songs".[133] Robeson's "finding himself" originated in song discovery, in learning new repertoire—art song, on this occasion—and in training his voice; in other words, in finding his voice. It is exemplary of the processes by which the voice functions as a technology of self-development.[134]

Eslanda's biography concluded with a promise. But in the early 1930s Robeson would fail to establish himself as a singer of art songs, and the passage of artistic self-discovery was, we have seen, fraught: despite Robeson's early successes as a singer, the viability of a concert career remained uncertain; regardless of the paeans to his voice, he struggled at times with vocal technique; and even the "essence" of his voice—the deep bass—was questioned. The process of finding an artistic voice thus continued, and would proceed in a different direction in the decade of the 1930s, a story that later chapters in the book pick up.

In this chapter I have outlined some of the contexts that led to the formation of Robeson's early singing voice. Looking ahead, we might ask: do the transformations of Robeson's voice in the early years of its formation also give us a glimpse of things to come, of the oftentimes antagonistic position the artist would assume against dominant ideologies, an oppositional politics that came to dominate Robeson's singing and life in later years? Many thinkers, most notably Jacques Attali, have sought to grant music an annunciatory power, and the prophetic (singing) voice would perhaps be the original protagonist in such a "prophetics of music."[135] Of the Black tradition specifically, Fred Moten has proposed that resistance is the "essence of black performance."[136] And theorists of the voice have shown how through singing the subject may oppose. Notes Eidsheim: "Entrainment can also take place within the choice to undertake a particular vocal practice, within a vocal practice's resistance against hegemony, and in a play whose vocal roles may be forced upon a person, within which the vocalizer may potentially redefine the very definition of that vocal practice."[137] For Meizel, finding one's voice can implicate the voice in processes that at once produce the neoliberal subject and resist it. Singers, she reports, often imagine that the individuality of the voice is "socially suppressed and in need of liberation . . . a call for freedom from one or more types of hegemony, from musical and/or political subjugation."[138] Finding a voice thus intersects with "other elements of identity . . . and the oppressive systems of race, ethnicity, and gender . . . which in turn dialectically influences the processes of finding a voice." In the chapters that follow, *Paul Robeson's Voices* charts this ongoing dialectal process of vocal and self-discovery, documenting some of the many ways Robeson's practice reworked aspects of concert singing in the first half of the twentieth century, and the many ways his voice resisted. More prosaically, my account of the development of Robeson's voice's in this chapter is one of a young singer finding his voice as he entered the concert world, exercising his registers in settling on a voice type, and exerting his vocal cords to arrive at a method of singing with which he was at ease. Voice-thinking demands also this of us.

2

"Negro Spiritual"

Voicing Desire

While starring in the 1924 New York revival of Eugene O'Neill's play *The Emperor Jones*, Robeson was invited to sit for a sculpture by the Italian émigré artist Antonio Salemme. The singer visited Salemme's Greenwich Village studio on and off for two years while Salemme molded a life-size nude bronze of the singer. Elizabeth Shepley Sergeant might have had the statue in mind we she compared Robeson to a "bronze of ancient mold."[1] Salemme was initially attracted to Robeson's actor's body on stage: "beautifully formed and glistening with sweat," he recalled, a gaze that exchanged the slave's sweaty body for the model body's muscled form. Of Robeson's singing in the play, Salemme enthused that it "was wonderful; his singing left me almost speechless. He had this magnificent voice."[2] The magnificence of Robeson's voice is experienced as numinous—almost beyond discourse—and, in the static medium of sculpture in which Salemme worked, is translated into the ecstatic subject. On completion the bronze bore the title *Negro Spiritual*—its two-year creation occupied the same period during which Robeson turned to song, and concretely captures that move. During a posing session Robeson began singing the spiritual "Deep River" and, in the sculptor's recollection, stretched out his arms "gesturing the song's deep emotions." The sculpture idealizes this pose: the standing subject, arms held high, looks upward (see the photograph in Figure 2.1). The artwork's title thus set the meaning suggested by the subject's supplicatory posture, and the statue conflated Robeson's private body with the genre of song—the African American spiritual—he had come to embody by the time of the work's completion.[3] *Negro Spiritual* aestheticized both body and song molding them in a discourse of religious beauty.[4]

As with the varied modernist artistic forms that took Robeson as their subject at this time, such as Salemme's sculpture, so too in the music criticism focused on his singing of spirituals was Robeson's reception characterized by an aestheticizing imperative; specifically, in Hazel Carby's account, by

Paul Robeson's Voices. Grant Olwage, Oxford University Press. © Oxford University Press 2024.
DOI: 10.1093/oso/9780197637470.003.0003

Figure 2.1. Photograph by Carl Van Vechten of Salemme's sculpture of Robeson, 1937. Beinecke Rare Book and Manuscript Library, Yale University. With permission The Carl Van Vechten Trust.

"modernist strategies of inwardness" that repressed the (slave) history of Black America that the Negro spirituals represented.[5] But the extensive critical writing on Robeson in the 1920s—when he first appeared on "the scene"—is also striking for the variety of interpretive moves by which his voice and singing were heard and made sense of.[6] The pretenders Paul Robeson and his accompanist Lawrence Brown—Black musicians staging only Black music in concert—meant something, demanding an explanation

56 PAUL ROBESON'S VOICES

in the early twentieth-century world. The New York *World* prefaced its review of the duo's seminal Greenwich Village Theater recital of April 1925 with a disclaimer of sorts: "A program of Negro music . . . cannot at this particular time in our history be considered apart from its racial origins and accompaniments, faulty as that intrusion may be on an aesthetic count."[7] Then—as now—would nation, history, and race intrude on Robeson criticism. How Robeson was heard during his formative artistic years tells us much about his listeners' desires; and as Eidsheim provocatively puts it, the voice's "source is not the singer; it is the listener."[8] How Robeson presented the spirituals in concert tells us also much about his own desires. He aspired to the example, for instance, of singer Roland Hayes (1887–1977), the lyric tenor hailed as the first Black American to succeed on the international stage of classical music.[9]

For the young Robeson, who confided in Salemme that he was apprehensive about singing as a career, Hayes's success was transformational.[10] Robeson spoke highly of Hayes in several fora. In an article that appeared in January 1925 in *The Messenger*, an important mouthpiece of the Harlem Renaissance, he expressed the desire to follow the older singer's example: "Today Roland Hayes is infinitely more of an asset than many who 'talk' at great length. Thousands of people hear him, see him, are moved by him, and are brought to a clearer understanding of human values. If I can do something of a like nature, I shall be happy."[11] Robeson's praise of Hayes is, to be sure, framed by the Harlem Renaissance, the flowering of African American arts and letters in the 1920s in New York. The aspirational thrust as well as race-consciousness articulated through the aesthetic domain were hallmarks of the Harlem Renaissance.[12] And Hayes, like Robeson, was taken to be a model—even if a contested one—of a Renaissance man.

The New Negro credentials of both singers were grounded in their performance of spirituals, which, along with folk song in general, were favored and recurring subjects of debates within the Harlem Renaissance.[13] Two of the leading protagonists in these debates were Alain Locke, foremost New Negro spokesman, and Carl Van Vechten, man of letters, sometime music critic, and patron of Black artists. Locke opened his essay on the spirituals in his 1925 handbook *The New Negro* with the Du Boisian declaration that the spirituals are "really the most characteristic product of the race genius as yet in America." Van Vechten, following Dvořák and others, extended the argument for the value of the spirituals, asserting that they "constitute America's chief claim to musical distinction."[14] Both of these claims—of the worth of

"NEGRO SPIRITUAL" 57

Black culture and the significance of Black culture for American culture—drove the aesthetic practice of the Harlem Renaissance, as well as Hayes's and Robeson's own work at this time. Hayes later stated: "It pleased me to believe that I was restoring the music of my race to the serious atmosphere of its origin, and helping to redeem it for the national culture."[15] The singing of the spirituals on the concert stage seemed even to enact the integrationist politics espoused by mainstream Renaissance propagandists. Before his literary career took off, a young Sterling Brown attested to the power of Hayes's song: "Roland Hayes sings. And as he sings, things drop away, the uglier apparel of manhood slinks off, and the inescapable oneness of all becomes perceptible. . . . Roland Hayes sings, and boundaries are but figments of imagination, and prejudice but insane mutterings."[16] Much the same would soon be said of Robeson's singing. A review of a Robeson recital of early 1926 articulated what would become a common position:

> Whether it was a particularly fine audience, or whether Robeson made them so, we don't know. However it happened, there was comprehension as perfect as this world allows between two races. . . . Those who hear him sing *feel* the solution of the "Negro problem" in a way they never could reach it through their intellects.[17]

Later that year the *Detroit Evening Times* conducted an interview with Robeson that it titled "Racial Harmony Goal of Negro Spiritual Singer." Robeson was reported to have said, "No one can hear these songs as our people sang them and not understand the Negro a little better."[18] In broad terms, then, Hayes's and Robeson's aesthetic-political purposes for the spirituals coincided with the ideology of the Harlem Renaissance. But the spirituals and their singers occupied a contested space in the movement. In fact, Hayes and Robeson have been consistently upheld as examples of opposing visions for the Harlem Renaissance: crudely, the former's elite cultural cosmopolitanism was perceived by some as a compromised representative of Blackness, whereas the latter was judged to embody Blackness more authentically in the 1920s. As Langston Hughes put it in his Renaissance manifesto "The Negro Artist and the Racial Mountain": "the singing of Robeson, it is truly racial."[19]

But what, if anything, is "truly racial" about Robeson's singing? Does this formulation stem from an understanding of the voice as essence? Is it Hughes's and other (Harlem Renaissance) critics' appropriation of the Black

58   PAUL ROBESON'S VOICES

voice as a tactic of what has been called strategic essentializing? This chapter seeks to show that Robeson's "Black voice" is entrained through style, rather than existing as what Eidsheim calls the "figure of sound," that is, "a constellation of beliefs in a stable, knowable sound"—an essence. Student of the spiritual Marti K. Newland writes that even today "concert spirituals may still summon racist fantasies about the peculiarity of a black bodied performing subject."[20] As Matthew D. Morrison has written about Blacksound, the historical embodiment of racialized sound may be traced through "scripts of racial 'authenticity.'" Here, authenticity does not point to a natural phenomenon but is a conventional way through which race functions.[21] My task then entails, first, revealing how Robeson's voice is a function of critical writing about his voice; or, to put it another way, how it was listened to. This is because of how the figure of sound paradigm works: it is "listening that knows *only* how to listen for and through difference from a fixed referent."[22] Second, it involves listening differently—openly, without fixed ideas of what "Black" sounds like—and also listening attentively—drilling down to a level of granularity—to the various types of sound-voice data, which voice-thinking asks us to do. Following these endeavors we may reconsider the (identity) politics of criticism that has informed representations of Hayes and Robeson, and to think anew specifically that aspect of Robeson's identity that was in the foreground in the 1920s: race.

Robeson, we have seen, was deeply indebted to Hayes during the time of the young singer's formative artistic years, and so I "listen back" to Hayes to map the paths that Robeson followed and those from which he departed, considering three aspects of their performance of spirituals: the strategies of programming spirituals in song recitals; the practices of arranging spirituals as folk song for concert performance; and the singing of these arranged songs in recital. Through these concert practices Robeson voiced—indeed, he became the voice of—the Negro Spiritual.[23] Let us proceed to consider Robeson's spiritual voice.

Programming beyond the Veil

For critics in search of an authentic Black experience, Robeson's "all-Negro programs," as Van Vechten described them, more securely fit the bill than Hayes's recitals of art songs that included a selection of spirituals. Whereas Robeson initially did not present the spirituals in relation to Western art

"NEGRO SPIRITUAL" 59

song, Hayes, as Locke argued, "has given this racial material [the spirituals] a balanced background by which it has commanded more respect than when separately" performed.[24] Hayes himself put a slightly different spin on his practice, claiming that spirituals, if interpreted properly, were classics.[25] For Hayes the juxtaposition of European art song and spirituals was just as important as the reconceptualization of the spirituals as classics.

Hayes had grown up singing spirituals and studied at Fisk University, Nashville, the crucible of the spiritual revival in the late nineteenth century. He had also sung with the Fisk Jubilee Singers, who were pioneers in performing spirituals in the concert hall. It should then be no surprise that, although Hayes was trained in the classical tradition, he presented concerts of only Black-authored music before Robeson, as he would do again later in his life.[26] In late 1919, Hayes performed a selection of arranged folk songs and newly composed songs by African American composers at Steinert Hall in Boston (see Box 2.1). At that time Robeson's future collaborator Lawrence Brown worked as Hayes's accompanist, and the program included such categories of African American folk song as Sorrow Songs, Negro Love Songs, and Songs of Joy, aptly concluding with Harry T. Burleigh's "Ahmed's Farewell" from the cycle *Saracen Songs*. Two years later, Hayes, still accompanied by Brown, performed another program of Black music at the Chapel of Savoy in London.[27] Contrary to the claims frequent in literature on Robeson, he did not pioneer recitals of all-Black music.[28] His singing of spirituals was part of a nascent practice, even though he narrowed his recitals to exclusively Black spirituals and secular arranged folk songs, and was a driving force in the popularization of the all-spiritual concert in the mid-1920s.[29] Similarities between Robeson's and Hayes's early recital programs are such that we can appreciate in Robeson's appreciation of Hayes a more specific artistic debt.

Robeson's professional career began with a series of concerts (on April 19 and May 3 and 17, 1925) at the Greenwich Village Theater sponsored chiefly by Van Vechten. Van Vechten and other critics based their comparison of Robeson and Hayes on these concerts, which consisted of arrangements of Black spirituals and secular folk song, and provided the model for Robeson's concerts for the 1920s. But, as Paul Anderson has noted, Robeson's concerts "fell far short of Van Vechten's primitivist fantasy."[30] Programming was also less uniform than Van Vechten's reviews would suggest. Most items on the "all-Negro programs" were arrangements for one or two voices and piano (Brown occasionally joined Robeson in song), and many were by Burleigh, the elder composer of African American art music. The concerts at the Greenwich

60 PAUL ROBESON'S VOICES

Box 2.1. Program, Roland Hayes, Steinert Hall, Boston, December 10, 1919. Lawrence Brown Papers, microfilm 4. The Schomburg Center for Research in Black Culture, New York Public Library.

PROGRAMME

Sorrow Song

The Crucifixion (African)	
No More (American)	L. B. Brown
Nobody Knows	L. B. Brown
Steal Away (Spiritual)	

Readings

Negro Love Songs (Dialect) Lyrics by Dunbar

Down Lovers' Lane	Will Marion Cook
Lil' Gal	J. Rosamond Johnson
Florida Night Song	Nora Douglas Holt

Songs of Joy

I Stood on the Ribber of Jordan	H. T. Burleigh
Bye and Bye	H. T. Burleigh
Witness	Roland W. Hayes
Song of the Sea (Dunbar)	L. W. Brown
African Maid (Dunbar)	L. W. Brown
Longing (Johnson)	L. W. Brown

Reading

Thou Art Risen	Coleridge-Taylor
Ahmed's Farewell (Saracen Song)	H. T. Burleigh

"NEGRO SPIRITUAL" 61

Village Theater began with a group of four arrangements of spirituals by Burleigh, and more songs by Burleigh followed later in the program.

The presence of Burleigh's music attests to the contradictions that marked Robeson's all-Black programs and critics' reception of the singer. In the previous chapter we glimpsed how Robeson's and Burleigh's aesthetic positions were not completely aligned. And although Robeson was already singing Burleigh's modernized versions of spirituals in 1920, according to his son, "more to Paul's liking" were the simpler arrangements by Rosamond Johnson that he felt were closer to the "pure, original" spirituals. His Black middle-class audience, however, deemed Johnson's arrangements "embarrassingly crude," so Robeson "quickly dropped them from his repertoire." Robeson's collaboration with Burleigh, who acted as a musical supervisor for the singer's debut recital at the Copley Plaza Hotel in November 1924, was short-lived, ostensibly because the "decidedly classical European concert style, favored by Burleigh . . . didn't suit Paul."[31] Despite these artistic differences, Robeson continued to perform Burleigh's works throughout his career and accorded them a privileged place in the concerts at the Greenwich Village Theater.[32]

Opening his recitals in Greenwich Village with Burleigh's songs, Robeson established from the outset the seriousness of his intent and ability. Moreover, he situated his recital within the tradition of the concert spiritual that Burleigh had pioneered. Burleigh's arrangements at the recital displayed the diversity of Black song, a feature Van Vechten and others praised as a novelty of Robeson's concerts. The audiences, Van Vechten wrote, "will doubtless exhibit considerable amazement over the degree of variety . . . introduce[d] into their all-Negro programs." The "chief interest, if not chief joy" of the concert, claimed the critic of *The World*, was its "variety of mood and musical treatment."[33] The "tragic utterances" of the opening number, "Go Down Moses," were juxtaposed with the jubilatory, hallelujah-shouting in "I Don't Feel No Ways Tired," which was followed by the hymn-like "Weepin' Mary" and the "wistful resignation" of "Bye and Bye" (and, for variety, there was also the "sardonic, secular humor" of "Scandalize My Name" in the second group).[34] This selection of Burleigh's arrangements neatly contradicted the idea that, as Zora Neale Hurston wrote, "the whole body of spirituals are 'sorrow songs,'" underlining the reality that spirituals "cover a wide range of subjects from a peeve at gossipers to Death and Judgment."[35] In their variety, Burleigh's arrangements had a synecdochic relationship to the program as a whole. The program's range of subject and mood was a further debt to Hayes's example. Sterling Brown's partly fictionalized account of a Hayes concert is almost

62 PAUL ROBESON'S VOICES

exactly contemporaneous with Van Vechten's for Robeson. The parallels between the two descriptions are worth noting:

> a few inescapable spirituals, one definitely comic, one an amusing but
> sympathetic portrayal of our primitive beliefs—and one a tender picture
> of a Lynchburg (why not) mammy, whose heaven is where at last she will
> Sit down. . . .
> Then, the dynamic, syncopated
> Every time I feel de Spirit
> and the wierd [sic]
> You hear de Lambs a-cryin'
> and then the quiet consummation—renunciation. Negroid faith in an-
> other better world where one can
> Steal away to Jesus.[36]

For Robeson's Greenwich Village Theater programs, the Burleigh songs functioned as a yardstick, assigning artistic significance to other items on the program. Although Johnson's arrangements of spirituals, which were purportedly more authentic examples of spirituals in Robeson Jr.'s view, did not feature at the Greenwich Village Theater recitals and appeared only seldom on Robeson's future programs, Robeson did sing Johnson's popular love song "Lil Gal" in Greenwich Village. Robeson had previously sung the song in the chorus for a review starring Florence Mills at the Plantation Room in 1922, for which he had donned the "minstrel mask."[37] (Hayes too had sung "Lil Gal" at Steinart Hall.) It could be argued that the elevation of the popular song from the cabaret hall to the concert stage, where it stood alongside Burleigh's art songs, worked in the same way as the juxtaposition of classics and spirituals in Hayes's programs described by Locke. Certainly, in his concerts Robeson aspired toward Art with a capital A, an aspiration repeatedly thwarted in the popular theater (and in due course in his work in mainstream film), where his and other Black performers' agency in self-representation was limited. Black and white audiences alike still occasionally denied the value of spirituals in the 1920s.[38] "He might have gone on indefinitely singing ballads in cabarets," noted Van Vechten, "but he aimed higher."[39] On the thirtieth anniversary of his debut as a concert artist, Robeson recalled that he and Brown "staked our careers-to-be on the concept that the songs of the Negro slaves were concert material, ranking in musical stature with the acknowledged classics."[40] An aesthetic ideology

"NEGRO SPIRITUAL" 63

of art and a comparative framework organized by the concept of the classic guided Robeson's thinking at this early stage, even if at the time Western art song had not yet appeared on his programs.

Alternately, one could view Robeson's program of Black song in its relation not to a normative white repertory, as has been argued for Hayes, but to other Black musical styles. This changed perspective would replace the telos of race for that of (intra-racial) class—critics of the Harlem Renaissance have long exposed the cultural elitism and bourgeois biases that marked its proponents' politics of progress.[41] Robeson's programs could thus be viewed as furthering the Harlem Renaissance ideal of race progress while ignoring, to some extent, aesthetic considerations championed by Renaissance forerunner W. E. B. Du Bois, which were developed by Locke and enacted in song recitals by Hayes.

Du Bois in particular cast an enduring shadow. His work foreshadowed central ideals and ideas of the Harlem Renaissance, and he would become a lifelong friend and intellectual mentor of Robeson. In *The Professor and the Pupil*, Balaji Murali charts their relationship in some detail, casting Robeson as the student of Du Bois. Ronald Radano argues that the concerns raised in Du Bois's magnum opus *The Souls of Black Folk* (1903) are still relevant today.[42] Du Bois famously proclaimed for the "Gentle Reader" that "the problem of the Twentieth Century is the problem of the color-line." *The Souls of Black Folk* is also well known for the prominence it gives to the sorrow songs, treating them as expressive of Black subjectivity and history, and as a uniquely national cultural product. The "sole American music," the sorrow song, Du Bois declared, is "the most beautiful expression of human experience born this side of the seas."[43] More to the point, Du Bois argued that spirituals depicted not only the lives of African Americans past and present, but that their development also presaged African American progress. For Radano, Du Bois's formulation is a perfect example of the dialectical process of racial identity formation. It "celebrates the difference that produces the realness of Black experience while simultaneously exposing that realness as an invention of racial ideology that, when brought into the conscious mode, is capable of being transcended." What Radano calls the textualizing of spirituals, the "inscription, the re-ordering, re-making, and re-membering," as exemplified by Hayes's and Robeson's performances, thus allow for the "transcendence of racial identity": "the songs of black folk, refashioned as black art," concludes Radano, "play an emancipatory role in the making of America. They do so not simply in fashioning a new, more modern national

64 PAUL ROBESON'S VOICES

vision but by uncoupling white racial logic in order to supply African-Americans with greater claim on American culture as a whole."[44]

Du Bois's own textualizing of the spirituals in *The Souls of Black Folk* is emblematic of his politics of racial progress. Each chapter of the book is headed with an incipit, the first few measures of a transcribed spiritual, which is then juxtaposed with a quotation from European and Euro-American literature. Commentators have read these epigraphic pairings as a critique of white discourse on racial ordering, the message of the juxtapositions being one of racial parity rather than hierarchy.[45] Because, according to Du Bois, "progress arises from blacks' rightful claim on all realms of knowledge," from Blacks participating, as Du Bois himself wrote, as "co-worker[s] in the kingdom of culture."[46] As many have noted, Du Bois's "kingdom of culture" was populated by European cultural heavyweights:

> I sit with Shakespeare and he winces not. Across the color line I move arm in arm with Balzac and Dumas. . . . I summon Aristotle and Aurelius and what soul I will, and they come all graciously with no scorn nor condescension. So, wed with Truth, I dwell above the Veil.[47]

In Du Bois's famous metaphor the veil distorts perceptions of the racial other, whereas the Black man's mastery of European culture functions as a veil-removing act. Hayes's practice of combining spirituals with Western classical repertoire approximates Du Bois's imperative to participate in an elite cosmopolitan culture and thus further racial progress; more so, it might seem, than Robeson's programs of all-Black music. But Du Bois, and later Locke, offers us another way to understand Robeson's programs.

Du Bois identified three stages in "the development of the slave song." In the first stage the slave song is African, in the second it is "Afro-American," and in the third Negro music blends with the music "heard in the foster land." In this third stage the spiritual is "distinctively Negro and the method of blending [is] original, but the elements are both Negro and Caucasian."[48] It would be a pointless exercise to classify the repertoire Robeson performed in his all-Black program according to Du Bois's developmental schema, but it is worth noting that the program in its totality demonstrates a similar progress. Du Bois, for example, named "Steal Away" a second-stage sorrow song, that is, Afro-American. He used the song as a heading for the chapter "Of the Faith of the Fathers," pairing it with two verses of the poem "Dim Face of Beauty" by Fiona Macleod (the pseudonym of Scottish writer William

Sharp).[49] Lawrence Brown's arrangement of "Steal Away," which both Robeson and Hayes performed, demonstrates the texting process by which folk culture becomes art. The same process concomitantly brings Black subjectivity into self-consciousness, which, according to Du Bois, is a necessary condition for progress. Brown's "Steal Away" is therefore a third-stage sorrow song: it lifts the veil—the "Dim face of Beauty haunting all the world," to borrow the poem's opening line—thus enabling Robeson's programs of Black music to enact the racial progress Du Bois espoused.

Inspired by Du Bois, Locke developed a theory of music history, which progressed from folk to formal music (by which he means individually authored and texted music), and in which the spirituals are granted the status of classics:

> This universality of the Spirituals looms more and more as they stand the test of time. They have outlived the particular generation and the peculiar conditions which produced them; they have survived in turn the contempt of the slave owners, the conventionalizations of formal religion, the repressions of Puritanism, the corruptions of sentimental balladry, and the neglect and disdain of second-generation respectability. They have escaped the lapsing conditions and the fragile vehicle of folk art, and come firmly into the context of formal music. Only classics survive such things.[50]

In this reasoning, in which the spirituals are classicized and aestheticized, Robeson's programming of Brown's and Burleigh's arrangements of spirituals did not then have to refer to Western art music on the program; they are themselves classics. Elizabeth Sergeant concluded her biographic portrait of Robeson with the statement that he and Brown, "who are consciously and lovingly working in an unconscious folk art, are establishing a 'classic' Spiritual tradition."[51] The upshot was that by the middle of the decade it was commonplace to describe the concert spiritual as classic. As leading art music critic Herman Devries, who considered the spiritual standard in the contemporary American musical landscape, put it: "The Negro Spiritual scarcely needs any 'apologia' at the present period of musical history. It has become almost an accepted and standard factor in the arrangement of a typically modern recital program in America."[52]

We should therefore be wary of claims, made according to competing aesthetic and political agendas of the Harlem Renaissance, that too easily pit Robeson's and Hayes's programming practices against each other and present

66 PAUL ROBESON'S VOICES

Robeson's all-Black music recitals as novel and expressive of a more authentic Black folk practice. Not only did Robeson lionize Hayes and follow his programming, but, as I noted, the two shared similar political ideals for the spiritual in the 1920s. By the end of the decade, Robeson would also begin to explore tentatively the Western art songs he first seemed to shun, and his engagement with this repertoire resulted in a highly selective, small body of art songs that would remain on his programs throughout his career.

The synchronic comparison of Robeson and Hayes in the mid-to-late 1920s has ignored the perspective offered from a longer view. When in the 1940s and 1950s Hayes recorded LPs of spirituals and edited *My Songs* (1948)—his own arrangements of what he called "Aframerican religious folk songs"—Robeson's recordings and recital programs were thoroughly cosmopolitan (as I explore in chapter 4).[53] The long view also allows us to consider how their programs changed at different moments in their careers. A younger Hayes undertook programs of Black music in the late 1910s and early 1920s in addition to the Western programs he is said to have performed exclusively in his early career. And later Hayes opted for more varied programs. New to the concert stage in the mid-1920s, Robeson presented programs of Black music at first, which a little later he supplemented with repertoire from other traditions. We might keep in mind the prediction of the Detroit critic Russell McLaughlin, who heard Hayes and Robeson in recital in the space of a few days and commented that it was likely that "when Robeson is as old as Hayes his art will be as comprehensive."[54] Focusing only on the 1920s and the Harlem Renaissance obscures the similarities between Hayes's and Robeson's career trajectories.

Nor should it be a surprise that Robeson sang only Black secular and spiritual songs early in his career. His choice of repertory depended less on his personal political views or on the ideology of the Harlem Renaissance than on his limitations as a singer. He had little vocal training when he started professional concertizing, so he chose to sing repertoire with which he was familiar and which he had been singing in the theater in the years immediately preceding his appearance in the recital hall. In practical terms, the inexperienced singer turned to songs he was confident his voice could carry. As the *Detroit Evening Times* noted, Mr. Robeson was aware of his limitations.[55] By contrast, Robeson would begin to broach repertoire from other song traditions after the relatively extensive, if ad hoc, voice training he undertook during the latter part of the 1920s that I chronicled in the previous chapter. Voice-thinking reminds us that Robeson's vocal competence is a not unimportant consideration when accounting for his choice of repertory.

Arranging the Evangelical Spirit

A common presence in both Hayes's and Robeson's early concertizing was the accompanist Lawrence Brown (1893–1973), the pianist in Hayes's recitals who also collaborated with Robeson on and off until becoming his permanent accompanist in 1925 (see Figure 2.2). The Greenwich Village Theater concerts of that year were not Robeson's professional concert debut, but they were the debut of the partnership of Robeson and Brown. The extent of Brown's hand in Robeson's early success has not always been acknowledged. In one sense the

Figure 2.2. Photograph of Paul Robeson and Lawrence Brown. London News Agency, 1938.

68 PAUL ROBESON'S VOICES

move from Hayes to Robeson must have been liberating for Brown because the unknown and inexperienced singer offered the professional musician a second creative start. Years later, Robeson put their professional experience into stark relief: "I with no concert experience, Larry with years of rich and varied professional experience at home and abroad."[56] Brown's experience included studies in piano, voice, and composition at the New England Conservatory, Boston, and Trinity College, London, and private mentoring by, to cite two notable examples, the English composer Roger Quilter and the *Lieder* master Raimund von zur-Mühlen. By the time he came to work with Robeson he was an experienced accompanist and a published arranger of spirituals.

Hazel Carby has been one of the few scholars to have recognized the significance of Brown's work, noting that Robeson's singing should not be isolated from the work of his accompanist-arranger, and that an examination of Brown's contributions to Robeson's performances can help unsettle early twentieth-century modernist visions of Robeson. "The musical partnership," she argues, "mounts a powerful challenge to interpretations of the spirituals which attempt to denude them of their historical, political, and cultural complexity." Carby is surely correct in concluding that the allegedly more authentic approach of Brown and Robeson was a "very carefully crafted performance strategy," even if her hermeneutic efforts are directed elsewhere: she attempts to illuminate a performance of resistance.[57] Carby's insight opens the door to further investigate how Robeson and Brown's performances crafted authenticity, focusing specifically on the arranging practices they used to present and reinvent spirituals in concert. Commentators have pointed to Brown's arrangements as the chief marker of the difference between Robeson's and Hayes's performances and thus the singers' positions in the Harlem Renaissance.

Van Vechten acknowledged the significance of Brown's arrangements from the outset, noting that "Lawrence Brown's versions of the Spirituals are in many instances remarkable." Yet the critic focused on only one mark of exceptionality: racial difference. In the process of authenticating Robeson and Brown's performance of spirituals, Van Vechten returned the concert spiritual to the Black church, to one of its original performance spaces. Brown's work, he wrote, captured "the traditional evangelical rendering of the Spirituals": it was "the evangelical, true Negro rendering." Moreover, he claimed that Robeson and Brown's purpose was "to restore . . . the spirit of the original primitive interpretation to these Spirituals." Van Vechten tellingly set this mode of interpretation against "the pseudo-refinement of the typical concert singer," specifically contrasting it with "the more refined performances of Roland Hayes."[58]

"NEGRO SPIRITUAL" 69

To be sure, Van Vechten's hyperbole was that of the publicist. By this time he was a seasoned critic of catholic taste, an advocate of European modernism, who also championed the concert presentation of folk and contemporary popular music, with a particular interest in Spanish and African American music. But if, as Anderson argues, Van Vechten was no purist in his thinking about folk music, he preferred that his singers display their primary national or ethnic identity.[59] As one of Robeson and Brown's promoters and the financial sponsor of the Greenwich Village Theater concerts, he thus endeavored to situate the artists uniquely in the crowded market of singers of spirituals by drawing on a complex of discourses issuing from the racial imagination. One instance of that logic is grounded in what Van Vechten called "the evangelical" or "the true Negro rendering" of spirituals. Van Vechten's descriptive use of the term "evangelical" did not refer to particular denominational doctrine or even religion in general, but rather to aesthetic matters: to an imagined style of religious expression practiced in African American churches. And a core feature of evangelical expression for Van Vechten was freedom.

It was not the freedom of the post-abolition slave, "the passing of slave days," that Van Vechten celebrated. On the contrary, for Van Vechten the denial of freedom seems to have been the condition for continued Black creative energy: "Conditions in the South for the Negro are still sufficiently oppressive to keep him in a state of emotional ferment extremely favourable for the inspiration of religious folksong."[60] By the 1920s, locating the genesis of the spirituals in the domain of pathos had a long critical tradition; Van Vechten described the spirituals as the "spontaneous outpourings from the heart of an oppressed race."[61] The critic's invocation of evangelical emotion was employed to summon a musical freedom. Thus he remarked specifically on the "evangelical abandon" of Brown's "Every Time I Feel the Spirit" and other "joyously abandoned melodies."[62]

For Van Vechten, Brown's evangelical spirituals recalled, and partly enacted, the practices of performance in "little Negro churches or at camp meetings," practices missing in the concert arrangements for piano and voice. The organizing principle of authentic practice was, according to Van Vechten, the idea of vocal communing, of one voice with chorus, a preacher with a congregation. The "Negro Spirituals were—and still are under primitive conditions— sung in harmony by a chorus, one voice leading with a verse to which the chorus responds," Van Vechten noted.[63] Replicating this ideal, Van Vechten wrote, Robeson "undertook the solo parts while Lawrence Brown sang the choral responses, the piano filling in the harmonies." Brown's structural

70 PAUL ROBESON'S VOICES

interlocutions were authentic also by dint of the mood in which they are voiced, for his spirited responses to Robeson's solo lines were deemed by Van Vechten to be suitably exuberant and befitting of evangelical expression. Van Vechten also called attention to Brown's ethnographic fieldwork in further support of his authentic performances: "he had visited many other of the southern states and, wherever it was possible, he had jotted down notes of the Spirituals as he heard them sung in the churches or on the plantations."[64] The racial knowledge Brown innately possessed, in other words, Black singers' capacity for authentic performance, was something on which most commentators on the Harlem Renaissance agreed regardless of their aesthetic orientation. Brown's scholarly endeavors gave further authority to his performance, bringing what he described as vocal practices in Black churches into the concert hall.

Listening to Robeson and Brown's recordings of the evangelical arrangements, it is difficult not to get caught up in the spirit of their performances. Their "Ezekiel Saw de Wheel" is a rollicking ride, infectious because of its exuberance, especially when compared to Hayes's arrangement and gently rocking performance of the same spiritual.[65] The effect of spontaneity— a much-noted mark of racial authenticity in the Harlem Renaissance and another marker of musical freedom—is generated by a dazzling array of responses, interjections (as African American shouts?), and contrapuntal duetting that Brown added to the performance. That they are uttered in a voice that is not melodically songful (though remaining firmly within the bounds of rhythmic and tuneful rectitude of professional performance) serves only to enhance the claim for authenticity. But interpreting the Robeson-Brown version as "primitive," as Van Vechten did, and which at once situated their performance within an aesthetic of primitivism governed by instinctual emotion free from the rules of the concert stage denies the spiritual the subtlety and therefore depth of interpretation that Hayes gave the song.

For Hayes, "Ezekiel Saw de Wheel" is a simile, like "a smile that can accompany serious matter," an example of the lyric type in which humor is "not lacking in serious import." In his book of arrangements Hayes describes the song as "a child's delight": "we lift, temporarily, the realism of the object out of the context of a poem." This sense of play guides his arrangement. The object, in "Ezekiel Saw de Wheel," is the "big wheel"; Hayes summons the image of the big circus wheel as the child's point of reference by evoking feelings of "motion, gaiety, wonder."[66] The piano simulates the perpetual motion of the wheel by the ascending and descending arpeggiated chords, accented second and third beats (mm. 1–2 in Example 2.1). The same motion continues in

Example 2.1. Roland Hayes, "Ezekiel Saw de Wheel," *My Songs* (Boston: Little, Brown, 1948), mm. 1–18.

Example 2.1. Continued

"NEGRO SPIRITUAL" 73

the accompaniment, transformed first into an expression of gaiety, and then momentarily suspended to express amazement. The piano's ascending scalar runs in measures 11–13 are both sonic representations of the text ("The big wheel runs . . .") and means of musical humor: if the big wheel's run is at a lower register, then the run of the little wheel, "a wheel in a wheel," contains both in its "doubled time." As the piano's runs interact with Hayes's voice, the listener can only smile (to quote Hayes) in the resulting playfulness. A new section, marked *Lento, declamatory quasi-recitativo* (mm. 15–17), disrupts the playful mode. The exchange of levity and gravity, of humor and serious-ness, Hayes argues, is a structural trait of spirituals. "Often, in the songs of my people, a light humor, not lacking in serious import, however, can enter very aptly and deftly into reverence."[67] Hayes thus countered that his "Ezekiel Saw de Wheel" is no less faithful to the spiritual tradition than Robeson and Brown's. As Hayes's example shows, Robeson and Brown's performances were not the only ones that can be considered authentic.

Another of Brown's evangelical arrangements was "Ev'ry Time I Hear de Spirit." By the time he came to perform it with Robeson, it had become the preferred concert version of the spiritual.[68] As with "Ezekiel," it is Brown's vocal interpolations and dialoguing with Robeson in performance that are the primary markers of its evangelical mood. When Robeson "throws out a line," as Van Vechten styled the practice, Brown "tosses him a response."[69] Robeson's singing of the chorus melody "E-v'ry time" is counterpointed by an extemporized repetition of the words by Brown, who interrupts the line with a shouted "Lord" (e.g., at 0:28–0:40).[70] This ecstatic, melismatic shout takes the place of the words "I feel de spirit," which Robeson continues to sing, before Brown takes up the chorus's words again, "movin' in my heart," in harmony with Robeson; "rocking with a mighty, harmonized chorus," in Van Vechten's inimitable phrase.[71] For the critic of the *Ohio State Journal*, Robeson and Brown "managed to put over the idea of a whole camp meeting. Those spirituals sound better when a whole crowd is singing them. These two gave the crowd impression, and retained the musical standard of the individuals."[72]

Tellingly, here and in other spirituals the evangelical arranging is a function of performance. The choral effects are absent from Brown's own published arrangement of the spiritual, although its upbeat tempo, marked *Allegro con moto*, and propulsive syncopations are contributing factors. Transcribers and arrangers of spirituals during the Harlem Renaissance rou-tinely acknowledged what Radano calls the "partiality" of the transcriptive

74 PAUL ROBESON'S VOICES

act. In the introductory remarks to *The Book of American Negro Spirituals*, to which Brown contributed several arrangements, James Weldon Johnson pondered whether it was "possible with our present system of notation to make a fixed transcription of these peculiarities [of spiritual song practice] that would be absolutely true; for in their very nature they are not susceptible to fixation."[73] The inscription of the spirituals was at once an assimilationist move made in order to bring them into the Euro-American song tradition and, in its fixation, a fetishizing of racial difference. In short, as Radano writes, the "partiality of text had an enabling effect": it implied "the possibility of encounters with a sound world existing beyond the transcriptive act."[74] Drawing on the discourse of partiality, Robeson himself remarked that "negro music . . . defies expression in formal printed arrangements."[75] It was the sound world beyond his own texts that Brown endeavored to arrange in performance—voices freed from texted strictures—and which so fired Van Vechten's and other critics' imaginations.

Brown's arrangements had already been considered authentic by the time he started to collaborate with Robeson. The first occasion at which we know Brown and Robeson performed "Ev'ry Time" together was at the Village home of theater director Jimmy Light in March 1925, as part of an impromptu post-dinner entertainment. As Brown recalled, he joined Robeson as the second voice completely spontaneously. The combination excited Light, and he suggested the duo give a concert, which resulted in the concert at the Greenwich Village Theater in April, with the debut of "Ev'ry Time."[76] But the spontaneity central to the evangelical performances was something of a *trompe l'oreille*. Supplementing the textual arrangements, the performances themselves became fixed in their repetition, operating against the tradition in which, as Hurston observed, "no two times singing is alike, so that we must consider the rendition of a song not as a final thing, but as a mood. It won't be the same thing next Sunday."[77] Brown's vocal improvisations to Robeson's singing are exact replications. For example, the 1938 HMV studio recording of "Ev'ry Time" does not differ from the live recording of the song at the 1952 Peace Arch concert.[78] There is little evidence of the Black vernacular practice of the "changing same," and thus the musical freedoms celebrated in the evangelical arrangements turn out to be enslaved by processes of reification similar to those from which their fixed notated arrangements are said to suffer and from which their performances supposedly permit escape. By listening closely to historical performances alongside critics' accounts, one is able to challenge the premise of spontaneity and freedom that are said to constitute authentic practices and identities. Under scrutiny, the claim of authenticity turns out to rest on shaky ground.

Although Van Vechten and other critics heard Brown's singing as the primary carrier of the evangelical tradition, in Brown's arrangements the piano accompaniment also functioned as a substitute for the lost voices. As James Weldon Johnson explained, Brown and his brother J. Rosamond Johnson, who arranged *The Book of American Negro Spirituals*, had "sincerely striven to give the characteristic harmonies that would be used in spontaneous group singing" in their piano accompaniments. More specifically, what they had "principally in mind was to have the instrumentation approach the effect of the singing group in action."[79] Arrangers of art songs, such as Burleigh, strove to achieve a similar effect. Brown's piano-as-voice interjections in "Ev'ry Time" (right hand at mm. 14–16 in Example 2.2) recall Burleigh's similar treatment of the piano in his arrangement of the same song (mm. 16–18 in Example 2.3). In both cases the piano engages in rhythmic and registral dialogue with the voice; its syncopations (more pronounced in Burleigh's than in Brown's version) stand out because they harmonize the voice in another register.[80] The piano accompaniment in both Brown's and Burleigh's arrangements shares with the voice the task of evoking Black vocal practice. Yet both are invented residues, neither being able to fully substitute for the tradition. Aware of the problem, Van Vechten wrote that Brown and Robeson "restore, *as far as they are able*, the spirit of the original," capturing "as much of the traditional evangelical renderings of the Spirituals as would be consistent with the atmosphere of the concert hall."[81]

Example 2.2. Lawrence Brown, "Ev'ry Time I Hear de Spirit" (London: Schott & Co., 1923), mm. 14–16. With permission, Schott Music.

Example 2.3. H. T. Burleigh, "Ev'ry Time I Hear de Spirit" (New York: G. Ricordi & Co., 1925), mm. 16–18.

There are other reference points too for Robeson and Brown's evangelical spirituals, such as the vaudeville tradition of performing spirituals. The vogue for spirituals was not confined to jubilee groups or solo art singers in the first few decades of the century. Although the biographical narrative presents Robeson's concert career as a move away from the popular stage, and his aesthetic program for the spirituals as one of "uplift"—a ministration of rescuing the spiritual from minstrelsy—his singing within several popular vocal traditions must have prepared him well for his duetting with Brown. In his youth he sang in glee groups, and in the spring of 1922 briefly joined the Four Harmony Kings, then appearing in the hit Broadway musical *Shuffle Along*, as the replacement bass. This, one could argue, was the setting for Robeson's first professional vocal apprenticeship. Here he extended his knowledge of the popular song repertoire, which he would sing and record for the following two decades: a body of work that has been almost entirely displaced by the narrative of the spirituals in Robeson scholarship. Stephen Foster's "Old Black Joe," for example, was the closing item of the Harmony King's segment in *Shuffle Along*, and a Robeson favorite that he later recorded in a solo version as the renamed "Poor Old Joe" for HMV in 1930.[82] The Harmony Kings who first performed as a jubilee group were also known for their performances of spirituals. Listening to the group's recordings of the early 1920s, Tim Brooks notes their meticulous harmonizing and tenor-quartet "modified call-and-response" patterning.[83] Surely Robeson's day-to-day work in the quartet familiarized the young singer with the variety of voice relationships and interactions characteristic of multi-part singing that in turn shaped his performances with Brown on the concert stage. Indeed,

"NEGRO SPIRITUAL" 77

the spiritual was articulated through a number of different vocal traditions, genres, and styles in the early twentieth century. We gain a sense of how these articulations played out in Robeson's programming by considering the following cases.

Burleigh's arrangement of "Deep River" quickly became a staple of the solo concert singer's program and was performed by Robeson throughout his career. The spiritual was also reworked by Turner Layton of the popular cabaret duo Layton and Johnstone into "Dear Old Southland" (1921). Burleigh was not pleased with this development, decrying the popularizing of the spirituals as "prostitut[ing] the inherent religious beauty" of the genre and "polluting [its] great, free fountain of pure melody."[84] Robeson would record both Burleigh's "superb art-song" (the first of several recordings of "Deep River" made in 1927) and its "polluted" alter ego "Dear Old Southland" (sometime later in 1939), a practice more in tune with the workings of the music market in the interwar years, and more in keeping with the intersections and mutual transformations of art and the popular at this time than Burleigh's purist agenda. It should not surprise, then, that Brown's arrangement of "Steal Away" was a favorite of both art singer Hayes and vaudeville artists Layton and Johnstone. In the latter's performance of Brown's arrangements, we hear another tradition in which the spirituals were globally performed.

Robeson met, befriended, and heard in performance Layton and Johnstone in mid-1925 when in London to act in *The Emperor Jones*. Eslanda recalled that "Paul heard his host and friend, the famous team 'Layton and Johnstone,' sing to crowded and enthusiastic houses."[85] The similarities between the vaudeville duo and the new partnership of Robeson and Brown are worth pointing out. Layton, the senior musician, composer, and pianist, accompanied the singer Clarence Johnstone and sometimes joined him in voice. Known for their slick act and polished sound, their performances of spirituals invoke the parlor rather than the camp meeting. For instance, their undoubtedly jaunty "Ev'ry Time" is more measured than Robeson and Brown's spirited tempo and the second, responsorial voice is limited to harmonizing the soloist in the chorus rather than "spontaneously" dialoguing, as Brown does with Robeson.[86] Yet, with one ear we can also hear the parlor sounding in Robeson and Brown's "Ev'ry Time" and, with the other ear, recognize the remains of "authentic" practice in Layton and Johnstone's performances. The cabaret duo thus follows, in "Ev'ry Time" and "Steal Away," the typical form of a "class" of spirituals in which James Weldon Johnson argued the "lead and response are still retained, but the response is

78 PAUL ROBESON'S VOICES

developed into a true chorus." The chorus in this spiritual type dominates the song, which begins with the chorus, and is sung by the congregation in part harmony, features which Johnson demonstrates through an analysis of "Steal Away," and which Layton and Johnstone perform (but which Robeson and Brown do not).[87] Moreover, in Layton's harmonizing with Johnstone in the chorus of "Ev'ry Time," Johnson would probably hear the duo's participation in a tradition of Black male singing that informed the performance history of spirituals. In African Americans' "instinctive" harmonizing, Johnson locates the origins of the barbershop quartet, which in turn provided the foundation for the close-harmony all-male singing that characterized the minstrel and vaudeville stages. In this lineage, he upholds the Four Harmony Kings as the most recent model of close-harmony perfection.[88] It is as part of this tradition, as it moved on to the popular music stage, that we can hear Brown's smooth harmonizing with Robeson; in "Ev'ry Time" in the phrase "movin' in my heart I will pray" (1:03–1:15). The *New Yorker* deemed Brown's habit of "chucking in a few snatches of informal close harmony" charming.[89]

The influence of these contemporary popular vocal practices is as important to recognize in Robeson and Brown's performances in the 1920s as those of the primitive church that Van Vechten and the critics celebrated. Critics failed to acknowledge the popular as one fount of origin for Robeson's voice because it muddied the waters of spiritual and racial authenticity; it polluted, to draw on Burleigh's metaphor, the field. It was precisely at this time, in the 1920s, that America's musical landscape became increasingly segregated: "racial and class lines in performance styles were redrawn industrially and culturally"; voices were racially essentialized.[90] Robeson's critics participated in this move. But through the intersections of and crossovers between the popular and classical, and sacred and secular vocalities, Robeson sang multivocally. And one of the potential effects of multivocality, of singing plurally, is to challenge: such voices, argues Meizel, do "more than switch between two styles of music; they undertake a complex process of code-switching between cultural histories, interrogating the racialization of genre in the global music industry."[91]

If Van Vechten's first point of comparison for Robeson was the art singing of spirituals rather than popular music performances thereof, and Hayes rather than Layton and Johnstone his foil for Robeson, it is because the art song tradition is seemingly furthest removed from Robeson and Brown's evangelical performances. By invoking it the critic attempts to overstate their difference, in observance of the "musical color line."[92] But the art song tradition is also the primary context within which Robeson and Brown concertized and to which they aspired. As much as their performances evoked "the atmosphere of the concert hall" (in Van Vechten's phrase), the critic also sought to distance them from that tradition. He did the same when he attempted to redirect criticism away from the dominant interpretive move of the spirituals as sorrow songs: Brown's "Ev'ry Time," Van Vechten argued, was "entirely at variance with the slow-footed arrangements made by other musicians," of which Hayes's "sanctimonious, lugubrious manner" was an example.[93] In so doing, Van Vechten situated the spirituals within a discourse on Black music-making long in the making. Where postbellum discussions of the spirituals continued to foreground their melodic character, by the 1920s Black music had been reinvented as rhythm music, a turn that colored the analytical literature on the spirituals and informed Van Vechten's conception of Robeson and Brown's evangelical arrangements.[94] According to Anderson, Van Vechten "championed Robeson's less refined but more rhythmically propulsive style."[95] His penchant for the exotic no doubt encouraged such an interpretation.

In preferring the evangelical arrangements, Van Vechten gave prominence to a certain image of Robeson, one that is by no means fully representative of his art even in the 1920s. A cursory glance at programs for the Greenwich Village Theater concerts shows that there were as many slow sorrow songs as upbeat evangelical arrangements in Robeson's repertory (see Box 2.2). The two groups of spirituals arranged by Brown on the program of the first concert are organized by contrasts, with each sorrow song followed by a faster arrangement. Both the logic of the grouping and the organizing principle of contrast were typical of song recitals. The final group of four songs begins with the singing subject expressing his sorrow in "Nobody Knows de Trouble I've Seen." The mood is then lightened in the gently comforting "I've Got a Home in-a-dat Rock." Centrally placed in the group is "Swing Low, Sweet Chariot," the chorus and verse of which respectively draw on the moods of the previous two songs. And the program concludes with the evangelically treated "Joshua Fit de Battle of Jericho." But if the Greenwich Village Theater programs contain as many sorrow songs as evangelical numbers, Robeson would in time prefer slower songs. Of the fifteen spirituals he recorded for Victor between 1925 and 1927, the majority—nine of the fifteen—are slow.[96] What Van Vechten chose to hear in Robeson and Brown's performances reflects, as is often the case, the critic's own aesthetic agenda, and we should therefore treat his unfettered celebration of Brown's "remarkable" spirituals

Box 2.2. Recital Program, Greenwich Village Theater, New York, April 19, 1925. Lawrence Brown Papers, microfilm 4. The Schomburg Center for Research in Black Culture, New York Public Library.

PROGRAM

I.   NEGRO SPIRITUALS

Go Down Moses . . .

I Don't Feel No Ways Tired }   Arranged by
H. T. Burleigh

Weepin' Mary . . .

Bye and Bye . . .

II.   NEGRO SECULAR FOLK and DIALECT SONGS

Water Boy . . . .   Arranged by
Avery Robinson

Scandalize My Name . . .   Arranged by
H. T. Burleigh

Lil Gal . . . .   ~~Arranged by~~
J. Rosamond Johnson

Down de Lovah's Lane.   ~~Arranged by~~
Will Marion Cook

III.   NEGRO SPIRITUALS

Steal Away . . .

I Know de Lord's Laid His
Hands on Me . . .   }   Arranged by
Lawrence Brown

Sometimes I Feel Like a
Motherless Child . . .

Ev'ry Time I Feel De Spirit . . . . .

IV.   NEGRO SPIRITUALS

Nobody Knows de Trouble
I've Seen . . . .

I've Got a Home in-a-dat Rock }   Arranged by
Lawrence Brown

Swing Low Sweet Chariot . . . . . .

Joshua Fit de Battle of Jericho

"NEGRO SPIRITUAL" 81

with some caution. We might recall Hurston's response to the critics who tried variously to present the arranged spirituals as authentic. She called the arrangements "neo-spirituals": the "works of Negro composers or adaptors *based* on the spirituals" are all "good work and beautiful," she wrote, but they are not spirituals. "This is no condemnation of the neo-spirituals," she proceeded. "They are a valuable contribution to the music and literature of the world. But let no one imagine that they are the songs of the people, as sung by them."[97]

Singing Ecstasy

Program compilation and arranging practices were important aspects of the debate surrounding the performance of spirituals during the Harlem Renaissance. So was the singing of spirituals. Hurston's original people's voice, the "untampered-with congregation," was "bound by no rules" in its singing. Her theory of vernacular expression, grounded in ethnographic work, attempts to describe the way this Black collective body voices the spirituals properly. Concert artists and singers in glee clubs, who never performed what she considered genuine spirituals, occupy the other end on her spectrum of authenticity.[98] Hurston failed to acknowledge the different singing styles practiced by the choirs, quartets, and solo singers of the neo-spirituals, and one has to listen only to contemporaneous recordings by the Fisk Jubilee Singers, Tuskegee Institute Singers, Harmony Kings, Hayes, Anderson, and Robeson, to name only a few Black artists, to hear these various vocal styles. Comparisons of Robeson's and Hayes's singing were thus routine, and their voices allowed for different conceptions of the Black subject.

I have suggested that Robeson's programs were in part organized to accommodate his (at the time) limited vocal abilities; although his aesthetic-political aims also guided his programming choices, as did his life history: he frequently used his singing of spirituals in childhood to establish his racial right to perform the repertoire authentically. Unlike Hayes, Robeson was in no position to perform the literature of Western art songs at the beginning of his concert career; and both the program of all-Black music and Brown's arrangements of spirituals gave him not only a technically appropriate repertory but also helped him develop his technique. The faster tempi of the evangelical arrangements, for instance, eliminated the need for the type of breath and tonal control required for slower singing. Brown's choral duetting with

82 PAUL ROBESON'S VOICES

Robeson, "after the Negro manner," also served to show the singer's voice in a better light.[99] The accompanist's rough tenor, concluded the *Morning Telegraph*, "suffers by comparison with Robeson's great pipe organ."[100] Indeed, the sound and style of Brown's singing voice were a necessary and "admirable foil for his colleague's luscious, slow moving voice."[101] In the first years of Robeson's concertizing, Brown seems to have nurtured the young singer's voice not only by presenting it in a repertoire that did not unduly expose its shortcomings, but also by placing his own untrained voice against Robeson's. As Robeson developed as a singer, Brown's vocal contributions decreased, both in the number of duets he performed with Robeson and in the increasing prominence of Robeson's voice in the duets.[102] With the decrease in duets over time the evangelical arrangements also decreased in Robeson's repertoire.

It is perhaps unsurprising that, with training and experience, Robeson would come to prefer slower singing, a heavier and more dramatic voice, and what music critic Noel Straus called a "gorgeousness of tone"—in other words, a mode of vocality different and even contrary to the one Van Vechten and other critics favored at the outset of his singing career. Robeson's singing of "Deep River" demonstrates this nicely. Annotating his own arrangement of the spiritual, Hayes wrote about the workings of repetition in the song: the "musical phrase, '*Deep river, my home is over Jordan*,' lies deeply rooted in the consciousness of mankind. It has a suggestive quality of inescapable power." Its repetitions of phrase, continued Hayes, function as "a sort of incantation . . . not unlike the litanies of the Catholic Church. Repetitions are phenomena of imaginative, poetic intoxication that, choosing word sounds irrespective of meaning identifies the person with the mood."[103] The repetitions of Robeson's voice in "Deep River" (and in his wider repertory) afforded a hearing of his voice as a deep bass while also making it an object of sheer sound. Critics often commented that the spiritual was an effective vehicle for the display of Robeson's voice,[104] and the singer's voice in "Deep River" reveals the extent to which Robeson would be heard *as voice*. Thus, one of New York's most celebrated critics Straus observed that Robeson's singing now "ignored those salient traits of all Negro music—its spontaneity and intensity of feeling"; his reading of "Deep River . . . failed to be anything more than a series of empty phrases which interested merely because in them Mr. Robeson's splendid lower tones had ample play." It was what Charles D. Isaacson called Robeson's "ocean of tone" that became the singer's vocal calling card (the anatomy of which I dissect in chapter 3).[105]

"NEGRO SPIRITUAL" 83

Hayes's spiritual voice must also be heard in the context of his own voice's history. By the time he was singing spirituals professionally, he had a classically trained voice, schooled particularly in the music of the concert rather than opera stage. In the mid-1920s Hayes's singing of spirituals was heard in the context of his career as a singer of art song, whereas Robeson's was heard outside of a single and homogeneous tradition; it was multivocal. Vocal practices of the popular stage, Burleigh's short-lived art song mentoring, childhood singing in his father's churches, and Brown's coaching were all part of his vocal practice at this time. It was easier to invent a context for Robeson's voice and discover an authentic way of singing in his mixed lineage. Van Vechten thus measured the "true Negro rendering" of Robeson against "the pseudo-refinement of the typical concert singer," a comparison that took racial authenticity as a yardstick and came to characterize criticism of the spiritual as venues for its performance broadened.[106] Johnson agreed that singers "who take the Spirituals as mere 'art' songs . . . are doomed to failure, as far as interpretation is concerned." But he and other Black critics redeemed Hayes's interpretations, conferring on them also the stamp of authenticity. Hayes's Black credentials were argued by various means. Unlike Van Vechten, Johnson believed that concert singers—even white singers— could sing authentically provided they "*feel* the Spirituals deeply," a romantic guideline to which Hayes adhered in spite of his technical facility with the Western *Lied* repertoire: "notwithstanding all his artistry," Johnson wrote, Mr. Hayes "sings these songs with tears on his cheeks."[107]

Locke's apology for Hayes took a less broad route. Comparing performances of the same spiritual, "God's Goin' to Set Dis Worl' on Fire," by Hayes and the "cowboy composer" David Guion (who was a "careful and appreciative student of the Spirituals"), Locke presented musicological evidence to reveal African American practices in Hayes's singing that were lacking in Guion's performance. He pointed out that the rhythm of the "great Negro tenor" was "subtler," he linked phrases more closely, included rhapsodic voice glides, and moved in a "dramatic recitative." He described Hayes's singing of spirituals as recitatives, marking thus the kinship between spoken and sung Black vocal modalities. For Locke, these features of Hayes's performance demonstrated not only a greater familiarity with the material and its practices but also the existence of an instinctive feeling for it.[108] Locke advocated a natural feeling for idiomatic performance as the hallmark of authentic practice. Van Vechten's claim that Robeson "indulged in the characteristic vocal peculiarities of Negro

84 PAUL ROBESON'S VOICES

inflection" held true, Locke showed, also for Hayes.[109] Cautioning against insisting "upon an arbitrary style or form . . . in the name of the folk spirit," Locke contended that the distinction between what Van Vechten described as Robeson's "evangelical renderings" and Hayes's "subdued, ecstatic and spiritually refined versions" was based on a false premise because "the folk itself has these same two styles of singing." Like Van Vechten, Locke too was concerned with "the purity of the tradition," but he proposed a tradition that encompassed a broader aesthetic gamut: "So long as the peculiar quality of Negro song is maintained, and the musical idiom kept unadulterated, there is and can be no set limitation."[110]

Like my discussion of Hayes's arrangement of "Ezekiel Saw de Wheel," which was no less, if differently, grounded in the vernacular than Brown's, Hayes's singing of Brown's "Ev'ry Time I Hear de Spirit" can be heard to carry other aspects of the spirit and idiom of the vernacular than those celebrated in Robeson and Brown's performance of the spiritual. Hayes's ecstatic interpretation, surely appropriate in the evangelical tradition, is located in his voice: in his forceful reaching for the first vocal syllable; the near forcing of his voice as he moves from "feel" to "the spirit"; and the exaggerated and crude approximation of a sort of *messa di voce* on "mo-ving," all indicating that the art singer's voice is a little "out of" (the "ek" of ecstatic) its standard classical voice position (0:03–0:08 and 0:39). The repeat of the phrase that follows (at 0:11) presents ecstasy in another mode: in the *subito piano* and hushed voice in which the excitement is barely contained. Rapture erupts at the start of the repeat of the chorus when Hayes, his rhapsodic voice gliding, creates a liaison between the concluding word of the verse, "please," and the refrain's "Ev'ry time" (0:33–0:36).[111] The singer's forceful crescendo on the quick upward glide is a bursting forth of the energy that has been simmering in the verse and which can now express in unbounded joy the text "the spirit moving in my heart." Hayes's "Ev'ry Time" is exemplary, by turns, of the ecstatic and subdued spirituality that Locke and others heard in his interpretations of the spiritual, and which they argued was part of the vernacular tradition. Authority for this interpretation lies in Du Bois's description of the "religion of the slave," expressed in Frenzy or "Shouting" (the scare quotes are Du Bois's), which encompassed a range of expressive means from "silent rapt countenance" to "mad abandon."[112]

Listening to a contemporaneous performance of the spiritual by Robeson, one is struck by its comparative blandness, the dynamism of his early

"NEGRO SPIRITUAL" 85

recording with Brown long forsaken for the sonorousness for which his voice had become known.[113] But Robeson's early performances of spirituals were also heard within a discourse of the ecstatic. This was especially true of the slow spirituals, what the *Philadelphia Bulletin* termed plaintive songs, such as Burleigh's arrangement of "Were You There?"[114] Accounts of this song type offer another way to hear Robeson, one more akin to the reception of Hayes's singing of spirituals and less accommodated by Van Vechten's evangelical model. For the critic of the *Indianapolis News*, Robeson's "Were You There?" was as "magnificent a presentation of a single mood as the reviewer has ever had the good fortune to hear":

> There were in it a discerning understanding of its profundity and a fine expression of its stark, yet exalted, simplicity. There were, too, a burning emotionalism, all the more impressive because of the quietness, the restraint of the singing. . . . The song stood alone, elemental, agonizingly poignant. It was as startling and vivid a disclosure of reverent feeling of penetrating pathos as one could imagine. For once, at least, the Negro spiritual stood forth in all its true beauty, true force.[115]

One can listen to Robeson's recording of "Were You There?" from the previous year and attempt to hear what the critics heard in his singing. We can certainly appreciate the contrast pointed out by the *Indianapolis News*: exaltation expressed in stark simplicity, burning emotionalism executed quietly with restraint. This calls to mind the work of another scholar of the Black voice: in Jason King's readings, soul singing, he argues, "is more than grit"; for key to its "rapturous vibe" is a "slow-burn aesthetic" tending toward "softness, quietude, tenderness, restraint, and understatement."[116]

These qualities, typical of Robeson criticism in the 1920s and 1930s, are all the more apparent when listening to Robeson's recording aside that of Hayes's unaccompanied performance of the song.[117] Every musical event in Hayes's performance is in some way exaggerated, the emotion burned into the listener's ear far more viscerally than in Robeson's reading. In both recordings the thrice repeated word "tremble," which ends the phrase "Sometimes it causes me to tremble," intensifies with each repetition, but each of Hayes's utterances of the word is tremulous in ways that Robeson's are not (see Example 2.4 and compare 0:54–1:09 and 0:42–1:02 in the recordings).[118] Robeson's first utterance of "tremble" is neutral, that is, without audible emphasis on the word, whereas Hayes's aspiration of the initial consonant

86   PAUL ROBESON'S VOICES

Example 2.4. H. T. Burleigh, "Were You There?" (New York: G. Ricordi & Co., 1924), mm. 15–18.

and the subsequent dying away of the voice on the second syllable sonically marks the utterance as one of hushed awe, an interpretative choice on which he builds in the subsequent repetitions.[119] By the third and final repetition of "tremble," the voice exaggeratedly aspirates the "tr-," after which it leans into the remainder of the syllable "trem-," then falls away onto the "m" and the next syllable "-ble." All the while his voice lays bare a wide breathy vibrato, heightening the impression of a voice in wonder. Hayes achieves this through a subtle play of breath. Robeson's singing of the final "tremble" is also an intensification of its earlier utterances, but the expressive means by which he achieves this is tone rather than breath. As the phrase that starts "Sometimes it causes me . . ." descends to its lowest point at the final "tremble," Robeson's bass tone is enriched (1:04–1:09). Indeed, the concentration of the voice-as-tone, as it revels in the low register, makes the word forcefully emphatic, and the trembling is rendered as fear rather than quiet awe.

Hayes's and Robeson's different interpretations of the same song illustrate the gap between the sounds of Black singers voicing an aesthetic of religious ecstasy and their critics' discursive accounts of this aesthetic. Robeson's singing in "Were You There?" penetrates the listener with pathos, presenting his voice according to an alternative aesthetic to the evangelical freedom celebrated by Van Vechten. The singer's vocal expressiveness achieved through the beauty of his tone is in fact more aligned with Hurston's "white vocal art"—"European singing is considered good when each syllable floats out on a column of air, seeming not to have any mechanics at all"—than with the "characteristic vocal peculiarities of Negro inflection" that Van Vechten heard.[120] Robeson's voice, even in the 1920s, thus sounded more complex than almost a century of criticism has suggested. In her study of the Fisk Jubilee Singers' performance of concert spirituals, Newland cautions of "the protracted and politically fraught misunderstanding and miscategorization of concert spirituals as either 'art' music or 'black' music, and the essentializing of the conflation of these two categories."[121] Eidsheim generalizes this point: "'black voice,'" she observes, is "born from an encultured notion of sound that expects fidelity to a referent and listens for difference. When voices are reduced to fixed sounds and undergo assessment, they cannot help being heard within binaries or scale degrees of fidelity and difference."[122] To resist this binary thinking, and to attend to sonic Blackness in its complexity, we must pay closer attention to the varieties of Robeson's and Hayes's sounds and to the contexts in which they were produced.

We have seen that one of the contexts against which Robeson's aesthetic Blackness was regularly measured was the classical tradition. His first encounter with performing in this tradition was probably during his brief apprenticeship with Burleigh, who mentored him in preparation for his debut recital at the Copley Plaza Hotel in Boston in late 1924. I noted earlier that Robeson Jr. claimed that Burleigh's "classical European concert style . . . didn't suit" his father," and others have contended that Robeson set out to concertize with the explicit intention of performing spirituals, according to Anderson, in a voice different from "formal European styles" or, as Van Vechten put it, "in the characteristic vocal peculiarities of Negro inflection."[123] But might it be that Robeson's initial withdrawal from Burleigh and the classical tradition was the result of a young amateur singer's daunting first meeting with that tradition? Robeson's vocal insecurities, frequently admitted by him, must have been further exposed in the unfamiliar discipline of classical singing. Rather than presenting Robeson's singing style at the very outset of his concert career as an aesthetic-political choice—an argument that may more convincingly be made for the mid-1930s on—I suggest we consider it in the more mundane terms that voice-thinking asks of us: to focus also on Robeson's vocal abilities at a particular career moment.

Sometime later, in 1934, Robeson himself spoke out against his performance of the art music repertoire and its style of singing: "I have no desire to interpret the vocal genius of half a dozen [European] cultures which are really alien cultures to me," Robeson told the Black press.[124] This statement too has a specific performance context. By this time, Robeson was a global singing star on the path to finding his mature voice, both artistic and political. His aesthetic-political stance on his voice and repertoire, occasioned by

88 PAUL ROBESON'S VOICES

what Sheila Boyle and Andrew Bunie have called his "professional ambivalence" in the early 1930s, was wrought as much by the pragmatics of voice-thinking as by a nascent political engagement.[125] Robeson's revelation was in part a consequence of his serious study of the Western art song repertoire in the last years of the 1920s and early 1930s, which entailed listening to *Lieder* on gramophone while rehearsing to a metronome, continued voice training in the classical style (as I outlined in chapter 1), adding art song to his repertoire, and first performing it in concert in 1930. Yet his was a thwarted learning of the art song canon—he was "not intellectually oriented towards great classical music," observed Hayes's accompanist Reginald Boardman—and critical reception of his singing thereof was often lukewarm. The mastery of the classical cannon was "a great cliff I cannot climb," Robeson himself confessed.[126] Disappointment borne of frustration at his voice's failings when faced with the art song repertoire is the context in which we might evaluate Robeson's statement of declining to perform "alien" European art song. The technical demands of Western art song were indeed strange to Robeson's voice, already in its early thirties by then.[127]

Attributing a conscious aesthetic of the Black voice to Robeson in the 1920s thus fails to take into account the historical record and the pragmatics of vocal performance. It misattributes intention to Robeson while ceding agency to others, whether critics like Van Vechten and Anderson, or even Robeson's wife, Eslanda, a keen promoter of her husband's early singing career. (Robeson did not always agree with Eslanda's presentation of his voice.) In her 1930 biography of Robeson, Eslanda presents herself as the agent for Robeson's voice training, her authority signaled by the use of the third-person narration:

> Essie wanted to find a teacher who would not touch his voice as such; it seemed to her quite perfect. The more recitals she heard, the more prejudiced she became against the so-called "trained" voice. The technique seemed to level all the voices to one uninteresting mould; it seemed to her lay mind that the more perfectly, technically, one sang, the less interesting the voice became. There was just a well-placed, well-handled vibrant voice which was so absorbed in being produced properly that it lost all the colour, roundness and personality which distinguish voices individually. She didn't want Paul's voice to sing to this mould.[128]

In short, Eslanda did not want Robeson's voice "opera-ated upon," to borrow Johnson's term for the procedures to which spirituals were subjected in art

"NEGRO SPIRITUAL" 89

music arrangements.[129] She emphasized the difference between schooled and natural voices, as did many who wrote about the performance of spirituals during the Harlem Renaissance. Eslanda's concern was the preservation of Robeson's vocal distinctiveness, the marketing of its artistic uniqueness, which she feared would be compromised by conventional vocal training. This is exemplary of the commonplace idea of the "vocal thumbprint," that singers possess a unique voice that they need to find, and that their vocal authenticity will position them well in the music marketplace.[130] Perhaps surprisingly—because, after all, the title of Eslanda's biography, *Paul Robeson, Negro*, points to race—Eslanda did not represent Robeson's voice by recourse to race, as many other critics did. As she proudly declared to a prospective voice teacher, she had married "the most beautiful Voice" she had ever heard.[131] In this personification of Robeson-as-Voice, the aestheticized ideal displaces the Black subject.

There is another biographical account of the voice that we might consider, one in which race is re-inscribed into the voice. A 1942 biography of Hayes recounts the singer's vocal self-discovery at the beginning of his professional career and in the wake of his conservatory training in the late 1910s. The account betrays an anxiety of classic Du Boisian formulation: "I had been working in a cloud of depression," Hayes confessed, "because my voice had not come out as 'white' as, in the beginning, I must have hoped it would." He attributed this failure to the "racial habit of imitation." Hayes's epiphany that "the voice I was born with was colored" resulted in aesthetic action: "I felt I had a motto for my career: to understand the beauty of a black voice."[132] Perhaps these reflections on his voice led to the brief period, at the very end of the 1910s and the beginning of the 1920s, during which Hayes performed the Black-authored programs, as if his newly discovered Black voice required Black song.

We have then a case of contradictions. In the 1920s some critics did not hear Hayes, whose vocal identity crisis occasioned an awareness of the racial voice, as a Black artist. Instead, they held up Robeson, who did not consciously ground his singing at this time in an aesthetic of the Black voice, as the epitome of Black performance practice. In these contradictions is a moral. What critics hear in the voice, their interpretation of the sounds that flow from the singer, is determined by their own aesthetic convictions and ideology. The voice is desired. But the voice is also enabled and constrained by its history, contexts, training, and the repertoire it sings. The voice thus desires. As Meizel writes, "singers *will* their voices in the search for self."[133] There is often a gap between the voice as object and subject of desire. It was

90　PAUL ROBESON'S VOICES

easy for critics to disregard Hayes's racial background when he sang Western art songs in a conservatory-trained voice. It was equally easy for critics to hear Robeson as sounding Black when he performed all-Black programs. Our task is to move beyond the obvious categories by which the voice is circumscribed and to hear Robeson's voice in its complex tangled contexts and histories.

The Rhapsodic Voice

Robeson criticism in the mid-to-late 1920s, particularly of his singing of spirituals, is overdetermined in its interpretive prolixity.[134] No doubt, critics were caught up in the novelty of Robeson. But their flights of interpretation overstrain to explain the singer. In one sense this should not be, because Robeson's singing of spirituals occurred within a tradition of interpretation. While his critics draw on this tradition they also extend it, and in this closing section I briefly outline further lines of interpretation. In the spirit of voice-thinking, I propose that critics' listening was in part enabled because of the way Robeson's voice operates as sound in song form.

It is well known that the church featured prominently in the lives of the Black singers of spirituals who have been the subject of this chapter. Perhaps this is unsurprising given the prefatory statement with which Du Bois commenced his sociology of the Black church: "The Negro Church of to-day is the social centre of Negro life in the United States, and the most character-istic expression of African character."[135] Roland Hayes's commitment to the faith of the fathers was by all accounts more profound than Robeson's, who has typically been cast as something of a secular humanist. But Robeson's ties to the church, with which he would reconnect at crucial points during his life and career, were fundamental and, as we saw in chapter 1, formative of his singing. His account of his first encounters with the spiritual was tied to his father the preacher and the church and its people, as he explained to a British audience about to hear him in a series of matinee recitals at Drury Lane in London in mid-1928: "My father was a slave who escaped from a plantation in North Carolina. He became a minister and encouraged his coloured congregation to sing their native folk-songs in church. There I first heard them."[136] Raised on spirituals, it was, Robeson insisted, his right to perform them: "I heard these spirituals sung by Christian Negroes from my youth and by *every law* was fitted to render them as they should be."[137] The laws that Robeson invokes are several. His right is hereditary, passed on by the father-preacher, and by the church; it is a right inherited from family and community. But the law that gives Robeson the right of performance is also informed by the ideal of social justice and divine law. This burden of complexity of expectation that the spiritual bore accounts for its contested status in the Harlem Renaissance—and in Robeson's reception.

Jon Cruz has written the longer history of the spiritual's reception, in which, from the mid-nineteenth century, the spiritual displaced "other grammars of [Black] discontent" to become, for whites, the preferred expression of Black subjectivity. In turn the spiritual "was transposed from its status as a moral item or testimony to that of an abstract object or artefact," encouraging what Cruz calls a circumscribed "ethnosympathy" of sentimental listening "that remained largely silent about lynching."[138] Along the same line, for Carby white modernist artists used the spirituals' artistic value to dissociate the songs from the material conditions of their production, and held Robeson up as a symbol who offered "the possibility for unity for a fractious age."[139] Robeson's own utterances of the time, however, do not divorce his ideals for the spiritual from their critical reception so much as feed that reception: the critics' desire for Robeson as unifying symbol correlates with the singer's position on racial uplift and unity, a hallmark of mainstream Renaissance thinking and the initial impetus for Robeson's concertizing. Put another way, his performance of spirituals colludes with his modernist invention because the ideology of Renaissance aesthetics is itself a function of modernism; albeit a particular brand of Black modernism.

Carby contends that Robeson's critics heard art (rather than slave history) in his performances, although I think she overstates her case. For instance, it was not uncommon for critics to connect Robeson's singing to the spiritual's origins. As the Boston critic "D. McC." wrote, in Robeson "there is the voice of the original singer, the Water Boy, the camp-meeter." If he had lived in the days of slavery, conjectured Elizabeth Sergeant, he "would surely have been one of the unknown and tragic creators of the Spirituals."[140] Attributing this vocal lineage to Robeson is of course an authenticating strategy but it also brings something of the material history of the spirituals into Robeson's popular reception. Lest we forget, Robeson's life was only one generation removed from slavery, and throughout his life he experienced slavery's legacies in lynching, Jim Crow, and other forms of racialized violence. His commitment to the repertory of Black religious music was his conscious engagement with that history.

92 PAUL ROBESON'S VOICES

Carby also does not make sufficient point of the fact that Robeson's concert performance of spirituals asks us to hear the songs, and his voice, as art. The aestheticizing, what Carby calls "classicizing," of Robeson is a process that the artist initiated, concretized in the statue *Negro Spiritual*, and one that, for Robeson to be recognized as a concert singer, he conscientiously worked at. Robeson desired, at first, to be an artist. One might argue that materialist critiques of the concert spiritual fail to consider the *material voice* that voice-thinking requires of us, and which this chapter endeavors to do. When critics insist that the spirituals were "turned into an aesthetic commodity for white consumption," we should bear in mind both the reality of the music marketplace in which Robeson was trying to make his way as an emerging artist and earn a living, and the dominant aesthetic ideology of the Harlem Renaissance which sanctioned his mode of artistic production, and also deemed it political.[141]

At the same time, as Carby and others have noted, Robeson and his singing of spirituals functioned as "representative of metaphoric negroness . . . [he] was stamped . . . with the signs of authenticity."[142] The sacred was one such complex sign. It had become a marker of Blackness while signifying also the transcendence of race. Radano has described how, in its transformation from the slave song around the time of the Civil War, the renamed spiritual (from the slave vernacular "sperichel") epitomized the alignment of Blackness with the sacred.[143] This set in motion a tradition of interpretation for the spiritual, one in part continued in Du Bois's "sorrow songs." As the foremost purveyor of spirituals in the concert market, Robeson's singing was surely invested with the signs of the spiritual's sacredness. "Listening to Paul Robeson," rhapsodized one critic, "is to undergo an experience more spiritual than aesthetic and to start a train of reflections and speculations which lead far from the concert hall."[144] But as was often the case, Robeson's voicing the spiritual encouraged a wider range of responses. For Sergeant, Robeson was properly a "preacher, a seer, who . . . must out of the mystic and authoritative understanding of his own heart, sing his message."[145] In the same vein the *Wichita Beacon* discovered in Robeson's singing "the voice of a prophet and an artist," and critic James Douglas granted Robeson the gift of "seership," for his "was the art of the actor, the singer, the poet, and the prophet in one." Douglas begins his account of attending a Robeson recital with the mundane—"I went into Drury Lane Theatre to hear Paul Robeson singing negro spirituals"—but is helpless to doing anything other than wax metaphysical for the rest of the review: "We are caught up into a seventh heaven of faith by these cadences of the grand voice that carries like a violin from depth to depth and breadth to breadth of vision. The man sees what he sings, and we see it as he sees it and sings it."[146] Carby has charged this non-materialist tradition of interpretation thus: it hears the singer as "a premodern conduit, capable of transporting America's soul to other worlds of experience by denying and repressing its brutal history."[147] But the desire for Robeson's voice as an idealized alternative to Western materialism also works dialectically because, at times, it was also a rebuke for the processes by which that world was constructed. Robeson's voice was thus fantasized by white critics as a voice of conscience. More than "the oracle of an oppressed race," Robeson was "the Moses in a Transatlantic Egypt appealing to a white Pharaoh."[148] The moral here is a Black voice, articulated through the spirituals, that serves as notice to a West writ large—an Egypt become transatlantic—of its ongoing politics of enslavement. An artistic corollary is that the spirit of ennui that was said to have infected Western culture in the early twentieth century shaped modernist engagements with assorted Others as a strategy of revitalization; or as Robeson put it: "Europe is now trying to import vitality for its art and music from primitive sources."[149]

The encounter with Robeson's voice as spiritual was enabled by two aesthetic processes, of which voice-thinking requires mention. It was informed by a romantic aesthetic that accompanied the rise of art song interpretation in the early twentieth century, and which in turn supported the interpretation of spirituals. And it was grounded in a reversal in the order of knowledge between voice and word, or *logos*. A feature of the Western philosophical tradition has been what Adriana Cavarero characterizes as the "devocalization of logos," which "radically denies to the voice a meaning of its own that is not always already destined to speech."[150] Thinking about the voice in this way has infiltrated criticism of the voice even in its musical forms. Lawrence Kramer pointed out that the "experience of song as enveloping voice has not, by and large, entered into theorizations of word-music relationships, which tend to assume intelligible utterance as the sine qua non of song."[151] Cavarero outlines a time prior to the triumph of the word when the voice was unharried. Here the poet, whose voice gave to speech a carnal body, was attended by what Cavarero names the rhapsode, the acoustically performing voice, so that thinking and vocalizing were one. In this regime of knowledge, "poetry is a song and the song is a vocalization." More to the present point,

94 PAUL ROBESON'S VOICES

Cavarero describes how the rhapsode "vocalizes a song that in turn produces *enchantment.*"[152]

Robeson's singing of spirituals, and the voice therein heard, functioned as a rhapsodic voice—a "spell that is inescapable," wrote one critic.[153] Often critics paid little attention to the spiritual's lyrics in Robeson's singing. "The words are not particularly illuminating," mused the esteemed Chicago critic Karleton Hackett. It was rather his vocal tone of "searching beauty" that attracted: the "tone challenges you. . . . It is like the searching question."[154] Even more, oftentimes the music Robeson sang was deemed unimportant, the song a mere vehicle for the voice; and this applied to the spirituals too. Celebrated English musicologist Ernest Newman penned a "personal confession" after hearing Robeson in concert: his diatribe against the spirituals—"these mostly despicable melodies"; "the thinnest, barest, flattest commonplace" airs—was undone by Robeson's "fine bass voice": "so engaging" was Robeson's voice, Newman confessed, "that for the moment I can almost find it in my heart to forgive him the wretched material on which he chooses to exercise his gifts."[155] Already by 1929, then, when Newman penned his critique, Robeson's voice was being distanced from the song repertoires it sung. This would be a feature of much Robeson criticism from then on. The power of Robeson's voice overturned the reign of *logos*. It brings to mind Kramer's account of "songfulness": the "fusion of vocal and musical utterance judged to be both pleasurable and suitably independent of verbal content; it is the positive quality of singing-in-itself: just singing." The songful voice moreover permits "both an aesthetic relationship (that is, an embodied fiction)" and a "fantasy-structure that underlies the experience of songfulness."[156] The desire for Robeson's voice in its first public soundings was, as this chapter has shown, structured by race. The (white) reception of Robeson's spirituals turned on the desire for pleasure and profit—and exposed also white guilt. And the ways in which songfulness operates also permitted other hearings of and desires for the spiritual. What these varied fantasies show is that already in the early years of his concert career Robeson's voice challenged: racial identity, aesthetics, and song practices.

3

Natural Acts, or To Sing Simply

Toward the end of 1929, at the time of Robeson's first two Carnegie Hall recitals of November 5 and 10, the singer kept something akin to a diary; entries spanned a brief period of five days and were jotted down in a compact black notebook. Back in the United States—Robeson was then residing in England—and with his debut at the august venue behind him, the diary entries tackle weighty matters, revealing by turns a hesitancy and confidence in their expression and a fervent imagination. It was a time, wrote his son, "exhilarating but unsettling."[1] In the diary, notes biographer Martin Duberman, Robeson "mulled over the pros and cons of learning additional technique as an artist, remarking that 'Water Boy,' his 'best record,' was made 'when I was untrained.'"[2] What, we might ask, did Robeson mean by this occluding statement? Was "Water Boy" a favorite song; his preferred recorded performance of the song; or cherished for being one of his very first recordings, and his first solo recording?[3] We must, moreover, be slightly wary of the singer's declaration, of linking (as if in afterthought?) the untrained voice to the recording. When as a trial artist Robeson first entered RCA Victor's New York studio on April 21, 1925, he had already received some coaching. The first five takes of "Water Boy," made on July 16 and 27 of that year and January 17, 1926, were destroyed, and it was only the sixth take from the last session that became the master from which the commercial releases followed.[4] In the intervening half-year Robeson had done significant further concert work, under the guidance of his accompanist Lawrence Brown and in consultation with several voice coaches. His voice, on the "Water Boy" record, was by no means completely untrained, even as it would undergo further, more systematic training during the ensuing years. In these private moments, as Robeson reflected on his voice and singing, the singer participated in a discourse on "the natural" that had characterized Robeson criticism from the outset. As Richard Middleton puts it of Robeson's performance of Joe in *Show Boat*: "he was Natural Man incarnate."[5]

This chapter begins by considering the singer as subject of criticism, as reported in the pages of the contemporary popular press, in order to explore

---

Paul Robeson's Voices. Grant Olwage, Oxford University Press. © Oxford University Press 2024.
DOI: 10.1093/oso/9780197637470.003.0004

96 PAUL ROBESON'S VOICES

how the idea of the natural was deployed in the reception of Robeson's early concert career. As Eidsheim has said, "by listening to listening we can trace voice back to ideas. And by doing so, we can consider the sound and the meaning attached to it."[6] The natural is one of the most potent signs by which the racial subject is constructed—and made to sound authentic. It is another figure of sound, as Eidsheim would say. What my excavation of the critical writing reveals is the longevity of a discourse that racialized natural singing, and the specific articulations the discourse assumed vis-à-vis Robeson. Some critics proffered the revelatory idea that Robeson's natural song was a product of art, and so I assay an analysis of the singer's voice that attempts to locate its "natural" sounds within the practices of concert singing. Of course, singing conceived as an embodied act highlights the materiality of the voice. As Bonnie Gordon reminds us, this involves a different kind of listening, "one that takes into account the physical activity of singing and inserts the performer's body into a mode of musical analysis."[7] Such an endeavor is exemplary voice-thinking. It invites us to venture yet further: to consider not only the body's singing acts but the materiality of the voice's resultant sounds too. Tuning in to somatic and acoustic epistemologies, I argue, helps to further unmask the racial ideologies that have constructed Robeson as subject and voice.

What the Critics Said

Critical writing on Robeson in the 1920s is notable for the extent to which it draws on a discourse of the natural. It traverses the terrains of race (Robeson as Negro), the subject (in Robeson's person and personality), and the aesthetic, and forms around a set of oft-iterated tropes: emotion, simplicity, sincerity, and authenticity. These tropes, among others, were deployed to construct the threefold terrain of race-subject-aesthetic.

Occasionally, the old (and racist) romantic equation of race and nature surfaced in Robeson criticism. A *Glasgow Evening News* review of a Robeson recital was headlined "A Gifted Child of Nature," and the London *Daily Mail* sought fit to remind its readers that it "would be an error, however, to think of him as a child of Nature 'warbling wood-notes wild.'"[8] The child of nature trope is instructive for what it tells us about the whole discourse of the natural. For one, the strategy of infantilizing privileges a non- or pre-rational mode of being, and therefore the world of emotions. The same *Daily Mail* critic explained the power of Robeson's performance: if even "the hardened concert-critic feels its power," the critic imagined what "the effect of such dramatic emotionalism on a highly impressionable race" might be. Several years later the *Manchester Evening News* stated the race-nature-emotion equation in its starkest terms: "Paul Robeson is a negro. That is to say, he is one of a race whose natural emotions have been as yet little affected by that cramping and de-humanising process that we know as civilisation."[9] Routine discursive violence like this was a function of slavery's legacy: Robeson as Black subject/voice is reduced to emotion, to a function of pure nature. This line of criticism continued an earlier tradition.

In a broader sense, African Americans, and in the colonial imagination Black subjects in general, had long been considered children of nature; and in this habit of thinking were said to be naturally musical. The discourse would in due course inform the interpretation of spirituals too, the mainstay of Robeson's repertoire in the 1920s. By the time of the Civil War, and under the impress of the ideologies of New England romantic thought, Ronald Radano has shown how the spiritual reduced to "pure sound the suprarealities of God and nature . . . culminating in a sacred splendor that finally rejoined black folk with an original, natural world."[10] Illustrative of this alignment of Black singers of spirituals with the discourse of nature is the reception of the jubilee movement, which popularized the concert performance of spirituals starting in the 1870s. Of the Fisk Jubilee Singers from Nashville, the best known of the jubilee groups, the *New York Journal* enthused that they were "all natural musicians," and *Dwight's Journal of Music* commented that the "character of the music is purely natural as contradistinguished from artistic."[11] Radano summarizes the situation as such: "If the jubilees were products of studied practice following the rules of European music, they were also unadulterated wholes of natural purity."[12] This tension between the ascription of (racialized) naturalness and acknowledgment of artfulness characterized Robeson criticism too, as I explore more fully at a later point.

Robeson's naturalness was also mapped onto the subject. As many have noted, "Robeson's sound could not be divorced from his body, his body from his gender, his gender from his race," such that his singing seemed to give listeners access to "his qualities and qualifications as a person and performer." Shana Redmond refers to the "corporeal technology of sound" by which Robeson's voice presented itself to listeners.[13] Explanations of Robeson's natural artistic expression were thus underwritten by the belief that the singer's naturalness was nothing more than an expression of his self.

98 PAUL ROBESON'S VOICES

"His is not a simulation of sentiment and feeling," noted the *Musical Courier*, "but a simple, unaffected expression of what lies deep within him—an integral part of his nature, the nature of his race."[14] If the magazine's primary argument was to locate the naturalness of Robeson's art in "his nature"—"what lies deep within him"—that nature, it seems, needed to be qualified by also accounting for it as the nature of his race. In short, the subject of Robeson was that of his race. Thus Eslanda Robeson would title her biography of her husband *Paul Robeson, Negro*. Some accounts of his naturalness went so far to suggest that he did not merely express his self in song but that he could only but do so: "Music is the essential element in which he breathes and moves, and he expresses himself in song as easily and naturally as a beautiful woman expresses herself in grace and form."[15] In play here is the old trope of Black musicality.

Two related features of naturalness linked the terrains of the subject and the aesthetic: simplicity and sincerity.[16] As Matthew D. Morrison has noted, an "ontology of blackness *as* simple" has been a common device in scripts about Black music.[17] For the *Register*, Robeson was "a true black man," in part because the "great thing about him is that he has retained this simplicity" in spite of his education and accomplishments. It was the very "possession of this latter quality"—simplicity—that made him "a perfect medium for the pathos and the humor of his race." Across the Atlantic, critics attributed the attraction of Robeson for the throngs who turned out to listen to his matinée recitals of spirituals at Drury Lane in 1928 to the fact that audiences "like the utter simplicity of the man—a simplicity which seems not at all to rest upon stage artifice."[18] (The reference to the theater is telling, as Robeson was appearing in *Show Boat* at the time, and his acting was also noted for its simplicity.) Having fashioned the man as a simple person, it was no complex leap to describe his art in similar terms.

The repertoire Robeson sang suggested such an interpretation. Patron of African American arts Carl van Vechten had described the spirituals as "these simple songs of the Negro people,"[19] and as spirituals increasingly took their place alongside other folk song repertoire on the concert stage they took on the character of simplicity that folk song in general was said to embody. In the 1930s when Robeson began to add songs from other folk repertoires to his programs, it was not only spirituals that were described as simple music. "There are very few foreign vocalists of any class at all who have the slightest idea of how to sing a perfectly simple English folk song," commented a provincial pundit on Robeson's successful foray into English

NATURAL ACTS, OR TO SING SIMPLY 99

folk song.[20] But it was easy to sing such simple song un-simply, and to the ears of the majority of Robeson's critics it was an error he avoided. "He sang simply" became a much-penned line in Robeson criticism.[21] It was then also his simple manner of performance that was praised, and by which his naturalness was further confirmed and constructed.

Frequently the terrain of race entered that of the aesthetic, as in Karleton Hackett's observation in the *Chicago Evening Post*: Robeson "sings with the unaffected simplicity that makes negro music from the lips of the negro a thing apart."[22] Critical discourse often made recourse to a negative opposite to make this point. Reviewing a Robeson recital at Carnegie Hall in late 1929, Samuel Chotzinoff drew on an old foil: "Mr. Robeson's art embodies the traditional simplicity of Negro musical art kept clean of sophisticated 'white' influences. Mr. [Roland] Hayes, on the other hand, consciously subjects his native musical gifts to this alien influence. . . . Mr. Robeson's singing of spirituals is natural where Mr. Hayes's is artful."[23] Robeson's simple (Black) singing encouraged his listeners to introduce, as one critic put it, the twin "virtue" of sincerity to the discourse of nature, thus more expressly imbuing aesthetics with ethics. In most instances, Robeson's sincerity was taken as a marker of racial authenticity. But sometimes the simplicity of his singing was presented merely as artistic sincerity. Even as harsh a critic of spirituals as Ernst Newman, for whom the spirituals were "despicable melodies," was engaged by the "sincerity of [Robeson's] manner" to the extent, confessed Newman, that "for the moment I can almost find it in my heart to forgive him the wretched material on which he chooses to exercise his gifts."[24] The *Glasgow Herald*'s account of Robeson's appearance in the city in early 1930 adds a more explicit moral to the comparative framework. Noting the "childlike quality of expression" of the spirituals, the newspaper contrasted Robeson's singing thereof with the "sophistication in treatment with which they are so often presented." Whereas the "tendency [was] to make too much of them on the part of both singers and arrangers of the accompaniments," "Mr. Robeson's direct singing—associated as it is with sincerity of feeling and a very high standard of vocal performance"—bore the "stamp of authenticity." It made "itself felt as right."[25] Robeson's sincerity marked his voice also as thoroughly contemporary, a witness to the shift, in the 1920s and 1930s, "from singing styles prioritizing virtuosity to more intimate styles that privileged the vocalist's genuine feeling."[26]

For the critics, Robeson's singing felt right for several reasons. It was racially right, authentic for the repertoire he sang, and appropriate for his voice

100 PAUL ROBESON'S VOICES

and artistic means. In short, the sincerity for which critics so praised Robeson formed along a threefold formation of race-repertoire-performance, and on all counts was explained by its lack of artifice. In reviewing Robeson's successful concert series in Budapest in the spring of 1929, a Hungarian newspaper wrote that his "caressingly warm and soft bass gushes forth naturally from within him, *without the slightest pose*, and it is for that reason that he is particularly suited to interpret the fervent sincere childlike naïve and directly appealing Negro song." This prevailing position on Robeson was summed up by a Manchester daily: "Mr. Paul Robeson stands outside art."[27]

One line of criticism, then, continuing in a tradition of criticism of Black musicking, took the position that Robeson's natural singing stood outside art. Critics taking this line could be charged with uninformed or lazy listening (in contrast to the alternative hearing of Robeson's performance of the song "Water Boy" I pursue below), or we could conclude that their "outside-art" position was an inability to hear beyond race. Another line of criticism offered a more complex assessment. Though still on occasion summoning the racial discourse of nature to explain Robeson's singing, it acknowledged its intellectual and artistic foundations. In doing so, this branch of criticism, with its core insight the idea of the natural-as-art, introduced distinctions into the discussion on aesthetic naturalness not made by the outside-art critics, and extended the terms of reference by which Robeson's naturalness was argued.

The banal observation, both commonplace and obvious, was that nature had gifted Robeson with his voice. "Mr. Robeson's natural vocal endowment is stupendous," enthused the *Columbus Citizen*. "It is impossible to imagine more virile, more richly resonant and beautiful tones." Here, it should be noted, the voice as object of beauty was not a racial gift, even if its natural provenance was at times attributed to another, higher order, a voice from the Father: "what the Lord so generously bestowed."[28] For these critics, however, it did not follow that Robeson sang outside art because he employed his vocal gift naturally. Quite the contrary. Importantly, this line of criticism typically gives a nod toward Robeson's vocal training, whereas the outside-art position more likely ignores or disavows Robeson's history of voice training as the primary evidence for his natural singing.[29] For the natural-as-art critics it was noteworthy that the training did not undermine the natural vocal gift. "Nor has his training been permitted to spoil what the Lord so generously bestowed," noted one critic, while for another, Robeson's singing was free from "the rather devitalizing polish which trained singers impart to Negro

NATURAL ACTS, OR TO SING SIMPLY   101

music."[30] Remembering Robeson's search for a compatible voice teacher in the late 1920s Eslanda too voiced her "prejudice . . . against so-called 'trained' voices," which "level[ed] all the voices to one uninteresting mould."[31] The "voice-help" she and her husband sought would thus align with schools of "natural singing" and protect Robeson's voice against the homogenizing effects of training.

But it did not follow, as the outside-art critics would have, that Robeson was an untutored singer, and critics acknowledged this place of vocal in-betweenness in different ways. For the *Boston Globe*, Robeson occupied a "middle ground":

> His work is free from both the exuberant roughness of that of untrained singers, and the rather devitalizing polish which trained singers impart to Negro music. Thus his interpretations stand on middle ground, and are interesting for their liveliness, their spontaneity and imagination, and pleasing for their appropriate degree of refinements.[32]

The Hungarian daily *Pesti Hirlap* explained Robeson's "vocal art" as a product of the folk music he cultivated, and which accounted for the naturalness of his singing style, but was at pains to note for its readers that "such natural-ness should not be confounded with naturalism: Robeson sings with infinite culture and, from the musical viewpoint, with perfection."[33] If these types of distinction, here between naturalness and naturalism, sometimes strike us as arbitrary, they are a recognition that "the natural" is an aesthetic, a con-sciously worked out—and worked on—style of singing. It is also a case of a performer's multivocality; the voice, in part trained through classical singing, is styled by its remembrance and practice of Black folk musics.

The rhetorical move employed by the natural-as-art critics presented an exposition of Robeson's naturalness followed by an explanation of its artful construction. Thus for the *Columbus Citizen* his singing "is as natural, as sincere, as if he were all alone, singing just for the fun of it." But the *Citizen* cautioned that "to create such an effect requires the highest sort of intelligent artistry." Similarly, the London *Daily Chronicle* noted that Robeson's singing "has that naturalness and simplicity," yet this was a "characteristic of great art" and as such "there is plenty of subtlety and refinement in the treatment of the songs."[34] The proposition of an artfully fashioned naturalness could ring true even for critics who ascribed naturalness to race, whether to a generic Black vocal aesthetic or to the song-type of the spiritual. "Mr. Robeson's [singing]

102 PAUL ROBESON'S VOICES

pleases chiefly by its engaging simplicity and its naïve but racy imperfection, its honest and unashamed racial quality." But if the "*effect* is undoubtedly of untutored singing," it was, the *Boston Herald* clarified, "intelligently desired and artfully achieved."[35] Here, we are presented with an explicit statement of how "the natural" itself is constructed—and thereby race, too.

One type of listening, then, heard Robeson as subject and singer according to the (racial) discourse of nature. But his singing was also heard according to other logics, which could, at times, contradict the logic of the natural. Richard Dyer traces how, on the one hand, the images of Robeson that drew on racialized discourses of the natural, ideas of Blackness as folk-like and atavistic, for instance, were, on the other hand, accompanied by strategies of "deactivation," of passivizing Robeson in order to contain him: "there was the contrast between the potential bodily power and his actual stillness [in his acting] and, most movingly, between the potential vocal power and his soft, gentler, careful actual delivery of speech and song." Dyer notes that the media's discursive containment and Robeson's and his collaborators' creative practices of restraint were necessary for his success as a global cross-over star in the 1920s and 1930s. Hazel Carby argues the point more forcefully: "The formal qualities of control and discipline over voice and body gain political resonance precisely because Robeson is presented as a controlled and disciplined Negro: the consumption of his art could not threaten to disrupt the national constitution."[36]

While the idea of (vocal) power in check is certainly present in representations of Robeson in the 1920s, a closer look at reviewers' language reveals a broader application of the idea of restraint.[37] There is, for example, the idea that vocal restraint heightens affect, as when "the burning emotionalism" of Robeson's performance of Harry T. Burleigh's "Were You There?" was considered "all the more impressive because of the quietness, the restraint of the singing."[38] Then there is the art music critic applauding restraint as a model of classical vocal rectitude. Seasoned commentator Herman Devries found Robeson's voice, in 1926, to have "been well and intelligently trained" and, "while vigorous, is handled with restrained, refined discretion."[39] A few years later, Robeson's vocal restraint was again yoked to his training: "Now that he has persuaded his voice to move more easily, and has got much better control over it, he has become a real singer. . . . His restraint is a lesson to many."[40] Finally, Robeson's restrained singing is also, as I discuss later in this chapter, a function of vocal quartet practice that he learned when he performed with the Four Harmony Kings. The lesson here is twofold and

NATURAL ACTS, OR TO SING SIMPLY   103

permits a more nuanced understanding of the natural. Robeson's restrained singing, in part a product of his vocal training, was uttered against vocal excess and therefore artifice. In that sense, his singing partook of a natural aesthetic. But there is also a more basic lesson: precisely because he sang with restraint meant that he was not a natural singer. As the London *Evening Standard* put it, he sang "with a touch of restraint, with a careful direction of tone quality which proved that he is not merely, in the limited sense, a natural singer."[41]

By acknowledging the primacy of the world of concert singing, in which Robeson indubitably if tentatively sought to make his way in the 1920s, we gain another perspective. Where the outside-art critics celebrated the racially natural in Robeson's singing, the lament of postmodern critics (such as Dyer and Carby) at the singer's aesthetic of restraint is perhaps a sublimated wish for a more natural Robeson; a desire for a freer racial subject and art. Both positions take this stand because they choose to take race as the starting point for their interpretive flights and fail to acknowledge the importance of the practices of the concert stage in fashioning Robeson's voice. These collective critical acts produce what Eidsheim calls a "phantom genealogy" of the voice, in which listening practices materialize an idea—natural singing—about vocal sound "even if it is not found in reality."[42] Through these means, ideas about the racialized voice are perpetuated. But if we listen closely to the material sounds of and musical contexts that produced the singer in the mid-1920s, we might learn something else about Robeson's singing.

"Water Boy": What a Song Can Tell Us

Robeson, we saw, presented his first recording of "Water Boy" as exemplary of his natural singing. But it is also an exemplar of how the natural is artfully crafted. The song was a staple of Robeson's repertoire: sung at his first appearances on the concert stage and programmed throughout his career, used in his "trial" for Victor, and then for his "first engagement" proper for the record company, and recorded numerous times throughout his performing career.[43] It even made an appearance on screen: playing the chain gang convict Brutus Jones in the 1933 film adaptation of Eugene O'Neill's *The Emperor Jones*, Robeson leads the gang in a diegetic singing of "Water Boy," a song aptly about hard labor. As much as Robeson came to be associated in the popular imagination with "Ol' Man River" from *Show Boat*, he

104   PAUL ROBESON'S VOICES

probably identified more with "Water Boy." It is an example of the secular Black folk songs he programmed together with the spirituals at the start of his career, and specifically it is a work song. As such it thematizes Robeson's presentation of African American history and Black slavery, reminding us of the relationship of popular music texts like "Water Boy" and the history of racial violence. Fred Moten notes that the slave's "scream is diffused in but not diluted by black music." In supplementing Saidiya Hartman's observation that the aftermath of slavery is located not only in "invocations of the shocking and the terrible," Moten reiterates that the diffusion of violence continues to be "perpetrated under the rubric of pleasure"; in other words, also in Robeson's artful singing of spirituals and work songs.[44]

The version of "Water Boy" Robeson sang was, like his voice, a mediated object. It is by no means a folk song per se, despite its reception as such in the Robeson archive. Composed by the Romanian-born American songwriter Jacques Wolfe, who took an interest in African American music when his military band was posted to the South, it is an example of Wolfe's many popular songs penned "in the style of" African American music.[45] The introductory and concluding chant of "Water Boy" is based on a putative field call uttered by parched laborers for the water carrier. It was not Wolfe's composed reimagining of a water call and prison song that Robeson drew on but rather Avery Robinson's "jazz" arrangement of Wolfe's song, a jazz vaguely gestured at in the gently swinging refrain that lightens the serious business at hand, as the note to the sheet music explains: "By a hot, white road in Georgia, the Negro convicts are sitting astride the rock-piles, breaking rock. . . . The convicts sing this rhythmic song to lighten their labor."[46]

Robinson's arrangement circulated as a popular text, specifically among concert singers of spirituals and African American song. Robeson might have sung "Water Boy" before he began serious concertizing,[47] but it likely entered his concert and recording repertoire through the influence of established Black performers' promotion of the song. The sheet music cover is thus headed with the endorsement "As sung by Mr. Roland Hayes," and the Black American British-based popular singer and choral conductor John Payne, who provided Robeson with access to London society and letters on his first visit to the city in 1922, also performed the song.[48] The common denominator in this concert tradition of performing the song is Lawrence Brown, then Hayes's accompanist, and friend of and part-time collaborator with Payne, and who met Robeson at Payne's London home. With Robinson's score of "Water Boy" under his hands, it is instructive to listen to Brown's

NATURAL ACTS, OR TO SING SIMPLY   105

recordings of the song with Payne in 1924 and then Robeson; there is no record of Hayes having cut a disc of "Water Boy" despite his association with the song.

The sheet music of Robinson's arrangement is the starting point to consider the recorded performances of the song. It was certainly the version both Robeson and Payne used: Brown's piano accompaniment follows the score in every detail save for the rolling of chords, as do the singers follow the vocal line but for the addition of an ornamental note or two related to the delivery of the lyrics and the loosening up of the notated straight rhythm for the sake of swing. In other words, we can safely take the scored arrangement, and the tradition of its concert performance, as our reference point rather than an unwritten folk tradition.[49]

The arrangement of "Water Boy" and its performance relates to folk practice in contradictory ways. In James Weldon Johnson's discussion of "Negro rhythms and 'swing'"—the scare quotes an acknowledgment of the elusiveness of the swing-concept—he observed that the "'swing' of these songs is governed by the rhythmic motions made by a gang of men at labor," adding a cautionary note that "the ballet of bending backs and quivering muscles . . . is all in rhythm but a rhythm impossible to set down" (and Johnson's aestheticizing of labor is a telling instance of Moten's insistence that slavery diffuses through pleasure). The problem of notating Black music is in recording the irregularity of the rhythms of work, as Johnson explained:

> A phrase is sung while the shining hammers are being lifted. It is cut off suddenly as the hammers begin to descend. . . . Each phrase of the song is independent, apparently obeying no law of time. After each impact the hammers lie still and there is silence. As they begin to rise again the next phrase of the song is sung; and so on. Just how long the hammers will be allowed to rest cannot be determined; nor, since the movements are not governed by strict time, can any exact explanation be given as to why they all begin to rise simultaneously.[50]

For Johnson, "a fine illustration" of this point was Robeson's rendition of "Water Boy" in *The Emperor Jones*. He could only have been referring to the stage (rather than film) version of the play, in which Robeson appeared in the 1924 revival, because Robeson's singing of "Water Boy" in the 1933 film version and his (and Payne's) recordings of the song demonstrate the converse: they are models of rhythmic regularity that, unlike the laborers' work rhythm, strictly obey time, specifically the law of common time meter in which the popular song's refrain is arranged. It is likely that Robeson's singing of "Water Boy" in the play was *a cappella*, and that freed from the piano his voice accompanied the motions of work he enacted.

Robinson's arrangement of "Water Boy" contains two *a cappella* moments, the four-measure water call set to the text "Water Boy where are you hiding" that introduces and concludes the song. In these moments, the song, in both its arrangement and performances, gestures toward the folk practice of a work song. The fact that the vocal line is unaccompanied in itself suggests a reference to the unaccompanied field call or holler, the solo expression in turn permitting rhythmic and metric freedom. But the temporal freedom of the field call is awkwardly and incompletely captured by Robinson. The changing meter, from 6/4 to 4/4 and back (see Example 3.1), is surely indicative of the arranger's struggle to force the call into song time. It is an instruction the singers of "Water Boy" chose to ignore. Both Payne and Robeson chant the call freely, accepting the broad rhythmic outline of the notated phrases while shortening and lengthening notes, holding back and pushing them along,

Example 3.1. Avery Robinson, arr., "Water Boy," mm. 1–6.

NATURAL ACTS, OR TO SING SIMPLY   107

although not in the practice of *rubato* in which meter and beat still guide the performer, but rather such that meter and beat perceptually retreat. The overall effect of the sung call is a sense of temporal freedom not indicated in Robinson's arrangement. That both Payne's and Robeson's performances of these *a cappella* moments (and of the refrain too) are broadly similar suggests a preferred interpretation in performing "Water Boy": passed on by their accompanist Brown, it may have been initiated by Hayes, the first interpreter of Robinson's arrangement. Although there is no recording of the song by the tenor, Hayes's own arrangements of African American folk song are studious in their notation of chant- and call-like modes of vocalization, made explicit also in the expressive markings used to guide his and others' performances. His arrangement of "Lit'l Boy," a solo-type folk song heard "sung by a traveling Aframerican evangelist," thus specifies above the voice part "Exclamatory—Voice ad lib."[51] Robinson's score is headed simply "Andante."

In "Water Boy," Robeson's and Payne's ad-libbing is heard primarily in the dimension of musical time, but they depart from the score in other areas too, such as in their elaborations of the scored melody. While the broad strokes of their performances suggest a close affinity, constituting a tradition of preferred interpretation I mentioned, comparing their ad-libbing in detail gives us insight into how they respectively construct a natural aesthetic. How they translate speech into song in the prisoner's call for the water boy in the opening *a cappella* measures might be taken as one measure of the naturalness of their performances.[52]

Payne's singing approximates speech, which in my current argument aligns with naturalness, more closely than Robeson's in several respects. First, Robeson's lyrical language is more "highbrow" than Payne's. He tends, for example, to use African American dialect selectively: sometimes, as with Payne, he converts the lyrics into dialect: "That's on-a this mountain" is sung "Dat's on-a dis mountain" (0:41). But other times he eschews the published lyrics' vernacularisms—"Yo Jack-o Di'monds" is sung by Robeson as a deliberate and proper "You" (1:26) while Payne sticks with the variant "Yo"—and elsewhere Robeson follows the standard English of the lyrics whereas Payne vernacularizes them, as when "You robbed my pocket" is turned to "Done robbed my pocket" (1:27). Robeson's ambivalent attitude toward dialect (which I discuss in more detail in chapter 5) characterized his singing of Black song throughout his career, whereas the effect of Payne's consistent use of dialect is to create the impression of a more authentic, and therefore

108   PAUL ROBESON'S VOICES

natural, aesthetic. As we know from the history of American popular culture, however, dialect is no simple sign of natural speech, and the relationship of dialect in popular songs such as "Water Boy" and the varieties of Black vernacular speech is complex.[53] This is so for the singing of spirituals too: Marti K. Newland notes that the incorporation of dialect in concert spirituals, which happened alongside its use in literature, "destabilizes the concept that dialect usage in concert spirituals is a product of the 'natural' singing of black Americans."[54]

Robeson's inconsistent recourse to dialect in song suggests a degree of what sociolinguist William Labov termed "linguistic insecurity," as if the singer preferred not to fully embrace the African Americanisms the song's discourse requested of him for fear of straying too far from standard English.[55] The insecurity is demonstrated further by considering the sounds of the sung lyrics. Robeson's diction is more studied than Payne's; and it was an area of his singing that critics consistently lauded throughout his career. Writing in the *Chicago American* in early 1926 soon after the release of the "Water Boy" record, Herman Devries noted that Robeson's "excellent diction" didn't sacrifice "the timbre of the tone" for it; and that is was therefore an "ideal diction."[56] More to the point, it was an ideal *singer's* diction, one often uttered at odds with the phonology of spoken language and in the interests of songfulness. Even in the chanted opening of "Water Boy" where the expectation of approximating a speech-like mode is greatest, Robeson's singer's diction is in evidence. The clarity of the enunciation of his (British English) "t" in "water" is in contrast with Payne's swallowed American English pronunciation of the "t" as a "fast d"; and Robeson's rolled "r's" in both "where" and "are" (in the phrase "where are you hiding") is a classic instance of the singer's liaising of phonemes for the sake of sustained tonal production, what Richard Miller has called "vocal legato (the unrelenting flow of tone)."[57] Payne instead sings the "are" as a conventionally spoken "ah." Robeson's preference for dictional rightness in song results also, for example, in a propensity to conclude final consonants, a practice sometimes contrary to the workings of African American dialect. He thus adds a meticulously voiced "d" to the dialect "ol' " (in the phrase "Yes, know yeh of ol' ") (1:38–1:42), whereas Payne sticks with the liquid "l" (1:23–1:27).

Robeson's singer's diction maximizes the tonal ideal of classical singing. For the same end, he understates the declamatory moments of the "Water Boy" call, which is constructed in two parts. The water carrier is first summoned, "Water Boy where are you hiding," and then, as the prison laborer becomes increasingly desperate for a drink, threatened: "If you dont-a come, Gwine tell-a yoh Mammy." The note to the sheet music explains that "To 'Tell your Mammy' is a real threat, as the rebuke is often vigorous." Yet in Robeson's singing of this line there is no indication of a telling-off. The promise of vocal vigor is gestured at in the quickening of tempo with which he sings the eighth notes of "If you dont-a . . ." (m. 3) only for the energy to dissipate as he settles and then lingers on (far longer than the notated half note), the phrase's concluding ". . . come," reveling in the timbral space the open vowel affords and seemingly not wanting to let go of his voice's sound as he prolongs the closing of the word on to an extended hummed <m> (0:20–0:23).[58] Payne too sings "If you dont-a" quickly, but his voicing of the protagonist's frustration with the water boy's nonappearance gains force both in the forcing of his tone and, importantly, in the clipped "come" that he abruptly ends as if in annoyance, an action more in keeping with the expression of such sentiment in speech. Indeed, Payne's vigorous vocalization in the ensuing "Gwine tell-a yoh Mammy" (m. 4) is easily heard as a rebuke (0:15–0:18), whereas Robeson's singing of the phrase continues in the same unharried mode and mood as the rest of the call.

Payne, in other words, sings the call rhetorically, which he does in part by following the contours of emotive speech. In Robeson's interpretation, the call-as-song wins out. These different conceptualizations of the call are also heard in the durations of their respective performances: as we might expect, Robeson's lyrical song-call is a significant five seconds longer than Payne's declamatory one.[59] There are then a number of indications to suggest Payne's version is more "natural," in the many ways in which it aligns with speech, than Robeson's. It is also more natural in its sounding, in the audibly obvious fact of Payne's untrained voice. Traces of the "exuberant roughness of that of untrained singers" that critics noted as absent in Robeson's singing are easily detected in Payne's performance.[60] For this reason, and despite the tradition of interpretation their performances of "Water Boy" share, perhaps the comparison with Payne is to a small degree amiss. We might rather pursue, as I do below, how listeners heard Robeson's singing as natural in terms of the partially trained concert singer he aspired to be. Although Robeson was by no means a conventional art singer and his voice was fashioned through his participation in several vocal traditions—he sang multivocally—critics at the time for the most part placed his concert singing in the context of, and assessed it in terms of, art singing.

110   PAUL ROBESON'S VOICES

One particularly intuitive listener who was less than convinced by Robeson's "Water Boy" was the African American woman of letters Anna Julia Cooper. In fact, she was somewhat vexed by it: "I heard Paul Robeson sing 'Water Boy' and I have not yet made up my mind whether it was the real Robeson I heard or the actor impersonating a ... chain gang Negro." Cooper's unease stemmed from her inability to easily locate Robeson's art, either in the singer's self, "the real Robeson," or in his impersonation, and she grudgingly conceded that "the perfection of art is to conceal art."[61] Like the critical discourse on Robeson explored earlier, the difficulty to which Cooper points is grounded in the terrain of race-subject-aesthetic, but it is her foregrounding of a problem arising from that terrain that is noteworthy. The possibility of a problem is only entertained because the idea exists that the natural voice may be compromised in its artful presentation. In the song world of "Water Boy," Robeson's singing is, as I have argued, less than natural. How might we hear his singing instead?

An Anatomy of Simple Singing

In the spring of 1930, Robeson embarked on an extended tour of the provinces of the British Isles, a tour he would undertake many more times in the ensuing decade when London was his base. By and large, the pundits reproduced the discourse of nature with varying emphases and to differing degrees in reporting on his performances as he worked his way through the British counties. In Glasgow, Montague Smith heard Robeson's reading of the spiritual "Steal Away" in terms of an already well-established trope in Robeson criticism: the song was "deeply impressive by reason of the simplicity and sincerity of its rendering."[62] What I am interested in dissecting is something akin to an anatomy of simple singing, itself one of the core features of an aesthetics of the natural. Roger Freitas reminds us that at least since the eighteenth century, naturalness in music has in large part being defined as simplicity.[63] What, we might ask, constituted Robeson's simple singing?

As he made his way from Scotland to the Midlands in 1930, Robeson arrived in Birmingham in early March to much fanfare, as was the norm for his reception in the provinces throughout the 1930s. There, as elsewhere on the tour (and again during the fall tour of August to October), he presented what the London *Evening Standard* later in the year characterized as a "rather peculiar" "mixed entertainment." Consisting of "the least interesting act

NATURAL ACTS, OR TO SING SIMPLY   111

of a full-length play [*The Emperor Jones*], some *lieder*, which Mr. Robeson does not sing very well, and some spirituals, which he sings superbly."[64] The Birmingham critic A. J. S. focused on the concept that Robeson's concert demonstrated the "abnegation of artiness," or, as the critic phrased it elsewhere, a "lack of sophistication." The racial imagination seems to be in play here, for want of sophistication often stood in Robeson criticism for Black naïveté. But A. J. S. was sure to note that "abnegation of artiness need involve no exclusion from the domain of art." The critic continued: even though "we may rightly declare Mr. Robeson a natural singer," art was very much evident in Robeson's performance, to the extent that "one might go further, and ascribe genius to the manner in which [Robeson's voice] was used."[65] The refusal of artfulness thus marked Robeson's singing as simple, but more specifically it is the refusal of an explicit *art singing* presentation of artfulness that we must consider in assessing Robeson's simple singing, for such was the critics' experience of it. The *Daily Telegraph* pronounced: "it is as the most unsophisticated of all sophisticated singers of Negro spirituals that many of us will remember him."[66] Placed within the field of the art singing of spirituals, Robeson occupied its edge.

The most obvious, aurally evident, distinction between Robeson's voice and the classical voice is that he does not sound like a *Lieder* or opera singer, whether singing art song repertoire or spirituals. His classical voice training did not, to draw on the original senses of the word, "sophisticate" his voice: it did not corrupt the original, natural voice by mixing it with something foreign, such as voice training. As the *Oxford English Dictionary* has it, to be branded as sophisticated is to be "altered from . . . simplicity or naturalness." By the turn of the nineteenth century, "sophisticated" took on its more contemporary sense of being "experienced, worldly-wise; subtle, discriminating, refined, cultured," but its usage in Robeson criticism still contained traces of its archaic formulation. It also had class and race connotations. In the British context, as the distinction between popular or light classics and serious art music became more delineated during the interwar period, sophisticated became also an indicator of serious art. At a Robeson concert in Birmingham a few years later, the "curiously composed" audience was thus characterized as "two separate audiences, one of considerably greater cultural sophistication, the other, no doubt, very much larger in bulk."[67] In the American context, sophistication could also function as a marker of race. Thus for Samuel Chotzinoff, writing in the *New York World*, "Mr. Robeson's art embodies the traditional simplicity of Negro musical art kept clean of sophisticated

112 PAUL ROBESON'S VOICES

'white' influences."[68] It is less these social meanings that accrued to the adjectival form "sophisticated" than the aesthetic sense of the original verb that I pursue.

One marker of Robeson's unsophisticated singing, or its rejection of artfulness, was its cautious approach to, and at times avoidance of, the dramatic singing voice, at least in the first decade or so of his concert career. As critics became used to Robeson's singing and repertoire after several years of hearing him in concert, their criticism, by the end of the 1920s, often pointed out this lack. Reviewing the Carnegie Hall recital in late 1929, the *Wall Street Journal* wished that he "might, perhaps, have been more dramatic," hastening to add, however, that "this was never felt to be a serious defect in the singer's art."[69] The so-called shortcoming was particularly apparent in the art song repertoire he started to sing around this time. Of a Crystal Palace concert, an English critic commented, "curiously enough, in the case of an actor, Mr. Robeson made very little of the dramatic aspect" of Schumann's "*Ich grolle nicht*."[70] But by the end of the 1930s, and by the time he had "found" his voice, for Russian song among other repertoire, things had changed. Critics began to praise his dramatic sense. A 1938 performance in London's Royal Albert Hall, a cavernous venue of which Robeson was not fond, led the *Daily Telegraph and Morning Post* critic to remark that in "the more dramatic pieces, too, he made use of an incisive tone that effectively set off the suavely lyrical style in which he has always excelled."[71] His dramatic sensibility had caught up with his lyrical style. Bearing in mind Robeson's mixed vocal lineage—church choir, glee group, quartet singing in musical revues, and then classical voice training—we should be wary of drawing on the classical voice categorization of the *Fach* system, specifically its distinction of lyric and dramatic voice types, in considering Robeson's voice, even as his critics occasionally employed the discourse of classical vocal practice. But the dramatic-lyric distinction is useful in exploring the nature of Robeson's singing.

In Robeson's youthful voice, in evidence from the mid-1920s to roughly the middle of the following decade, we hear a voice that in several of its aspects stands removed from the dominant line of development of the classical voice. Historians of Western singing chart a long-term shift toward a new vocal episteme, gaining momentum throughout the nineteenth century and which continues its reign today. This newly dominant voice exhibited "the new taste for greater volume and more dramatic expression," in part occasioned by the singer's need to project across larger spaces and over larger

NATURAL ACTS, OR TO SING SIMPLY 113

instrumental forces as the nineteenth century wore on.[72] Vocal strength thus became a hallmark of the dramatic voice. But these features were not at first fortes of Robeson's voice, whose singing was non-dramatic: in his non-rhetorical rendering of the "Water Boy" call described earlier, the muted first recording of "Steal Away" in 1925, and the unconvincing dramatic recitative of "Exhortation" recorded in 1930.[73] Robeson's "restrained" delivery and lyricism were a function of the state of his voice in the 1920s, one that was still in formation: through formal voice training and entrainment by the practices of concert singing. It was also a voice that was in-between: the popular vocal styles he performed in the theater, for instance, and the mature solo concert voice under development. For example, Robeson's early lyrical style must be heard as sounding, in part, from the African American quartet tradition. He was the bass singer for a short stint with the Four Harmony Kings, one of the most prominent Black quartets of the era, prior to his turn to professional solo singing. The Harmony Kings were exponents of an older style, in the tradition of the university jubilee quartets (before the genre transitioned to gospel repertoire and its more exuberant style of the 1930s and 1940s), which employed a "lyrical style of singing" characterized by "harmonic and vocal restraints."[74]

In several respects, Robeson's young voice aligned with the popular quartet style. Where the dominant classical voice favored the chest voice and increased volume in the upper register,[75] Robeson, by contrast, tended to approach the upper register with caution, falling back on the head or falsetto voices, and often presented *sotto voce* or in a reduced dynamic. Thus in "Steal Away," at the first emotionally heightened moment as the voice leaps up a sixth to attack "My Lord he calls me" (from 0:43), Robeson switches to the head voice where others, like Hayes, continue with the chest voice in open throat (from 0:53). Robeson's refusal to up the volume here results even in a semantically contradictory reading: he gets quieter as he sings the succeeding lyrics, "He calls me by the thunder / The trumpet sounds . . ." (0:48–0:55), where Hayes duly thunders to the point of forcing his voice (0:58–1:06).[76] In general, at the start of his concert career, Robeson tended to switch (perhaps too readily) between register and sing softly in the upper registers, favoring a lighter and sweeter high sound. This was in tune with the style of popular quartet singing. The Four Harmony Kings, which "lived up to its name, emphasiz[ed] meticulous harmonizing," requiring careful tonal blending of the ensemble, and were known for "their 'pianissimo' passages" demonstrating "a triumph of voice control." The shifting of register and use

114   PAUL ROBESON'S VOICES

of falsetto can be heard in the extant recordings of the quartet, as in their rendition of the barbershop favorite "Sweet Adeline" (1922).[77] More broadly, throughout the 1920s male pop singers routinely sang in falsetto, counter-tenor, and high tenor; "in fact, the higher a man could sing, the more he was celebrated by popular audiences."[78]

We can hear evidence of this in Robeson's early voice, for instance in the 1926 recording of the spiritual "Swing Low, Sweet Chariot." In the famous opening phrases of the song, Robeson switches back and forth between vocal register, with the higher notes sung falsetto, quietly and carefully, such that as the phrase "Coming for to carry me home" ascends in pitch Robeson departs from the chest voice, registrally splitting "car-ry" as he heads into falsetto (0:17–0:21).[79] But this also highlights a gap in Robeson's developing technique in another tradition: in failing to produce a uniform sound across registers, the *zona di passaggio* is not doing the work demanded by classical vocal pedagogy. By contrast, the preferred interpretation of these phrases in "Swing Low," which the dominant vocal episteme facilitates, favors tonal expansion of the voice as it heads toward "home." Robeson's later recordings of the song read it thus, and in his 1933 record for HMV he maintains both the dynamic level and tonal fullness of the phrase in the ascent to "home."[80] Also from the same year, his second recording of "Steal Away" demonstrates the foundations of a dramatic voice in a stentorian upper register. Here, and in marked difference to his first outing in the studio with the song in 1925, Robeson gives full voice to the refrain "My Lord he calls me" (0:38–0:53).[81]

We might also consider the gendering of male voices at this particular moment in the intersecting histories of Robeson's own voice and popular singing. Allison McCracken's social history of crooning charts a "key period in pop music" because it sheds light on the construction of American masculinity. Whereas male singing that was high-pitched and emotionally intense was naturalized by the 1920s, the rise of crooning as a mass cultural phenomenon was accompanied by the stigmatizing of this aesthetic by the early 1930s. Crooners were condemned as "unfit representatives of American manhood." Bing Crosby would redeem the crooner as an acceptable model of white masculinity in part because the baritone into which he developed distanced his voice from higher singing.[82] The shift in Robeson's developing voice from lighter and higher in the 1920s to the deeper, weightier, and more dramatic voice it became maps on to these changing ideals of vocal masculinity. In what follows I document that shift in some detail.

NATURAL ACTS, OR TO SING SIMPLY   115

Key to the production of dramatic voice types are the weight of the voice, for example the chest voice in the upper register, and its volume. So is a rhetorical mode of utterance, a preference for oratory over plain speaking. Thus in the 1933 "Steal Away," when Robeson summons a powerful chest voice in high volume to declaim the phrase "My Lord," it is accompanied by— and perhaps demands—an intensification of the dramatic in other features of the performance, notably in the more declamatory mode achieved by sharpening the dotted rhythms and the theatrical ending of final notes by crescendoing toward them. Listen to the flourish with which he concludes "soul" (0:50–0:53), whereas in the early recording the voice unceremoniously dies away (0:57–0:59). Rather than delivering song texts in a rhetorical manner through recourse to hyperbole, that is, dramatically, Robeson's young lyrical voice tended to opt for understatement as expressive restraint.

It is for this reason that critics heard Robeson's singing as "smooth," a core term in the critical vocabulary on his voice. Pianist Olga Samaroff enjoyed the "smooth, mellow beauty of Mr. Robeson's voice . . . a sheer loveliness of sound which might well arouse the envy of most opera singers," and critic Grena Bennett enthused that the "Roberson voice resembles a velvet of burgundy hue, so smooth, rich and warm it is in its entire range. He opens his mouth and tones of the most engaging quality seem to flow of their own volition. His is an artistry so flawless that it utterly conceals technic."[83] Smoothness here describes both timbre and sustained, legato singing, a feature of the lyrical voice type. Exemplifying the latter, the London *Daily Telegraph* noted his "smooth linking of phrase to phrase," and the *New York Times* "the smoothness with which [he] delivered some of the long phrases of 'Were you there?,' 'Deep River' and 'Water Boy.' "[84] Smooth singing was no doubt a goal of the classical voice training Robeson received. It was also a feature of quartet singing. Tim Brooks's description of the Kings' singing highlights their "practiced and smooth" style.[85] I would argue that Robeson's focus on tonal legato, and the "long line," was achieved at the expense of rhetoric, which perforce disrupts the smooth flow of sound. A comparison of the same vocal line from Hayes's 1922 recording of "Steal Away" and Robeson's 1925 version, both with accompaniment by Lawrence Brown, reveals how subtle rhetorical moves may affect smoothness in song.

The chorus of "Steal Away" is a model of smooth melody. The opening phrase is repeated thrice, each phrase uttered on a single pitch and iterated in the same rhythm, and each repetition ascending a third to outline a major triad (mm. 2–4, Example 3.2). This demands smooth lyrical singing, and

Example 3.2. Lawrence Brown, arr., "Steal Away" (London: Winthrop Rogers, 1922), mm. 1–9.

both Hayes and Robeson oblige; the piano part bears the instructions *ben legato* and *Con Ped*. In the second half of the chorus, however, Hayes's more explicit use of time as a rhetorical measure marginally interrupts the temporal smoothness. While Robeson minimally, though noticeably, slows down from measure 6 he maintains an overall temporal regularity (00:22–0:42): smoothness in another sense, against which Hayes's expressive lingering pauses mitigate. Hayes reads the scored fermata on "home" literally (where Robeson glosses over it), remaining there for a protracted five seconds (m. 7, from 0:32), and similarly lengthens his stay on "long" (in m. 9, at 0:40) well beyond its notated duration. These instances of rhetorical singing, of what a Boston critic referred to as Hayes's "subtly modulated singing," make him sound dramatic—and artful.[86] If naturalness, as Freitas has suggested, is projected through interpretive restraint, "performing the notes without obvious intervention," then Robeson's smooth singing, devoid of the intervening rhetorical gestures Hayes imparts, is simple singing par excellence.[87]

Robeson's is also a simple singing for the new century, a voicing of more contemporary notions of sonic naturalness, which is clear to hear if we listen to a slightly earlier exemplar of "naturalness," the soprano Adelina Patti. On at least one occasion Patti's natural singing was taken as a point of comparison for Robeson. The *Yorkshire Post* noted that the bass used his voice "with such consummate art that one cannot tell whether, like Patti, he is a vocalist by birth, or whether he has cultivated it to such a point that any sense of artifice is concealed."[88] In his discussion of naturalness in Patti's 1905 recording of the Henry Bishop song "Home! Sweet Home!" Freitas cautions that "the artlessness of the nineteenth century now 'reads' as affected, that earlier naturalness has come to sound unnatural." In Patti's case, naturalness is first and foremost a function of her lyrical singing approaching dramatic declamation. One strategy by which she achieved this was to avoid regularity of tempo, so that her "text-inspired wavering of tempo . . . sound[ed] less like a *musical* effect than an accentuation of key words."[89] Hayes's practice, as I have described it, is closely aligned with this aesthetic, and as a conventionally trained art singer slightly closer to the nineteenth century than Robeson we might expect this. That Robeson's less rhetorical singing, rather than Patti's and Hayes's speech-inspired art, was upheld as the preferred model of aesthetic naturalness in the 1920s indicates a turnabout. Robeson's singing is simple in part because it avoids drawing speech into song, remaining more resolutely in the mode of song. It is for this reason that contemporary listeners can more easily identify with his voice than those of singers of the preceding generation. Thus Freitas summons the conceit of a "foreign language" to account for Patti's vocal strangeness: her "dialect of interpretive nuance," he emphasizes, "is not ours and so can be read as artificial."[90]

Vibrato is another dimension of the voice that places Robeson's singing in the transition toward the contemporary voice. Already in his first recordings in the mid-1920s his voice is marked by a relatively consistent use of vibrato, rather than an earlier vocal aesthetic that considered vibrato an expressive

118 PAUL ROBESON'S VOICES

ornament to be applied sparingly. Employing vibrato in this way marked Robeson's voice as thoroughly modern—and artistic. An early "scientific" investigation into the use of vibrato conducted around this time concluded that "almost every artistic tone has a vibrato."[91] More specifically, in the new vocal episteme vibrato was crucial to the production of a heavier, dramatic voice.[92] But while Robeson uses vibrato consistently his voice's vibrato profile does not remain constant over time. Vibrato in his young voice tends to be slightly quicker and smaller than his mature voice's slower and larger vibrato, and this correlates with the broadest trajectory of vibrato use during the course of the twentieth century: "the well-known slowing down of vibrato rate from the dawn of voice recordings to our days," and conversely an increase in vibrato size.[93]

We get a sense of the change in Robeson's vibrato profile if we continue to dwell on the various recordings the singer made of "Steal Away." I do so by following in the tradition of early scientific work on vibrato, conducted by the Carl Seashore group at the University of Iowa in the 1920s and 1930s, at the time of the Robeson recordings, which sought to accurately measure vibrato acoustically. The 1925 recording of "Steal Away," which Robeson sings in E-flat major, yields the following information.[94] The quickest rate is around 7.2 cycles per second (cps) (or 0.139 seconds per vibrato cycle), the slowest at 6.7 cps, with most notes vibrating in the area of 0.145 seconds per cycle. In the later recording of the song in 1933, performed a semi-tone lower, the rates at the extremes (6.9 and 6.4 cps) and average (around the 0.15 seconds per cycle mark) are slower.[95] It would be placing too great an interpretive burden on these data to attribute every variation in vibrato rate within a single recording to a specific expressive intent. And although the change to a slower rate in the later recording is slight, it does situate Robeson's singing in the earlier recording made in the mid-1920s closer to an older order of singing. Of more significance is how the vibrato rate interacts with the frequency size of the vibrato.

In the earlier recording, the extent of Robeson's vibrato varies between about three-quarters of a semitone, at its smallest, to just over a tone, at its widest. On average it is 1.5 semitones. In the later recording his vibrato size increases: varying between 1.25 semitones and just over a rather sizable tone and a half, its average is almost two semitones.[96] This quite significant increase in the size of the vibrato is perceptually heightened by the modest decrease in its rate. In other words, we hear Robeson's wider vibrato in the later recording more markedly because it is also slower. The impact of vibrato

NATURAL ACTS, OR TO SING SIMPLY   119

rate on vibrato size is brought into sharper relief if we compare Robeson's mature voice, from the 1940s and 1950s, with his younger voice. His vibrato rate during the chorus of the 1926 "Swing Low, Sweet Chariot" is much the same as for the contemporaneous recording of "Steal Away," the concluding "home" in "Comin' for to carry me home" oscillating at a quick 6.9 cps (at 0:33). Three decades on, in a recording of 1956, the same "home" is sung with a very deliberate rate of 5.5 cps (at 0:30), and Robeson's average vibrato rate, at around 0.16 second per cycle, is longer yet than in the recordings from the 1930s.[97] But the vibrato size on the "home" notes is not significantly different: one semitone in 1926 and one and a quarter in 1956. What makes the vibrato seem so more prominent in the later recording is, among other things, the longer time during which it cycles. On average, however, the size of Robeson's mature voice vibrato is larger, as is the extent of its variation: between one and three semitones in the "Swing Low" of 1956 and only one and one-and-three-quarter semitones in 1926.

A bigger vibrato was a necessary additional component of the voice that permitted the shift in hearing Robeson's voice as increasingly dramatic.[98] Already by the late 1920s, recognition of a more explicit vibrato—ever slower and larger—accounts also for a bigger voice. As the *New York Evening Post* noted of a performance given at the tail end of 1929: "His voice sounded larger in the big hall and perhaps it has grown in volume from the exercise of much singing, or by reason of further study. It . . . seemed somewhat more 'edged' last night than heretofore, with an occasional tendency to depart from the pitch and a leaning toward vibrato."[99] Acoustically, a larger vibrato does of course render the tone more "edged" or, and to return to the discussion above, less smooth. It also perceptually increases the size of the voice—Robeson's voice had "grown in volume," surmised the critic—independent of any actual increase in amplitude there might be.[100] Like his use of vibrato, the volume of his voice was an aspect of Robeson's singing that required work for it to conform to, and grow into, the dominant art voice type. By his own admission he had an "embarrassingly delicate" voice. It was in part for this reason that he preferred performing in smaller, intimate theaters and concert halls.[101] How, then, do we account for contradictory statements on his voice size in the archive of Robeson criticism?

An early theater review of his performance in *The Emperor Jones* observed what became commonplace in criticism on his acting. Captivated by Robeson's "splendid physical presence and a voice the like of which is rarely heard," the reviewer imagined that "if he turned loose his full vocal powers

120   PAUL ROBESON'S VOICES

the walls of the tiny Provincetown theater would fairly bulge." He "is a true son of Stentor," concluded the reviewer.[102] If we unpack these truisms we find deductive errors and circumscribed truths. Robeson's bodily size and commanding physical presence were not, as many writers assumed, proportional to his voice size, especially his singing voice. Indeed, this visual-aural disconnect may have contributed to the trope of restraint that characterized Robeson criticism: the singer's modest vocal strength seemed to belie the body from whence it issued such that the exercise of vocal restraint was a necessary explanatory invention. Even as astute an observer as Richard Dyer, who first laid bare the politics of containment that characterized Robeson's early career, falls into this trap. Dyer speaks of the contrast between Robeson's "potential vocal power and his soft, gentler, careful actual delivery of speech and song," or that the singers' voice in the mid-1920s, "*as later*, is *capable* of great power."[103] The assumption of vocal power does not distinguish between Robeson's spoken and singing voices. Whereas theater criticism tended to note the strength of his actor's voice, music critics often observed the opposite: a "voice of great beauty, small perhaps, but unfailingly pleasing to the ear."[104] The attribution of "potential" vocal power is also made according to a retrospective listening, of hearing the singer's early recordings through his better-known later recordings in which vocal strength—a heavier, bigger, louder voice, all the adornments of a dramatic voice fashioned by the new vocal episteme—is on display. In this error of teleological listening, the mature voice is heard to be latent in the young voice. In addition to the mode of voice (spoken or sung) and time (early or mid-career, for instance) of Robeson's performances, we need to consider also the media and spaces of their making.

Critics who heard the actor and singer in small venues were more likely to comment on the voice's strength. In the tiny Provincetown theater his voice sounded stentorian. Not so in Carnegie Hall. Reviewing a Robeson concert of late 1929, Manhattan man of letters Pitts Sanborn noted with concern the singer's ability to adjust to "the big concert room more satisfactorily": "I repeatedly felt that effects which would have come off splendidly in the Town Hall, for instance, were minimized or virtually lost in Carnegie Hall." For Sanborn, Robeson's shortcoming was not a lack of volume per se, but the voice's projection, "the use of it, so to say, [is] short range."[105] The limits of his voice's carry made his initial appearances at the Royal Albert Hall in London daunting affairs. He fretted about his first performance in the Hall in April 1929, canceled a concert of late 1931, and Eslanda told Larry Brown that the

NATURAL ACTS, OR TO SING SIMPLY   121

singer refused to play the venue—he "said about R.A.H. 'never no more.'"[106] Not all large venues presented problems for Robeson's young voice all the time. Sometimes he seemed able to project a resonant voice satisfactorily in large concert halls. But even in these instances, critics observed his vocal restraint as a reluctance or inability to sing loudly. Thus Edward Moore of the *Chicago Daily Tribune* wrote that "his voice was something to grow rhapsodic about. It never rumbled, never seemed even to grow loud, it was always velvety, but it filled the whole expanse of [the 2,500-seat] Orchestra Hall." The *Daily Mail* critic similarly enthused over the "sheer quality of his resonant bass voice" in the 2,000-seat Drury Lane Theater. But as "richly and fully as he sang, he never sang loudly. . . . Plenty of reserve strength was felt to be there."[107] For the same reason Robeson favored small concert spaces that suited his vocal strength. He was, the singer proclaimed, "really a drawing-room singer."[108]

In chapter 6 I explore Robeson's engagement with, and uses of, sound technologies in the production of his voice. One of the effects was a recorded voice that sounded "bigger" than its unmediated self. The point here is that the small voice of Big Paul, as he was nicknamed, was another aspect in ascribing the voice as natural: its modest projected volume, colored by a discreet vibrato, stood in contrast to the dominant art voice, whose training permitted an acoustic power that Robeson's young voice could not muster. When critics portrayed his voice as powerful, as they were wont to do, it was not necessarily a reference to vocal size and strength but to the communicative and affective efficacy of Robeson's singing. A review of an early recital noted that "Mr. Robeson is a singer of genuine power. The voice is ample for his needs, mellow and soft, but it is his intense earnestness which grips his hearers."[109]

A final point to consider in Robeson's simple singing, and which returns us to the distinction between lyric and dramatic voices, is the "weight" of his early voice. It is surely telling that those critics who identified the young Robeson as a bass (rather than a baritone) heard him as a light bass. Chicago composer and critic Herman Devries labeled Robeson's voice a "basso-cantante," that higher and lighter bass singer of lyrical operatic roles and often said to have baritone qualities.[110] It was not uncommon for critics of Robeson's young voice to enthuse as much over his upper register as his trademark low voice. Montague Smith, of the *Glasgow Evening Citizen*, was enthralled by the singer's "skill in singing high notes pianissimo, which is astonishing in a bass," concluding that the "upper part of his voice . . . is

122   PAUL ROBESON'S VOICES

just as fine as the lower part, and some of the finest effects obtained were when he used it."[111] On occasion, as for the *Ohio State Journal*, Robeson's higher voice was even heard in preference: "It was more pleasing in the upper registers."[112] The singer's sometime willingness to sing higher was not in itself what constituted the lightness of his basso-cantante. Rather it was Robeson's exceptional use of the fullness of the chest voice in the upper registers early in his career that lightened his voice in this region.

We saw in the first chapter that one consequence of Robeson's facility in his upper register was the difficulty in classifying the voice type of the young singer. For the *Chicago Herald Examiner* it was thus "not possible to classify Mr. Robeson as to voice, since his range includes the compass of the bass and the tenor, or at least the high baritone."[113] But the reality, as several listeners noted, was that his voice's base in a lower register, despite critics' sometime praise of his upper voice, often meant that he forsook higher singing, an increasing occurrence as his career progressed. It was not so much the limited (pitch) range of the repertoire Robeson sang in the 1920s, that is spirituals, but that he "elected to sing in keys which led him down among the low G's and F's much of the evening," which denied "Mr. Robeson great opportunity to use his vibrant upper voice."[114]

Such observations would become more frequent in reviews of the singer's mature voice. Two reviews of a Robeson concert in Springfield, Massachusetts, in early October 1945 serve this point well. While the town's *Daily Republican* commented simply that "Mr. Robeson did not venture into the upper range and some of the songs seemed a bit low," the *Springfield Union* sought to categorize Robeson's voice specifically: "It was a basso-profundo that one heard last night. Mr. Robeson plumbed the lowest vocal depths." As we might expect from the character of the *profundo Fach* (and for the Springfield concert Robeson sang the "weightier" parts of Sarastro and Boris), the voice type's heaviness resulted in some unidiomatic interpretations of the lighter fare Robeson had been presenting in concert for a decade and a half: opined Willard M. Clark of the *Union*, the "voice was inclined to be wooden with the result that such charming texts by Shakespeare, arranged by Quilter, [such] as . . . 'It Was a Lover and His Lass' were entirely too heavy. Quilter's 'Over the Mountains' also lacked the requisite lightness of touch."[115] Lightness is indeed in short supply in the only recording we have of Robeson singing "Over the Mountains." His reading of the song, in a live performance at the Tchaikovsky Concert Hall in Moscow on June 14, 1949, and broadcast on Soviet radio, is ponderous and cumbersome, and, unusually for

NATURAL ACTS, OR TO SING SIMPLY   123

Robeson, crude in its lack of nuance and care; "Oh, No John No," also on the Moscow program, fares a little better.[116]

The reclassification of Robeson's *basso* from *cantante* to *profundo*, from lyrical to dramatic voice, is audible in several aspects. For one, the lightness and agility of voice associated with the former type is increasingly absent in Robeson's later singing; for the *Union* critic, it was "wooden." While Robeson never attained, nor in his account did he aspire to, coloratura-type agility of the classical tradition, his young voice was sufficiently flexible to deftly navigate the fast-paced evangelical spirituals we encountered in chapter 2 and that formed an important body of his early repertoire. But works that require lightness of voice gradually became less prominent in the repertoire of his later career. Accompanying the leaden movement is a heaviness of voice we would expect of a *profundo* bass, a perception of vocal weight resulting from Robeson's preference for singing at lower pitches and the lower register's physiological action, and resulting in a more resonant, richer quality of tone due to the distribution of harmonic "energy" in the composite sound.

Robeson's increasingly low singing as his voice matured is evident in the chronology of the keys in which he recorded and is also, I argue in a later chapter, a function of advances in recording technologies. In "Swing Low" he thus sings low in later recordings. The 1926 recording is performed in E-flat major, that of 1933 a tone lower, and a late recording of the spiritual in 1956–1957 is in B major.[117] The descent in pitch by a third from the early to late recording lends weight to the voice, with its "heavy mechanism" (to use William Vennard's term) increasingly coming into play. Named for the thickness of the vocal folds in the lower register, the heavy mechanism describes the chest register and is characterized by, among others, "great" amplitude of vibration and being "rich in harmonic partials."[118] It is the idea of heaviness as timbral percept that I here explore further, a terrain well mapped (unsurprisingly) by scholars of heavy metal.

For the metal community, heaviness and sonic weight are fundamental to the identity of the genre and are achieved, in part, by the practice of "down-tuning," the lowering of the guitar strings' pitches. As Mark Mynett explains: "Pitch can be seen as vital to the overall sonic impact of metal, and down tuning provides a deeper, heavier and darker tonality."[119] The progressive lowering of Robeson's performing pitch was similarly instrumental in the production of heaviness in his voice. But heaviness is overdetermined, the result of several interrelated acoustic phenomena and not only produced by low-end frequencies. In heavy metal, for instance, heavier timbres correlate

124 PAUL ROBESON'S VOICES

with the introduction of, perhaps counterintuitively, more high-frequency energy.[120]

Something similar is at play in the later, and lower-pitched, recording of "Swing Low." It is not simply that the 1956 recording is a third lower than Robeson's first record of the song of thirty years earlier. For the 1956 recording exhibits a different spectral, and therefore timbral, profile too. In the first utterance of the refrain, Robeson's voice is colored by a prominent high-frequency band entirely absent in the 1926 recording. As broad as between 4.5 and 7.5 kHz at times, though typically a little narrower, it is constituted of harmonics not individually or collectively audible, but which shape by enriching the overall sound of Robeson's voice.[121] If we hear the "ca-" of "carry" in the final phrase of the refrain, "Comin' for to carry me home," as particularly resonant, it is in large part because the voice here holds a bounty of harmonics, with continuous bands of acoustic energy fading away up to the early 8k Hz region (see Figure 3.1, 0:43; and listen to Sound Recording 3.1 ▶). The same point in the early recording is notable for its lack of significant acoustic material above 3 kHz—the blackness in Figure 3.2 (0:30; and listen to Sound Recording 3.2 ▶)—and hence the voice's relative perceived lightness.[122]

Advances in recording technologies, specifically the capturing of an ever-larger frequency spectrum after the advent of electrical recording in the mid-1920s, allowed for both the louder level at which the bass voice's lowest register could be convincingly recorded and the high-frequency bands prevalent in the later recording.[123] How the intensity, or loudness, of the acoustic material relates to the distribution of frequencies in the spectrum is significant for how we hear the voice's resultant timbre. Charting intensity-frequency relationships in the 1926 "Swing Low" explains, among other things, why sounds accrue certain timbral attributes, why in this case Robeson's lower notes are heard as louder and richer.

Take, for instance, Robeson's singing of "low" in the very first "Swing low" phrase, which sounds louder than the "home" that follows it a little later, and which at a fifth higher concludes the first sentence. The former's fundamental volume (at between −28 to −30 dB) is in fact quieter than that for "home" (−25 dB).[124] One of the reasons we hear the lower note "low" as louder than the higher "home" is due to the distribution of the intensity of the harmonics

NATURAL ACTS, OR TO SING SIMPLY 125

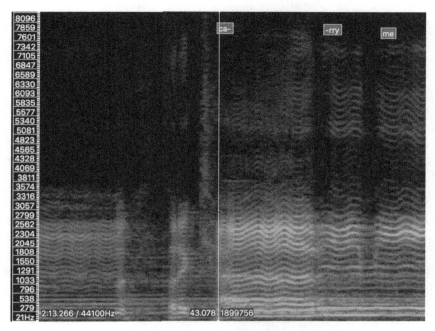

Figure 3.1. Spectrum for "ca-" of "carry" in "Swing Low" (1956).

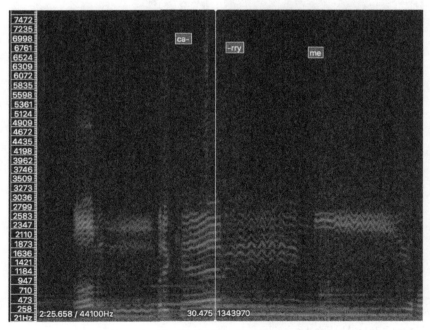

Figure 3.2. Spectrum for "ca-" of "carry" in "Swing Low" (1926).

above the fundamental. Daniel Leech-Wilkinson reminds us that the human ear is varyingly sensitive to different frequencies: "It's true that we seem to hear the fundamental most clearly: it's not interfered with by the vibrations of the harmonics to the same extent as the harmonics are by other harmonics, and so it's easier for our ears to identify with certainty. But strictly speaking, the loudest information is often from the harmonics."[125] Indeed, in this case the first harmonics are acoustically louder than the fundamental: for "low" the first harmonic is between −22 and −24 dB, the second a little less strong, and the third the same level as the fundamental. For "home," the intensity of the harmonics exhibits a different profile. Although the first harmonic at the octave is likewise louder than the fundamental, the other harmonics are all less intense than the fundamental. As is evident from Figures 3.3a and 3.3b, there is also less acoustic energy in the 2–3 kHz band range for "home." It turns out that the human ear's greatest sensitivity to loudness is precisely in

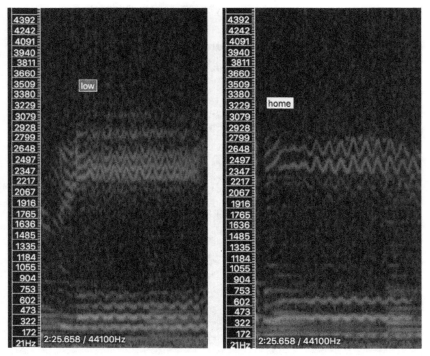

Figure 3.3a and b Spectra for "low" and "home," respectively, in "Swing Low" (1926).

the 2–3 kHz range, and that the acoustic material in this area is important for the sonic identity of a tone.[126] Robeson's voice on "low" thus sounds louder and richer, heavier if you will, than on "home" because its harmonics display greater intensity (see also the color graphs ▶). And this is true for the acoustic profile of his lower range in general.

Robeson's vocal heaviness is a function in large part of the activity of the partials, and this is demonstrated even more clearly by the later recording of "Swing Low." Here too the fundamental of the first "low" is acoustically less loud than its harmonics; it ranges in the low −20 dB compared to the first harmonic's −15 to −17 dB, and the second and third harmonics' range of −12 to −15 dB and −10 to −14 dB (see Figure 3.4, 0:05–0:06). But here, in the later recording, the fourth to sixth harmonics are also louder or as loud as the fundamental (whereas in the earlier recording these harmonics retreated in intensity), and compared to the 1926 recording there is yet more acoustic energy in the important 2–3 kHz range. Significantly, the non-octave harmonics—the fifth of the second harmonic and the third of the fourth harmonic—come more strongly to the fore in the later "Swing Low" (marked

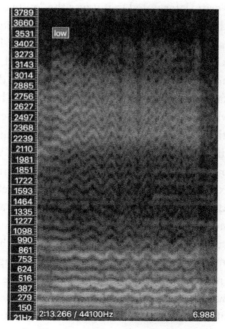

Figure 3.4. Spectrum for "low" in "Swing Low" (1956–1957).

128 PAUL ROBESON'S VOICES

in the color graphs by the intense orange ⓑ), providing additional timbral weight to Robeson's voice.

The presentation of the anatomy of Robeson's simple singing that I have undertaken reveals a voice that, in its early years, resists in part the structuring of the dominant art voice episteme. Many of the vocal calling cards of that regime—a fat vibrato, stentorian chest voice, dramatic flair— are recognized by the manifest "work" required for their production, or, in other words, as product of a visibly kinetic singer's corpus. By contrast, Robeson's natural voice was routinely described as occurring without bodily effort. From the outset of his concert singing career, critics heard his voice as flowing easily from his body rather than being produced as an exertion of the self: "His voice is rich in tone, powerful, but produced apparently without effort." The *Wall Street Journal* drew on what by the end of the 1920s had become a refrain in Robeson criticism singling out the singer's performance for its "utter lack of exertion, an absolute ease . . . sung with a feeling of freedom from effort."[127] Such freedom from vocal effort, it seemed, aligned the voice with nature, such that vocal ease in turn constituted a natural voice. Listening to the singer in Carnegie Hall, Charles D. Isaacson found the "effortless singing . . . alluring because of its almost entire lack of sophistication." A *Guardian* critic later noted that it was the "quite easeful and natural delivery that saved the music from any suspicion of rankness."[128]

For many critics, then, Robeson's singing epitomized an ideal of vocal ease. But we know that the singer often struggled with his art. Concert singing, for Robeson, required effort, and his commitment to the discipline periodically flagged and faltered.[129] His own fond recollection of his early recording of "Water Boy," which introduced this chapter, might be viewed from the vantage point of the seasoned professional singer reminiscing about easier times. The immediate context of Robeson's nostalgia for "Water Boy" makes this patent. His first two performances at Carnegie Hall in early November 1929 received mixed critical reception: the first recital left Robeson somewhat disappointed, while the second, five days later, was a triumph, indeed, to the singer's mind, one of the best recitals of his career to date.[130] The critical misgivings occasioned by the first concert, and which traversed at least two areas of commentary—the singer's vocal shortcomings, and his limited repertoire—were not new, exceptional, nor would they be easily dispelled in the years to follow. Is it these mundane travails wrought from the working life of a young professional singer that account for Robeson's enthusiasm for "Water Boy"? Representing an earlier time, at the outset of his career, when

NATURAL ACTS, OR TO SING SIMPLY   129

his singing received more uniform (if sometimes uncritical) praise, when he was fêted as the latest musical talent, the "Water Boy" disc stood for a time lost, thrown into stark relief by the occasion of the Carnegie Hall recitals.

The memory of the "Water Boy" moment, of a time "prior to," should, however, not be confused with Robeson's less-than-natural vocal practices in performance of the song. An informed listening, as I argued in my discussion of the song, reveals the fault lines along which ideologically burdened constructs such as "the natural" in art are deployed. Indeed, my critique of the critical discourse on the place of nature in Robeson's art sought to point out the lines along which it was constructed, and the collective will to account for Robeson's natural art in "other" terms. Rather than proceed from the racial subject, and the discourse of nature by which that subject was construed, I offer another undertaking proceeding from a different point of departure: to lay out an anatomy of the voice, and to dissect its vocal gestures as they were structured by song practice. By considering also the aesthetic contexts of the production of Robeson's voice—by practicing voice-thinking—we gain a more complete understanding of his singing, and of his ambivalent place in the song world of the early twentieth century. We can make yet further sense of Robeson's natural voice if we heed the insights of the philosophy of voice.

The Voice in the Time of Fantasy

The mouth is denaturalized by speech, diverted from its natural functions as it is claimed for the signifying process.[131] Even more so can this be said of singing: a cultivation of the lungs, vocal cords, mouth, among others—and, in the age of recording, the microphone—a gross elaboration of mere breathing and pre-linguistic utterance. Yet, as we have seen with the varied reception of Robeson's voice, the always-already cultured singing voice is situated along a discursive continuum, one that extends from imagined natural voices to art(ful) singers. The distribution of voices along this continuum is often aligned with broad traditions of music-making, style, and genre. Placing the natural singing voice in this emporium of voices is a fraught undertaking, attested to by the range of critical opinion on Robeson's early voice we encountered in this chapter and the last. Robeson's singer's voice typifies what Mladen Dolar claims for the voice more generally: a paramount feature of the voice is that it "opens a zone of undecidability, of a between-the-two"; or, to cede the voice greater agency, it "presents a short circuit between

130 PAUL ROBESON'S VOICES

nature and culture, between physiology and structure."[132] Robeson's voice is structured first by the repertoire it performed—in the 1920s Black song dominated by spirituals arranged for the concert stage—and second by the disciplinary codes of traditions of singing, such as the vocal quartet and classical singing. His not-quite art song voice falls short of a normative classical music ideal, as much as the arranged spirituals he sang fell short: both as art song and "the real spirituals," to summon Zora Neale Hurston's phrase; and the trenchant Renaissance debates on the spiritual we encountered in chapter 2 must in large part be attributed to the song form's position of intermediacy.[133] Robeson's was very much an in-between voice.

It is a commonplace to say that the voice implies a subjectivity that expresses itself; as Dolar says, the voice is "the intimate kernel of subjectivity."[134] Ascribing interiority to the voice had of course ancient precedent. For Aristotle, (human) voice was a special category of the acoustic: specifically, sound with a soul.[135] And the romantic aesthetic that governed art song expressivity (and the singing of concert spirituals too) in the early twentieth century was a continuation of that tradition. We encountered numerous instances of this conception of the singing voice in this chapter. Robeson's voice was heard to be expressive of his self, personality, body, and race, and therefore an exemplary natural voice. The very idea of the singing voice as expressive of presence informed his wife's opposition to the dominant art voice type. What Eslanda termed her "prejudice" against the "so-called 'trained' voice" was due to her observation that in training the voice was "level[ed] . . . to one uninteresting mould." The result which she feared for her husband's voice was that loss of "personality which distinguish[es] voices individually."[136] Eslanda's anxiety over what Dolar calls the "fingerprint quality of the [singing] voice" is a desire for the natural voice, one, however, that is already compromised by the practices of professional singing as the voice is imbricated in the "disciplinatory assumption of the code" of art singing, and other traditions of vocalizing.[137] That code disrupts the possibility of a natural voice being heard on the concert stage, a scission we encountered in the discourse of the art-as-nature critics as they argued, against the outside-art position, that Robeson's "natural" singing was artfully crafted. Certainly the idea—or better yet, fantasy—of Robeson's natural voice is evoked by his acoustically sounding voice, even as the idea and the voice's soundings are non-equivalent. The acoustic bits of the voice nevertheless enclose the fantasy of a natural voice.

NATURAL ACTS, OR TO SING SIMPLY   131

What is the relationship of the voice to fantasy? Dolar reading Freud has this to say: "The voice, the noise, things heard, are at the core of the formation of fantasy; a fantasy is a confabulation built around the sonorous kernel, it has a privileged relationship to the voice, as opposed to dreams which are, supposedly, visual." And, moreover, the voice as an enigma persists because there is a time lag between hearing it and understanding it, and this Dolar emphasizes is the time of fantasy: "Fantasy functions as a provisional understanding of something which eludes understanding."[138] The sheer volume of critical writing on Robeson, the will to explain the singer's voice in the 1920s and early 1930s, might productively be thought of in terms of the workings of fantasy. Robeson's initial moment of appearance as a concert singer had to be made sense of, and in the process of sense-making fantasy enters. Indeed, the operation of the voice itself facilitates fantasy, for the voice is both address and enunciation in that it need not bear a discernible statement. Hence "the drama of the voice is twofold": for the voice as enunciation, the listener is compelled to interpret the voice's demands, and as address the voice is already an attempt at interpretation by the singer: "the voice is something which tries to reach the other, provoke it, seduce it, plead with it; it makes assumptions about the other's desire . . . it tries to present itself as an object of its desire."[139] Robeson's young voice, always in development in the process of discovering his concert voice, at first perhaps performed more on the side of enunciation in listeners' hearing/interpretation thereof. As we have seen in the last two chapters, fantasies of race, often articulated through proxy tropes such as the spiritual and natural, loomed large in understanding Robeson's voice. As the singer arrived at a mature concert voice, the anatomy of which I presented in this chapter, and as Robeson also advanced a political outlook for his work as an artist, his voice presented more resolutely as address. It is to the provocations, seductions, and pleas of Robeson's voice to which I turn now.

4

A Voice for the People

Soon after Robeson returned to live in the United States in 1939 he was lauded "an American institution." By the start of the next decade he was the "Most Controversial Negro" of the time, and a much-maligned figure in the imagination of mainstream America.[1] It is well known that Robeson suffered greatly for his progressive politics and civil rights activism, although the extent of his persecution and the consequences thereof are not always fully appreciated. Perhaps the most forceful image of the place he came to occupy in America at mid-century is the part he assumed in "the American lynching imagination": in 1948 Robeson was invited to Birmingham, Alabama, to be welcomed by a twenty-foot-tall burning cross and hanged effigy of himself.[2] Amid the culture of paranoia that characterized Cold War America, Robeson supporters—from child fans to world leaders and cultural heavyweights, in private letters and public media—rallied around the singer. Robeson's song voice loomed large in these offerings.

One of Robeson's champions was the Turkish poet Nâzim Hikmet who, like many writers as we glimpsed in the Introduction, eulogized Robeson in verse. "To Paul Robeson," written from a prison cell in Turkey in 1949, is Hikmet's offering:

> They don't let us sing our songs, Robeson,
> Eagle singer, Negro brother,
> They don't want us to sing our songs.
> . . .
> They are scared, Negro brother,
> Our songs scare them, Robeson.[3]

Hikmet's words were prophetic of the censure and censoring of Robeson that would gather momentum in the 1950s, and which would result in the singer's "imprisonment" in the United States when his passport was confiscated. The Turkish poet sent Robeson the verse for three songs on the subject of peace, one of which, "The Little Girl" on the Hiroshima bombing, Robeson

Paul Robeson's Voices. Grant Olwage, Oxford University Press. © Oxford University Press 2024.
DOI: 10.1093/oso/9780197637470.003.0005

A VOICE FOR THE PEOPLE   133

sang at the Peace Arch concert in 1955. This was the fourth and last in a series of annual concerts, commenced in 1952, that took place at the Peace Arch Park on the Canada-US border in Washington state. One of the many consequences of Robeson's blacklisting by the state, it was also one of the many workarounds in response to the blacklisting. In this case Robeson had been barred, by presidential executive order, from leaving the United States to perform in Canada in early 1952, whereas typically American citizens did not need a passport—Robeson's had been confiscated—to enter Canada. By performing in an international park that straddled the two countries, from atop a "flat-bed truck within one foot of the border," Robeson was able to sing to a dual US-Canadian audience.[4]

We might consider one further instance of this transnational network of voices. In March 1952, soon after Robeson had been denied entry to Canada and just prior to the first Peace Arch concert, the singer received a letter from the Soviet actor Mikhail Nazvanov, "Honored Artist of the Republic, Stalin Prize Winner."[5] It was an "open letter," a common form employed to articulate international support for Robeson. Nazvanov, who had not met Robeson, reported back on the occasion of the hundredth performance of the play *John—Soldier of Peace*, then on at the Pushkin Dramatic Theatre in Moscow, which took Robeson as its subject with Nazvanov playing the title character John Robertson. The central plot point involved "the bitter political struggle" that played out around a concert presented by a "progressive political leader and remarkable Negro singer." It was the actor's task, Nazvanov told Robeson, to "embody your features . . . to reproduce before the audiences your words, your voice, your songs":

> Throughout the play I sing your songs which are so well known to millions of Soviet people. "Whence these [*sic*] deep bass timbre—you've never had it before?" my friends frequently ask me after seeing the play. "I don't know," I tell them, "I needed it in order to recall to the people of Robeson's voice, and that is how it appeared." It was in the same way that your specific diction, the soft elasticity of gestures and motions native to you, and your remarkably musical speech appeared in the process of my work on the part.

Nazvanov also recounted his appearance—as Robeson—in concert, which he had often done. In November of the previous year he was invited to "enact" extracts from the play for the delegates of the Third Soviet Conference for Peace in Moscow's Hall of Columns. To complete

134 PAUL ROBESON'S VOICES

the illusion for his ventriloquizing act, Nazvanov appeared "in make-up" (blackface?),[6] sang Robeson's songs such as "Water Boy" and "Joe Hill," and recited Hikmet's poem on Robeson. It "was not so much for me, for my modest art, that the applause of the delegates were [sic] meant on that evening, but rather for you." By such performative means was Robeson's (and Hikmet's) voice heard in the hall in which Robeson had previously sung when he could travel.

What do these vignettes on the subject of Robeson's voice tell us? For one, they highlight further the idea of Robeson-as-voice. The voice is revealed, more specifically, to be a transnational object; heard, to be sure, as Robeson's own voice on occasion, but also appropriated by others—in texts and sound acts—in other places. Robeson-as-voice is also thoroughly political and politicized by this time. In the Introduction I outlined how Robeson's art has almost always been located within the domain of the political, and it has always represented: the self, the race, the human spirit, among other things. As the celebrity became an activist during the course of the 1930s, Robeson's art increasingly performed politically within sites of diverse struggle politics.[7] And so it has become something of a truism in Robeson scholarship to appropriate the arena of politics to his voice. Shana Redmond writes that "his voice as a technology developed into a powerful tool within his later political agenda." More suggestively, Tony Perucci has explored the idea of Robeson's "radical black voice."[8] There is one specific iteration of the political voice that I consider: Robeson as voice of the people. When the singer infamously pronounced that art was "a social weapon" which worked for "one side or the other," he qualified that his singing was done "at the service of the people."[9] My interest then is to focus on two, related dimensions of Robeson's politics: to chart, first, how the idea of the voice of the people emerges through the development of the singer's international outlook; and then to delineate the aesthetic dimensions of Robeson's people's voice. In undertaking the former I emphasize, more strongly than other scholars have, that Robeson's international politics emerged from his song practice, and in the latter endeavor, pursued in the chapter that follows this one, I interrogate the contradictions of the political voice that come to the fore when we listen closely to its sonic dimensions; that is, when we practice voice-thinking. I begin by considering one, albeit complex, component of Robeson's politics—that is, internationalism—and I do so by parsing the distinction between Robeson's voice as transnational object, which we have been considering, and his voicing of internationalism.

A VOICE FOR THE PEOPLE 135

"The Internationale," or Toward Internationalism

It was during Robeson's tenure in Britain, from the late 1920s through much of the 1930s, that he became a global star, and that his voice became an international object of audition and representation. It is also to the time of his stay in the United Kingdom that scholars attribute his political awakening— and his internationalism. Robeson's internationalist politics has a complex genealogy and expressed multiple allegiances with different emphases at different times, sometimes contradictorily. One event in particular seems to have galvanized him to action: the Spanish Civil War that began in 1936, and which Robeson called "a dress rehearsal for World War II."[10] His involvement in the war, which included regular appearances at rallies in Britain and singing to the troops in Spain in early 1938, was, he reflected, "a major turning point in my life." It was during a radio broadcast to a rally in London made while Robeson was touring in Europe that he famously articulated his position of the artist as activist: "Every artist, every scientist, must decide *now* where he stands. He has no alternative. . . . There are no impartial observers. . . . The battlefront is everywhere. . . . The artist must elect to fight for Freedom or for Slavery. I have made my choice."[11]

The Spanish Civil War brought together several of the constituencies and ideals that constituted Robeson's political world and imagination at the time. For one, he viewed it as a cause of the "common people." On the battlefield he observed that "it was the working men and women of Spain who were heroically giving 'their last full measure of devotion' to the cause of democracy." Similarly, the volunteers of the International Brigades, the Soviet-backed multinational paramilitary units that included Black and white Americans, and which fought for the Spanish Republican Army, came from "the ranks of the workers of other lands." Second, the British labor movement, to which Robeson had drawn increasingly close in the second half of the 1930s, was at the forefront of the war effort. Third, the war revealed, for Robeson, the commitment of the Soviet Union and of socialist action in general to human justice and equality, and especially to anti-fascism. The "Western powers," at first, "were calm and unmoving in the face of the agony."[12] For these reasons the singer's biographers conclude that it was during his Spanish sojourn that he arrived at "a personal, artistic, and political way of being that would replace the years of self-doubt and floundering with a clear-cut moral and ethical direction, a passion that satisfied his need for a higher calling, a passion that added a new and compelling spiritual dimension to his life."[13]

136 PAUL ROBESON'S VOICES

One of the songs Robeson performed to the troops in Spain was the so-cialist anthem "The Internationale," with words by Eugène Pottier set to music by Pierre De Geyter.[14] Robeson's wartime singing is documented in Cuban writer—and music critic—Alejo Carpentier's 1978 novel *La consagración de la primavera*, which presents a leftist argument for an anti-elitist conceptualization of cultural goods set against the backdrop of the Civil War. Carpentier's writing is particularly productive for understanding music and culture during the War. A musicologist, he was a war corre-spondent during the war, and analyses of his wartime writings, and the later novel that was based on wartime texts, have noted "the large number of sono-rous and musical references, remarkable in warlike context but fundamental in Carpentier's writing."[15] The novel's heroine, the Russian ballerina Vera, visits the Spanish village of Benicàssim, where Robeson sang to wounded soldiers. There she hears Robeson sing "The Internationale" with "the par-ticipation of a multitude of partisans in many languages." Vera is skeptical of the song's politics but is entranced by Robeson's voice: "I found a dif-ferent power, that of firm belief, totally independent of the words that he was conveying: the power of art, of transcendent eloquence, magnificent, uni-versal and timeless."[16] Vera hears Robeson's voice according to an aesthetics of transcendence—that art operates independently of politics—although later she supports the socialist cause; her volte-face perhaps occasioned by hearing Robeson's "Internationale." Such listening denies the voice's po-litical if not sonic materiality, and it is not a position with which Robeson would have agreed at the time. For others, the aesthetic power of Robeson's voice reinforced and even enacted the political. The significance of "The Internationale" is that it topically and symbolically brought together several of Robeson's political interests and allegiances, much as the Spanish Civil War did, and unsurprisingly the anthem was popular during the war. "The Internationale" is an imperative to the "wretched of the earth," the "enslaved masses"; it is an anti-imperialist socialist call to action, with the chorus proclaiming "This is the final struggle / Let us group together, and tomorrow / The Internationale / will be the human race." The song's message was easily understood by those receptive to it. Carpentier's hero Enrique, a Cuban ar-chitect enrolled with the Brigades, also heard Robeson sing the anthem in Spain. He recalled: " 'L'Internationale' . . . the one that Paul Robeson sung for us in Benicassim; the one that was chanted, in twenty languages, by the combatants of the International Brigades. . . . 'L'Internationale.' The title says everything."[17] As the anthem of international socialism "The Internationale"

A VOICE FOR THE PEOPLE   137

signified multinational cooperation in the Spanish Civil War and transnational action beyond the war (and involved multilingual singing in Robeson's performance).[18] Robeson's "Internationale," as performed sound and literary topos, is thus a fitting index of his emerging internationalist politics.

A Politics of the Comparative: The Four Strands of Robeson's Musical Internationalism

Hazel Carby's 1998 essay on Robeson concludes that the singer's "unwavering commitment to an internationalist politics of social transformation eventually placed Robeson in opposition to the national discourse of race, nation, and manhood."[19] Others have elaborated on this insight, pursuing the different threads of Robeson's internationalism and its internal contradictions. On his return to the United States in 1939, Robeson was involved with the cultural work of the Popular Front, a broad "radical social-democratic movement forged around anti-fascism, anti-lynching, and industrial unionism."[20] As Michael Denning has argued, Popular Front culture was "a paradoxical synthesis of competing nationalism and internationalism—pride in ethnic heritage and identity combined with an assertive Americanism and a popular internationalism."[21] I want to delineate, and elaborate on, four song strands to Robeson's musical internationalism. In doing so I privilege the place of the aesthetic, of Robeson's song practice, in his developing internationalism, focusing at first on how his musical internationalism was articulated through his engagement with different types of song repertoire.

First, and oldest in Robeson's repertoire, was the African American song tradition, constituted primarily of spirituals and secular folk songs. Lisa Barg has noted that Robeson's contribution to the Popular Front demonstrated the centrality of African American culture to the Front's pan-ethnic Americanism. Whereas his performance of folk song during the Popular Front period has typically been narrated in terms of the broader urban folk song movement, Barg points out that this places Robeson in a largely white discursive space and ignores his place in Black Atlantic history; and, one might add, other axes of global Black experience.[22] Also noteworthy, by this time Robeson had reconstructed the spiritual's history, both in his statements on the spiritual and in his programming practice. No longer only a sign of the Black American experience, the singer reframed "the spiritual as an international symbol of freedom." Barg thus speaks of Robeson's

138 PAUL ROBESON'S VOICES

"performative black internationalism."[23] As many have noted, Robeson's rethinking of the spiritual was indebted to his encounters with what Alys Weinbaum has called "racial globality," the expanded horizon of an "internationalist goal of black belonging in the world."[24] In Robeson's case this took shape during his time in Britain in the mid-1930s when he fraternized with African, Caribbean, and Asian artists, intellectuals, and workers, many of whom were anticolonial activists, and who have collectively been designated the "Black Internationale."[25] The singer's encounters with the multinational International Brigades in Spain presented an opportunity to witness the ideals of the socialist (Black) internationale in action, perhaps more so because of his meetings in Spain with many Black Americans, who fought in the Abraham Lincoln Battalion, the first racially integrated military unit in US history with Black leaders.[26]

It was during this time that Robeson "discovered Africa,"[27] although we should not forget that the Harlem Renaissance, with which Robeson was loosely associated in the preceding decade, was not uninterested in Africa. Robeson's discovery is documented in several of his own writings on the topic—what I call the African Letters—from late 1930 to the middle of the decade.[28] Africanist readings of the Letters, such as Sterling Stuckey's early work on Robeson, have focused on, among other things, his (re)valuation of African culture; arguing for its place within global culture; and, especially through the discourse of "survivals," its connection to African American culture so as to foster an awareness of African heritage for Black Americans.[29] The African Letters are a statement of cultural pride; they occasionally present essentialist notions of culture, and therefore are of their time; and they include the first articulations of Robeson's emerging anticolonialist politics. For these reasons he has been described as a "black nationalist."[30] But the claim that his turn to Africa influenced his song practice is overstated and the singer's desire to perform African music would go unrealized: he did not program African song, nor do the sounds of his voice and singing style exhibit any affinities with African music.[31] His interest in Africa was perhaps more profound, and also more self-serving.

The insight of Africanist readings of Robeson's Letters is that they reveal his increasing interest in the links between culture and politics from the early 1930s, which had been largely unstated in the 1920s. But they fail to point out the extent that Robeson's Letters speak to internationalism, and specifically how Robeson's African "research" is the ground for his internationalism. In 1933 and 1934 the singer enrolled at the then London School of

Oriental Studies to undertake comparative studies of African languages, an endeavor outlined in an article for the London *Spectator*, which concluded with an ambitious declaration: "I intend to make a comparative study of the main language groups: Indo-European, Asiatic and African, choosing two or three principal languages out of each group, and indicate their comparative richness at a comparable stage of development."[32] As with many of Robeson's stated plans the large-scale project did not materialize; although copious, disorganized, shorthand notes totalling around 10,000 words, many on matters of sound, on phonetics and phonology, indicate the extent of his interest in the topic.[33] The African language studies did, however, mark the beginning of the singer's lifelong interest in world languages, and was soon common knowledge. One reporter thus noted that the "ambitions of the builders of Babel brought the curse of many tongues upon the world, to the regret of all, except, perhaps, a few professors of philology—and Paul Robeson."[34]

Robeson's essay "I Want to Be African" first appeared in a 1934 collection of writings by prominent British personalities compiled by E. G. Cousins, *What I Want from Life*. It begins with a twofold declaration "I am Negro. The origin of the Negro is African," and concludes with a desire: "in my music, my plays, my films I want to carry always this central idea: to be African." In the seven intervening pages Robeson presents an argument for an expansive Black identity politics. Proceeding from the "problem" that the American Negro is "without a nationality," Robeson's logic is, first, grounded in the idea of national culture, while second, acknowledging a network of connections between different cultures, and third, for purposes that supersede national interest. In the "world-community every nation will contribute whatever it has of culture" for the "world-necessity": "an understanding between the nations and peoples which will lead ultimately to the 'family of nations' ideal." Here, the Harlem Renaissance ideal of interracial cooperation between Black and white American has undergone global expansion. By the time of the African Letters, Africa's contribution, for Robeson, was its culture's basis in spiritual life, in contrast to the "blind groping after Rationality" and materialism that characterized Western society. Robeson sought rather "a more fundamental, more primitive, but perhaps truer religion," which he defined as "the orientation of man to God or forces greater than himself," and which he argued "must be the basis of culture." This ideal of a spiritual culture Robeson located in the Orient and Africa, and throughout the essay he points to similarities between particular instances of cultural practice—language, a musical feature—of Black American, African, and other societies.[35] Thus

140   PAUL ROBESON'S VOICES

rather than attempting to seek out in Robeson's repertoire and performance practice specific African songs or aspects of African vocal practice (other than that which informed the African American music he performed), we might instead acknowledge that Robeson's ideas on African (and Oriental) culture shaped the spiritual and emotional foundations of the ethical art he desired; and that this basis for his song practice informed his increasingly political singing. Put another way, the desire Robeson articulated in "I Want to Be African" was the desire for an ethical art.[36]

The African Letters, and the comparative network of non-Western cultural correspondences they propose, also served as an apology for Robeson's own developing performance practice, and for his failings to successfully perform the repertoire of the Western art song tradition. After several years of battling to learn and perform in public, to mixed reviews, the canonical art song repertoire in the early 1930s, he confessed, "I will not do anything that I do not understand. I do not understand the psychology or philosophy of the Frenchman, German or Italian. . . . So I will not sing their music or the songs of their ancestors."[37] Rather, he could only "render well in art" what he understood thoroughly, and the connections he imagined to exist between Africa and the East drew forth repeated witness in the African Letters of both intention and action to perform the music of what Robeson called the Easterns: Russian, Hebrew, and Chinese song.[38] Since at least 1931, Russian art song began to appear regularly on his concert programs.[39] It was the spirit of African culture, rather than the sounds of African music, that pervades the African Letters, and which guided Robeson's repertoire experimentation as he moved from the familiarity of African American spirituals (dominant in his recitals until 1930), via Western art song (which appeared on his programs between 1930 and 1932), to Russian and English art and folk song, and folk musics of the world (which assumed increasing importance in concert from 1933).

Unlike the sounds of Africa, Russian music came to occupy a central place in Robeson's song practice, and, like Africa, the Soviet Union was central to the development of Robeson's internationalism. Amid the African Letters are accounts of the singer's first visit to the Soviet Union undertaken in late 1934 and early 1935, which reproduced a striking confession: "This is home to me. I feel more kinship to the Russian people under their new society than I ever felt anywhere else."[40] The Soviet argument would provide a second strand to Robeson's musical internationalism. Black Americans, as Kate Baldwin has documented, conceived of their encounters with the Soviet Union "as

A VOICE FOR THE PEOPLE 141

a means of transforming exclusionary patterns into an internationalism that was a dynamic mix of antiracism, anticolonialism, social democracy, and international socialism." It is another plot line in the story of Black transnationalism, which tends be dominated by the narrative of the Black Atlantic. Importantly, a Soviet-inspired Black internationalism was less concerned with doing away with the idea and practices of the nation and rather contemplated "linkages between peoples of the African diaspora and their nonblack allies—those bound together by a shared sense of exclusion from the nation-state, from citizenship."[41] Particularly inspirational for Robeson, Baldwin argues, was the Leninist doctrine of merging a nationalist discourse of minority self-determination with a cooperative internationalism in order to extend the proletarian revolution; and on the terrain of culture this turned on fostering the idea of *narodnost'*, the collective identity of a people, or a folk-based nationality.[42] (The pan-ethnic internationalism of Popular Front cultural politics has points of similarity.)[43]

Robeson's writings on his Soviet experience are shot through with these ideals. In an interview of 1935 he expressed "a keen interest in the Soviet minorities, their culture and the policy on national minorities." The Soviet Union, he claimed, was the only place where ethnology, the comparative study of cultures, was "seriously considered *and applied*." Soviet policy therefore affirmed and gave further impetus to the comparative project on which he had already embarked, and which the African Letters detailed. The interview's conclusion linked the singer's identity politics to his internationalism and comparative interests: "Paul Robeson's activities have been put, with the enlargement of his interests, on an international scale, including studies and experiments in Eastern cultures along with his participation in African and American affairs. In correlating racial cultures, he sets a standard of awareness, saying, 'The Negro must be conscious of himself and yet international, linked with the nations which are culturally akin to him.' "[44] Critics have attributed Robeson's performance of a network of national folk songs to the "transnational formations of a Leninist tradition,"[45] but Robeson's discovery of the Soviet concept of *narodnost'* was not necessarily generative but rather reinforced an already emerging aesthetic position.

The year prior to his first visit to Russia, the British press reported widely that the singer would "concentrate on the folk songs of the world," with local newspapers giving varying details of Robeson's plan. For a Cambridge readership he pointed out that in singing Russian, Hebrew, and Slavonic folk songs, together with spirituals, he was demonstrating "a deep, underlying

142   PAUL ROBESON'S VOICES

affinity." "Swing Low, Sweet Chariot" was "very near to the Hebrew spirit." A Sheffield newspaper informed its readers of Robeson's contention that it was "the Highland and Hebridean folk music" which formed "the very root of the whole hierarchy of folk idiom," and that Robeson vowed to study the shanties for their influence by Negro melodies. The previous year, in 1933, he had told a reporter from the Isle of Man that he would be turning his attention to Irish and Manx music. At this time, and to aid his study of folk song, he collected records from "nearly every country in the world," which in the singer's listening revealed "a wonderful common feeling about them, a common folk basis."[46]

Assuming increasing prominence in Robeson's discourse on folk music, in the African Letters, and his utterances on the Soviet Union, is the nebulous category of "the people." Until the start of the 1930s, before which the singer's attention was focused on African American music, the people was figured narrowly as "his people" for the critics, or "my people" for Robeson. His voice was representative of the race; or as one critic put it he was an "ambassador of the Negro people."[47] The expansion of the singer's politics and repertoire in the early 1930s resulted in a concomitant enlargement of his audiences and the identity of the people; and in his own identity: an early biography *Paul Robeson, Negro* is refashioned, in a later version, as *Paul Robeson: Citizen of the World*.[48] Of course, folk music takes it very name from its connection to the people. Thus Robeson explained that folk songs "are the music of basic realities, the spontaneous expression by the people for the people of elemental emotions." Because he was interested in performing not only for the "serious music-lover" but also for the "man in the street," folk song seemed the most apt communicative means for the task.[49] His explanation of the foundations of and purposes for folk music chime with his call for a return of the emotional and spiritual in art articulated in the African Letters. And Robeson's interest in folk music was, I suggest, less for what it said about national, ethic, and minority identity than for how folk song allowed him to communicate through its emotive content with diverse peoples around the world, and how in turn it functioned to connect them with each other; I pursue this line further in the next chapter. It is probably significant that the discourse on Robeson's songs of the world project changed in the press from "songs of the nations" in 1933 and 1934 to "songs of the people" by 1937; and in time he would of course gain the moniker "the people's artist."[50] Another people's poet, Neruda, recognized this:

A VOICE FOR THE PEOPLE 143

It would be small praise
if I crowned you king
only of the Negro voice,

. . .

No,
Paul Robeson,
You sang . . .
not only for Negroes,
for the poor Negroes,
but for the poor,
whites,
Indians,
all peoples.[51]

The people Robeson thus sought out and for whom the singer desired to perform as the 1930s progressed were peasants, the man on the street, the common folk, the masses; or in a specific instance, Russian workers of the Kaganovitch Ball Bearing Plant.[52]

The aesthetic and music stylistic links Robeson made between the musics of the world he sang has been interpreted as formalizing solidarity among an international working class, "by conjuring class (and not singularly racial) consciousness," a position shaped by a nascent internationalist socialism.[53] Indeed the singer's well-known participation in the politics of international labor is the third significant strand to his internationalism. The labor historian Mark Naison thus wrote of Robeson's "pantheon of laboring peoples," and Jeffrey Stewart that he forged "a transatlantic body based on the figure of the international worker."[54] His associations and involvement with institutional labor have typically been addressed from the early 1940s on after his return to the United States, and it was a commitment that intensified in the following years. He marched on picket lines, organized, sang in union halls, becoming a celebrity within the American and international labor movements. It was in fact in America during the 1940s that his designation as a "people's artist" gained traction, no doubt because of the rhetorical importance of the people to the Popular Front.[55] Robeson's formal alliance with labor, however, took shape during his final years in Britain, as did his initial cultivation of the artistic persona of the people's artist. In general, his interest in labor accompanied his move to the left in the mid-1930s. Formal artistic associations include his involvement with

144   PAUL ROBESON'S VOICES

the workers' theater collective Unity Theatre in 1938, and his starring role in *Proud Valley* (1939), a film on oppressed Welsh mine workers fighting capitalist greed.[56] Labor-themed and union songs also began to appear on his concert programs at this time.[57] Before this, select African American work songs and music that took work as its lyrical subject matter, such as Alexander Kopylov's "The Laborer's Plaint," occupied a marginal place in the singer's repertoire, their selection almost certainly not primarily for the subject of work or workers' politics.[58] It was only later, from the final years of the 1930s that workers' songs would become "a permanent fixture of his musical repertoire."[59]

My argument is that Robeson's comparative aesthetics, and specifically his emerging interest in folk song, were fields of thinking and practice that led him to "the people," and thereby to the politics of labor and its musics. His turn toward ethnology and folklore studies, moreover, was occasioned by his turn away from art song. In Robeson's failure to sing properly the canonical literature of the Western art song repertoire—primarily *Lieder*, but also *mélodie* and aria—was his discovery of and warming to the music of its peripheries—English and Russian art song—and thereby his introduction to folk music. At the same time that critics were unconvinced by Robeson's performance of *Lieder*, "which Mr. Robeson does not sing very well," grumbled the London *Evening Standard* in 1930, they were more generous in their estimation of his singing of Russian and English art song, which he seems to have started performing in public around the same time.[60] A Carnegie Hall recital of January 10, 1931, advertised that "Mr. Robeson will sing for the first time in this country classic Songs in German and English in addition to Negro folk and spirituals" (see Figure 4.1). The notice might have added Russian art song, for Robeson's repertoire for the tour included at least two such items: Borodin's "Dissonance," more commonly known in its English translation as "The False Note," and Gretchaninov's "The Captive."[61] By the time of the American winter tour of the following year Robeson seems to have shifted his focus to Russian and English art song, with *Lieder* getting the chop.[62]

Two factors account for Robeson's preference for Russian and English song: linguistic facility and mentorship. His learning of Russian music, and the language, was facilitated by his contact in London with the Russian émigré composer Alexandre Gambs and his sporadic work with the accompanist G. Ruthland Clapham, a Russian music specialist.[63] His long-term accompanist Lawrence Brown offered the English connection. Brown had studied

A VOICE FOR THE PEOPLE   145

Figure 4.1. Advertisement for Robeson recital at Carnegie Hall. Lawrence Brown Papers, microfilm 5. Courtesy of Carnegie Hall Rose Archives.

privately with the English composer Roger Quilter in the early 1920s, with whom he had a close friendship, and who acquainted Brown to the world of English art song composition and performance.[64] Quilter also introduced Brown to the folk musics of the British Isles, and in 1930 Robeson, through Brown's introduction, would himself work with Quilter.[65] Such intimate

146   PAUL ROBESON'S VOICES

tutorship—by friends and accompanists—must have eased his way into the repertory of English and Russian song that stood in contrast to his learning of the Western canon of arias and *Lieder* practiced in lessons with a long line of institutional vocal teachers he employed from the mid-1920s discussed in the first chapter.

Important for Robeson's learning of song was his mastery of a song's verbal language, and the singer often spoke about the connections between spoken and sung word throughout his life, a matter I turn to in some detail later in this chapter and the next. When informing the press that he was learning Russian, he claimed the language as "almost his own tongue," and for that reason: "I know that I am going to be able to sing the music of Moussorgsky as if I had been born in Russia."[66] Perhaps drawing on his experience in the dramatic theater, the singer's way into a song was through its lyrical text. An extended account of his learning of "Ol' Man River" makes this plain:

> In his London home he was constantly reciting the words. They had to be spoken at first, every possible meaning put into them, every advantageous emphasis discovered. At first the music didn't matter. It was not a song in early rehearsals. It was a poem to be recited. He would thunder the phrases; roll them in his tremendous voice with no thought of the tune. . . . Day and night the lines of the song ran through his mind and whenever he could he let them come out in resonant vocal expression. Over and over he would chant one single line. He would try it in a rumble; he would whisper it. The accent here, the accent there. Hundreds and hundreds of times he would say just three or four words over and over. Then it was time to sing the song, and gradually the words fitted themselves into the melody. It was when he was putting the two together that Robeson discovered the happy kinship of this song to the spirituals. Just as these folk songs started from just words that took on the proper pitch and tone through religious fervor, so it seemed the words of "Old Man River" had picked up just the right musical score to preserve the meaning that can be sound in musicless recital.[67]

If Robeson struggled to speak a language, or didn't have a feeling for it, it affected his learning of a specific song tradition. "I found that I—a Negro—could sing Russian songs like a native. I, who had to make the greatest effort to master French and German, spoke Russian in six months."[68] His preference for English art song was also based on the common ground he established with the language. He "lacked feeling," he explained, "for the English language later than Shakespeare,"[69] and much of the English song he performed, whether folk song or Quilter's settings of Shakespeare lyrics, harkened back to antique modes of the language. It is perhaps no coincidence that Robeson's enjoyment of English song, which he would perform throughout his life, was established at the moment the actor was learning the part of Othello for Maurice Browne's truncated production that played at the Savoy Theatre in mid-1930. Robeson recalled that his greatest difficulty in acting Othello "was in mastering the English of William Shakespeare," a solution to the pronunciation of which he alighted on when he encountered the orthography of early modern English in old editions of English literature in the publisher Alfred Knopf's library: "As I read the beautiful lines in their early English spelling, I knew that I could master Shakespeare's English. So it proved. I had only to learn to pronounce the early English as it is spelled. Not only was been spelled 'beene,' but dew was spelled 'diew' and most of the other difficulties ironed out."[70]

Through Robeson's learning of English and Russian art song, encouraged by advocates of the repertoire (accompanists and composers he worked with) and an affinity for their languages, he would come to folk music. Later the singer would explain the connections that the select art songs he sang had with folk song. For example, Quilter arranged many folk songs—Robeson sang at least one of these, "Over the Mountains" (published in the *Arnold Book of Old Songs*)—the composer was a student of folk music, and his melodies took on the shape of folk song's singability; Stephen Banfield has written of Quilter's "easy and rewarding manner of writing for the voice."[71] The network of connections between English art song, folk song, and the comparative method favored by Robeson and pursued by some of the folklorists Robeson studied is demonstrated by the singer's performance of sea music, an enduring theme of English art music. Sometime in the early 1930s Robeson began performing John Ireland's popular ballad "Sea Fever," although he only recorded it late in the decade.[72] Robeson's performance for the recording provides for a study of his training: the very first note is delivered deliberately, well prepared and supported, and sounds in the full tone of a dark bass. The *messa di voce* on the held notes that conclude the verses is another instance of classical training (0:38, 1:17, and 1:58).[73] At the same time, the performance reveals perhaps a folk aesthetic in the spoken-like mode by which Robeson performs the melodic line—and one can imagine him reciting the lyrics before singing them, as he had done in learning "Ol' Man River." The

148   PAUL ROBESON'S VOICES

speech-like quality is in part due to the rhythm of Robeson's performance (and also the articulation), which is not always indicated in the score. For instance, Robeson has a tendency to read the prevailing even triplets as dotted, the result of which makes his delivery sound closer to the rhythmic patterns of speech.

A couple of years later, "Shenandoah" appeared on his recital programs. Conventionally considered a sea shanty, Robeson alighted on the song through Sir Richard Terry's arrangement in *The Shanty Book* of 1921.[74] Robeson's recording of "Shenandoah" would "suit the popular taste," noted a review,[75] and in his singing of the song he made good his promise to study the shanties, at least in part for the comparative song knowledge they held.[76] The middle years of the 1930s would witness an escalation in Robeson's folklore studies, with his findings being reported regularly to audiences and the press. At a press conference in Edinburgh in early 1935, he demonstrated both his reading of British folk music research and his own understanding and application thereof. For the gathered reporters he hummed sections of Marjory Kennedy-Fraser's arrangement "Kishmul's Galley," another sea song that appeared in her multivolume *Songs of the Hebrides*, a major work of collecting, transcription, and interpretation published between 1909 and 1925. Robeson studied *Songs of the Hebrides* closely both for its music and its theories of folk music. Kennedy-Fraser's most popular tune "An Eriskay Love Lilt," named for an Hebridean island, would become a standard on Robeson's programs, and his annotations to the folklorist's "Notes" in his copy of the *Songs* reveal his keen interest in matters other than the performance of its songs. He thus highlighted the following hypothesis: if "the Mediterranean civilization penetrated into Ireland and the Western Isles over 3,000 years ago, it is not too fanciful to suggest that musical forms of the Aegean Isles and of the north shores of Africa might be recoverable to-day in the Hebrides."[77] No doubt inspired by Kennedy-Fraser's dictum that "traditional music [is] a valuable medium for ethnological research," Robeson sang next for the press the spiritual "He Shall Feed His Flock" to demonstrate its similarities to "Kishmul's Galley." Robeson's point was that "If the Hebridean fisher folk and the African fisher folk are doing precisely the same work, under conditions which are very similar, they express themselves similarly." And his moral had broader implications; it was nothing less than the "international significance and value of folk music": "If people knew how closely they were related to each other in speech, song, and expression, the world would be happier."[78]

A VOICE FOR THE PEOPLE 149

By at least 1935, then, Robeson's reputation as a "master" of folk music, as the *Yorkshire Telegraph* referred to him, was well earned as both amateur student and professional singer. Moreover, the comparative framework that informed, and perhaps initiated, his interest in folk studies, lent it an explicit political thrust by the mid-1930s, confirming an internationalist and specifically cosmopolitan view: "the differences between civilisations disappear in folk-music," he contended.[79] It is tempting to speculate that Robeson was first directed to the comparative method, at least in part, by chance encounters of an itinerant professional artist prior to his formal ethnological studies at the School of Oriental Studies and his reading of the folk music literature. Several anecdotes suggest the possibility. The singer's interest in "the origin of the negro airs" was energized by meeting a Polish musician during the 1930 tour of continental Europe who "proved" to Robeson that music from central Africa influenced European music by moving with the Moors and Spaniards to Poland. On another occasion, a year later, Robeson heard in his co-actor Sidney Morgan's singing of Irish songs "strange plaintive airs" that had "much in common with the song of my people," just as he recalled being struck by the "likeness to Negro music" of the "native songs" sung by Russian students at college.[80]

The bent for cultural comparativism that Robeson showed early on, initially through lay observation and then, a few years later, with keen anthropological intent with a firm basis in folk song (and language), would form the ground for his thinking about song and for how the singer would relate to the world through song for the rest of his life. In the 1950s he formalized his scattered utterances on the topic in several published and unpublished writings, the very basis of which was underpinned by the comparative method. Robeson-the-historian "found great satisfaction in research into the origins and the inner ties of the folk music of different peoples" and argued, for example, that "the black music of African and American derivation . . . belonged to a great inheritance, to the great folk music of the world":

> These songs, ballads and poetic church hymns are similar to the songs of the bards of the Scottish Hebrides, the Welsh bards of the Druid tradition and the Irish bards which inspired Sean O'Casey. They are similar to the unknown singers of the Russian folktales, the bards of the Icelandic and Finnish sagas, singers of the American Indians, the bards of the Veda hymns in India, the Chinese poet singers, the Hassidic sects and the bards of our African forebears.[81]

150   PAUL ROBESON'S VOICES

This virtuosic cataloguing is a veritable statement of belief in the global comparative method.

My point is that we might grant a strong influence to Robeson's musical practice on his developing internationalism. This was not only persistently demonstrated through song but in part *emerged* in song. Robeson's internationalism and his musical internationalism were of course thoroughly overdetermined. Robeson scholars have tended to read his choice of musical repertoire as representative or reflective of one or several political positions and affiliations. My counter is that we also consider how his song experiences, with repertoire and traditions that he partially failed at and was frustrated by as much as the music he was at ease with, championed, and celebrated for, constituted an aesthetic field that would accommodate the varied politics he advocated. This is not to imply that his comparative folk song practice developed during the first half of the 1930s led him to, or generated, the labor activism or critiques of imperialism and fascism that followed. The comparative method and the field of folk song, however, would illuminate topoi—on universalism, humanism, "the people"—that formed, together with other factors, a crucible for Robeson's political internationalisms, and which would attune his varied politics to his song practice. Much later, Robeson himself would state that his "first glimpse of this concept"—the "belief in the oneness of humankind"—"came through song."[82]

This was certainly the case with the fourth strand of Robeson's musical internationalism: protest or anti-fascist music. The singer's involvement in anti-fascist politics, which later coalesced into a forceful critique of imperialism, first occurred during the Spanish Civil War, a moment that occasioned internationalism in action and sound, as I discussed earlier, and it was at this time that a more explicit message of protest was introduced to Robeson's singing. Robeson was of course initially known for his performance of African American spirituals. But his early singing of spirituals, from the mid-1920s to the mid-1930s, can be attributed first to his familiarity with the repertoire—he grew up singing spirituals—and second to his argument, in line with Harlem Renaissance cultural politics, that spirituals were art and thus to be presented in concert as "serious" music. It was only later in the 1930s that Robeson was drawn to Black music that enunciated a more explicit protest than the spirituals and secular songs he programmed earlier. The emancipation lyric "No More Auction Block for Me" thus first appeared on Robeson's programs in the late 1930s, as did two work songs collected in *Negro Songs of Protest* (1936).[83] The impetus for the singer's reconceptualising of spirituals and work songs as protest music was in part the result of his introduction to a wider body of protest music he encountered during the Spanish Civil War.

While singing to soldiers in Spain in 1938, Robeson heard there the German actor-singer Ernst Busch performing with the Thaelmann Battalion, a multinational group of volunteers. Robeson recalled of Busch that he "was a great artist, with a magnificent feeling for the folk song. And he was one of the first artists who found that, as an artist, he had a part to play also." It is unsurprising then that the American would borrow some of the songs Busch promoted, later introducing Busch's *Six Songs for Democracy* (1938), recorded in the field of war, to an American public on radio:

> And at the end of the program, as the last note of the Song of the Peat-Bog Soldiers as sung by the Thaelmann Battalion Chorus dies away, Robeson took it up, his rich, living voice carrying on from where those other now-silenced voices left off, affirming with all his massive vigor that their spirit has not died, can never die.[84]

Robeson would continue Busch's performance of "Peat Bog Soldiers" (in Hanns Eisler's arrangement) in concert and through his own recording of the song released in 1942 in a box set of 78s pointedly titled *Songs of Free Men*, a collection of eight songs "inspired by social and international upheavals preceding and during the early years of World War II."[85] The singer's incorporation of protest music into his recital programs hastened critics' reception of his art as political, such that a Robeson concert began to attract the qualification "propaganda recital." In these programs the African American, English, Hebrew, Mexican, and Russian music he performed at a Carnegie Hall concert in late 1940 "projected an unwavering theme of protest and revolt against oppression."[86] Indeed by the time of his return to the United States in late 1939 his musico-political internationalism was commonly accepted (if not always deemed acceptable concert practice). The *Saint Paul Pioneer Press* headlined its review of a concert "Robeson Stirs Audience with Songs of Oppressed," Portland's *Sunday Oregonian* reported that "Robeson Sings of Humanity," and the *Seattle Times* found his recital "international in theme, with emphasis on the common people."[87]

The four primary threads of Robeson's musical internationalism—protest, socialist internationalism, labor, and the Black internationale—were often interrelated and overlapped, and informed by overarching political and

152   PAUL ROBESON'S VOICES

humanist ideals. The different strands have received fairly thorough scholarly interest, although to varying degrees—the repertoire of non–African
American protest song is neglected—and, much as in my own account,
scholars have pursued the relationship between Robeson's politics and song
through his choice of repertoire.[88] Voice-thinking requires us to shift the
emphasis from a concern with repertoire to consider also the performing
practices and sounds of the voice of the global people's artist, and thus pose
the question: beyond the songs he sang, might we further consider how
Robeson exercised, in song performance, the voice of the people? I begin by
exploring how "the people" received his voice and the politics it envoiced.

Vox Populi; or Paul Robeson, Friend!

Robeson worked out his developing song practice, and thereby his emerging
politics, on the recital stage, a domain of artistic expression over which he
exerted greater creative control than on record (or in film). Much of the "bad
music" he sang, recorded for the HMV stable, was issued in the 1930s, precisely the time when Robeson the people's artist emerged. A comparison
between the singer's HMV catalog and the repertoire for the independent
records he made in the early to mid-1950s, when none of the major labels
would sign him, underscores what music was personally meaningful for
the artist: very little of the bad commercial music of earlier survives in the
independent recordings. The concert format allowed Robeson to shape
audiences, to sing to the people, and also to structure the song practice of a
people's artist in ways not possible on record alone.

The singer's utterances on his ideal audience mix first surface during the
time of his turn to performing folk musics of the world, in the mid-1930s.
During his 1934 British tour, Robeson attempted to broaden his appeal,
in his words "to steer a middle course. . . . I am appealing not to the highbrow and not to the lowbrow, but I am singing for all." To the *Cambridge
Daily News* he expressed the conviction that he could "retain the interest
of the serious music-lover, but also entertain the man in the street."[89] This
was not Robeson's first outing singing for everyman—his "first music-hall
appearance," two years earlier at the London Palladium, was proof for the
Times that "there is no need for a fine singer to play down to such surround-
ings"[90]—but it did begin a process by which he rethought the allegiance
of his concert practice to the traditions of classical music. By no means

A VOICE FOR THE PEOPLE 153

a conventional art song recitalist in either training or repertoire selection, Robeson's concertizing partook in other features of the tradition, such as the venues in which he appeared and the "serious" audiences he courted. He was thus snapped up by the South African-born British impresario Harold Holt and presented under the umbrella of Holt's International Celebrity Concerts series, noted for introducing the British public to the world's leading classical artists. For at least one pundit, Robeson's 1934 program was therefore confusing: whereas the Celebrity Concerts were

> usually associated with a programme of music above the understanding of the usual audience . . . Paul Robeson's recital was certainly an exception, for it was definitely of universal appeal. The most humble listener and what has now become known as the "high-brow" must have left the hall at the conclusion of the concert feeling that a profitable evening had been spent.[91]

As the decade wore on, Robeson became less accommodating, less interested in the demands and expectations of elite audiences: of the few artists who could fill the Albert Hall in London, Robeson was the only one who made "no concession to the highbrow public."[92] His biographers chart the singer's changing ideals for concertizing at this time, signaled in his partial rejection of the status of celebrity singer and his embrace of the role of the artist as activist. During the final years of the 1930s, and increasingly in the 1940s, Robeson was thus concerned with audience accessibility, performing at free events or keeping ticket prices affordable, and appearing in nontraditional recital spaces—in music halls, outdoors, in churches, and factories— to maximize opportunities for access for the diverse peoples with which he affiliated.[93]

Before I consider the means of song communication by which the artist's message was delivered to the people, identified by one writer as Robeson's "skill at turning concert-going people into partisans,"[94] I document how ordinary listeners heard the people's artist. I do so through a reading of Robeson's fan mail, presenting a micro historical ethnography of listening.[95] My focus is to attend to what Tia DeNora has called "musical affect in practice," uncovering the meanings Robeson's listeners attributed to his singing, identifying what they felt and experienced, and how their listening effected their actions. This history of everyday listening contrasts with the archive of critics' professional listening consulted in the previous chapters. It is also an opportunity to consider the popular reception of Robeson's internationalism.

154 PAUL ROBESON'S VOICES

xOx

You have given me joys and happiness—sounds and emotions—wings to my spirit that I remember like yesterday.

You were my friend ["immediately!" inserted above "friend"]—when I just heard you sing . . .

I just wanted to let you know—how much you have meant to me—all these years.

You have been thru the mill on a public stage—& millions of people know & love you—& are indebted to you—like me—who never met you—& call you friend.

—Louise R. Franks, August 20, 1973, Virginia.[96]

During the years of Robeson's retirement, from the early 1960s, the singer received regular fan mail from around the world. One such correspondent was John Dickens from Auckland, New Zealand, who began with an explanation for his address: "I have sent you this card 'to a dear friend' because you have been a friend to me, my parents and grandparents for almost as long as we can remember, although we have never met you in person." Dickens recalled his first encounter with Robeson, when as a boy of nine he listened to Robeson's voice on record issuing from the family's newly acquired gramophone player; and he remembered his mother's particular interest in the singer: "I wondered why she cared so much. After all, she never said these things about Bing Crosby or Gracie Fields. What made you so different?"[97] Three features mark Dickens's note to the singer that are common to Robeson fan letters: the imagining of Robeson as a friend, the recollection of first hearing the Robeson voice, and a discourse on artistic exceptionalism. None of this is itself exceptional; in fact, as scholars of fandom have shown, they are stock rhetorical moves of fan writing. But the explicit naming of the fan-artist relationship as friendship is, perhaps, less usual. More typically fans deploy the open term "love" to express their devotion to a hero. In interrogating love as a keyword in fan talk, Mark Duffett notes that love subsumes all manner of positive identification—admiration, affection, lust, affinity, and friendship, to be sure—and allows fans to avoid having to specify a particular meaning or mode of identification.[98] Robeson's correspondents were certain enough of their relationship with the singer to name it as friendship.

Indeed, it was the imagined relationship of friendship in which Robeson's letter writers cast themselves that caused many of them to question their

A VOICE FOR THE PEOPLE 155

position as fans. (This is especially true for the correspondence of the 1950s and 1960s, framed possibly by an awareness of the associations of teenage fandom and the new popular music, which at the time was often cast in pathological terms. It is also true for older writers. Jo Love, a seventy-four-year-old widow from the mountains of Colorado, warned Robeson that the singer should "not expect a Teenage-Beetle[sic]-Rhapsody" from her.)[99] If "fan" itself is a keyword in discussions of fandom, it is productive to explore Robeson's correspondents' disavowal of the term for what it tells us about their perceived relationship with the star. Mona Frame, from Huntsville in Australia, considered it anathema to be counted a fan because she was a friend: "I can no longer think of myself as a 'fan,' that is too superficial a word. You are my friend, the friend of my almost-grown-up family and all the people you met (and many you could not) while you were in Australia."[100] The fan letter too seemed ill-suited for the purpose of Robeson's correspondents and many thus presented their letters as alternative modes of writing. Twenty-six-year-old David Miller, from Saskatoon in Canada, proposed that rather than conceive of his letter as fan mail it was more properly a thank-you note: for Robeson's music, and the records that made up the soundtrack of Miller's childhood, but more pointedly for what Miller learned from Robeson's songs.[101]

It is not only how fans perceived themselves vis-à-vis their hero—not as fans, in the case of many of Robeson's correspondents—or how they conceived of their epistles—not as fan letters, or as exceptional writers thereof—but also how fans addressed the singer that sheds light on the nature of their relationship with him. The epistolary salutation announces from the outset the fan's desired relationship with the star. Robeson's correspondents forgo formality in their address, almost always omitting an honorific, and often simplifying the vocative to the singer's first name. To cite but two of many instances from Australian fans. Don Johns, from Victoria, commenced thus: "I call you Paul, for after seeing your concert . . . I feel we are friends and as you said brothers." And Sydneysider Sylvia J. Lamond's apologetic opening was a familiar move: "Please excuse the familiarity of the address," she began, "but I feel so much a friend of yours that 'Mr.' seems out of place."[102] The apology accompanied salutation is indicative of, among other things, the letter writer's generation and the broad tradition of music-making associated with the singer, for these shape the practices of fan-being. On the one hand, Robeson's correspondents were often adult writers—although he also courted many younger fans—no doubt schooled in a tradition of formal letter writing. For these fans, addressing a world figure in writing by first

156 PAUL ROBESON'S VOICES

name necessitated an apology and explanation. On the other hand, the artist's long association with the song recital located his listeners within a musical practice that encouraged a certain formality of relationship between audience and artist. While Robeson would revise many of the practices of the song recital, some of which I discuss in the following section, a Robeson recital nevertheless remained a world apart from performances of the popular youth musics of the day, and the types of fan relationships those musics encouraged.[103]

Fan correspondence sets out clearly that the fan-as-friendship relationship was primarily entered into through listening to Robeson's singing and the sounds of his voice; it was not constituted through fans' reading of the singer's extensive political writings or their participation in his organizing, for example. When Jess Andrews, who introduced herself to the singer as "a young busy housewife" from Belfast in Ireland, heard Robeson in 1959 it was, she described, "like hearing the voice of an old friend again."[104] We might thus ask, how did Robeson envoice friendship, and how did his listeners hear friendship in his singing?[105]

One quality that Robeson's listeners heard in his voice was sincerity, on which feelings of friendship could be firmly founded. A Swedish émigré to the United States explained to the singer that "you have become my friend over the years": "your voice, which used to boom out from your heart and soul . . . made an everlasting impression on me: I felt that there was a sincere man."[106] In hearing sincerity, fans drew on an older discourse, established in the 1920s, by critics who identified sincerity as core to the natural aesthetics they attributed to Robeson's singing that I explored in chapter 3. Listeners to the singer's hit Sunday evening BBC radio broadcasts of 1958 and 1959 wrote of the artist's "sincere and homey" presentation, his "obvious sincere delivery."[107] Indicative of truthfulness and directness, Robeson's vocal sincerity welcomed a relatability that allowed fans to imagine a relationship of friendship with the people's artist.

The singer's performances also fostered feelings of intimacy with his audiences, and fans commonly expressed a sense of closeness to and of personal address by the singer. On the death of her father, one Elizabeth Perkins listened to Robeson records as a source of comfort: "It was as if *you sang to me alone*," she wrote, signing off as "Your living friend."[108] The changes to consumption practices wrought by the new recording and broadcasting technologies in the early twentieth century, which included the creation of intimate, domestic listening spaces and the production of intimate microphone

A VOICE FOR THE PEOPLE   157

voices, are well known.[109] Thus Mrs. W. Smith of Yorkshire explained: "I don't know how you do it. Perhaps it's because you were a very friendly person but I've felt as if you were *in our home just talking to my husband and myself* instead of miles away in a B.B.C. studio."[110] The Robeson records U. Sunny Nwogu from Lagos played not only kept the memory of the singer "green" but, emphasized the twenty-two-year-old, "They bring you near me."[111] The record mediated the intimacy of Robeson's voice but it was unlike that of other recorded voices. The crooner's voice, for example, positioned listeners in a relationship of imagined romantic intimacy,[112] whereas Robeson's vocal intimacy was heard for its enveloping sonic warmth, and the effect of communing that this facilitated. One correspondent, after apologizing for his informality—"the liberty of addressing you in this manner because that is the spontaneous approach that springs from a profound and natural fondness which all members of my family and myself hold for you"—commented on the "warmth and closeness" of Robeson's singing on radio.[113] The affect of intimacy was a product of recording technologies and specifically high-fidelity, but also of familiarizing strategies of performance the singer cultivated in concert.

For these ends, Robeson endeavored to speak to fans in their language, sing their songs in the vernacular and with their accent, and to involve them in the performance, thereby connecting with audiences to create a sense of community. These features characterized his "homecoming" concert at Carnegie Hall in 1958, his return to the mainstream concert stage after his blacklisting. Critics noted that "it was more than an evening of singing . . . it was more like an evening in the living room."[114] And so fans' sense of familiarity with Robeson's voice and singing afforded feelings of friendship. A Hungarian correspondent wrote of the "millions of Hungarians who . . . think on you with love and friendly feelings. When we hear your voice we feel that you sing for us personally."[115] Here, the personal address is not private (as Perkins experienced it in her time of loss or the Smiths heard it at home), but a collective public address, made personal because of Robeson's recordings of Hungarian music, which included György Ránki's "Song on the Friendship between the People." The expectation of familiar address led one listener to express his disappointment in Robeson's performance of the traditional Scottish song "Loch Lomond": "Knowing that you have great linguistic ability and a great regard for the authentic folk-song," the writer began, "I would have thought that you would have kept nearer to the Lallans in 'Loch Lomon', e.g. 'gae' instead of 'go', 'yell tak' instead of 'you'll take.'"[116] (In extant recordings of the song Robeson typically sings it in dialect.)

158 PAUL ROBESON'S VOICES

Fannish familiarity with Robeson's voice was also brought about through repeated listening, often across spans of time entailing a fan's lifetime. Enabled by the repeatability of recorded sound, Robeson's voice, letter writers often informed him, was on repeat play in their homes; sometimes, they confessed, to the annoyance of neighbors. Many made a point of informing Robeson of their lifelong listening to his voice, as if the constancy and commitment were evidence of their friendship. Because he had been brought up on Robeson's records, Miguel Fonseka, from Ceylon, claimed that "I feel that you have been a friend and one of the family for as long as I can remember."[117] It is telling that fans' discourse on friendship is often framed by their family context. In other words, rather than imagine a relationship of individual friendship with Robeson, fans profess him to be a friend of the family. The familiar dovetails with the familial. And by extension, letter writers often discussed Robeson's voice in terms of the home, as both locus of the family and sentiment of belonging. In one sense, a Robeson record functioned as placeholder for the singer's person. One fan wrote that when her family played the singer's records it was "like having you visit us in our own home."[118] Many others, often self-identified as ordinary people and workers in the correspondence, extended an open invitation to Robeson that should he be in town he should pop in for tea or dinner.[119] These acts of welcome and hospitality, certainly never realized, are of course basic acts of friendship.

Other fans conceived of his voice as sounding home. This recalls Cornel Sandvoss's understanding of fandom as a form of *Heimat*, which encompasses not only a physical space but also an emotional and even ideological space.[120] A Mrs. Charles Peard recounted an anecdote of her family's "musical friendship" with the singer. A Czech visitor to the Peard's New Jersey home heard there a record of Robeson singing a Smetana song—probably *Píseň svobody* (usually translated as "Song of Freedom"), and one of the international protest songs in the singer's repertoire. In a fit of nostalgia the guest began to weep, exclaiming: "This brings home to me." For the host the sentiment applied more broadly: "Your voice surely means home to people everywhere." The record was played again and again with the guest singing along, and the connection made and shared through Robeson's singing resulted in the host and guest becoming friends: "He has since become our cherished friend and my husband says that we must give you the credit." In similar vein, on the singer's return to the United States in the mid-1960s a well-wisher noted:

A VOICE FOR THE PEOPLE   159

"I will not say 'Welcome home,' for the world is your home."[121] This artic-ulation of Robeson's vocal friendship as affirming yet complicating and expanding the idea of home is key to understanding how fans thought of Robeson's place in their world and his place in the world at large. In the artic-ulation between those two spheres, the cosmopolitan imagination—another axis to Robeson's internationalism—is energized.[122]

It is a truism that fans imagine themselves as belonging to a social commu-nity of fans. As much as Robeson's fans wished him to be part of their imme-diate circles of family and friends, his letter writers conceived of themselves as belonging to and participating within larger communities of friendship that often extended globally. Regretting his inability to be with the singer on a celebratory occasion, the civil rights lawyer Martin Popper explained that although "I shall miss being with you, I find some comfort in the knowledge that wherever I happen to be, I'll be among your friends." He continued: "It's true that the peoples of all the continents have adopted you as their own, which is as it should be, for you are the embodiment of our belief that we are all brothers."[123]

This humanist discourse—on brotherhood—is as prominent as that on friendship in the Robeson archive, and accompanies yet is also dis-tinct from it. For one, the friend-as-brother is more explicitly politi-cally marked, aligned in the 1950s and 1960s particularly with the peace movements (mobilized against the Cold War), and also with anticolonial and workers' movements, all of which counted Robeson as a passionate advocate. Emerging already in the mid-1930s alongside and perhaps out of the comparative method and folk music studies, the idea(l) of frater-nity would inform Robeson's political thought and artistic practice for the remainder of his career. He presented the purpose of his tour of the Spanish War as such: "Je ne suis pas allé en Espagne par curiosité," he told French journalists, "mais pour apporter aux combatants républicains le témoignage de mon amitié" ("I did not go to Spain out of curiosity but to bring to the Republican soldiers the testimony of my friendship").[124] It was a message keenly heard by his fans. Writing to Robeson in sympathy when Eslanda Robeson passed away, Jo Love from Colorado recounted her own mourning practice: "All these day and weeks I have not played your records. They are so like your very presence, and I knew this could not be a time for singing." (Fannish friendship is also evident in the voluminous wishes for wellbeing Robeson received on the occasions of his birthday, and at times

160 PAUL ROBESON'S VOICES

of illness and family tragedy.)[125] Love then turned to consider the broader effects of Robeson's singing:

> Your music too, it doesn't only win popular applause, it makes world-wide brotherhood. We don't only lushly hear the sound of your "velvet tones." Nothing so easy as that. You make us live vicariously, till the cry: ". . . an end let there be, / To all this sorrow and suffering," is torn from *our own* hearts. And this brotherhood bond that you call into being is the only thing that can save our very earth itself and its people.[126]

For Robeson's ordinary listeners it is important to reiterate that the message of brotherhood was primarily heard in song, rather than accessed through his writings or political organizing. J. B. Neumann recalled that even when he first encountered Robeson, in the mid-1920s, "it was clear to me that you were 'das Lied der Welt.'" (The conceit of Robeson *being* the song of the world, or some variation thereof, is not uncommon.)[127] Some twenty years later this was reinforced, such that Neumann wrote, "you are still more the voice of the people of the whole world"; and he urged the singer to "speak up for the brotherhood of man wherever you will appear in the future." Above this typewritten plea is a point of clarification written in by hand: "I mean in your concerts!"[128] In hearing Robeson's message of the cosmopolitan ideal of universal brotherhood on radio, record, and in concert, ordinary listeners broadened the terms of their friendship with the star, thereby situating themselves within a larger community of fans.[129]

In numerous fora Robeson elaborated on the value of friendship as a tool for effecting political and social change. For instance, writing to the philosopher and anti-racism campaigner Lionel Kenner, Robeson laid out in nutshell his political philosophy: "the essence of my world outlook is that it is entirely possible for men and women of differing political viewpoints to join hands in the common search for peace, equality and freedom. . . . The cornerstone of any effort to achieve them must be friendship and understanding."[130] Friendship, Robeson argued, was facilitated through (cultural) exchange, which in turn would allow for an understanding that was both intersubjective and cross-cultural. During the singer's protracted battle with the US government in the 1950s to secure his right to travel the world, his legal team took the following position: through cross-border cultural exchange Robeson's music contributed to "the advancement of man's universality, brotherhood

A VOICE FOR THE PEOPLE 161

and humanism," thereby consolidating and growing, they argued, "the friends of the U.S. abroad."[131]

Robeson's practice of song exchange, and the relationship of friendship and understanding he hoped it would enable, was based on another instance of exchange: the gift. We can think of the gift not as a utilitarian form of giving, nor in the contractual terms of commodity exchange (as we might consider the purchase of concert tickets and records). Rather, following Paul Ricoeur, the gift is imbued with a "logic of superabundance [that] exceeds the logic of reciprocity." In Ricoeur's formulation the "economy of the gift touches every part of ethics" and stems from, on the one side, "creation, in the most basic sense of an originary giving of existence," to, at the other extreme, "the source of *unknown* possibilities," and thus of hope.[132] In art critic Marsha Meskimmon's reading, the gift is thus a form of generosity that engenders an "ethical commitment to others that is future-orientated." It is potentially transformative, and encourages social relationships that are predicated on the understanding of difference. Put another way, because the locus of the gift is aesthetic-ethics it has the potential to interpellate its receivers as response-able, that is responding and responsible subjects. Ricoeur states this unambiguously: "the gift turns out to be a source of obligation."[133] Redmond's theorization of Robeson's singing as vibration—"Robeson was vibration," she emphasizes—functions similarly to this conceptualization of the gift, for vibration is "a call, a reminder, an alert deserving attention and response, leaving a 'something to be done.'"[134]

Robeson's fans invite us to think of his voice as a vibrational gift of such typology. More than the prosaic formulation of his voice being "a very special gift" (as a talent) bestowed on him,[135] fans wrote of his gifted voice, given to the world.[136] Many fan responses to the voice-gift are of the order of affective listening that does not pass beyond aesthetic reification (and sometimes in Robeson's case, deification). But other responses reside in the domain of ethics. For these fans, Robeson's voice was heard as a call to action, which some answered, and in different ways. For some listeners, Robeson's voice encouraged a sense of self-realization that, if we take the correspondence as the only evidence, seems not to exhibit consequences beyond that. It was not uncommon for fan responses of this order to empathize with Robeson's message of friendship but to cast him as a surrogate for the acts they desired but could not, and sometimes dared not, undertake. A South African–born Australian resident lamented her lack of social courage "back home," where she had been at odds with family and friends "who seemed to think that the

162   PAUL ROBESON'S VOICES

natives were lucky to spend their lives being exploited by their overlords." She signed off in resigned confession: "All I can do now is to hail people like you, Mr. Robeson, who courageously fight for what they know to be right."[137] For other correspondents, hearing Robeson led to the transformation of intersubjective social relationships, and fans commonly admit to reconsidering their racial, class, and national positions.[138] And for yet others their response to the gift-voice is to embark on social (and sometimes political) action. The numerous anecdotes fans relate to Robeson tell how they heard the ideal of reciprocal obligation in his song message and how they in turn gave to others. Two brief anecdotes will serve as example.

From Christchurch, New Zealand, Mary Donnell presented Robeson with a picture: "Maori and Pakeha [white New Zealanders] gathered in a simple farm kitchen listening to [your] voice on an old gramophone." Robeson's singing, she explained, offered them a "lesson": "to stop thinking about our own petty, trivial slights, to stop being armchair socialists and to get out as you are doing and make a heaven for our Family of Man right here on earth." "You see," she concluded, "now that you have given us hope and courage we can no longer be quiet."[139] From the other side of the world, in England, and as with many listeners to Robeson's Sunday evening BBC radio broadcasts of 1958 and 1959, Eileen Gibson wrote a letter of thanks to the singer. She and her husband listened to Robeson on a "little portable radio," such that it "was just as if you were . . . in our little cottage, singing to us." Prefacing her thoughts with proclamations that she hated the "colour bar" and the goings-on in apartheid South Africa, she confessed that she rejoiced in Robeson's music for its beauty, but also because it "make[s] the mind *think*." For her own immediate context—"this rural place"—she endeavored to learn from Robeson, to "always speak a word of friendship or give a smile to those people who are obviously 'the strangers within our gates.' "[140]

These fans-as-friends' responses to the gift-voice evince cosmopolitan thinking in action. The "cosmopolitan imagination" is premised on "an embodied, embedded, generous and affective form of subjectivity," all of which Robeson's fans heard in his voice, and takes effect "in conversation with others in and through difference."[141] As Robeson's fans listened to difference (in his voice and the songs of many lands he sang), they listened with others (Māori and Pākehā together, for instance), for the sake of understanding and engaging with others (the strangers within).[142] The effect of hearing Robeson's voice within the terms of friendship permitted the mediation between what Seyla Benhabib has described as the "generalized

A VOICE FOR THE PEOPLE   163

other" and "concrete other," where the former (a moral person endowed with universal rights) is served by demands of justice and the latter (a unique individual, with "a certain life history, disposition and endowment") exists in the domain of virtue. Robeson's fan-friends heard the virtues of his being expressed in song—"you have been a symbol to me of all that is best and most heartening in mankind," wrote one fan[143]—as an argument for social justice, and therefore as cultivating qualities of what Benhabib calls "civic friendship."[144] The nature of the friendship the singer envoiced thus exceeded the domain of the personal. It spoke of the moral contract that binds the world's citizens together. Redmond's vibrational theory puts it thus: Robeson "sang to and for communities whose equilibrium was disrupted through the act of participatory listening, being charged by and reactive to the stimulus of song through which the movement of bodies—those both politic and individual—was produced."[145]

The power of Robeson's voice to affect ordinary listeners' lives and their relationships with others is indeed a powerful function of the voice. As I write about a "great" voice and the voice of a "great man," it is a salutary reminder that fans and fan practices—letter writing and record buying—are the grounds through which Robeson's internationalism and cosmopolitan ideals find local expression. By listening to Robeson's listeners, a different perspective on the people's artist's internationalism comes into focus. Less concerned with the various strands of political theory and ideology that constituted Robeson's internationalism that I explored earlier, the people's hearing of the artist's message through its affective dimensions emphasizes rather its effects on their individual lives as concrete others.

"Brothering Song": Performing Cosmopolitanism

Robeson's message of friendship was borne of a cosmopolitan imagination. The insight of recent scholarship on cosmopolitanism has highlighted its embeddedness in the ethics and behaviors of everyday practice, including fan practices. It is thus in the features of a mundane cosmopolitanism, rather than in the hallmarks of internationalism as grand global politics, that Robeson's fans heard the call of his voice. And it is from the field of the singer's concert practice that a people's voice may be discerned.[146] Indeed, Robeson instructs us on the ethical imperatives and practical actions that arise from a cosmopolitan way of being in the world in the songs he sang.

164 PAUL ROBESON'S VOICES

The topoi of cosmopolitanism presented in a typical late-career Robeson program of songs included lessons on the practice of hospitality (in Parry's "Jerusalem") and neighborliness ("Balm of Gilead"). This concretizes social relations in specific localities but is also a model for action beyond the local. Unity (in Smetana's "Svornost") and brotherhood (sung in "All Men Are Brothers" to the choral melody from Beethoven's Ninth Symphony) were also common lyrical themes. Nor did Robeson experience a contradiction between these universalist tenets and the politics of the particular. The historian David Hollinger presents a case for cosmopolitanism as being doctrinally positioned between universalism (expressed in the sentiment of "All Men Are Brothers") and pluralism (presented, e.g., in the diverse children's songs, from China, Mexico, and a Schubert lullaby, that Robeson sang). Determined to "maximise species-consciousness," to fashion tools of understanding and acting on problems of a global scale, cosmopolitanism also promotes diversity, recognizing the power of the ethnos and nation, and other group formations, in non-dogmatic and fluid ways.[147] Robeson thus argued that his "belief in the oneness of humankind . . . existed within me side by side with my deep attachment to the cause of my own race."[148] As with Robeson's internationalism, the origins of the cosmopolitan imagination that characterized the singer's mature political thought and concert practice can be traced to the comparative folk studies of the 1930s, and also to the Harlem Renaissance.[149]

The very structure of a Robeson recital program expressed an international outlook that offered a cosmopolitan argument, with programs organized to demonstrate the unity of humanity and its song cultures:

I have found enormous satisfaction in exploring the origins and interrelations of various folk musics, and have come to some interesting and challenging ideas . . . there is a world body—a universal body—of folk music. . . . Interested as I am in the universality of mankind—in the fundamental relationship of all peoples to one another—this idea of a universal body of music intrigued me.[150]

Radically juxtaposing songs of different genres and from different traditions, and from across the globe, Robeson "very deftly included . . . the folksongs, chants, hymns, and spirituals of the Africans, colored Americans, Chinese, Asians, Russians, and Jews to demonstrate that all can be 'brothers.'"[151] The actress and sometime critic Dorothy Dandridge explained further: "The

A VOICE FOR THE PEOPLE   165

artist talks to his audience and explains how closely related are the folk musics of many peoples. He then illustrates the relationship with songs." Robeson's message, she concluded, was that "such ethnical bits of culture are blood brothers—no matter what their geographical source of origin."[152] Robeson's programming strategy was an act of cosmopolitan intent, an endeavor to "build bridges of cooperation across difference," proceeding from the belief in and pursuit of commonalities.[153] British critic Edward Goring aptly referred to Robeson's practice as "brothering song": through song, listeners were to be placed into a relationship of kinship.[154]

Brothering song had several consequences for the recital format. Robeson's programming had always challenged the repertoire conventions of the recital by including song traditions from outside of the art song recital. As I discussed in chapter 2, his formal recitals of all-Black music were novel (although not unheard of), as was his rethinking of the relationship of the spiritual, and in time folk music, to Western art song. It was common practice already by the time Robeson was making his mark as a singer, in the 1920s and 1930s, for art singers to include folk songs and spirituals in recital; hence Ernest Newman complained about the "vogue" for spirituals in 1929.[155] Whereas folk song typically appeared at the end of art song recitals, in the final group of songs, Robeson accorded them a more prominent place. He routinely promoted the "value of folk music"—"I do not consider that they constitute an inferior art form"—arguing also for their "international significance";[156] he programmed a greater number and selection thereof; and dispersed folk song throughout his programs rather than organize them into a distinct group separate from the rest of the repertoire.[157]

Robeson also deconstructed, for cosmopolitan ends, the idea of song grouping itself, an organizing principle of art song recital programming that his own recitals drew on, and which he learned as he entered the "concert field," as he termed it, in the 1920s and 1930s.[158] In this tradition, songs in a group affine, commonly through chronological telos, linguistic uniformity, and national kinship, and for much of his career Robeson's recital programs tended to adhere to this logic. A selection of programs from the early 1940s is exemplary: an all-English group of four songs commenced the Purdue University Hall of Music recital of February 14, 1942, and a group of four spirituals concluded it; a selection of four Russian songs formed the central group in a McMillin Theater concert of January 1943.[159] But already in the mid-1930s there are signs that the singer had begun to depart from these conventions of national and ethnic song grouping. A New York Town Hall

166   PAUL ROBESON'S VOICES

concert of October 19, 1935, concluded not with a group of spirituals, as would have been the case a few years prior for the singer's concerts, but with spirituals, a song by Rimsky-Korsakov ("O Ivan, You Ivan"), and a prayer from Palestine arranged by Sir Arthur Somervell.[160] A more thorough loosening up of the group logic by which song recitals are structured happened more consistently only during the time of his national arrest in the 1950s. This is particularly evident in the explicitly oppositional events to which Robeson lent his voice. The third annual Peace Arch concert of August 1954 opened with two spirituals, "Didn't My Lord Deliver Daniel" and "Jacob's Ladder" (arranged by his past and present accompanists Lawrence Brown and Alan Booth), followed by Roger Quilter's arrangement of the English folk song "Over the Mountains," Schubert's "Cradle Song," Parry's "Jerusalem," and concluded with the English ditty "O No John!"[161]

Robeson's son recalled that during the mid-1950s his father developed "a new concert format—a presentation . . . appealing to a broad section of music lovers."[162] The format seemed to perplex some, as this 1957 review suggests:

> It was an unusual program, not so much in content as in *arrangement*. It ranged from folk songs to opera, with Othello's final speech tossed in as an encore; it offered an initial group which was mainly religious, but within this unity it placed Bach next to Roger Quilter and a Negro spiritual alongside a Jewish chant in disregard of long standing, if perhaps unnecessary, concert tradition.[163]

Similarly, the song groups for the Carnegie Hall recital in 1958 (see Figure 4.2 for the first group of the program) display a diversity that undermines the conventional coherences of a recital group but accommodates—indeed is necessary for—a presentation of cosmopolitanism, and for the ideal of brothering song.[164] In structuring the programs of his late recitals as such, Robeson created what in cosmopolitan theory has been called a "deterritorialized locality," a social—and here, concert—space that is deterritorialized (from national or music historical era) and thereby reterritorialized as a cosmopolitan space, a place based on multiple civic publics "opened to the world."[165]

This cosmopolitan repertoire, which less generous critics thought "a motley program," permitted Robeson to reach diverse audiences—there was something for everyone—while presenting his central message distilled in the idea of brothering song. Taking no chance that the program would speak for itself, however, the singer spoke for it. The combination of song and explanatory

A VOICE FOR THE PEOPLE   167

Figure 4.2. Program for Robeson's May 9, 1958, Carnegie Hall recital. Courtesy of Carnegie Hall Rose Archives.

speech constituted the new format, "the presentation" as Robeson's son termed it. Some critics referred to it as a sermon, in which Robeson assumed the role of preacherman; and here we might recall Robeson's family history of preaching. Still others thought his recitals akin to a lecture; the singer was also

168   PAUL ROBESON'S VOICES

a "scholar and anthropologist."[166] Music historian Irving Kolodin described in some detail the practice as Robeson employed it in the Carnegie Hall recital of 1958. After the opening group of songs it was evident to the critic that it "was less a recital than a preachment":

> The implicit became explicit towards the end of the next group when, after persuading the audience to join him in song, he digressed to a lengthy explanation of why he juxtaposed Hebraic material with African, and African with Chinese. They were, he explained, part of a long-range affinity which manifests itself in the music of folk around the world. This basic musicological truth was received by his audience as a revelation, aided no little by Robeson's histrionic talent for vivifying the commonplace by an inflection of speech, a thrust of the head or even, when pertinent, a bit of truckin'.[167]

The preaching and teaching served two purposes: it allowed Robeson to drive home—to keep on truckin', in Kolodin's use of the vernacular—the message of his songs and programming. For one East Coast critic, Robeson was primarily concerned with "delivering a message": "'Let us think of the entire earth and pound the table with love,' he recited as he brought the formal program to a close. It was the keynote. He was pounding truth, as he saw it, through his own gifts."[168] Talking also enhanced communication, and therefore the singer's connection, with audiences. It was in part through the performative manner of Robeson's talking—his histrionics, inflections, gestures—for which he had long been known that the singer engaged audiences, and by which a sense of familiarity and friendliness was established with them. Critics thus noted Robeson's "allergy to formality": "The informality of his performance was largely responsible for the genuine delight his singing created."[169]

Robeson's late-career informal recitals attempted to further undo the performer-audience barrier by invoking and enacting the congregational ideal. By the 1950s, critics routinely commented on the singer's habit of inviting the audience to join him in song, often several times during a concert. "I came here to sing and for you to sing with me," the singer announced to an audience in Dundee, Scotland.[170] *Variety* noted how Robeson brought his audiences "completely under his spell": "A simple 'Join me' caused the sympathetic throng to sing with him on several occasions, after which Robeson applauded the audience's vocalism."[171] The invitation ("join me"),

A VOICE FOR THE PEOPLE   169

the resultant communal singing, and the artist's return applause functioned as gestures that enabled affective exchange by which different listeners who may not be positioned as a unified community experience connections. They also serve as familiarizing, or friend-building, strategies. Thus for one critic, a Robeson recital "was more than an evening of singing": "The artist was so at home with his audience that it was more like an evening in the living room. . . . And he let us sing with him, too, not once but two or three times."[172]

Often the communal singing took place during the encore section of the concert. Since the start of his concert career, and throughout it, Robeson had elaborated the encore into a distinct and extended section of the recital. Reports of half a dozen encores—on occasion, half an hour of additional singing—were common, and by the time of the Carnegie recitals of 1958, ten items of encore were sung.[173] The singer's choice of encores was as diverse as his main program repertoire. In reviewing a Hartford, Connecticut, recital Carl Lindstrom commented on the "three salmagundian groups of songs whose mixed nature was accentuated by generously given encores of similarly assorted nature."[174] This unusual emphasis placed on the encore section allowed Robeson to connect with audiences through the joint recollecting of specific song-moments of his career, and as the conventionally less formal moment of a recital it encouraged greater artist-audience interaction. One instance of congregational singing was recorded at the 1958 Carnegie Hall recitals. At the start of the penultimate verse of the spiritual "We Are Climbing Jacob's Ladder," Robeson interrupts his own singing: "We are . . ." he sings, but breaks off to invite the audience to "Join me" in song, and then continues singing ". . . climbing Jacob's ladder" (1:45).[175] In doing this, Robeson connects with the audience, and the listeners-become-singers join Robeson as a community of "soldiers in this fight," to borrow Robeson's altered lyrics for the spiritual. Such moments, legion in Robeson's performance history, allow for a participatory, potentially transformative, "dimension of belonging."[176] Robeson begins the final verse of "Jacob's Ladder" in a hushed *sotto voce* (at 2:20), compelling his auditors to listen closely, to become more intimate in their communal performance. The massed singing then leads to a thunderous climax, and the Robeson-audience voice becomes pure sound stripped of audible word (2:52–2:56). It is tempting to hear this as the dissolution of Robeson's self into the (concert) community, a final gesture of affiliation and unification. Such was the experience of one fan's listening of the live

170   PAUL ROBESON'S VOICES

recording. She rhapsodized about the "mystic overtones" that "lift[ed] the Spiritual far beyond mere song," sympathetically hearing what another fan referred to as the "singing audience" as an act of communing: "The big crowd felt that transcending, fusing something that made them one with Robeson and his winning conquering power . . . the conglomerate-whole of that American-ized assembly knew brotherhood."[177] I am reminded again of Redmond's reading of Robeson's practice as vibration. The type of call-and-response technique, evident in Robeson's concert congregational singing, is an example of what Redmond calls the Black antiphonal method: "as Robeson sings to the world and they affirmatively reply in kind": "His vibration was often the initial call or catalyst that brought them together, while theirs affirmed his recognition of a laboring world coordinated in its pursuit for unity."[178]

As with Robeson's internationalism, his communal singing had several strands of influence. The first context of communal singing is the Black congregational ideal. Eslanda wrote of his youth: "He led the singing in church with his big, unmanageable, but beautifully moving bass voice, and was often carried away by the religious emotion which swept the congregation with the music. He became an essential part of the church, and, in turn, the church, the music, and the people became an essential part of him."[179] Kate Baldwin has noted that Robeson's concerts were a collective ceremony, in which "ritualized participation [was] an affirmative project" drawn from the singer's childhood experiences of his father's church. Baldwin concludes that "Robeson's concerts used the black congregational model and adapted it to an internationalist project. His process of performative reflexivity relied on the involvement of its audience members, each of whom could come to reflect on themselves . . . creating new social composites or a previously unthinkable coalitional alliance."[180] My description of Robeson's program as a reterritorialized cosmopolitan space in which, at times, he united audience members through collective singing chimes with these ideas.[181] But Robeson's embrace of the congregational model received more immediate impetus. One consequence of the singer's blacklisting in the 1950s was that concert halls increasingly shut their doors to the singer, as the "Don't Still His Voice!" poster for a birthday concert in 1952 makes plain (see Figure 4.3).

Not able to sustain a conventional recital career under such conditions, Robeson managed, often with difficulty, to continue singing in alternative venues: in the Black church, at union events, on college campuses, at civil

Figure 4.3. Poster for Gala Birthday Concert, New York, May 8, 1952. Paul Robeson Collection, microfilm 4. The Schomburg Center for Research in Black Culture, New York Public Library.

rights demonstrations.[182] The singer spoke about this turn of events at the second Peace Arch concert of 1953:

> Whenever I go into a city . . . The wrath of all the powers that be descends upon one single poor minister who wants to give me his church, or descends upon the people who rent the halls. They are told by all the forces in America, the strongest business forces . . . told that banks would no

172   PAUL ROBESON'S VOICES

longer honor their mortgages. Everything, to keep just one person from appearing in a concert in this church, or this hall.[183]

One can imagine that reconnecting with Black churches, and their performance practices, during this time must have suggested anew the possibility of incorporating congregational singing into his concert practice. One outcome of Robeson's outreach to the Black church community at this time was the record *Solid Rock: Favorite Hymns of My People*, released c. 1954. The singer's notes accompanying the LP acknowledged that the spirituals were no longer popularly sung but "presented by concert soloists" like himself. In the Black church, "it is the hymn rather than the spiritual that is sung by the people." Scholars of Black sacred music concur. Patricia Woodard notes not only that by the mid-twentieth century African American congregations had "left the spiritual behind," but that "educated and upwardly mobile African Americans embraced hymn singing" while eschewing the emerging gospel tradition and its emphasis on the "service of feeling."[184] Like the spirituals Robeson had championed since the start of his concert career, hymns were a part of his upbringing; indeed, claimed Robeson, they were "the first songs that I knew." And he continued to sing them in church later in life, at the Mother AME Zion Church in Harlem, New York, at which his brother the Reverend Benjamin C. Robeson was pastor, and he was an active member.[185]

Robeson acknowledged the significance of the church by beginning and ending his comeback concert tour of 1958 at the Mother AME Zion Church. It was, the singer stated, a concert of thanks, "back home where I began," for the hospitality and succor of Mother Zion and the Black church at large during the time of state and public hostility. The singer concluded the June 1 concert with a performance of "Jacob's Ladder," the spiritual become hymn and which appeared on *Solid Rock*. In his performance of the hymn Robeson utilized the congregational model. Indeed, the Mother Zion audience-congregation joins in much earlier, in the second verse (at 0:38), than the Carnegie Hall audience had done and without audible prompt.[186] If the African American congregational tradition is in play here, it is a practice that had transferred to the civil rights movement's singing activities at the time. Bernice Johnson Reagon explains that most of the singing in the movement was congregational "in the tradition of the Afro-American folk church." The are several parallels with Robeson's church concerts. The Black church hosted the civil rights movement as it provided a venue for Robeson in the 1950s, with "activist songleaders," rather than church officers, conducting the singing and delivering the message. The songleader "raises the song [which is] caught by the congregants and raised higher into a full life," with an effective songleader being both organizer and musical leader, "the galvanizer, the person who starts the song and thus begins to pull together a temporary community formed in the process of that specific song rendition." In concert settings in which Robeson deployed the congregational model he functions something akin to a songleader.[187]

The Mother Zion concert was Robeson's final public performance in the United States. It was both a fitting and poignant swansong: celebrating the Black community and church as the birthground of his own singing and focusing on Black American song, it was more inward-looking, less cosmopolitan than his typical late career program. But if the hymn's message of "overcome" told a narrative of personal triumph—as a preface to the song Robeson told the audience that much of the hard struggle was over, and that his concert career was re-established—it was something of a pyrrhic victory: in the coming years state security would continue to surveil and harass the singer, and according to the biographic record psychologically and physically break the man, and so end his career. Neither was Robeson's fight—to "walk this . . . earth in unity" (4:25), he told the congregated, and which the collective performance of "Jacob's Ladder" expressed as a hope[188]—near done, as the struggles of the civil rights movement and against global capital gathered pace. It is tempting to hear the extreme *morendo*—the dying away of sound—that concludes Robeson's performance of the song as an expiration not only of the singer's breath but also, in the years immediately following, of his life as a singer and of his ideals.

The congregational model fulfilled a performance ideal that Robeson had long professed and aspired toward. Already in 1935, before he incorporated communal performance in his own concerts, he expressed the desire that "the artist should be in close contact with his audience," having been inspired by a visit to Moscow's Realistic Theater where he witnessed the audience "participating in the performance."[189] A few years later, collective singing would mark Robeson's own performances associated with the Spanish Civil War. Perhaps Robeson was inspired by hearing Busch's practice, in which the German singer performed with a soldiers' chorus in Spain. Another model of participatory singing can be found in the nascent American urban folk song movement of the early 1940s, with which Robeson would in time develop a loose relationship that is yet to be fully explored. From the outset, urban folkies developed a participatory aesthetic typified in the practice of

174   PAUL ROBESON'S VOICES

the Almanac Singers (1940–1943), which counted Pete Seeger as a founding member. The group's informality and conscientious nonprofessionalism provided a new sense of audience access, explains Robert Cantwell: "the entire performance space being redefined to bring audience and musicians together into active participation."[190] Years later, Seeger wrote to Robeson recalling a performance Seeger had given in Moscow, one that in repertoire and participatory aesthetic might have been given by the elder singer: "In Moscow I sang as a final encore a request: Joe Hill, and you would have been moved to hear people sing along with me on the last verse, repeating the first. How much I and all my generation owe to you!"[191] Such spontaneous audience participation was not uncommon in Robeson performances.

Several scholars have explored Robeson's connections to his audiences and how he effected these associations. Redmond describes Robeson as an "organizer": "the individual who brings workers into communion with one another around a more perfect vision and then mobilizes them in service of it." The thrust of her analysis turns on the lyrical alterations Robeson was well known for making to many of the songs he sang; the "zipper" song practice not uncommon in the folk and labor song traditions. Textual alterations "highlight Robeson's respect for the insider knowledge of his audience," demonstrating an "affinity for and engagement with the populations in attendance."[192] Robeson's messages, though often engaging global themes and audiences, were at the same time thus tailored to specific communities in local address.

The singer's revising of songs, especially their lyrical texts, to agree with his developing protest politics dates from the late 1930s and can be traced directly to his involvement in the Spanish Civil War. The best-known case of Robeson's revising of a song text is his performance of "Ol' Man River." On December 19, 1937, Robeson took part in a pro-Republican rally at the Royal Albert Hall in London, which drew a crowd of 12,000. It was reported that Robeson canceled another engagement to take part in the rally, an indication of his commitment to following the path of an engaged artist. The high point of the rally, according to one biographer, was his performance of "Ol' Man River." But for the first time, Robeson altered the song's words, transforming it from a "'white-person's spiritual'—a poignant lament of unchangeable fate—to a strident, unapologetic protest."[193] In Robeson's version "Ah gets weary an' sick of tryin' / Ah'm tired of livin' an' scared of dyin'" becomes the rallying cry "But I keep laughin' instead of cryin' / I must keep fightin' until I'm dyin.'" A Scottish volunteer soldier, Alec Park, heard Robeson's revision

A VOICE FOR THE PEOPLE   175

thus during the war: "Robeson rendered to us many of his songs, but he gave 'Old Man River' to new words, words of hope and struggle and not of as in the past defeatism and helplessness."[194] Robeson's involvement with the Spanish Civil War not only introduced him to the genre of war protest song as I discussed earlier, thereby expanding his repertoire, but it also provided a context for revising some of the repertoire that he had performed for some time, and in so doing articulating a more explicit position of protest.

A less well-known instance is Robeson's singing of "Join in the fight," a reworking of the spiritual "Heaven-bound Soldier." In its incarnation as "Join in the Fight" the song appeared in Busch's wartime songbook *Canciones de las Brigadas Internacionales*, accompanied by a portrait of Robeson.[195] As far as can be established, the Spanish Civil War was the first time the singer presented the spiritual in its new guise as political protest song. Carpentier recounts how Robeson gave the soldiers his "personal version" of the spiritual in Spain, an account that again serves as testament to Robeson's experiences and enactment of a wartime song aesthetic: protest (in the altered lyrics and "aggressive" style), communal singing, and united multinational audience:

> with us there were people from Jamaica, Australia, Canada and the Philippines, and even South Africans who, with their action in the Brigades, were fighting. . . . But soon, wherever they came from, everyone around me, carried away by the rhythm, by the almost liturgical repetition of a phrase, they joined the chorus, in groups, like an "amen" of religious office.

Robeson's rendition, Carpentier concluded, was at once aggressive, uniting, and signified "beyond borders" ("a la vez agresivo, unánime y fuera de fronteras").[196]

Robeson also connected with audiences by endeavoring to speak to fans in their language, and sing their songs in the vernacular. His felicity for languages, as I noted earlier, is well known. Probably dating to the time of his comparative studies in the early 1930s, he became a lifelong student of language, and something of a polyglot. As late as 1946 he professed a "secret ambition . . . to master languages at the rate of one a year": "This is my real hobby. I can't get away from it. Even on tours, I while away my travel hours studying languages. That's how I mastered Hebrew and Chinese."[197] In addition to including songs in the language(s) of the local audience on his recital programs, he recorded entire albums of works by local composers in the language of the listenership in the mid-1950s. It was, I suggest, Robeson's

176   PAUL ROBESON'S VOICES

experience of multilingual musicking during the Spanish Civil War, a function no doubt of the multinational makeup of the International Brigades, that led the singer not simply to program an increasing number of non-English-language songs in his recitals but to translate song lyrics for local audiences. Busch's *Canciones*, first published in Barcelona in 1937 by the Propaganda Committee of the Brigades, brought together Spanish songs and works in other languages representative of the soldiers' diverse national identities. Writing from Paris in 1938, the war correspondent Egon Kisch recalled that when Robeson sang from an improvised stage, soldiers joined in the refrain singing in their respective languages. The result was a war song performed "in twenty languages yet united/unanimous" ("en veinte lenguas y aun así, unánime").[198]

One consequence of this experience for Robeson's practice was that for English-speaking audiences the singer often presented foreign-language songs as macaronic texts. There is no evidence he did this prior to the Spanish Civil War. As early as 1940, critics commented on what was, at mid-century, unusual art song performance practice. Editor of *Musical America* Oscar Thompson noted the practice in a Carnegie Hall recital of 1940: "Songs that began with English words and ended in Russian, German or Spanish supplied a new solution for the translation problem at last night's recital. . . . This bilingual procedure is not one to be recommended to other vocalists, save as they may be concerned more with audience reaction than with the artistic integrity of the music in hand."[199] It became Robeson's practice to sing the first verse or two in English and the latter part of the song in the original language. This is how he presented, for instance, Smetana's "Svornost" at Carnegie Hall in 1958.[200] It was a telling tactic of cosmopolitanism: the English translation, often preceded by a spoken introduction to the song, served to familiarize listeners with the music, preparing them for the foreign text to come, and allowing them better to relate to the foreign. At the same time, as the song unfolded in performance it enabled a sharing of sentiment and message across languages and cultures, a feeling of unity, of "svornost." Meskimmon suggests that in the cosmopolitan imaginary the process of translation is not one of loss, but rather of generative desire: to connect across national, cultural, linguistic limits, across the historical residue that reinforces people's isolation.[201] Robeson's macaronic songs became contact zones, interfaces that brought difference into connection. In this regard, one critic noted that "his many world tours have given him such close kinship with the people that when he sings their songs in their original language he so completely

A VOICE FOR THE PEOPLE   177

lowers any barrier which might exist between the stage and the audience that each person in the auditorium feels that he personally is the recipient of each song."[202]

Such was the importance of the singer-audience connection that it was produced on record. For this reason, among others, many of Robeson's late recordings were live concert recordings. Ever particular about the sound of his recorded voice, as I explore in a later chapter, the singer was displeased with the quality of the field recording of the first Peace Arch concert of 1952 but wanted to salvage the event's unique atmosphere for the commercial record *I Came to Sing!* To this end, Robeson rerecorded the songs but the taped speeches and audience participation sounds from the concert were used.[203] The outcome is an aesthetically jarring work with low-fi quasi-canned applause spliced onto Robeson's studio recorded singing. But, as a review in *Sing Out!* noted, "the most impressive thing about this album, however, is the sound of 40, 000 people honouring our generation's greatest People's Artist with their presence and their response."[204] By employing an aesthetic of liveness the (sonic) presence of the people validates the identity of the People's Artist.

Historians of recorded sound have argued that the qualities of liveness in music performance are phenomenological rather than ontological, "they are not characteristics of the performance itself but things experienced and felt by performers and spectators." The liveness of *I Came to Sing!* permits its listeners to experience a sense of community through the audience-community that sounds on the record.[205] More specifically, and following Paul Sanden's typology of liveness in recorded music, *I Came to Sing!* is heard as live because it presents "corporeal liveness," in the collective sounding body of the concert audience, and "interactive liveness," between Robeson and his listeners.[206] Liveness, in this instance, is also a dimension of what Nicholas Cook has called the "musical diegesis" of recorded music.[207] It is necessary to compellingly narrate the People's Artist's connections to the masses and his ideology of brothering song. And it seems to have been properly heard. A Canadian fan wrote that she had played the record "countless times, lent it out to the neighbours, and had many people in to hear it. And how many tears of sympathy and comradeship it has stirred! It is impossible for me to describe the strength of that record and the bond of solidarity with which it reaches out to encompass all its listeners!"[208]

Cataloguing the many departures from standard recital practice at mid-century that Robeson developed by the time of his late-career performances

178 PAUL ROBESON'S VOICES

draws attention to their singularity. No less seasoned a concertgoer than Moses Smith, director of Columbia Masterworks, could thus write of a 1940 Carnegie Hall recital:

> what thrilled me as a professional and itinerant observer of concert hall proceedings for almost twenty years was the wholesome lack of stuffiness apparent in the selection and arrangement of the program, a stuffiness which is so commonly regarded as a necessity in connection with the conventional art recital. I was all the more thrilled by the enthusiastic response with which the enormous audience greeted your attitude.[209]

The distinctiveness of a Robeson recital was routinely commented on by critics: "It would be forcing a point to call this event a recital," opined Harold Schonberg, one of New York City's most influential commentators, of a later Carnegie concert.[210] In Robeson's "recital" the repertoire of brothering song was presented as a program of universal musics of the world to demonstrate a shared humanity, to foster cultural exchange and understanding, and was enacted by remaking the song recital group for cosmopolitan ends. And the extensive elaboration of the encore moment of the concert, inviting audiences to sing along, and singing in the vernacular, all served the purpose of community-making and friendship-building. Through these collective practices Robeson was able to voice the friendship fans heard in his singing. In short, through the novel format of the late recitals, the people's artist performed for the people.

5

Voices Politic

Soon after the hit song "Sonny Boy" charted at number one, Robeson recorded it in London in 1929, as had a slew of performers in the wake of Al Jolson's success with the song a year earlier.[1] The British society magazine *The Queen* (later rebranded as *Harper's Bazaar*) observed that Robeson was but the "latest to prostrate themselves before that horrid urchin . . . that insufferable but unavoidable Sonny Boy," concluding that "Mr. Paul Robeson with his magnificent bass voice . . . might so much better serve better purposes." Thus did Robeson's choice of repertoire receive bad press. So did his performance. The weekly trade magazine *Variety* was of the opinion that Robeson's "Sonny Boy" lacked "the boff and sock which makes Jolson what he is." Robeson sung it "straight, sans color, sans pathos, sans nuance." It was delivered, the reviewer noted disappointingly, "conventionally." *Britannia*'s summation of the disc was perhaps the most pointed: in singing "Sonny Boy," Robeson "shows that he is white, clear white inside."[2] This is an instance of the bad music I summoned in the Introduction: trivial song, humdrum singing. But the hearing of Robeson's singing as "white" is interesting for another reason. In the 1920s and into the 1930s the critics' collective ear invariably heard Robeson's singing as Black, and for a variety of reasons: some invented, others based to varying degrees in sonic reality, as I discussed in earlier chapters. As Robeson aspired to an internationalist politics, expanded his repertoire toward world song, and developed a musical cosmopolitanism, his voice, over time, was heard increasingly less as (only) Black.[3] What was it about Robeson's "Sonny Boy" that prompted the *Britannia* reviewer to reverse the racially received wisdom of the time on Robeson's singing? There are probably several signs of whiteness we could identify. By this time Robeson's voice had begun to bear the marks of formal training, and in the history of vocal criticism the trained voice has often borne the qualification of whiteness.[4] Another marker is Robeson's pronunciation, upon which I dwell at some length in what follows, and which leads to a consideration of accent. Mladen Dolar identifies accent as one of the modes by which we most commonly access the voice and, one might add, assess the voice.[5] Listening to

---

Paul Robeson's Voices. Grant Olwage, Oxford University Press. © Oxford University Press 2024.
DOI: 10.1093/oso/9780197637470.003.0006

180 PAUL ROBESON'S VOICES

accent compels us to reckon with the materiality of the voice, with the voice's sounds. Armed with acoustic knowledge, I want to listen anew to the people's artist, and, more broadly, consider the relationship of the voice to the domain of the political.

Pronouncing Accents

From the late 1920s, when Robeson first moved to Britain, and during the ensuing decade when he was resident there, instances of certain types of rhoticity (that is, the pronunciation of r's) increase in his singing. Robeson's "Sonny Boy" offers an example of this, albeit in a tentative and inconsistent usage. As he sings "For me right here on earth," which leads into the refrain (1:32–1:57), a casual listening makes plain the several occasions Robeson inserts an /r/—"for," "here," and "dear" receive articulated r's—in what are termed postvocalic environments in which the historical /r/ has been lost in standard spoken English, and in some American English accents notably African American and East Coast speech.[6] Robeson's rhoticity is not simply a function of vocal modality, of enunciation in song (rather than in speech). In his earliest recordings, of the mid-1920s, Robeson seldom articulates r's in general, nor specifically provides terminal r's. Nor are the r's as prominent in contemporaneous recordings by American popular singers, such as those made by Gene Austin and Ruth Etting who both recorded "Sonny Boy" in 1928. In singing "For me right here on earth," Austin, for example, concludes "for" with a long vowel rather than an /r/; both he and Etting, as we might expect, provide a "linking r" for "here" to the next vowel-initial word "on"; and while Etting systematically provides terminal r's, hers are the conventional spoken r's of what would become standard American English or the "network standard," called the alveolar approximate <ɹ>. Robeson's, by contrast, are trilled or rolled r's (alveolar trills <r>). At this point in time his use of the trilled r is inconsistent: "promise" gets the treatment prominently while "stray" escapes.[7]

It is difficult to know the extent of the use of the rolled r and especially its reduced version, called the flapped or tapped r (as in "veRy"), in older forms of British English received pronunciation (RP), a term given currency by the foremost English phonetician of the day Daniel Jones, and which, in the early editions of Jones's *English Pronouncing Dictionary*, was variously referred to as the dominant accent of Southern England, public school English, and

VOICES POLITIC 181

that which was socially acceptable. Jones reported "some use of a rolled or semi-rolled (flapped) <r> in many words" for the early decades of the twentieth century.[8] Soon after his permanent move to London, Robeson moved among the city's elite society: he acquired an apartment in St. John's Wood and was "received," he recalled, "in English society . . . mostly 'high society'— the upper-class people . . . and I found myself moving a great deal in the most aristocratic circles."[9] Robeson was thus surrounded by elite British pronunciation of the type Jones documented and prescribed in his *Pronouncing Dictionary*. In America, the rolled r was not a marker of regional or racial identity but was associated with British and upper-class speech. Jonathan Greenberg argues that Black orators' and popular singers' cultivation of the tapped r, a "prestige-based phonetic marker," demonstrated "through physical action the ideology of uplift," and notes that the rolled r was part of a style acquired through training, in singing, acting, and even elocution.[10]

Pronounced forms of rhoticity in singing and actor's speech, specifically in theatrical declamation, were not uncommon in Britain too.[11] Historical recordings of British thespians from the first half of the century allow us to hear this clearly, perhaps no more than in *Shakespearian Records by John Gielgud* made for the Linguaphone Institute, London, as a model of correct pronunciation in the 1930s. Robeson owned several of Gielgud's records.[12] The singer, in his own words, was "a real gramophone fan" and had an impressive and varied collection of records that he used for comparative research and language learning, among other things.[13] Gielgud's voice on the Linguaphone records and on stage—for Robeson saw Gielgud in *Hamlet* at the Old Vic while Robeson himself was in rehearsal for *Othello* at the Savoy— must surely have been on Robeson's mind when the singer played Othello in London in 1930 for the first of several times in his career.[14] Robeson's Desdemona then was Peggy Ashcroft, who would work in Gielgud's companies for several years (and with whom Robeson had an affair).[15] This network of vocal correspondences with elite British actors encountered in the professional theater within which Robeson worked is one line of possible influence on his developing voice.

There is no recording of Robeson's portrayal of Othello in 1930, but his participation in the production gives us insight into his stance on English in Britain.[16] Theatre critic C. B. Purdom summed up the problem of Robeson's Othello for a British audience: "Here we have a negro playing a Moor in a part written for an Englishman, in an English company. This is matter for endless controversy."[17] In the terms of Purdom's formulation, however,

182 PAUL ROBESON'S VOICES

critics overwhelmingly focused on the problematic of race, of a "negro playing a Moor," rather than the matter of an American playing Shakespeare in England.[18] It was, I suggest, in part Robeson's attempt at mastering the language of thespian England broadly conceived that forestalled such criticism. Robeson spent months, he told the London *Daily Herald*, "striving to eradicate his American twang," which he did by several means.[19] One was to receive coaching in "his English accent" from the fashionable London voice teacher Amanda Aldridge, daughter of the American-born British thespian Ira Aldridge, a noted Othello of the nineteenth century. We might assume that aspects of the histrionic style of oratory and acting that dominated the British stage, including matters of pronunciation, were passed on to Robeson through the Aldridge lineage.[20] He also attempted to make sense of English pronunciation, and to facilitate his learning thereof, through familiarizing strategies, both speculative and practical. He informed the press, for instance, that he had a "fortunate" advantage in learning the English accent because, he claimed, the "negro accent is nearer the English than the ordinary American is. In such words as 'here,' for instance, and 'service,' the sound which negroes give the words is much akin to the English sound."[21] The veracity of Robeson's argument of phonemic proximity is not here important. His logic demonstrates a will to connect with British English; and was another instance of the comparative method that informed his political internationalism and aesthetic cosmopolitanism I explored in the previous chapter.

A more practical strategy that Robeson employed in his attempt to acquire an English acting accent was to draw on early English orthographic practices. In an interview with the *Evening Standard* the actor spoke about the "difficulty of my American accent": "English ears naturally find it offensive when an American says 'noo' for 'new' and 'doo' for 'dew'; 'can't' (to rhyme with rant) instead of your 'can't' with its long vowel. I felt that it was more of an ordeal to play Othello in London than to play it in New York."[22] Robeson's particular problem, it seems, was vowel sound recall, and his solution, which involved a sort of phonological recoding of accent, was to learn his part from a facsimile of the original *Othello*, which aided him in remembering "the way to pronounce [the] words":

> I did some research. I bought Shakespeare's plays with their original spelling. I read back beyond Shakespeare: Wyatt and Spenser and other Elizabethans. And then I understood why you put in all those vowels

VOICES POLITIC   183

Americans leave out. The old way of spelling "new" was "nieue," "dew' was 'dieu," "can't" and "chance" were "caunt" and "chaunce." In time you dropped the vowels; from your written tongue but kept them in your spoken one.[23]

Robeson's efforts seem to have paid off with his studied English accent favorably received. Few of the reviews focused on vocal failings, with those that did drawing attention to the monotony of his recitations rather than problems of pronunciation. The *Daily Herald* thus headlined a profile of Robeson's role in the production as "Paul Robeson's New Accent," concluding that he spoke "with a cultivated English accent."[24]

In a rare television interview, probably from the time of his third performance as Othello for the Royal Shakespeare Company in 1959, the actor rehearsed his method for learning the language. The segue Robeson makes in the interview from pronunciation in *Othello* to performing English art song indicates how his concern for accent extended to his singing. In the TV interview Robeson specifically mentions working with Roger Quilter, an influential artist mentor to Robeson and a catalyst for his learning of English folk and art song as I discussed in the previous chapter.[25] Three sources—a memoir, a performing score, and a record—suggest that pronunciation, and especially the ubiquitous rolled r, was central to Robeson's learning of English song. The memoir is that of Robeson's accompanist's (Lawrence Brown's) student, Ruth Reese, and suggests the long reach of Quilter's influence in performing English art song well into the century. Upon retiring from accompanying Robeson, Brown had settled in New York to teach voice and piano. When Reese left for Europe in the early 1950s, Brown arranged a study schedule in London for her with Quilter, among others. Reese recalled that the "last thing Larry said to me was, 'You must learn to sing in the King's English. Say hello to Madam Aldridge and Sir Roger Quilter,'" noting that Quilter "would help me perfect my English diction." Quilter was, Reese reminisced, "somewhat of a collector of famous people."[26]

Brown's and Robeson's performing copy of Quilter's "Now Sleeps the Crimson Petal" (published in 1904) suggests that much like Robeson's turn to early English spelling to learn pronunciation in *Othello*, he required learning aids in perfecting his English diction in song. To this end Robeson penciled in phonetic guides to pronunciation, a practice not limited to Quilter's songs. On both occasions that "nor" starts a phrase—"Nor waves the cypress..." (m. 6) and "Nor winks the gold fin ..." (m. 8)—the phonetic spelling of "nawr" is written in above the lyrics (see Figure 5.1). It is a composite sign to elongate

184   PAUL ROBESON'S VOICES

Figure 5.1. Roger Quilter, "Now Sleeps the Crimson Petal." Page 1 of Robeson and Brown's performing score. Lawrence Brown Scores, Box 8, New York Public Library for the Performing Arts.

the vowel and to roll the terminal r, which Robeson adheres to in the 1939 recording of the song. His singer's commitment to rhoticity is particularly conspicuous in his enunciation of the r's, quite elaborately trilled, in "porphyry" and "firefly." This was established practice in English singers' pronunciation for the first several decades of the century.[27] The English tenor Gervase Elwes, a keen supporter of Quilter and English art song and the first promoter of "Now Sleeps the Crimson Petal," gives similar articulation to the r's

VOICES POLITIC   185

in his 1916 recording of the song, as does John McCormack in his recording of a decade later.[28] While Robeson's recording of "Now Sleeps" does not bear all the hallmarks of these early twentieth-century voices—such as their temporal freedom and, to us, exaggerated rhetorical delivery—he does retain many aspects of their pronunciation. In short, during the time Robeson lived in England he learned to sing (and orate) in its received, elite language. (It is surely not insignificant that Quilter, Elwes, McCormack, and Harry Plunket Greene, the foremost authority in singing in English, were all of the gentry.)

None of this is perhaps surprising given the location of and contexts for Robeson's life and work I've outlined. His move to Britain was also accompanied by a shift in his primary market—a varied British audience—and a move from the American recording corporation Victor to the British HMV, such that he increasingly incorporated diverse British songs into both his concert repertoire and record catalog throughout the 1930s. Robeson had become so part of the English musical scene that his recording of *Jerusalem* was, for *Gramophone*, exempt from the magazine's dictum that for "a foreigner to sing Parry's *Jerusalem* almost invites a charge of blasphemy."[29] We might expect, then, that Robeson would attempt to perform English song, whether a national song, hymn-tune ("Nearer My God to Thee"), a Quilter or John Ireland art song (such as "Sea Fever"), or a folk song or ballad, in an English accent. But the recoding of his singer's accent affected (perhaps infected) his performance also of American song. We heard this, in a limited way, in "Sonny Boy," and it informed all manner of American song Robeson performed and texts he recited during this time.

How pronunciation colored Robeson's accent is evident in his recorded recitation of fellow Harlem Renaissance artist and friend Langston Hughes's short poem "Minstrel Man," which speaks of the slave's illusory mask and the pain it conceals. Topically, the poem served well Robeson's purpose of highlighting the effects of (global) slavery and authoritarianism, and it first appeared on a record the singer cut for the relief effort for children displaced by the Spanish War.[30] It is well known that Hughes's aesthetics was grounded in African American vernacular traditions, and his poetry is noted for drawing on Black American musics, notably the blues.[31] By contrast, Robeson's presentation of the subject matter is distinctly unplaced and, to an extent, raceless, in large part because of accent. He thus tends to lengthen the <a> vowel toward the British /ɑː/ sound in "laughter" (0:02), "after" (0:09), and "dancing" (0:21). But the elongated vowels also seem to sound short of the English ideal—plainly heard in "dancing"—and rather fall somewhere

186 PAUL ROBESON'S VOICES

between standard American and English accents. Indeed, in many instances the overall sound of Robeson's performing voice from the late 1930s on approximates what has been termed a mid-Atlantic or transatlantic accent. This was not a vernacular dialect but rather a hybrid of standard American and English received pronunciation, prevalent from the 1930s to mid-century, and cultivated by North American actors, broadcasters, and the Northeastern elite.[32] Like English received pronunciation, the mid-Atlantic dialect marked class and placelessness, in that it aspired to be a standard international accent. It is likely that Robeson incorporated aspects of the elite English pronunciation he learned for the stage and in song during the 1930s into an international American sound. Robeson's voice thus aligned with his developing politics: the mid-Atlantic English accent performs Robeson's emerging political internationalism. It is an international voice.

Masking Dialect and Preacherly Tones

The international voice also negates—and critiques—what Henry Louis Gates Jr. has described as the "racist image of Minstrel Man as absence of intellection."[33] As the singing Black man, Robeson unperforms the stereotype by, in part, performing in a cultivated international accent. (The star was all too aware of the stylistics of stereotyping, complaining of the "habit of 'minstrelising' the negro."[34] Indeed, throughout the twentieth century some Black classical singers have deemed "singing dialect in concert spirituals offensive and evocative of racist ideology.")[35] As Robeson revalued the spiritual, claiming it as world music, so he appropriated the matter of the Black experience—slavery—and revoiced it through an international accent as a topic of global concern. Both the worlding of the spiritual and internationalizing of the voice had been accomplished by roughly the same time, the late 1930s.

The poem "Minstrel Man" first appeared in the journal *Crisis* in 1925 and was reproduced in *The New Negro*, and as such was an exemplary product of the Harlem Renaissance. Robeson was acutely aware of debates on the proper representation of Black artistic expression—"the exact form that the signifier should take," in Gates's words[36]—and categorized the efforts of Harlem Renaissance artists into "two main streams": "One, whose outstanding exponents are Roland Hayes and Countee Cullen, abandons its Negro sources and merges in the torrent of the general scene; the other, best

VOICES POLITIC   187

represented by Langston Hughes and James Weldon Johnston, turn to those sources peculiar to the Negro for their inspiration." For Robeson, both were justified depending on the artist's worldview, a position not inconsistent given his own indebtedness to Hayes while at the same time being held as the counterexample to Hayes, as I explored in chapter 2.[37] And as I argued in the previous chapter, it was, in Robeson's words, the "psychological ... interior source of inspiration" of Black art, rather than the "anthropological" mode of "studying African arts and incorporating it," that came to inform Robeson's practice.[38] The singer was, therefore, perhaps less interested in the "ideology of mimesis" of the Black oral voice, to borrow further from Gates; in other words, he was more interested in its substance than its styles.[39] This is especially so for the 1930s on, after Robeson's initial focus in the mid-to-late 1920s on the spiritual and his association with the Renaissance, and from the time of his comparative thinking and his emergent internationalist politics. It is also evident in his ambivalent voicing of Black American dialect.[40]

Marti K. Newland reminds us that

> The subject of diction in black music has been a persistent theme in examinations of African American experience and identity for over one hundred and fifty years. Whether written on the page or vocalized in speech and song, the representation and performance of African Americans' language has politicized debates about the humanity, cognitive ability, creative assertions and specificity of black artists, listeners, readers, writers, and critics alike.[41]

Robeson's performance of Black texts was no different. The Renaissance poetry he recited, such as "Minstrel Man" and James Weldon Johnson's *God's Trombones*, avoided dialect in its poetic diction. This was not unusual given the connotations of dialect, which functioned as "the linguistic sign both of human bondage (as origin) and of the continued failure of 'improvability' or 'progress.'" For these and other reasons Johnson could claim by the early 1930s that "the passing of traditional dialect as a medium for Negro poets is complete."[42] In the "Preface" to *God's Trombones*, extracts of which Robeson broadcast for the BBC in 1931,[43] Johnson questioned the validity of dialect for *God's Trombones*. Dialect was too limited in its expressive capabilities, and the Black poet required a "form that is freer and larger than dialect, but which will still hold the racial flavor." For his source of inspiration Johnson turned

188 PAUL ROBESON'S VOICES

to the Black "folk sermon" as practiced by the "old-time Negro preacher" who "stepped out from [dialect's] narrow confines when they preached":

> They were all saturated with the sublime phraseology of the Hebrew prophets and steeped in the idioms of King James English, so when they preached and warmed to their work they spoke another language, a language far removed from traditional Negro dialect. It was really a fusion of Negro idioms with Bible English.[44]

One can imagine how these sentiments, which acknowledged the Black preaching arts, chimed with Robeson's own experience grounded in a family history of preaching. Perhaps for this reason a curious work entered Robeson's repertory, albeit briefly: Will Marion Cook's "Exhortation," introduced to Robeson's recital programs in 1929. For one reviewer, "Exhortation," which "purports to be the essence of a typical negro sermon," had "from end to end . . . a hollow and artificial ring."[45] Peppered with dialect, it is an awkward amalgam of a declamatory recitative-like introduction, "to be sung with unction and religious fervour," instructs the score, an uptempo popular tune, and a concluding ecstatic "A – A – A – A – A – A –men!" Departing from Johnson's description of the preacher's language and his injunction to poets to turn their pens from dialect, "Exhortation" places dialect front and center—"Kase ef you kaint 'turn good fu' evil" is a typical line—and recalls Hayes's critique of the exaggerated use thereof, as "vulgarities and malefactions . . . superficial parodies, because they simply fail to reach the profound religious expression which is the very heartbeat of the Aframerican religious folksong."[46] Unusually, Robeson performs much of the dialect in "Exhortation," although it is both unevenly sounded and voiced in the terms of the singer's English he was acquiring at the time: in the phrase "Turn roun' an' han' him de odder" Robeson returns the elided d's and rolls the terminal r (0:13–0:20).[47] One reason for Robeson's singing the work is that its expansive range and dramatic turns lent it to the voice training with which he busied himself at the time; that "Exhortation" fell from his repertoire two years later as he pronounced against the canonical art song repertoire is perhaps not a coincidence. And its dialect must have troubled him too, and for several reasons. Even as it aspired to be a serious composition indebted to the vernacular preaching tradition—the sheet music bore the subtitle "A Negro Sermon"—its aesthetic proximity to minstrelsy is all too obvious.

VOICES POLITIC 189

Furthermore, the tonal production and enunciation requirements of Robeson's voice-in-training clashed with dialect's own sound demands. These competing claims to the voice are clearly heard in Robeson's recording of Avery Robinson's "Hail de Crown" which appeared as the A-side of the "Exhortation" record (H.V.M. B 3409). The full tone in the high register, breathing for the long line, and singer's diction combine to suggest that Robeson is more concerned with 'proper' singing than in paying attention to the particulars of dialect. Most obviously the titular "de" is returned to "the" because the latter's softness is more conducive to sustaining the flow of tone. In similar vein, Newland comments on the university jubilee tradition's "varying adherence" to performing vernacular language in the singing of spirituals in a voice practiced in classical voice pedagogy: in the accurate performance of standard English, in diction and text clarity, the "singers perform a 'properness,'" but their "overarticulation" of consonants is such that it has become a feature of vernacular practice, which amongst other things, represents "bourgeois aspirations." Singing thus "embodies a critique of the objectification of their singing as essentially 'black' while performing blackness," a process heard in their diction.[48] Robeson too did not reject Black American dialect in performance fully. He sang dialect songs, particularly in his early career—some are of the order of bad music—and he did not always refuse to sound the phonetically inscribed instructions of dialect lyrics in preference for standard English. J. Rosamond Johnson's "Li'l Gal," which Robeson sang throughout his career, provides one such instance.

Based on a poem of the same title by Paul Laurence Dunbar, the "most accomplished black dialect poet,"[49] the lyrics of Johnson's song exhibit in isolated instances already a very slight shift away from Dunbar's more marked vernacularisms: the poem's "unnerneaf" is moderated to "underneaf" in the song. By and large, Robeson's 1931 recording sticks to Johnson's lyrics but on occasion it strays yet further from dialect. For "Dey's an' hones' hea't a-beatin' underneaf dese rags o' mine" Robeson inserts the r in "dey's" and "hea't" and returns "th" to "-neaf" and "dese" (1:38–1:46). And by the time of a 1957 recording, when his mature voice and mid-Atlantic singer's accent were dominant, the dialect is further unsung with "beatin'" and "o'" the only remnants of what in the original poem was a vernacular laden phrase (1:40–1:47).[50] Even in dialect-marked texts like "Li'l Gal" we can hear Robeson's ambivalence toward dialect in performance, and clearly Robeson did not follow too carefully Johnson's injunction that the spirituals "lose in charm when they are sung in straight English."[51]

190 PAUL ROBESON'S VOICES

Suspicion of the minstrelizing effects of dialect, combined with the dictates of vocal training and acquisition of elite English accents, served to distance the singer from a more complete performance of dialect. But signifiers of the Black voice could take other forms, such as the Black preaching arts. And perhaps the defining feature of the Black preacher was his voice. The vocality of Black preaching was thus much thematized in Harlem Renaissance discourse and artistic practice. The very title of Johnson's book of poems, *God's Trombones*, metaphorizes the preacher as sound: the old-time preacher Johnson heard and who inspired the poet

> brought into play the full gamut of his wonderful voice, a voice—what shall I say?—not of an organ or a trumpet, but rather a trombone, the instrument possessing above all others the power to express the wide and varied range of emotions encompassed by the human voice—and with greater amplitude. He intoned, he moaned, he pleaded—be blared, he crashed, he thundered.

Thus was the Black preacher—as voice—God's instrument. Robeson surely felt an affinity for Johnson's sound-orientated art. It accommodated his own vocal arts within a family and racial genealogy of preaching, and provided aesthetic justification for the singer's practice. Much like the "old-time Negro preacher," Robeson delighted in "the sonorous, mouth-filling phrase," modulating from "a sepulchral whisper to a crashing thunder clap," as Johnson put it.[52] Robeson's annotations to the script for the 1931 radio broadcast of his recitation of *God's Trombones* bear this out. Pencil markings guide Robeson to stress words and phrases, to pause, and to break the line. Verbal directions clutter the margin: "lift," "back to myself," "up," "change voice," and "sing." This is another instance of the fluidity of spoken and sung modes in Robeson's practice. And the instruction to sing occurs, notably, at the line "I am the Lord God Almighty."[53] Critics certainly noted the parallels between Johnson's sound aesthetic and Robeson's voicings: "The great Negro bass has a voice like the title of the late James Weldon Johnson's book, 'God's Trombone.' It is a voice as sonorous and full and deep as a prophetic brass choir, but it is capable of the utmost intimacy and sympathetic expression as well."[54] We might thus revisit and extend my earlier proposition: where Robeson's international English accent refused the Black voice of dialect, his vocal arts sounded in the tradition of the Black preacher's voice. In the remainder of this chapter I parse this formulation by drawing on Dolar's

VOICES POLITIC   191

distinction between accent, timbre, and intonation, the three modes by which we most commonly access the voice.

Vocal Resonances

Accent, Dolar contends, is "a distraction, or even an obstacle, to the smooth flow of signifiers" that are communicated by the medium of the voice; accent inhibits the hermeneutics of understanding. Refocusing Dolar's argument, we might add that the voice's accent also supplements understanding.[55] The (un)performance of African American dialect encourages a certain understanding of race, just as Robeson's endeavor to sing in other dialects, in Scots Lallans for example, and in non-English languages was heard as an act of cosmopolitan friendship. Because accent may interfere with meaning, it is often avoided by the voice. Here we find the reign of the "official voice," a "ruling norm . . . an accent which has been declared a non-accent in a gesture which always carries heavy social and political connotations."[56] Robeson's English accents—standard British and mid-Atlantic—are the sounds of an elite voice, an official voice par excellence; and similarly the system of art singing through which his voice was partly trained was also productive of an elite musical voice. These accents and the singing voice that carried them are also the sounds of an international voice that enabled the singer to communicate with a multitude of peoples. Through these means I suggested that Robeson's official voice performed his internationalist politics for a global audience. But the official English voice also purports to be a universal (Western) voice, the carrier of the humanist ethics the singer espoused in his cosmopolitanism as well as the imperialist politics he denounced. We might thus observe an aporia: in one listening, we hear the dominant accent of Robeson's voice, and, in another listening, the voice of the "people's artist," as the Aberdeen *Evening Express* noted: his "voice is more and more becoming the voice of the soil and the voice of the people."[57] Kate Baldwin's reading of Robeson's folk art as a "minority discourse" illustrates this problem well.

For Baldwin, Robeson's "folk-based performative praxis" entailed an intermixing of the "particularist and internationalist," the central principle of which was the juxtaposition of "radical differences," exemplified in the singer's performance of multinational folk ballads and, one should add, other varied repertory. Moreover, Robeson's folk praxis expressed an antidote, functioning as a minority discourse to the marginalization of "peripheralized

192   PAUL ROBESON'S VOICES

peoples," and recalls Pablo Neruda's ode to the singer as the voice of the silenced: "you have been the voice of man . . . the voice of all the silent."[58] Baldwin argues that Robeson's practice achieved this by inserting "otherness into previously denied territories of identity and selfhood" and "opened up a space [of] radical heterogeneity." In short, Robeson's performances "asserted a counterclaim to non-identity" against "the oppressive effects of Western philosophies of identity" and "collective whiteness."[59] A convincing case may be made for what Baldwin calls Robeson's "counteraesthetics" in several domains of the singer's practice—the multinational repertoire, innovations in concert practice, and foregrounding of the folk ideal. This reading chimes with my own presentation of Robeson's musical cosmopolitanism proposed in the previous chapter. But like most discussions of Robeson's folk aesthetics, Baldwin does not listen much to the sounds of his voice.

There is an argument to be made for folk song as a minority discourse in the field of the art song recital. In several senses Robeson's simple singing, the anatomy of which I outlined in chapter 3, aligns with, and in part constructs, the image of the singer as a folk artist. The singer's rejection of artfulness, partial avoidance of a heavy dramatic voice (the dominant episteme of art singing in the twentieth century), and the apparent freedom from vocal effort placed Robeson's voice at some remove from classical singing and its elite contexts of consumption. In short, Robeson's voice did not fit easily with the dominant practices and sounds of art singing. His singing also supplemented them, for example in its stylistic expression of Black vocalism. One such practice is what the literature on African American singing calls "melodic embellishment," a practice documented since the start of performances of the concert spiritual, by Black scholars and white ethnomusicologists alike. In his essay on the spirituals, Alain Locke drew attention to the "actual mechanics of the native singing, with its syllabic quavers, the off-tones and tone glides, the improvised interpolations," and Natalie Curtis-Burlin itemized the "vocal peculiarities" she heard in the singing of spirituals similarly as "the subtle embellishment of grace-notes, turns and quavers, and the delightful little upward break in the voice."[60] In these early "scientific" endeavors, Robeson's singing was taken as evidence. His recording of the spiritual "On Ma Journey" (1926) was the first in a series of examples Milton Metfessel used to demonstrate an alternative method of notation, called phonophotography, in order to describe African American singing "as it has never been described before." Metfessel's graphs illustrate "the excessive sliding of the Negro voice," the "peculiar grace-notes, voice-breaks, and sudden slides," which led him

VOICES POLITIC   193

to conclude that "one of the most obvious differences between Negro and artistic singing is in the attack and release of tones," which the Black singer achieved in "variety of type, extent, and duration."[61] But Robeson's vocal embellishments in the 1926 recording of "On Ma Journey" are, if not absent, somewhat muted, not abundant nor obviously audible (in part perhaps because of the pace at which he sings). Rather, crisp attack, clean approach, and discrete pitches are foregrounded, at least if we listen in comparison to later recordings made in the 1950s. Taken at an easy pace, Robeson's voice thus slides around in the 1957 outing of "On My Journey."[62] And if we listen closely to Robeson's only recording of "Amazing Grace" (1954), embellishments abound. A short catalog of these makes the point.

Robeson uses approach slides, although with restraint, and upper notes approached with a leap are more typically given a clean attack with large leaps seldom receiving slides. The hummed glide up (listen to the "-nd" of "found" [0:45–0:47]) is a Robeson favorite. The singer falls off pitches (quite a lot) at the ends of words and phrases, to liaise with the next word or phrase of a lower pitch, especially in descending lines (e.g., several consecutive off glides are prominently heard in the movement of "gra-ce," "ho-w," and "swe-et" [0:14–0:21], with the glide effected on the second phoneme). There are also off glides, what one might call an emphatic glide, for terminal notes at the end of some phrases (as in "me" in the line "that saved a soul like me" [0:31–0:33]). Ornaments appear with some frequency: the elaborate grace note on "be-" of "believe" (1:45–1:46), and added notes (such as that which the "-nd" of "found" receives [0:45–0:47]). The line "was blind but now I see" (0:47–1:00) is something of a microcosm of the variety and extent of Robeson's melodic embellishments. The phrase starts with an anacrusis approach slide on "was" as the voice moves to "blind"; adding a note to "blind," a third above on the second beat, and scooping up to it; followed by a microtonal glide off, called a "flatted tone," on the "-in' " of "blind" (the singer electing not to pronounce the "d"); with another quick descending glide on "but," this time a "straight-toned" glide as it occurs between two notes on the same syllable; which leads to a drawn out flatted tone on "now"; and concludes with a grace-note ornamentation in a cracked voice flourish as "I" leads to "see." These style elements have marked the singing of a long line of Black performers of spirituals.[63]

Robeson's singing of spirituals, then, partakes in and perpetuates a tradition of Black vocalism. He does so with propriety. The use of melodic embellishments is idiomatic, observing what Locke referred to as "the duty"

194   PAUL ROBESON'S VOICES

of the Black artist to maintain "spiritual kinship with the best traditions of this great folk art."[64] And if Robeson does not reserve embellishments exclusively for his singing of spirituals, they receive their fullest statement there, although they are more prominent in some songs than others. In his early concert singing the sounds of embellishment in his practice are subtle, even restrained. At this time, his voice was less certain, aspirant to be sure but still developing and in training. Perhaps the classical voice training of the 1920s and early 1930s muted a more robust presentation of Black style in Robeson's practice. By his late career, though, the style is striking and more pronounced. There are two possible reasons for this. By the 1950s, Robeson's was the voice of a mature singer, long settled, confident in its sounding and in artistic purpose. Moreover, as we saw in my account of Robeson's congregational singing, in the 1950s he had reconnected with the Black church, which provided safe harbor and a new audience during the time of his blacklisting. Singing in and for the church he introduced hymns to his repertoire: "Amazing Grace" appeared on the album *Solid Rock: Favorite Hymns of My People*. It is not unlikely that Robeson accommodated his singing to this context, and to the civil rights movement, singing for the people in a style familiar to and valued by them. Marian Anderson's performance of the African American tradition too was deepened during times of increased contact with Black communities.[65]

There are, however, other contexts to consider. As historians of art singing have noted, singing in the first half of the twentieth century involved extensive use of portamento, with pitch variation a primary means of expressivity.[66] We have only to listen to Robeson's recordings of "Now Sleeps the Crimson Petal" (1939 and 1957) to hear the scoops, sometimes "excessive" to contemporary ears, amid slides of various sorts. Another context is Robeson's thesis on the unity of talking and singing, specifically his argument that the genesis of folk song and art song based on folk music lay in spoken language. The singer's musings on what he called a "universal" theory of folk music, which received its fullest statement in the 1950s, included discussion on the influence of language on song. He concurred with Czech composer Leoš Janáček's "theories about the effect of speech of peoples . . . on their folk music and came to the conclusion that musical expression must be founded on the positive melodic and rhythmic elements of conversation." Exemplifying this practice for Robeson were Russian composers, and the "speaking-singing, singing-speaking" of the preacher and cantor in "any Negro church or in any Jewish Synagogue."[67] Robeson's declamatory style in his performance of Russian and Yiddish song (heard, e.g., in "Vi Azoi Lebt der Keyser" [early 1950s]) is thus as notable for its use of melodic embellishment as is his singing of spirituals and hymns.[68]

As so often with Robeson, his voice sounds complexly; he sings multivocally. The sources of otherness, to return to Baldwin's terms, we hear in Robeson's voice are overdetermined, and we should also attend to the otherness—an aural strangeness—of the historical forms of Robeson's practice. Even earlier styles of art singing, the "majority discourse" of the concert field, can sound foreign to contemporary ears. Lisa Barg makes a similar point about Robeson's relationship to Black folk performance practice: the singer "troubled . . . racialized aesthetic boundaries" because he did not perform an idealized Black folk authenticity.[69] It is a point that applies more broadly.

Several conclusions follow. The identity of the voice is complex, not easily reduced to a single, unified self, nor necessarily representative of one (political or social) position. We might, then, place a limit on the possibility for and efficacy of certain domains of the voice, such as Robeson's dominant accent, to perform oppositional political work. Neither should we seek to reconcile the different, sometimes contradictory, dimensions of Robeson's singing, or pursue every aspect of his voice on the terms of the singer's activism. To do so falls into the trap that has dominated Robeson scholarship: an imperative to align the singer's art with his ideology. The point is that not all aspects of the aesthetic can be claimed equally for the domain of the political.

The field of the song recital, one of the primary contexts in which, and for which, Robeson's voice was produced, makes this clear. The singer's elite English was a function of the trained singing (and acting) voice, the goal of which is to produce a uniform, standard pronunciation. It also aims to produce a relatively homogeneous tone: within registers, as the voice moves between registers (the *passaggio*), as it vibrates and modulates (as in the expansion of sound), and more. It must produce a recognizably "classical"-sounding voice; and it is through the production of this generic voice that the tradition is sustained. Robeson's voice, moreover, is also *his* voice. Dolar refers to this mode of the voice as its timbre, the "fingerprint quality" of the voice, its individuality; Adriana Cavarero elaborates on the "vocal ontology of uniqueness."[70] The sonic stuff of Robeson's voice is what makes his voice his. We hear his voice whether he sings an extract from a Russian opera, a Jewish prayer, a Chinese lullaby, a spiritual, or an English art song. The demands of both the generic voice and the unique voice may mitigate

196 PAUL ROBESON'S VOICES

against the production of radical differences and heterogeneity in the domain of sound. To put this strongly: the very ontologies of these voices are predicated on sameness; on identity rather than non-identity, to return to Baldwin's terms. In the field of the song recital, do the everyday experiences of singer's practice and the fashioning of a voice's sound mitigate against the voice becoming an object of radical sonic difference, from being a cognate to the minority discourse of a folk aesthetics?

Dolar notes that the fingerprint qualities of the voice do not contribute to linguistic meaning, even as they are "susceptible to physical description: we can measure their frequency and amplitude, we can take their sonogram"— as I did in dissecting the anatomy of Robeson's simple singing in chapter 3— and "they can easily enter the realm of recognition and identification, and become the matter of (dis)liking."[71] Cavarero's insight on the voice's uniqueness is that it implies relationality. Because of the "elementary phenomenology of the acoustic sphere . . . the voice is *for* the ear." The voice thereby operates according to what she calls "the law of resonance" in that it "invokes and convokes the other."[72] We have encountered, in this book, many of the variety of listener-others that Robeson's unique voice invoked and sometimes brought together. In its uniqueness Robeson's voice was heard by listeners to "represent." It represented not—or not only—as the sonorous articulation of the linguistic register of signification (e.g., in his repertoire and song lyrics), or as affect, but as an object of signification itself. For Cavarero, "the voice pertains to the very generation of meaning," which it effects through resonance: "resonance is musicality in relation; it is the uniqueness of the voice that gives itself in the acoustic link between one voice and another"—and, we might add, Others.[73] In the rest of this chapter I dwell on other instances of how Robeson's voice, in its sounding, represented; that is, how it further resonated with the people.

Heroic Tones

Throughout his life Robeson was eulogized as a hero. The biographic narrative of his life is often written in epic form with heroic plot elements, character traits, and physical attributes. "His story is a hero story," proclaimed Carl Van Doren in the Foreword to Shirley Graham's biography of the artist, *Citizen of the World*, adding blandly: "because it had to be."[74] He is, more specifically, the model artist as hero; a figure, as Lawrence Kramer has written,

VOICES POLITIC 197

forged in the romantic imagination, who "as a displaced form of the epic war-
rior, engages in quest and combat," and who latterly has assumed the roles of
social outcast and critic as "guarantee of artistic truth."[75] Robeson, too, was
the celebrity-hero of fans: "From the bottom of my heart I look up to you
as our hero," wrote a Japanese high school teacher. He was the hero of Pete
Seeger's youth.[76] More than this, the singer was a hero of the race, and of
labor too. Thus Robeson assumed to his own identity other folk heroes, like
Joe Hill and John Henry: "Paul Robeson IS John Henry," exclaimed the nov-
elist Roark Bradford when Robeson starred in the musical on the "legendary
giant Negro worker." And when Robeson sang the labor anthem " 'I dreamt
I met Joe Hill' it was Joe Hill in life."[77] Rather than elaborate on these varied
discursive accounts of Robeson-as-hero, I want to focus on how Robeson
sounded heroic. It has been the case that for Robeson's listeners, the stories
of his life, character, and body have found expression in his voice, and it is
through the mode of the heroic voice that the people accessed their hero.

Jeffrey C. Stewart has offered one reading of Robeson-as-hero. His starting
point is Harlem Renaissance thinker Alain Locke's recommendation of Walt
Whitman's heroic representation of the Black body (in the poem "I Sing the
Body Electric"), epitomized by Robeson. Importantly, for Whitman, the presence of the heroic Black body formed part of a democratic political vision for
the United States. The people, represented by the slave, were the heroes of the
land. Stewart notes: "For the heroic black body was always a critique of hegemonic Americanism"; that is, the idea of the Black hero was political. Two
facets of Stewart's reading of Robeson's heroism are noteworthy: it is mascu-
line and transnational; the singer breaks with a "race-based notion of cultural politics" to become a "transnational hero." In accounting for Robeson's
appeal—"his Black body magnetism"—Stewart suggestively attributes the
singer's "electricity" to eros, or a sexual energy, "the erotic love of the black
body."[78] Stewart does not countenance how the hero's magnetism might
sound through his voice, but it was not uncommon for listeners to hear
Robeson's voice itself as heroic.

In the early 1930s, composer, scholar, and music critic Clara Stocker
commented that Robeson's "voice calls for great and spacious arrangements
of sound" because of "his capacity for expressing the heroic in sound."
Isadora Smith welcomed the singer's return to the United States in 1940 by
hailing "the voice of the heroic artist."[79] Others were less enthusiastic about
Robeson's heroic style. The actor's 1943 portrayal of Othello was noted for
"his ponderous war club of heroic emotion," with one reviewer wishing that

198 PAUL ROBESON'S VOICES

he would "weep more humanly and less majestically."[80] Majestic effects are of course a hallmark of the heroic style.[81] And thus reviewers of Robeson's Othello commented on the majestic-heroic quality of his voice, which for many turned on the singer's voice intruding on the actor's stage. For Edwin H. Schloss, Robeson's performance was "lyrico-dramatic. [He] uses his superbly sonorous voice almost in singing his lines." The *Philadelphia Inquirer* noted how Shakespeare's lines "rise to operatic richness" in Robeson's rendition.[82] Robeson's musical recitation seemed to elevate the voice to the plane of the majestic, as the *New Yorker*'s review, titled "Black Majesty," made plain: "His voice, like his physique, is majestic, but sometimes it seems to me to be employed for meaningless organ effects. . . . When Mr. Robeson says, 'Put out the light—and then put out the light,' each word is a separate tombstone." The sonic weight of Robeson's voice at once makes the voice majestic and is a death knell to "proper" dramatic practice and signification; the voice's "meaningless" sounds kill the bard's poetry. *Time* magazine concluded that Robeson's "magnificent voice" "did not bring to the part poetry and drama so much as sculpture and organ music. He was not so much Othello as a great and terrible presence."[83] This is but another instance of the voice acting against *logos*, and it is a voice that performs the heroic style: as Aristotle said of the heroic style, it conduces to grandeur, thus diverting the mind of the listener.

Robeson's heroic voice is recognizable especially for its depth of register. Here gender and race intersect in the Black bass voice. Scholar of the gendered Black male voice Alisha Lola Jones notes that the "lower vocal range" of African American male singers has "represented masculinity, virility, potency, hardness, and manliness"; and, in Robeson's case, heroism.[84] For New York critic Brooks Atkinson, "the something heroic" that he identified in the "man of magnificence" was located in Robeson's "deep voice."[85] This timbral bass of course identifies the voice as Robeson's, as we saw in the profile of the voice I sketched in chapter 1, but it is through what Dolar calls the mode of intonation that the deep voice is performed into a heroic voice. Dolar itemizes intonation's parameters as including "the tone of the voice, its particular melody and modulation, its cadence and inflection," all of which contribute to the voice's meaning.[86] (Similar to the heroic voice, the Black preacher's voice—always deep in Robeson's own telling of his family's preacher-voices—operates more within the mode of intonation than accent.)[87] Robeson delivers his deep voice with strength. We can hear this in two of the many songs that are hymns to rivers and paeans to workers in

VOICES POLITIC   199

bondage that he sang: the spiritual "Stand Still, Jordan" and the Russian folk song "Volga Boat Song." As one critic noted, Robeson was best in "Song of the Volga Boatman" "where his prodigious lower register . . . was heard in its greatest power."[88] The mid-1950s recording of "Stand Still, Jordan" finds the singer in full-throated deep voice. From the opening descending phrase the weight of Robeson's highly resonant tone creates an impression of a terrible force. With a slight flattening of the vowels to darken the sound, Robeson glides down to the low tonic $F\sharp_4$ further reinforcing the sense of depth as he luxuriates in the lower reaches of the melody sliding up and down between the tonic and third (0:04–0:13). All of this receives a more emphatic treatment by the end of the performance. The final iteration of the refrain is taken at a more deliberate pace, the lyrics receive exaggerated articulation—striking sibilances and hum-extended final nasal consonants abound—and the tone is more forceful still (2:28–3:11). There is much in Robeson's expansive voice here that strikes a heroic note. And it is apt that he does so. In one hearing, it is God's voice that he utters: an instruction, passed on by the prophet Joshua, to command the Israelites to remain calm (to "stand still") as they cross the raging river Jordon to the promised land. In another hearing, Robeson is the voice of slaves, of workers of the world, who refuse to accept the master's command—"I can't stand still," he sings.[89] Here, he sings for the people.

With these insights into Robeson's performance of a heroic voice, we might return to Stewart's proposition. The singer, Stewart tells us, became a transnational hero by "embracing the worker's [*sic*] internationalist cause. . . . Robeson internationalizes his body and makes the black body a representative symbol of the aspirations of all oppressed workers of the world."[90] Following Dolar, we have seen that through the mode of accent Robeson's voice was internationalized, and also how through the operations of intonation he was heard as heroic. Indeed, in its heroic tones Robeson's voice was made "electric" (to use Whitman-Stewart's term), or, as Cavarero has said, it resonated with the people. The heroic mode thus permits an understanding of the voice's relationality, of the people to the artist. The hero is part born of the gods, and (like the Old Testament prophet) has direct access to the deity. (The conflation of the prophets as "Old Testament heroes" is made explicit in the notes to Robeson's recording of "Stand Still, Jordan.") So the hero (and hero's voice) bears a relation to the divine (voice). But the hero is also of the human world. His struggles and suffering, and superhuman attributes and acts (and voice), play out on earth, often in defense of everyman, a narrative

Figure 5.2a. Cover of *People's Songs*, June 1947, volume 2, number 5.

that drives much of the biographical writing on Robeson.[91] To return to my discussion in the previous chapter, the singer's heroic voice is thus also the voice of the friend. The simple singing by which Robeson's heroic voice was delivered across a range of repertoire rendered his voice an object to which the people related.[92] The cover of the folk publication *People's Songs* (Figure 5.2a), on which the singer appeared in 1947, makes this plain. Robeson is a picture of vocal strength, of a muscular voice; one can *see* the force with

VOICES POLITIC 201

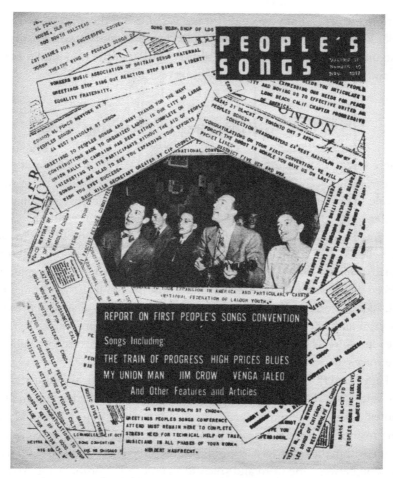

Figure 5.2b. Cover of *People's Songs*, November 1947, volume 2, number 10.

which the voice sounds forth. It is a heroic representation too (and in the style of heroic realism): the singing Robeson dominates the image, standing before the anonymous, international collective of workers as their leader; he is also the civil rights leader. (Compare the do-it-yourself montage featuring Pete Seeger in a sing-along for another cover of the same magazine [Figure 5.2b]. Nothing there says "hero.") Stewart concludes that Robeson's presentation of the Black body—and we can now add voice—as a transnational

202 PAUL ROBESON'S VOICES

hero made of it a body-voice that was desired.[93] But the force of Robeson's voice, and its ability to organize and energize protest and opposition, made it also undesirable for others. It is to this dimension of the voice's politics that I now turn.

"Old Man Mississippi Rages": Protesting Voices

There was another account of Robeson-as-hero.[94] In his brief memoir of the singer, fellow activist and author C. L. R. James hailed Robeson as a "truly heroic figure." James's interpellation turned on the immense personal and professional loss that Robeson's "devotion to the world revolution" caused the singer: he was a "relentless fighter who could not be moved from what he believed."[95] The image of Robeson as a fighter—a "Freedom Fighter of the first magnitude"[96]—was another facet of the Robeson hero complex and placed the singer in another relationship to the people. It also determined his art. As Robeson proclaimed: "I have protested vigorously against oppression, Fascism and war with songs."[97] Of course we hear the protest registered in the repertoire he sang, but I ask again: can we also hear the freedom fighter in the voice's matter?

I approach this line of inquiry by turning to three political formulations of the voice: Dolar's "authoritarian" voice, Steven Connor's "bad voice," and Fred Moten's fugitive listening to the Black voice as resisting object. For Dolar, "the very institution of the political depends on a certain division of the voice, a division within the voice, its partition." This division is based on a structural distinction between the word and voice, *logos* and *phone*, or following Aristotle between *zoe*, "naked life," and *bios*, life in the community that includes political life. Dolar reminds us that there is, however, no easy division, for *zoe*-voice is not outside of but central to *bios*-word, hence the voice is in a position of *extimacy*: the voice makes speech possible and is also a product of *logos*, "sustaining and troubling it at the same time."[98] While many functions of the political voice sustain the "letter of the law," the authoritarian voice performs to another logic: it "puts into question the letter itself and its authority." Dolar only considers negative instances of the authoritarian voice—those of totalitarian dictators—in which the voice, "not bound by the letter, [is] the source and immediate lever of violence."[99] But the politically "progressive" voice of protest is another instance of the authoritarian voice. It too questions the letter and its authority. This is Robeson's protesting voice.

VOICES POLITIC 203

And even more, following Moten's observation that the "history of blackness is testament to the fact that objects can and do resist," the protesting (or, in Moten's lexicon, "fugitive") voice also refuses the law/authority: Black fugitivity is "a desire for and a spirit of escape and transgression of the proper and the proposed. It's a desire for the outside . . . an outlaw edge proper to the now always already improper voice or instrument." If the historical grounds for fugitivity are slavery, the "material heritage" of the latter continues to cross the divide that separates slavery from freedom. And thus Moten concludes, "the resistance to enslavement is . . . the essence of black performance."[100] This insight is defining of Robeson's art, not "simply" because of his family's slave heritage, nor because of his lifelong dedication to the performance of the slave spiritual. It is his profound commitment to the fight against global slavery at mid-century that energized his protest. We can approach Robeson's voice as resisting object by recourse to Connor's "bad voice."

The bad voice is the substitute for a lack. It is more than substitute, though, because it is also a symbol of unsatisfied desire and agency of frustration of the desire. And thus the voice functions negatively, it is bad: it expresses rage and embodies the subject's fear borne from its destructive anger.[101] The bad voice operates through the following functions. First, "the action of the voice upon itself is clearly visible and audible," insofar as it attacks itself, "taking itself as an object or substance which may be subjected to injuring or exterminating assault . . . it may scatter or pulverize its own forms and tonalities."[102] Moten's metaphor for the "material degradations" of Black sound is more visceral: he speaks of "fissures or invaginations."[103] Second, the bad/fugitive voice's destructive bent is so because it must transcend its own condition, "forming itself as a kind of projectile, a piercing, invading weapon." Hence the dimension of elevation—of volume—is important to the bad voice;[104] and also for Moten, whose entire theory is predicated on the slave's scream: "Where shriek turns speech turns song . . . lies the trace of our descent."[105] And yet, Connor adds, the bad voice is also capable of what he terms "bracing or armouring itself": "the angry or demanding voice at once destroys and defends itself . . . yet it also reins and retains the rage it unleashes. Timbre and voice quality are bound in by the percussion and 'attack' of the voice itself." Finally, the angry voice is "a bringing up and out of what comes from below, or deep within." It is the "gesture and enactment on the body of a certain affective disposition."[106] All of this, Connor argues, results in the production of what he calls a "vocalic body," the idea that the voice, produced by a body, itself produces a body, which can take the form

204 PAUL ROBESON'S VOICES

of a "dream, fantasy, ideal, theological doctrine . . . a surrogate or secondary body, a projection of a new way of having or being a body, formed and sustained out of the autonomous operations of the voice." The bad voice, specifically, is "a desire for and hallucinated accomplishment of a new kind of body, a fiercer, hotter, more dissociated, but also more living, urgent, and vital kind of body."[107] Moten too is interested in desire and possibility (of freedom), which he invokes through the use of the subjunctive, pursuing the "interarticulation of the resistance of the object" with, following Marx, the "subjunctive figure of the commodity [that is, the slave] who speaks."[108] Robeson's freedom fighter's voice, I suggest, might be conceived of as the vocalic body of a bad/fugitive voice.

There are untold moments in Robeson's career in which we can discern his voice of protest. The singer's participation in a pro–civil rights event at Peekskill, New York, in 1949 brought to the fore the recognition of Robeson as a voice of protest and illustrates how this voice operated. By this time the singer was so well known for his "interracial organizing, his radical anti-capitalist and anti-imperialist politics, and his activism for racial equality," that he occupied a special place in what Tony Perucci calls the "American lynching imagination." At Peekskill, Robeson and his supporters were stoned, besieged, and abused by local resident mobs, and abetted by state security forces and a whitewashed investigation of the violence.[109] Robeson responded—"My Answer" he titled his epistle—in the *Negro Weekly*:

> I am well equipped now, though I have not always been so, to make the supreme fight for my people and all the other underprivileged masses wherever they may be. . . . God gave me the voice that people want to hear, whether in song or in speech. I shall take my voice wherever there are those who want to hear the melody of freedom or the words that might inspire hope and courage in the face of despair and fear. . . . I will go North, South, East or West, Europe, Africa, South America, Asia, or Australia and fight for the freedom of the people. . . . This thing burns in me and it is not my nature to be scared off. . . . They revile me, they scandalize me, and try to holler me down on all sides. That's all right. It's okay. Let them continue. My voice topped the blare of the Legion bands and the hoots of the hired hoodlums. . . . It will be heard above the screams of the intolerant. . . . My weapons are peaceful for it is only by peace that peace can be attained. The song of freedom must prevail.[110]

Two features of the fugitive/bad voice may be detected in Robeson's civil rights statement: the quality of elevation—his voice "topped," it was "heard above"; and thus he called it a weapon—and the expression of an affective self: this "thing burns in me," he wrote. In an analysis of Robeson's appearance at the House Committee on Un-American Activities in 1956, Perucci notes how Robeson's speeches before the committee were received by its members as being always too loud, and that Robeson's volume was read as a symptom of his political insanity and treason: volume emerged as a "measure of his citizenship and as a concomitant incendiarism of his tonality."[111]

The conceit of burning is prominent in Perucci's account and captures the inflammatory nature of Robeson's politics and his fiery voice. It also permits an understanding of how Robeson's voice fulfills the first function of the bad voice, that is, it attacks itself. We can hear this if we move from Robeson's speaking voice to consider his singing. These modes of vocality, we have seen, were mutually informing of each other in Robeson's practice. Noted one critic of a St. Louis concert: "The vigor of introductory remarks was translated into his singing."[112] More generally, observed Carl Lindstrom, "creating words is Robeson's business—beautiful words, expressive words, terrifying ones and some so pregnant with meaning that you don't know whether he sang or spoke them."[113] Where loudness was one constituent of Robeson's angry voice, roughness was another. Starting in the late 1930s, critics begin to note the first signs of tonal roughness in the singer's live performances. Tellingly, this was during the time that his multivalent internationalist politics that I documented in the previous chapter began to emerge. A performance of the Jewish hymn of praise, the "Kaddish," at the Royal Albert Hall in London in 1938 drew the observation that "his voice throbbed, even turned harsh and rough, as he cried, 'Let there be an end to all these sufferings and woes.'" And the *Daily Mail* detected "an occasional gruff note" in a voice otherwise "as nobly resonant as ever."[114] Before this, notices of a rough voice were isolated, and attributed to problems of tonal production in the pre-trained voice or to ill health. After the singer's political turn, the rough voice appears not as a vocal failing or only as interpretative expressivity (as in the singing of the "Kaddish") but as a fundamental sonic attribute of Robeson's protest. And so it colored his normative voice too. By the end of his career critics thus routinely still heard "the same rich tone, deep, dark and firm," but it was now tinged, "slightly gritty."[115] Vocal roughness, one might argue, was the sonic correlative of Robeson's political protest and anger.[116]

The vocalic body of the fighter is presented in Robeson's performances of "The Four Insurgent Generals," a song the singer first encountered through his involvement in the Spanish Civil War, and which became a mainstay of his recital repertoire. It was sung at a "Victory Concert" in Albany, in upstate New York, soon after the events at Peekskill and after city authorities had initially banned Robeson from appearing at a local high school "on the ground that his artistry was not mere singing." The local mayor Erasmus Corning cited "The Four Insurgent Generals" as evidence: the emotions roused by the song was "very disturbing," and when he sang the "'fighting' line . . . repeating it in Spanish with even greater emphasis" a "wave of emotion swept the audience."[117] Robeson had first recorded the song in 1942 as part of the *Songs of Free Men* box set of 78s (see Figure 5.3). In this first outing on record, the voice on display is Robeson's trademark bass, strong and rich, and is a model of tonal rectitude. But the performance of the war song is innocuous, the voice at times even cloying; a hangover from the many sentimental songs Robeson recorded for HMV in the 1930s. It is only at the end of the song, when Robeson switches from the English verses to

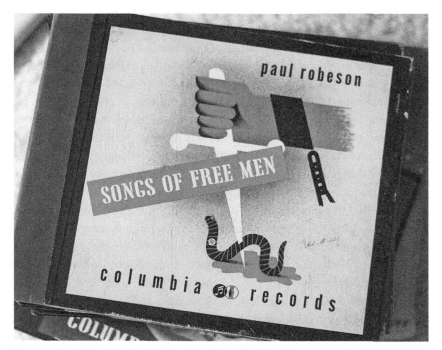

Figure 5.3. Album cover, *Songs of Free Men* (Columbia Masterworks, 1942).

singing in Spanish and proclaims that the treacherous four generals will be hanged ("Serán ahorcados"), that his tonal smoothness is momentarily compromised (2:05). By the time of the 1949 Moscow recital recording of the song, however, the rasps occur more frequently and the tone is consistently rough.[118] Critics noticed this too. "Robeson seemed to rasp a trifle on 'Four Insurgent Generals,'" observed one critic. Wrote Carl Lindstrom of the song and another protest song "Peat Bog Soldiers": "These are no bagatelles with Robeson. There is a subdued fierceness and vibrancy about them."[119] The "edginess" that characterized Robeson's mature singing is a product of forcing the voice for the purpose of emphasizing a (political) message. It is thus an exemplary bad voice that injuriously acts upon its ideal self, the smooth tone of the classical voice.[120] In this Robeson's protesting voice sings according to Moten's aesthetics of the Black radical tradition, which the theorist locates in the break in/breakdown of normative speech, in the "elevating disruptions of the verbal that take the rich content of the object's/commodity's aurality outside the confines of ['universal'] meaning."[121]

This development of Robeson's voice of protest was accompanied by his move out of the conventional recital hall, a move in part necessitated by his political blacklisting but which was also part of a strategy to broaden his audience base during the civil rights movement. These spaces of performance were more permissive, and even productive, of the freedom fighter's voice. Take Robeson's annual concerts at the Peach Arch Park in Washington state on the US-Canada border at which the singer performed outdoors from on top of a truck with a mediocre upright piano. Time and again in the songs he performed at Peace Arch, Robeson clearly forced his voice for interpretive force. In "Hymn to Nations," which appropriated the "choral melody" from Beethoven's Ninth Symphony for new words by Josephine Bacon and Don West, the forced voice accentuates particular words and thoughts but it also comes to characterize Robeson's sound more consistently in this recording, especially in the final verse.[122] The rough voice is thus interpretively a proper instrument but is also generalized, separated from its performance of any one song.[123]

The foreign-language songs in Robeson's repertoire make this clear. For the decade during which the singer was confined to the United States, from the late 1940s to 1958, he sang mostly for English-speaking audiences. The meaning of individual words in foreign-language works would have eluded most of his listeners, even if they might have had some idea of the overall sense of the song, for it was Robeson's practice either to give a brief account of

208 PAUL ROBESON'S VOICES

the song before he performed it or to sing a verse or two in English. The Peace Arch concert of 1953 concluded with Robeson singing "Chee Lai" ("March of the Volunteers"), written by Tian Han and Nie Er to protest the Japanese invasion of Manchuria in the 1930s, and which later became the anthem of the People's Republic of China. Robeson was introduced to the song by Liu Liangmo, a pioneer of using choral music to support the war effort and who had fled to the United States. It seems that Robeson first sang "Chee Lai" in concert in 1940, and recorded it the year after with several other Chinese songs in the three-disc set *Chee Lai: Songs of New China*.[124] While in the 1941 recording Robeson delivers the Mandarin Chinese in a tonally smooth and richly songful voice, by the time of the 1953 performance the "voice of rage," as Connor puts it, has intruded: it is percussive, gruff, and gritty (listen from 1:53 to 2:33).[125] And thus, without needing to understand the Mandarin in which it sings, the voice produces the vocalic body of a fighter.

Robeson's protesting voice highlights another operation of the voice's relational resonance that Cavarero proposes. The voice not only invokes and convokes the other; it also provokes others. Robeson's political voices— official, heroic, protesting—demanded different political responses from different listeners, and it sometimes provoked them too. Heard by the state, Robeson's voice sang against sources of authority, his fugitive voice performing against the letter/law banned by the state. In a different hearing, his voice's challenge invited responses by listeners from minority subject positions, sometimes encouraging them to radical action. Performing thus, the political voice itself politicizes. The possibilities for a fuller reckoning of the political voice that voice-thinking encourages, and that I've attempted in this chapter, allow us to hear the many grain(s), to summon the Barthesian cliché, of Robeson's voice(s), to observe that the many language-body-voice gestures that constitute the singer's abundant voice place it in different positions, for Robeson and for his listeners. The voice is indeed a resisting object.

6

A Microphone Voice

In 1954, while under "national arrest" in the United States, Paul Robeson appeared by proxy at the Second Congress of Soviet Writers in Moscow.[1] The writer Boris Polevoy witnessed the event, prefacing his account with a statement of impeccable Soviet aesthetic ideology: my writing, he announced, "adheres strictly to the realistic trend, and is not inclined to exaggeration":

> The entire Hall of Columns, with which you are familiar from your frequent appearances, was packed to the rafters. . . . There was no room for an apple seed to fall not to speak of an apple. The ushers carried out a large speaker and put it on the rostrum, the chairman introduced you, a deathly quiet came over the hall, and once more we heard the hearty sound of your unique bass.

The scene was an unlikely one for the neoclassically styled venue renowned for its art music performance culture: an empty stage but for a podium with a loudspeaker atop from which Robeson's recorded voice hailed forth. The "entire tremendous hall . . . at that moment probably held more people than it has held in a long time." As Polevoy relates it, Robeson may as well have been present: "a new wave of enthusiasm shook the hall, everyone jumped up and gave you a long standing ovation, greeting in your person . . . yourself, a courageous fighter for peace and friend of Soviet literature, whose voice, having flown across the ocean, had reached that hall."[2]

The rapport that Robeson's taped voice performed for his Russian listeners—no doubt in part established because the singer addressed them in Russian (in speech, poetry, and song)—was also a rapprochement of sorts: "We felt that no frontier cordons, no laws, no lying by the masters of the cold war, however refined and grandiose it might be, can raise a barrier between cultures, between people of good will. In those moments we, the Soviet writers, saw among us, as it were, a great American."[3] As Kate Baldwin has argued for the Russian reception of Robeson's recordings, the singer's "voice conveys a connection that Polevoi typifies as 'real.'"[4] And the

Paul Robeson's Voices. Grant Olwage, Oxford University Press. © Oxford University Press 2024.
DOI: 10.1093/oso/9780197637470.003.0007

210   PAUL ROBESON'S VOICES

afterlife of Robeson's "appearance" also worked to revivify the singer's career overseas, which had flagged in the wake of his international travel ban by the US authorities. Polevoy's nine-year-old daughter thus inquired of her father doubtfully, "You really mean Robeson is living now and didn't live long long ago?" Although Robeson had last appeared in Russia in person only five years earlier, he was, by the mid-1950s, already a "legendary figure"; hence the child's incredulity: "it is hard for her to even believe that you are our contemporary."[5]

This vignette reveals how the media and objects of sound technologies replaced the singer, substituting for his physical absence, particularly during the 1950s when Robeson was denied a passport to travel. As Shana Redmond has written, these "varied transmissions and proximities" of Robeson's voice animate him sonico-optically to "produce his hologram and its transit . . . in locations otherwise inaccessible."[6] Indeed, numerous accounts exist of the singer sending discs or magnetic tape of recorded spoken messages, a single song or several musical items across the world, and of a public address system delivering his voice at the output point. His recorded voice, concludes Baldwin, "defied containment, soared over airwaves, permeated and permutated to find homes on unlikely shores."[7] Mostly Robeson did this at the request of organizers of political events he supported. On other occasions his technologically transmitted voice was the main event. Rather than constituting one item on a larger agenda, voicing a message for this or that organization—and which, as Redmond has said of Robeson, "exposes the command of sound within political mobilizations"[8]—Robeson would use technology to present recitals from afar. To be sure, these were given under the auspices of politically progressive organizations, but their raison d'être was Robeson's singing, often undertaken in support of the singer's ongoing struggles with the state. As much as he sang for others, he sang for his own cause too.

One such event took place on May 26, 1957. Singing "direct from New York (by special trans-Atlantic hook-up)," Robeson presented a recital to a thousand-strong audience in St. Pancras Town Hall in London organized by the London Paul Robeson Committee, a lobby group that sought to publicize Robeson's case.[9] In the Moscow event Robeson's taped voice had ushered from the loudspeaker-performer, whereas in London the loudspeaker transmitted a live voice. The logistics of the "telephone concert," as the parties involved referred to the St. Pancras concert, are laid out in correspondence between the *Guardian* writer and activist Cedric Belfrage and the

A MICROPHONE VOICE   211

Robesons. It is revealing of the keen state surveillance that surrounded the singer, and of the innovative use of the most recent developments in sound communication technology.[10]

On both sides of the Atlantic a wire was reserved for the time of Robeson's appearance in London. Stateside the plan was to connect from California, where the singer was touring. That proved too costly, so he ended up singing into a telephone handset from an AT&T studio in New York. Robeson was asked to record an "insurance tape," in the event, one assumes, of a technological glitch—the concert was a relatively unusual use of telephony—or sabotage by the state security apparatuses. It was certainly with the latter in mind that Belfrage, who like Robeson had personal experience of the FBI's inquisitions and interceptions, requested multiple copies of the tape to be sent "by different routes and to different addresses" in the United Kingdom. The transmission began badly when Robeson was cut off before singing a note; "the man at your end said sourly that they wouldn't allow any conversation ahead of the call. We all thought Somebody was starting to sabotage the show." But thereafter the telephone concert proceeded to plan.

> Then suddenly Paul began to sing and did his several numbers. The quality was quite magnificent, absolutely without static of any kind and remarkable purity of sound. . . . Paul's voice continued from the empty stage with a blow-up of a photo of him hung at the back and the Union Jack on one side, Old Glory on the other.

The stage set up composed of the singer's image flanked by the two flags suggest that Robeson's performance connected the two countries, as did the new transatlantic cable, the TAT-1, which made the concert possible, and Belfrage had specifically requested that Robeson "confine the selections to American and English songs," an unusual restriction given a standard Robeson program at the time was purposively multilingual and multinational. As with the Moscow listeners who heard a taped Robeson in the Hall of Columns, the London audience responded enthusiastically to Robeson's telephone voice. Belfrage reported on "the full vigor of the storm of applause and shouting from the audience . . . the audience jumping out of their seats." What Belfrage called "our 'noble experiment' " was by all accounts a success.

The idea of a telephone concert was not new; its forebears can be traced to the late nineteenth century.[11] But there was something experimental about the Robeson telephone recital on account of its use of the latest

212 PAUL ROBESON'S VOICES

telecommunications technology. The TAT-1 submarine transatlantic cable had been completed only the year before, and improved the quality (and lowered the costs) of telephony between the continents. The press reported that the Post Office technicians involved in the concert indicated that it was the first time that transatlantic telephony had been used as the medium to deliver a "concert hall performance."[12] And Belfrage claimed that members of the St. Pancras audience who had heard Robeson in person years before enthused that the sound of the telephone concert was as good. There was, he concluded, "a very 'present' quality about the whole thing."[13] In recognition of Robeson's contribution to what the British Broadcasting Corporation (BBC) called "technologically-enabled free speech," the transatlantic concert and the technologies that made it possible appear on permanent display in the Information Age Gallery in London's Science Museum.[14]

The technological achievement that enabled the telephone concert and then informed its reception was also politically productive. For Belfrage the experiment was "noble"; for the BBC it fostered free speech. The *Manchester Guardian* review of the concert reported that "last night some of [Robeson's] words and music escaped, alive, through the new high-fidelity transatlantic telephone cable."[15] The promise of sonic escape—"a new means of communication from the jailhouse," wrote Eslanda Robeson[16]—animates Robeson's use of sound technologies in the 1950s. Indeed, a causal, if fanciful, relationship has been proffered between Robeson's increasingly productive deployment of sound technologies to escape the nation and commune with the world as the decade progressed and his eventual physical release in 1958 when his passport was restored. What this techno-triumphalist narrative ignores is the geopolitical and legal contexts of the Robeson case that gave impetus to its resolution.[17] These contexts also profoundly reshaped Robeson's work as an artist, both on stage, as we saw in the last two chapters, and in the studio. And in the section that follows I chronicle Robeson's recording work of the 1950s. This in turn provides a context for exploring what I call Robeson's "microphone voice," which is my task in the rest of this chapter.

Othello to Othello

The consequences of Robeson's "fall"—hailed as "America's Number One Negro" at the start of the 1940s and considered the "most persecuted man in America" by end of the decade—were many.[18] The folk singer Pete Seeger recalled that Robeson was "the most blacklisted performer in the history of America," and it is well known that this affected, and all but brought an end to, his mainstream public performance career at the time: concerts were canceled, venues were closed to him, audiences either stayed away or were scared off.[19] As Tony Perucci writes, "his American career [was] in distress."[20] Similarly did his status as a major recording star wane, at least in the United States. During the first two and a half decades of his singing career, Robeson was courted by and contracted to the world's major recording companies, RCA Victor, His Master's Voice, and Columbia. Upon his return to the United States in 1939 he recorded largely for Columbia Masterworks in the 1940s. (A release on Victor of the patriotic cantata *Ballad for Americans* (1940), which starred Robeson, was an exception. The album cover of that recording, on which the singer's image was festooned by stars and stripes, was an unambiguous message that all was well with Robeson and mainstream America then.) The string of critical and commercial successes for Columbia in the 1940s—the box set of 78s *Songs of Free Men* (1942), a cast recording of the Broadway production of *Othello* in three volumes and thirty-four sides (1944), and an album of spirituals and Robeson recital favorites (1949)—came to an end as the new decade dawned. After a meeting with the head of Columbia Masterworks, Goddard Lieberson, Robeson's son recalled: Lieberson "came back to us almost in tears and humiliation and said, 'The board told me flatly, not only can't I give you access to our studio, I can't let you get your records pressed in any facility that we control.'"[21] The recording industry thus participated in the broader (state) plot to silence Robeson. My interest, in what follows, is to chart the means by which Robeson would get his voice onto record again, and the ways in which the business of recording was rethought in the process. The details of these endeavors have not been well documented.

Around the time that agents of the internal security division of the Department of State called on Robeson at home in New York demanding he hand over his passport,[22] the singer's team was in correspondence with interested parties overseas on a matter that would become increasingly familiar as the 1950s progressed: how to obtain Robeson records. Charles Ringrose, the national organizer of the Workers' Music Association in London, informed Robeson, on the one hand, of the many inquiries about Robeson records his organization received but that, on the other hand, they could not "obtain supplies." And Collet's, the left-leaning British bookstore and publishers, reported on "the demand and popularity of Paul Robeson in this country"

214 PAUL ROBESON'S VOICES

while institutional machinations denied the public Robeson's voice: "As in the U.S., so in Gt. Britain, the official company—in our case H.M.V.—have for the past many years, not reproduced any records of Paul Robeson although they hold matrices of records issued in the years before the war."[23] Collet's temporary solution was to import records from the Czechoslovakian label Supraphon, but English demand fast outstripped Czech supply. Meanwhile, Ringrose's plan was to dub old commercial Robeson releases onto record under the association's own label Topic Records, a move Robeson's team put paid to due to the patent limitations on the right to copy such work. But the ethos and model of Topic perhaps inspired Robeson to pursue a similar venture, and he promised the label that he would make records directly for their use. Several years later the *Transatlantic Concert* (1957), which documented the telephone concert, appeared under the Topic imprint.

As the recording concern of the Workers' Music Association, an educational offshoot of the British Marxist Party, Topic Records sought to release "gramophone records of historical and social interest." Records were sold by subscription and the organizers shunned the commercial marketplace. It was an exemplary "independent" project, and remains the oldest independent label in Britain.[24] Soon after the interest from Topic, Robeson announced his return to recording in an open letter (see Figure 6.1), and the Othello Recording Corporation was born. The singer released three albums in the United States in the early to mid-1950s for Othello, funded by advance subscription.[25] What distinguished Othello Records from Topic was of course its raison d'être: a calculated move by a global star from big studio to self-publishing forced on the singer by his blacklisting. The first Othello release, on both 78rpm and long-play formats, was titled simply *Robeson Sings* (1953), a clarion statement that the singer was to be heard again. But both the production and distribution of Othello's records were complicated affairs as they endeavored to navigate what Perucci has called "the Cold War performance complex," an "assemblage of techniques of power" that regulated American life, and functioned by articulating discourses of difference (such as communism, Blackness, madness, and theatricality) as those of treason.

Perucci details how Robeson's performances, musical and other (e.g., his testimony before the House Un-American Activities Committee), disrupted the conventions, rhetoric, and policies of the Cold War complex, concluding that they were a "central domestic site for the waging of the Cold War."[26] While the state painted Robeson red, irrational, and a threat, *Robeson Sings*, in the words of the album liner notes, promoted "the mention of his name" as

A MICROPHONE VOICE 215

December, 1952

Dear Friend:

I am writing to you about a matter that is most important to me as an artist.

For the past several years a vicious effort has been made to destroy my career. Hall-owners, sponsors and even audiences have been intimidated. Recently, in Chicago, 15,000 persons who wanted to attend one of my concerts had to assemble in a park because the hall-owner had been threatened.

The outrageous denial of my passport bars me from accepting contracts to appear in England, France, China and many other lands.

Although I have recorded for nearly every major recording company and sold millions of records both here and abroad, these companies refuse to produce any new recordings for me.

What is the meaning of this? It is an attempt to gag artistic expression, to dictate whom the people shall hear and what they shall hear. It is an attempt to suppress not only me, but every artist, Negro and white, whose heart and talent are enlisted in the fight for peace and democracy.

There is a way to explode the silence they would impose on us. An independent record company has just been established that will make new recordings for me. This company will also release work by other artists banned because of their views, and younger artists often denied a hearing.

My first new album, described in the enclosure, is now in production.

But the making of records is only part of the job. The big task is to make sure that the records will reach a mass audience in every part of the country. To do this I need the active support of all my friends.

The first step is to assure an advance sale of thousands of albums. So, I am asking you to subscribe now to a special $5 advance sale of my new album, which I will autograph for you. I hope you will tell your friends about our new project and get them to subscribe now to this advance sale.

I am determined to defeat those who would imprison my voice. Your $5 in the enclosed envelope will help to break through the barriers.

Sincerely yours,

Paul Robeson

Figure 6.1. "Robeson on Records Again!" Typescript dated December 1952. Originally published in *Freedom*, December 1952. Paul Robeson Collection, microfilm 4. The Schomburg Center for Research in Black Culture, New York Public Library. With permission from the Robeson Family Trust.

bringer of "pride and joy, warmth and courage, to the hearts of men, women and children all over the world. . . . Paul Robeson is today the most beloved American in the world."[27] One of the ways in which Robeson countered the state's domestic performance was to remind the United States of his place in the world, and of his international standing. The regular flow of petitions and letters of support from world statesmen and international artists and

216   PAUL ROBESON'S VOICES

celebrities, often mobilized by Robeson's team, was an overt strategy—another mode of performance—to counter the US state's position. The force of this global support should not be underestimated. At the very least it was an annoyance to the security and legal apparatuses (as is evident from the FBI and MI5 files on Robeson), and most likely it was also an embarrassment to the state; and it is probable that concerted international pressure played at least a small part in the return of Robeson's right to travel. We should thus recognize the role played by international actors in the domestic Cold War drama, and also that Robeson's Cold War performance complex played out on other national stages with sometimes different plots.

It was thus imperative for Robeson to continue to perform for international audiences when he could not do so in person and during the time the global record companies had forsaken him. Othello Records therefore did not contend itself with only the US market. By 1954, and possibly from the year before, Othello Records had entered into agreements with agents and labels in several Eastern European countries, which in succeeding years included other European countries and beyond. A memorandum from Othello Records states the corporation's plans for overseas markets clearly:

> The continued denial of his passport has made it impossible for Paul Robeson to accept any of the numerous invitations that have come to him requesting concert performances in European, Asian and Latin American countries. However, through the Othello Recording Corp. . . . Mr. Robeson is now in a position to act upon the requests that he make phonograph records especially for audiences in the Soviet Union, The People's Republic of China and the New Democracies of Europe.

The strategy was to offer a series of records, rather than individual ones, with the specific intent that the series would "comprise a full concert program—a program of songs such as he would sing were he permitted to travel abroad."[28] Would-be agents could procure the masters for six groups of six songs each, either per group or as the entire "program," with each group constituting an album of three 10-inch 78s. The decision to package the records as a Robeson recital made commercial sense, but it also fulfilled the function of the record acting as proxy for the singer. At this point in Robeson's career an in-person recital would typically be constructed as several groups of several songs, with several items being in the language(s) of the host country. To this end the World Council of Peace reported on an "interesting move" by Othello Records: its albums for "foreign countries" would include "his famous songs and one or more songs of the country from which the request came. . . . The latter would be specially recorded by the great American singer and would be sung as far as possible in the national language."[29] The extent of Robeson's vernacular recording policy is clear: in 1954 for a Hungarian venture four of the six songs recorded (two by Kodály, and a song each by Bartók and György Ránki) were in Hungarian, and for a Soviet agent half of the thirty-six songs were in Russian.[30] Through the means of the self-recorded album-as-recital, Robeson was able to sing to foreign audiences in the format he would have used had he appeared in concert in person.

But putting his voice on record was no easy task. "The large record companies belong to Big Business and would flatly refuse to rent their studios," complained the singer, "and the smaller companies would be afraid." Robeson spoke cryptically also of "sabotage done by recording engineers whose ears, keenly attuned to the snarls of McCarthy, were deaf to a singer of Peace."[31] Denied access to recording company studio facilities, Robeson at first worked out of well-to-do friends' apartments. Helen and Sam Rosens' East Side Manhattan apartment with a generous living room and excellent grand piano was a favorite. Several small independent recording outfits and venues were also used: Esoteric Sound Studies, whose owner was harassed by the FBI for renting to Robeson; Nola Recording Studio, on the seventeenth-floor penthouse of the Steinway Building; and the Carnegie Recital Hall. Engineers and musicians sometimes refused to work with Robeson for fear of the implications for their careers: "Whenever we had union people," recalled Robeson's son, "they had to do it off the books and not get credit because they'd lose their union card."[32] An engineer graduate, with some knowledge of audio engineering and a "musical ear," Paul Robeson Jr. took on the role of producer[33] and managed to secure the services of several of the city's highly respected sound engineers: Peter Bartók, son of the composer; Tony Schwartz, a seminal figure who worked across multiple media technology platforms; and David Hancock.[34] The last was also expert in the pressing of discs. And after many refusals, a small plant in Yonkers, just north of New York City, agreed to manufacture the records. Another set of problems then arose: "no commercial distributor would handle [the records], no stores would display them, nor would any radio station play them." In the United States the independently produced records were sold by mail order, subscription, and through Black churches, the civil rights movement, and progressive

218   PAUL ROBESON'S VOICES

organizations.[35] Historian Robert Cataliotti concludes that Robeson's independent recordings, which totaled more than a hundred tracks, "stand as a stunning accomplishment. . . . There is no rival to the achievement that this body of work represents when the conditions under which this music was produced are considered."[36]

If we keep in mind the production challenges faced by Robeson's team during the time of his blacklisting by the recording industry, it is perhaps surprising that the audio quality of the records was a priority. There are several indications to suggest that this was so. New releases were promoted as much for the event of a new Robeson record as for technological achievement. Othello Records' second release, *Solid Rock: Favorite Hymns of My People* (c. 1954), aimed specifically at the local black market, was advertised thus: "The very latest advances in the art of High Fidelity have been employed. *We do not hesitate to say that this is the finest Robeson album ever offered from the point of view of Mr. Robeson's voice and art.*"[37] Ensuring that Robeson's voice was heard at its best, perhaps especially because his public seldom heard him in person, was important in representing a fit, healthy, and powerful voice at a time that the state sought to weaken Robeson and silence his voice. Such was the control the Robeson team exercised on his voice's sound that they would recall very recently released master tapes for succeeding ones that sounded better. Writing to the Workers' Music Association in London, Robeson Jr. noted that the singer was "anxious to have the distribution of his new records get started in England" but that of greater concern was how he sounded on record:

> Since I wrote you last, we have made a considerable number of new recordings, and have been able to achieve first rate all round sound quality. In view of this, Mr. Robeson and I both feel that many of the recordings which I sent you previously are not up to the technical standard of quality which we have now achieved. There [in the UK], Mr. Robeson does not wish records to be pressed from the 16 inch per second tapes which you now have, and requests that you destroy them.[38]

A "Technical Notes on the Recordings" thus accompanied the master records and tapes sent overseas, which included information on the packaging, lacquer cutting, playback (the speed and stylus suggestions), and equalization (AES standard was employed, with suggestions for the increase of radial equalization for some tracks).[39]

A MICROPHONE VOICE 219

Robeson's collaboration on the independent recordings with noted engineers working in professional studio environments, from sometime in 1955, no doubt facilitated the sonic advances the Robeson team advertised. Prior to this, the singer had been recording in friends' apartments with his son working as both producer and engineer. David Hancock's involvement seems to have been particularly productive of Robeson's sound. A classically trained pianist, Hancock was a celebrated engineer, and sometime producer, noted for his work on contemporary art music and avant-garde jazz projects. In audiophile circles his recording of the Donald Johanos and the Dallas Symphony Orchestra's Rachmaninoff *Symphonic Dances* in 1967 "attained near-legendary status . . . (both for sound and for the performances)." On that project, as with most others, Hancock used custom ribbon microphones and a modified tape recorder running at thirty inches per second, a setup that was something of a Hancock trademark.[40]

At mid-century, ribbon microphones were considered somewhat old fashioned. The technical notes on the album cover for Art Blakey's *Midnight Session* (1957), engineered by Hancock for Elektra, and contemporaneous with his work for Robeson, states as much: "These recordings were made at Carl Fischer Concert Hall by David Hancock on a modified Ampex, Model 350, employing two RCA MI-3025A bi-directional ribbon microphones, a type now generally considered 'obsolete.' "[41] Whereas in the 1930s and 1940s the standard microphone for recording voices were RCA ribbon mics, in the 1950s the condenser mic was preferred, a new allegiance epitomized by Frank Sinatra whose use of microphones is, unusually, well recorded.[42] In an article for *db: The Sound Engineering Magazine*, Hancock documented his practice of "updating ribbon microphones," through various "improvised modification[s]," and outlined his reasons for advocating for their usage, which included extended response for both low and high frequencies.[43] For Robeson the use of Hancock's microphone "proved far more effective in capturing the full range of Robeson's bass-baritone than condenser microphones."[44] Another feature of Hancock's work was his use of thirty inch per second (IPS) tape, "twice the speed of conventional tapes" at the time and which, recalled a fellow soundman, resulted in "a superior recording."[45] It is tempting to posit that Hancock's capturing of Robeson's voice on thirty-inch tape led to the Robeson team's withdrawing the sixteen-inch tapes mentioned earlier. It is also possible that the directions for cutting the masters specified in the "Technical Notes" sent out by Othello Records to its overseas clients bore Hancock's stamp, as he was also a "great LP cutter."[46] A little commented

220   PAUL ROBESON'S VOICES

on but crucial step in the production and mixing process of vinyl records, the cutting of the lacquer master is important for the resulting audio quality of a record. All in all, Hancock's combined skills can only have resulted in the superior audio of Robeson's independent records, produced in the age of high fidelity (about which I say more later).

The Robeson-Hancock partnership may have culminated in two LPs released by New York–based Monitor Records in the late 1950s. Hancock worked for Monitor at the time Othello Records licensed a selection of previously released and unreleased tracks—the independent recordings—some of which were engineered by Hancock, to Monitor in 1958. *Favorite Songs* and *Encore, Robeson!* (c. 1959–1960), which appeared on Monitor's "Music of the World" series, was a first tentative step by the Robeson team to re-enter the mainstream record business as the effects of the blacklisting eased.[47] Robeson Jr. recalls: "I have to give Monitor credit; they were the first up, and they were still taking a risk, although it wasn't the same as before. . . . I mean, after all, they weren't revolutionaries; they were businesspeople. So, you know, I was forever grateful."[48] Monitor was a minor label set up for the purpose of promoting music from the Soviet Union, Eastern Bloc, and other parts of the world, specializing in folk and classical music recordings.[49] It was a good fit for Robeson, politically and aesthetically, and was quickly followed by another partnership with a larger outfit: Vanguard Records.

The agreement with Monitor seems to have rested on profiting from the institutional networks and apparatus of a commercial label in order to re-sell previously recorded Robeson material. For Vanguard, Robeson recorded new work. The inveterate documenter of musical Americana Nat Hentoff attended a recording session for a new Robeson LP in the ballroom of a disused hotel in upper Broadway, in New York, in April 1958. Maynard Solomon, the co-owner of Vanguard, described the album as "real schmaltzy," and was emphatic that there be no "political songs": "We're recording Robeson the singer, one of the world's great artists." Solomon's profession seems naïve— any song can be political, after all—but the LP, titled simply *Robeson*, aimed to present a de-politicized singer. Some of the repertoire harkens back to the "bad music" Robeson recorded for HMV in the 1930s, and the chorus and orchestra that accompanies the singer emphasizes the schmaltz.[50] *Robeson* the Vanguard record was nevertheless a significant moment in the singer's public rehabilitation, and his re-entry into the mainstream commercial recording industry thus coincided with his re-introduction to the world. By this time the state had eased Robeson's travel restrictions and he was allowed to travel within continental America, and within months he would reclaim his passport and travel abroad. His Vanguard records, Hentoff concluded, "are likely to precede him." Indeed, the flurry of commercial releases c. 1958 stands in stark contrast to the independent recording work of the years prior: in addition to the Vanguard LP, HMV issued *The Incomparable Voice of Paul Robeson* and *Emperor of Song*, Philips released three EPs, all transfers from 78s, one of which was *Paul Robeson: Ol' Man River*, and Topic Records' *Transatlantic Concert* was advertised in January 1958. And this was only for the UK market.[51]

Robeson's return to public life culminated in his appearance as Othello in Tony Richardson's production for the Shakespeare Memorial Theatre's one-hundredth annual festival in Stratford, England, in 1959. It was a role he performed throughout his career. His Broadway Othello of the mid-1940s had been a triumph and presented to the nation "one of the three great voices in American public life," as one correspondent wrote.[52] In the wake of a record run for a Shakespeare play on Broadway, a nationwide tour, and a cast recording of *Othello* for Columbia Masterworks, Robeson's embrace by the United States was confirmed in his co-option by the state: in 1944 the US Office of War Information organized a broadcast of Robeson reciting the Moor's closing speech from Act 5, Scene 2, for the BBC on the anniversary of Shakespeare's death. Such was the institutional desire to ensure Robeson's participation that they offered to do it "live to London," pre-record the show, or even to "string microphones at the theatre, and record you during the performance."[53] The radio transmission was perhaps Robeson's first extracted performance of the final monologue, and at some point by the late 1940s he began performing it in concert, typically as an encore as it is not itemized on the formal printed programs. The recitation worked as a concluding item structurally to his late-career concert recitals, provided Robeson vocal relief from singing, and topically functioned as a rebuke to the state: "Soft you; a word or two before you go," begins Robeson's Othello, "I have done the state some service, and they know't."[54] Robeson's investment in the role was such that he would play no other Shakespeare. "The only Shakespeare role he has ever undertaken," explained Eslanda to Glen Byam Shaw, the artistic director of the Memorial Theatre, "was Othello and he did that only after great soul-searching . . . because Othello was a foreigner, dark, different . . ., and it was a foreign-ness which he thoroughly understood and actually *was*."[55] (In private correspondence Eslanda and Robeson's accompanist referred to the singer as "his Moorship."[56]) Of Robeson's many encounters with the

222 PAUL ROBESON'S VOICES

Moor, he employed *Othello* in the fight against segregation in the 1940s and as a "vital symbol of his right to travel" in the 1950s.[57] The independent recordings produced during that decade, we have seen, were the means by which Robeson's voice traveled. So it is unsurprising that when the state did Robeson a disservice, to invert Othello's famous lines, he would name his company Othello Records.

If we consider the conditions under which Robeson recorded for Othello Records for much of the 1950s, the attention to audio quality, the extent of recording activities—over 100 tracks—the three domestic albums put out by Othello Records, and the unknown number of foreign records pressed (and unheard by Anglo-American scholars), we might reassess the accepted account of the 1950s being creatively unproductive for the singer, a time when politics trumped singing.[58] Moreover, while all of Robeson's recording activity was political, the recordings were meant to appeal to a wider listenership, to everyman listeners. In this the independent records were unlike the taped messages and songs recorded for occasional (political) events that I discussed at the outset of this chapter and by which Robeson's voice was heard beyond the nation. The notice for *Solid Rock: Favorite Hymns of My People* advertised itself thus:

> Here in this album of six selections is all of the surging power and heartfelt longing, the moving faith and soaring aspiration of the old-time hymns.
>
> Here, with the matchless beauty and feeling that have thrilled audiences around the world, Paul Robeson sings the songs you love. You will play these records over and over again. . . . Here are hours of enraptured listening pleasure for your family and friends!

The sales pitch foregrounds the aesthetic just as sales were at the forefront of the project. Hence the recordings were released in multiple formats to appeal to as wide a market as possible. Listeners could purchase an album of three 78s each containing two songs in "high quality break-resistant material in a beautifully bound album-cover"; or a single 78 of a pair of songs; or a single LP record of all six songs.[59] "*The big task,*" Robeson emphasized, "*is to make sure that the records will reach a mass audience.*"[60] By such measure Othello Records was only partially successful. Five thousand "friends" subscribed to the first album; whereas at the start of his recording career a single 78 sold upward of 15,000 copies a year and Robeson typically released several discs a year.[61]

A MICROPHONE VOICE   223

Of course the significance of the independent recordings rests on more than their sales. The creation and dissemination by the Robeson team of a range of media that included recordings was "not about making Robeson reap millions in revenues but about restoring his basic civic rights." This "promotion of Robeson can be seen as an organized battle waged against not only major institutional blacklisting but also a tendency toward growing public ambivalence toward Robeson's Black radicalism and internation-alism."[62] For my technology-focused story the independent recordings are also interesting for the ways in which they conformed to the logic of pro-gressive sonic advancement that dominated the age of high-fidelity audio. Robeson's Vanguard records, which we may view as both the culmination of his entire recording career and the conclusion of his independent recording work, were advertised as "An Adventure in Stereophonic Sound": "the first and only discs in which full justice is done to Mr. Robeson's voice through the most advanced techniques of high fidelity recording."[63] Sound technologies, in other words, were instrumental in producing the sound of Robeson's voice and, we will see, his own sense of a vocal self in a more essential way than the stories I have told thus far about records and tapes circulating the globe. The voice-thinking I pursue in this chapter is less interested in the theorization of recorded sound or a hermeneutics thereof, and focuses rather on Robeson's technologically facilitated singing practices and the mediation of his voice by sound technologies. Concluding the book with a chapter on these subjects is a recognition of the importance of sound technologies to the production of his voice and to our hearing of it.

"You don't need the mike, Mr. Robeson"

Robeson's encounters with electroacoustic technologies collectively produced what I call the "microphone voice" and allow us to reflect on the relationship between live and recorded performance, or to borrow Nicholas Cook's formulation, between "concert and gramophonic" singing. This in turn permits us to consider what constitutes Robeson's 'real' voice.[64] What I am interested in documenting is how Robeson deployed sound technologies he had encountered in radio broadcasting, the recording studio, and the film sound stage in the mid-1920s and 1930s, and thereafter, for use in song recital on the concert stage in the decades that followed.[65] As the preeminent artifact of electroacoustic technologies, the microphone

224   PAUL ROBESON'S VOICES

assumes thus a synecdochic relationship to the array of sound technologies. The figure of the microphone voice is invoked not only to describe the resultant sonic quality of Robeson's technologically mediated voice (a task I undertake at the conclusion of this chapter) but more generally it places electroacoustic technologies centrally in his concert performance practice—in front of his voice.

The recording studio has been a productive site of study recently, although as Susan Schmidt Horning's work illustrates, accounts of the historical development of many specific sound technologies are still only partially told.[66] But little attention has been paid to the ways in which musicians working in the first half of the twentieth century employed emergent sound technologies in concert performance (rather than for recording and broadcasting).[67] Perhaps, as Schmidt Horning suggests, this was because very few performers were fascinated by technology until the 1960s, a domain they tended to leave to the technicians.[68] Robeson, by contrast, I hope to show was a technologically engaged musician. And perhaps this reflects the status of "live sound" itself in the field. In the experience of the McCunes, one of America's preeminent sound families, live sound remained "the stepchild of radio and recording" at mid-century and into the 1960s.[69] My account of the singer's changing uses of electroacoustic technologies in concert considers several moments in his career, and I begin at a time near the end of his singing life when his microphone voice was well established.

Upon the return of his passport in 1958, the singer's first trip abroad was to return to London, his home of the 1930s, and thereafter followed a tour of the British Isles and select European cities. The British media were all agog at the singer's appearance in the country after almost a decade's absence, with three items common to the reportage: Robeson was in Britain to sing, not to politic; he had a contender in Harry Belafonte—"It's Belafonte versus Robeson," shouted a *Daily Mail* headline—who was making his London debut on the same night as Robeson's comeback concert at the Royal Albert Hall on August 10; and Robeson used a microphone.[70] Almost every review of the Albert Hall concert made mention of the last matter. The singer's seemingly daring use of the little electric device not only caught the critics off guard but was cause for much consternation. At issue were propriety and necessity. On the one hand, it was deemed improper for a (classical) concert singer to use a mic. For Oxbridge-educated music critic Percy Cater it "was something of a shock" that Robeson sang with a mic: "Artists who sing at the Albert Hall are not wont to rely on this mechanism." Critic Noël Goodwin was more pointed: it was "unknown for concert singers" to use the device.[71] (By comparison, commentary on pop singer Belafonte's use of the mic was either nonexistent or positive; Cater describing "the controlled strength of his crouch over the microphone.")[72] Robeson's performance with a microphone, therefore, departed from the practices and traditions of concert singing, and affronted its high-minded custodians.

It was also, so the critics believed, a vocal self-betrayal. So, on the other hand, critics were puzzled by Robeson's use of a microphone because they could not fathom why the singer, who was assumed to possess a powerful voice, required amplification (although in fact, and as we will see later, Robeson did not have a "big" voice). "You don't need the mike, Mr. Robeson," chastised Cater. These sentiments were echoed by American critics. Earlier in the year, in preparation for his anticipated return to formal concertizing, Robeson had undertaken a brief tour of the West Coast of America, and as with his Albert Hall appearance comments on his use of a microphone peppered the reviews. Influential art critic Thomas Albright, for whom Robeson was "the greatest natural basso voice of the present generation," concluded that he was "the last singer around who needs a microphone."[73] These misgivings brought to the fore a more pressing problem for the critics: as they strained to hear Robeson's "true" voice, the singer's microphone voice thwarted their task of critique. Leslie Mallory cast the relationship of Robeson's voice to its amplified sounding as one of deception for the listener. The singer "hid" behind the mic, "making it quite impossible to judge how his voice, now 60 years old, has stood the test of time."[74] Others were less forthright, but always the microphone voice impeded the critic's judgment. Thus for the London *Times*, Robeson's recital "disappointed only in one important respect—he used a microphone, so that never could we tell just where we were with him. . . . With Mr. Robeson it is the actual voice itself . . . that provides our thrills, and still to-day his voice (in so far as the microphone allowed us to judge) seems totally unimpaired by the passing of time."[75]

Robeson's microphone voice contravened more than the practices of concert singing. It also altered the relationship, and a history established over several decades of concertizing, that his listeners had with his voice. Broadly grounded in an aesthetics of the natural (as I explored in chapter 3), Robeson's singing was noted for its sincerity and simplicity, which facilitated in turn an honest communing with his listeners, and British critics drew on remembered accounts of this voice on his return to Britain in the late 1950s.

226 PAUL ROBESON'S VOICES

The *Times'* review of a recital Robeson gave in late 1958, also in the Albert Hall, is exemplary of this discourse:

> Fundamentally, of course, what Mr. Robeson sings is immaterial; all his songs are sung with complete sincerity and are his way of making friends with an audience. There is abundant artistry in all his proceedings but it aims at creating a fellowship with his listeners. It is all simple, rather sad—our friendship with Mr. Robeson is a community of suffering and aspiration—but it is always, after two hours of simple music, a remarkably real experience.[76]

For some critics, if not the singer's lay audiences, the microphone voice undermined the terms on which a Robeson performance was founded: was it Robeson's "real" voice, could it still be considered the "natural" voice for which he had long been celebrated, and, with these in question, how could his singing be a sincere expression of his self? In the *Times* critic's words: "never could we tell just where we were with him."[77] So set adrift aurally by the sound of Robeson's microphone voice were the critics that, as one pundit put it, the singer "might as well have been still on the other side of the Atlantic as far as any musical assessment of his voice is concerned."[78]

The reference is likely to Robeson's transatlantic concerts of the year prior. Then he had been separated from his St. Pancras audience in London by an ocean yet his telephonic voice, recall, was received as sounding remarkably present. Ironically, when appearing in person in the Albert Hall his microphone voice distanced the singer from his listeners. The "problem" of Robeson's microphone voice points to the extent to which sound technologies had begun to impact the reception of his singing, and to how different performance media and modes conventionally practiced and theorized as distinct domains (certainly by art music critics and classical musicians) transgressed upon each other. Specifically, what Robeson presented at the Albert Hall was a conflation of the conventionally opposed concert and gramophonic voices: the field of sound technologies—the mic, amplification, a sound engineer—had encroached on the singer's practice.[79] And this was not meant to be. Conventional wisdom has it that at mid-century live performance continued to assume a normative position vis-à-vis its reproduction, a product of a discourse of fidelity that trades on the distinction between original (live performance) and copy (recording).[80] This is particularly true, as Cook notes, of classical music for which "the prioritisation of live performance is general."[81] Robeson's technologically informed singing not only conflated concert and gramophone practices, it undid long-established hierarchies of practice. Two further instances of the inversion of practice attest to this.

Much has been said on the effects of disembodiment in recorded music, of recorded sound being separated from the bodies that produce it, and the consequences of this for listening. There is, writes Paul Sanden, "an abiding understanding in musical discourse that electronic mediation—particularly recording—leads to disembodied representations of musical practice."[82] By the mid-twentieth century, recorded sound had long been normalized and techniques of listening in the West adapted to it. In concert, though, Robeson's microphone voice presented the challenge of listening to a disembodied voice anew. Rather than hearing his voice direct from his mouth listeners heard it amplified from speakers at some remove from the singer's body. One critic who attended Robeson's Carnegie Hall recital of May 1958 spoke of "the confusing 'voices' from the speakers."[83] On these occasions Robeson's microphone voice functioned as a technological other to his fleshy voice, his listeners' auditory disorientation a function of his "real" voice not being plainly heard. Additionally, in the history of sound reproduction technologies the gramophone voice has functioned according to a "narrative of vanishing mediation" in which the medium of recording attempts to erase itself in the desire to bring sound source and copy into indistinguishable identity.[84] Put simply, the record aspired to be an increasingly faithful reproduction of the live performance, and Robeson's high-fidelity records of the 1950s are exemplary of this process. In stark contrast, the mediating microphone, which had fully materialized in Robeson's concert singing by mid-century, performs to another logic: it does not pretend to vanish, and standing before the singer calls attention to itself and its operations. For these reasons we should not be surprised by the critical reception of Robeson's microphone voice in concert. Critics were not primarily concerned about the quality of the sound; their reviews were not post-concert "soundchecks." Rather, they objected to the ontological confusion that the microphone voice introduced into the field of the song recital.

The negative press on Robeson's microphone voice elicited a response. Reporting on the singer's subsequent tour through England, the provincial press normalized Robeson's practice of singing with a mic. In a move of journalistic one-upmanship over the metropolitan papers they reported on Robeson's history with the mic, often citing the singer. "A word might be added," the *Yorkshire Post and Leeds Mercury* informed its readers, "about

228 PAUL ROBESON'S VOICES

Robeson's use of the microphone which apparently has caused surprise to some critics. It is a fact that Robeson has always used a microphone, and would not appear without one, 'even,' he says, 'if I were to be invited to sing at Covent Garden.'"[85] It was also a fact that Robeson endeavored to get ahead of the press, no doubt due to American critics' comments on his microphone voice immediately prior to the trip abroad. As he set foot on British soil, Robeson held a press conference at Heathrow airport. He spoke about the "important" issues, that he was in Britain as an artist not as an activist, and he must have deemed it important enough to make a statement about his use of the microphone in concert. Robeson "revealed that for the past thirty years he has ALWAYS sung with a microphone. 'I used to hide it away among the footlights and things,' he said. 'Now I use it quite openly.'"[86] To be precise, Robeson had been using a microphone in concert for the past two decades, and not at first for the purposes of amplification. To understand Robeson's adoption of a microphone voice in concert we need to turn to an earlier phase of his concert career.

Synthea, or the Acoustic Envelope

In November 1931, Robeson canceled, at the last minute, an appearance at the Royal Albert Hall. So unprecedented was it for a major artist to abandon a celebrity recital at the hall that the *Daily Express* headlined its report on the singer's no-show "Incredible News." The 6,000-strong throng that queued outside the Hall was equally incredulous: "Round the pavement circling the building men and women were running, shouting out the news to each other. They did not seem to believe there was no entertainment for them."[87] The official line was that Robeson was too ill to perform—a cold become influenza—but it is likely the singer's dislike of the venue played no small part in the decision to cancel. Robeson's valet and confidante Joe Andrews admitted that the singer was "probably not too sick to appear on stage." He "never liked performing in Albert Hall," recalled Andrews: "It was too big and the acoustics inadequate. He had his usual worries about his voice and whether it would carry, and . . . so he backed out."[88] But five weeks after the canceled performance Robeson was back at the hall, and he would perform there many times more.

One such occasion was in June 1937, when Robeson shared the stage with other public figures at a political rally and fundraiser organized by the

A MICROPHONE VOICE 229

National Joint Committee for Spanish Refugee Children. The nature of the event, which included much speech-making, necessitated a public address system, which Robeson appropriated for his sung portion of the program; and the event was also due to be broadcast. A photograph of Robeson singing at the event is perhaps the earliest instance of the singer's concert microphone voice, and performing with a mic in concert must have mitigated the singer's strain; Robeson was "actually comfortable, with none of the paralyzing fear he usually felt" in the hall.[89]

Before this event, Robeson's concert performances involved no direct use of sound technology; his singing was "natural" also in its lack of technological mediation. But by this time, in the mid-1930s, he was a major recording star, and, while by no means a radio artist, he had some experience of radio broadcasting.[90] In fact, his first radio broadcast predated his breakthrough concerts at the Greenwich Village Theater, in New York City, of mid-1925. On December 18, 1924, he broadcast a scene from *The Emperor Jones*, in which he had recently appeared on stage, and sang spirituals, from the New York station WGBS. Of his radio debut the press enthused over his "excellent broadcasting voice," signaling that he "should be an interesting figure in front of the microphone."[91] While praise for Robeson's broadcast and recorded voice would be a refrain throughout his career—the British magazine *Gramophone* noted "the particularly fine microphone quality of his voice"—he was, like many singers first encountering sound technologies in the early part of the twentieth century, skeptical of it.[92] Reporting on a series of radio broadcasts Robeson undertook for the BBC in 1929, the *Daily News* remembered that there "was a time when Paul Robeson objected to having his voice broadcast, as he considered the microphone was not always fair to artists."[93] Familiar with microphone singing from over a decade's work in recording and broadcast studios, recourse to the technology in the Albert Hall concert in 1937 perhaps provided the impetus for his productive experimentation with and adoption of sound technologies on the concert stage in the ensuing years.[94]

As war brewed in Europe, Robeson returned to the United States from London in 1939. Two composite events, soon after his American homecoming, precipitated his adoption of a microphone voice in concert. The first was his starring role in the radio broadcast performances of the patriotic cantata *Ballad for Americans* for CBS, which premiered on November 5, 1939, and which radio historian William Barlow argues was the singer's "first major triumph on network radio."[95] This was followed by subsequent broadcasts, a recording, and a nationwide concert tour of the work. The concert tour

230   PAUL ROBESON'S VOICES

in particular resulted in sustained use of the microphone and sound reinforcement outside of the studio, with the singer performing in large outdoor
venues to record-breaking crowds: the Hollywood Bowl concert on July 23,
1940, attracted an audience of almost 25,000, and the Grant Park concert in
Chicago a few days later as many as 165,000 by some estimates.[96] For these
outdoor concerts Robeson's performance with a mic was both necessary—
to project over the orchestra and choir and to reach the listeners amassed—
and conventional, as the use of public address systems in stadia for large
gatherings was common by the late 1920s.[97]

More interesting to consider is what Emily Thompson has called the
"sound of space," and the reverberations of this for Robeson's adoption of
a microphone voice in concert. In designing the modern auditorium,
and in acknowledgment that performers and auditors required different
acoustic conditions, engineers aimed to acoustically separate the stage and
hall. According to the dominant acoustic wisdom of the 1920s and 1930s,
where listeners needed an absorptive environment, performers desired a
reverberant one. Two of the era's seminal researchers on electroacoustic
technologies J. P. Maxfield and Douglas Stanley wrote about the significance
of reverberation for singers specifically:

> the sound which is heard at any given position in an auditorium or room
> may be quite different from the sound which is actually produced at the
> source, and it is, therefore, necessary, from the listener's point of view, to
> consider the acoustics of the room either as part of the voice or as part of
> his pick-up mechanism—i.e., the ears or microphone. From the point of
> view of the singer, this reverberant sound produces a psychological effect,
> namely, it creates the impression in the singer's mind that his voice is pow-
> erful and that it is completely filling the auditorium. . . . The reverberant
> room is necessary to the singer if he is to interpret the song with its full
> emotional value.[98]

To some extent, the design of modern concert venues reproduced the
conditions of the studio as reverberation gained ascendency in the 1930s,
whereas previously a "dead" environment that denied spatial context
prevailed.[99] Both the Hollywood Bowl and Grant Park, the outdoor settings
of which exacerbated the problems of stage-auditorium acoustic separation,
are exemplary for creating a performers' space acoustically distinct from the
open-air seating. Their stages were constructed as a series of semicircular

A MICROPHONE VOICE   231

concentric arches to form what was called an orchestra or band shell and which enveloped performers in a reverberant space that at the same time amplified sound as it was directed out toward the audience.[100] As Robeson became familiar with performing under these stage shells, and also singing within the isolating "shells" and booths of the recording studio, he attempted to recreate these conditions on concert stages where they were absent. Robeson would thus describe his ideal performance condition as like singing in his "own private little orchestra shell."[101]

The second event that facilitated the singer's microphone voice in concert was his collaboration with Harold Burris-Meyer, the famed acoustician and director of the Stevens Institute of Technology in New Jersey. It seems they first met collaborating on another project with the conductor Leopold Stokowski, "the most sophisticated acoustician among the world's conductors."[102] Noted for his involvement with experimental sound technologies, Stokowski was working further with stereophonic recording and "three-dimensional music," called "enhanced" music by his tech partner Bell Laboratories.[103] Robeson's involvement entailed recording a scene from the Eugene O'Neill play *The Emperor Jones* stereophonically on film, which was played back in a concert that took place in April 1940 and distributed through several speakers spread across the stage. Tim Anderson has noted that these early demonstrations of stereo recording underscored one of the central ambitions of stereo: audio-spatial aesthetics. More particularly, at play are the "acoustic principles that constitute the audio sensation of space, namely, reverberation, echo, and source separation."[104] Robeson's experience of these phenomena, and of the "directional use of sound," led him to suggest to Burris-Meyer that "these fascinating new principles might be applied to the matter of directing some of his voice back to his own ear."[105] Whereas the history of stereo has typically been focused on sound *reproduction* and its reception in listening, Robeson's innovation was to redirect some of the principles of stereo for the purpose of the *production* of his own singing voice. Experiments were conducted in the Maplewood Theater in New Jersey, which had "many acoustic limitations," whereafter Robeson tried out a "simple set of equipment" in several out-of-town concerts before using it in a Carnegie Hall recital of October 6.[106]

It was thus that in late 1940 the US daily press covered the news of a new performance mechanism nicknamed Synthea (which the press misheard for the female name Cynthia), jointly developed by Robeson and

232 PAUL ROBESON'S VOICES

Burris-Meyer.[107] The Philadelphia *Evening Bulletin* introduced Robeson's Synthea to its readers:

> When Paul Robeson, six-foot-three and 240 pounds of top rank baritone, sends his giant voice rolling out over the Academy of Music audience a little friend named "Cynthia" stands unobtrusively in the wings calling encouragement.
>
> She doesn't do anything so ill-bred as to shout, "Attaboy, Paul, you're doin' swell," although she will shout if Paul shouts. She has a voice almost as big as the famous Negro singer's and she doesn't hesitate to use it.
>
> But the audience never hears "Cynthia," for her words of reassurance are Robeson's own, coming back to him as an instantaneous and private "echo."[108]

The trade magazine *Radio-Craft*, which included an insert of Robeson and Synthea on its cover for March 1941, ran a lengthy feature on what became known as the "Robeson Technique." That the electroacoustic system and its application in live performance were both named—as Synthea and Robeson's technique—suggests something of their novelty. And it would not be too much of a stretch to consider Synthea a prototype of the stage monitor system that two decades later would become standard in live performances of especially popular music. More specifically, Synthea was at first an early example of a side-fill monitor, the first component of what would develop into the onstage monitor system; side monitors were in common use only toward the end of the 1960s with the first well-known use thereof being in 1962 by Judy Garland. Robeson's ongoing experimentation with Synthea, however, resulted in the number, placement, design, and shape of speakers changing frequently.[109] Burris-Meyer and Robeson's Synthea is thus a forgotten moment in the history of live stage sound, and for this reason I explore in some detail how Synthea functioned, and why Robeson adopted it.[110]

From the diagram of the setup reproduced in *Radio-Craft* (see Figure 6.2), Synthea consisted of Robeson's amplified voice captured by a microphone in the footlights fed back to him by an offstage directional bell-shaped speaker. Functioning as "a sort of super-fine sound mirror," Synthea's development was, for Robeson as for any performer, an endeavor to control the singer's acoustic environment, in part by allowing the singer to better monitor his own sound. The first thing to note about Synthea is that it sought to overcome age-old difficulties concert performers experienced, associated particularly

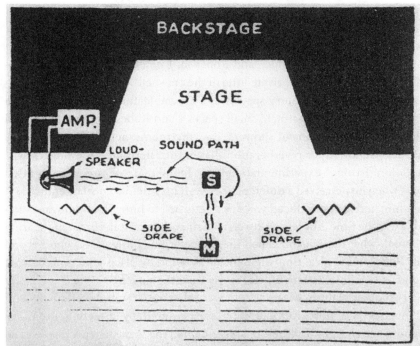

Figure 6.2. Diagram of Robeson Technique, *Radio-Craft* (March 1941), 561.

with large venues. *Radio-Craft* noted that concert singers "perform by choice in small, highly reverberant rooms since in them they are able to hear themselves easily. However, they deplore the acoustic conditions of most large concert halls and auditoriums." The magazine then presented a catalog of artists' (and these were also Robeson's) woes: "tension, inability to relax, a feeling of being ill at ease, of low vocal efficiency, forcing the voice in an effort to project, using a higher key than is best for the song in an effort to get out more volume and fill up the house."[111]

Synthea promised to overcome this litany of singers' complaints by creating what Burris-Meyer dubbed the "acoustic envelope," the virtual

234 PAUL ROBESON'S VOICES

transformation of the singer's stage-space into a "small, highly reverberant room." Burris-Meyer explained that the effect was "to surround the singer with the acoustic equivalent of a small reverberant studio, to enclose him in a small acoustic envelope," and Robeson, I noted earlier, described it as like singing in his "own private little orchestra shell."[112] The acoustic reduction of the singer's auditory space was a crucial feature of the system, with the theory presented as such: small spaces—and Robeson often mentioned the acoustic conditions of showers, drawing rooms, and recording studios as ideal—allowed for reverberation that in turn permitted the singer's self-audition. Through experimentation it was found that Robeson heard himself best when he perceived a difference between his original vocal utterance as it left him and his reproduced voice as it returned to him. The significant variable was the time difference between the singer's vocalization and his hearing thereof, what the *Bulletin* called the "voice of this Little Miss Echo,"[113] and for Robeson the ideal time difference was found by placing the speaker that returned his voice to him fifty feet away from the singer.[114]

Two other features of the system were also important: directionality and frequency selection. Auto-audition was ensured by directing Robeson's echo voice straight back to the singer alone. The acoustic envelope was so focused that walking a few steps out of it meant that one could not hear the reproduced sound. Importantly, the return of Robeson's voice to himself was meant for his ears only. And the ruse was complete by ensuring the soundware was out of the audience's sight: the microphone "nestle[d] unseen" in the footlight trough, the control box and bell speaker "in the wings."[115] The first major concert venue in which Robeson trialed the system was Carnegie Hall, in New York City, and there the loudspeaker was stationed discreetly offstage "behind the proscenium, stage right" (see Figure 6.3). Not only was Synthea's projection of Robeson's voice highly directional but it could be "at such a low level that persons other than the performer within its range will not notice it."[116] Hiding the singer's voice entailed also hiding a selection of its frequencies. Because low frequencies lack directionality and are not readily absorbed by the audience, among other things, argued Burris-Meyer, the system cut out frequencies below 500 cycles. Higher frequencies, by contrast, were found to be "directional enough to be kept away from the audience and are absorbed readily enough so that they are below background if they ever do get out."[117] All aspects of Synthea's construction and deployment worked to maintain the illusion of a technologically unmediated voice in concert, to present a concert rather than gramophone voice. Burris-Meyer

A MICROPHONE VOICE   235

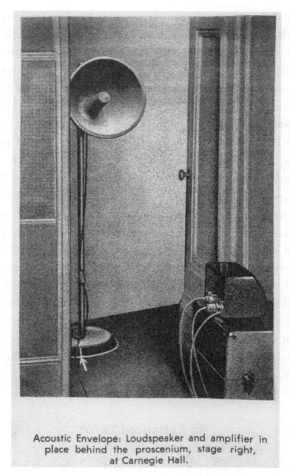

Acoustic Envelope: Loudspeaker and amplifier in place behind the proscenium, stage right, at Carnegie Hall.

Figure 6.3. "Acoustic Envelope," Carnegie Hall. Harold Burris-Meyer and Vincent Mallory, *Sound in the Theatre* (Mineola, NY: Radio Magazines, 1959), 40.

thus concluded his report to the Acoustic Society of America on a point of insistence: "It is important to note that the technique has no effect on the sound as the audience hears it."[118]

The phonograph effect exists in Robeson's desire to recreate the acoustic conditions of the recording studio on the concert stage, inspired in part by the insights afforded by his encounters with experimental stereo recording and demonstration. Historians of architectural acoustics have documented how,

236 PAUL ROBESON'S VOICES

from the mid-1930s, the aesthetics of recorded sound favored, among others, a more reverberant sound. The record was produced for a sense of physical space, whereas immediately prior to this recorded sound sought to deny spatial context.[119] Similarly, concert hall design strove to acoustically separate performers' and auditors' spaces, engineering the former for greater reverberation. There is no evidence that the Robeson technique and Synthea were adopted by performers other than by those who trialed it with its inventor. It was enthusiastically tested by a violinist and the bass Norman Cordon during rehearsals for a Met production of *Un ballo in maschera*, although Burris-Meyer assured Robeson that there were "no sets in use except yours." Synthea was undoubtedly a good fit for Robeson though: it mitigated his vocal limitations as much as it encouraged his bent for technological experimentation. Of this Burris-Meyer had firsthand experience, thus recommending Robeson, for his "interest in good recording," to Bell Laboratories as a test case for a new recording system the company was developing.[120] But if Synthea is a forgotten byway in the history of live sound, it was thoroughly of its time: it allowed Robeson to listen to his concert voice more easily, and so to sing more easily. In so doing he heard himself according to the dominant acoustic-spatial framework in which his recorded voice was located. Synthea permitted a synthesis of sorts of the acoustic conditions in which Robeson's gramophone and concert voices sounded forth.

An Enhanced Voice

In the early 1940s, Synthea was concealed amid the footlights and in the wings to allow Robeson's real voice to shine in the spotlight. To this end, Robeson noted that while Synthea had a crude equivalent in the practice of "ear cupping," by which singers cup their hand behind their ear in order to better hear themselves, the practice—"alright for rehearsal"—"certainly won't do for the concert."[121] But as the 1940s progressed, the microphone emerged from the footlights to stand before Robeson, and by the latter years of the decade it was routine for the singer to perform, in public, hand cupped to ear. These twin developments are captured in an undated photograph from the 1940s of Robeson in concert: from the front on angle, the singer's mouth (and much of his face) is fronted by the microphone, and accompanied with the hand cupped to ear. There is no more explicit image of the singer's voice become a microphone voice on stage. By the end of the decade it was not uncommon for Robeson to stand behind a bank of multiple microphones in concert.[122]

As with his use of sound technologies, Robeson's hand-to-ear habit drew response from the press. *The Ogden*, in Utah, commented on the "mannerism," which "had the audience guessing," and required the singer's explanation: " 'Holding my one ear is not because of an earache or deafness—it is just that it helps me to hold down my voice.' . . . Then laughingly, he added, 'I learned that trick from Bing in Hollywood.' "[123] It is unclear why Robeson assumed the mannerism when Synthea's aid was available to him. Perhaps the increasingly informal concert style he cultivated during the 1940s permitted the unconventional practice, and perhaps the spaces of performance he began to frequent, including those that were outdoors, did not always suit the use of Synthea.[124] As the hand-to-ear became routine it seems to have joined its high-tech substitute in Synthea, possibly even as a compensatory mechanism. Thus critics noted both system and mannerism in operation at a Carnegie Hall recital of May 1958. Music historian Irvin Kolodin pondered whether Robeson's "new mannerism" of cupping his right hand to ear was "to blot out the confusing 'voices' from the speakers," "a powerful complement" of which stood at either side of the stage.[125] As Robeson's amplified voice proliferated into plural instances of itself—in Synthea's return echo and the stage speakers' projections—the singer perhaps fell back on his hand in order to bend his ear toward better self-hearing of his unmediated voice. In other words, the addition of a public address system to the singer's private system of self-address that was Synthea seems to have introduced an element of confusion to the singer's acoustic environment, which the hand-to-ear practice endeavored to clear up.

When exactly Robeson started using a public address system regularly in concert is unclear, but it appears to date to after the introduction of Synthea. Robeson was emphatic that Synthea was "in no sense a 'booster,' so far as getting the voice out to the audience is concerned."[126] It was imperative, recall, that at first the audience was not to hear, nor see, Synthea. But shortly thereafter, in the early to mid-1940s, photographic evidence suggests that Robeson had started to rely on the amplificatory power of a public address system on a regular basis, at least for large venues and outdoor concerts. In time, this technological setup even become a condition of a Robeson performance, formalized in the contracts he signed, and specified in a "manual"

238   PAUL ROBESON'S VOICES

for hosting venues. Section 4 of the manual focused on the "Sound System and Piano":

> It is important that a good electrical technician be obtained to make certain that the public address system is in order and to be on hand throughout the concert to operate it. In addition to the regular loudspeakers, one speaker should be placed in such a position as to enable Mr. Robeson to hear his voice as he sings. Two microphones should be available, one near the piano for Mr. Lawrence Brown, Mr. Robeson's accompanist, who joins Mr. Robeson in several songs, and the other for Mr. Robeson.[127]

Such was Robeson's dependence on amplification at this point in his career that without it he would not sing. Thus, in 1954, when the local organizer of a Robeson recital scheduled for Chicago's Mandel Hall—hardly a large venue—reported that the "loudspeaker system in the hall is not good," and inquired whether it was "possible for [Robeson] to do without [the system] this time," Robeson's assistant replied that it was "*imperative* that the best available [system] in Chicago be set up in the hall, with a technician to operate it during the *entire* performance." He concluded with the injunction: "Mr. Robeson will be unable to perform if this is not complied with."[128] The equipment and the technician were duly acquired.[129]

Why, we might ask, Robeson's volte-face on sound reinforcement? At first he assured listeners that Synthea did not boost his voice, only later to refuse to perform in a venue without public address. It is unlikely his reliance on amplification was a result of declining vocal power as he aged, and more likely the consequence of several unrelated but ultimately linked circumstances, events, and influence, which collectively altered the conditions for a Robeson concert in the post–World War II years.

Certainly, the utility of Synthea and the slightly later addition of a public address system into the acoustic mix improved the conditions of live performance for the singer. But these sound technologies also created an environment that mitigated aspects of Robeson's vocal self, and the failings the singer perceived to flow from his vocal limits. For example, contrary to the popular image of the singer possessing a large voice, he had, what he called, an "embarrassingly delicate" voice.[130] As late as 1937, by which time his voice was that of a mature singer, he confessed that he was "really a drawing-room singer . . . and I really give of my best only in drawing-room conditions." Robeson explained that the "microphone provides these conditions. Film

A MICROPHONE VOICE   239

work and gramophone recording give me the best possible medium for my voice. I can sing naturally into the microphone." He also repeated his oft-stated dislike of performing in large venues: "In most big halls I have to produce my voice for the benefit of the guy in the back row of the gallery.... The strain on my nerves and on my voice is terrific." And so, he concluded, "I am trying to cut out the big halls."[131] Widely reported in the British press, these statements preceded Robeson's performance with a microphone in the Albert Hall—one of the very biggest of concert halls—for the Spanish Civil War event by only a couple of months. And when the singer returned to the United States two years later, he would have to contend with even more challenging performance conditions demanding sound reinforcement.

Indeed the singer's adoption of a regular microphone voice in concert accompanied the changing landscape of his concertizing that emerged on his return to the United States in 1939. In the wake of his newfound popularity in the United States, catalyzed by his starring role in the populist *Ballad for Americans*, and his growing politicization as advocate for the international working classes and oppressed minorities, Robeson gained the moniker, as we saw earlier in the book, the "People's Artist." Locations for his performance necessarily proliferated, and in addition to the concert halls with which he was familiar from the 1930s he increasingly sang also in large stadia, outdoor amphitheaters, and from makeshift stages set up in parks and factories. In these settings, sound reinforcement was required for Robeson's voice to reach the often sizable audiences that came to hear him. In these settings, too, Robeson cultivated a more informal performance presentation, which readily permitted the use of a mic as much as classical singing rejected it. The remove from the world of the art song recital is no more plain than in his appearance at the first Peace Arch concert, on the US-Canada border, on May 18, 1952. A flatbed truck, parked "within one foot of the border," provided the stage, with an upright piano and speakers mounted on the truck, with additional speakers "hooked up elsewhere around the concert area so a large audience could hear."[132] It is perhaps telling that the politicization of Robeson's voice—in speech and song—coincided with its amplification.[133] One of his first major political performances—the Spanish War Relief Concert—took place, recall, with the aid of a microphone. By the time of the Peace Arch event, the intimate association between political and microphone voices was normalized, captured on the album cover for the recording of the event. The artwork's crude montage aesthetic presents the singer and his microphone as a unity, whereas the electroacoustic artifact might as easily have been cut out. (And the disc label makes the larger point plain: the singer's voice on record is able to break free from the Cold War politics that imprisoned Robeson—see Figures 6.4a and 6.4b.)

The varied and changing contexts of Robeson's concert singing thus made his adoption of a microphone voice in concert a necessity, and the propriety for this act can in part be attributed to the practice of influential forerunners,

Figures 6.4a. Album cover for *I Came to Sing* (International Union of Mine, Mill, and Smelter Workers, 1952).

Figures 6.4b. Disc label for *I Came to Sing* (International Union of Mine, Mill, and Smelter Workers, 1952).

although there is limited evidence of Robeson being influenced by other singers' use of technology. Passing references by the singer to microphone voices par excellence Bing Crosby and Frank Sinatra—a "trick I learned in Hollywood from Bing and Frankie"—in the mid-1940s are unspecific, and at best indicate Robeson's awareness of popular singers' practice.[134] The example of Stokowski, with whom Robeson collaborated in 1940, is more intriguing to pursue further. Similar to Robeson's use of the TAT-1 for his transatlantic telephone concert, Stokowski participated in Bel Labs' experiments with the "long-distance wire transmission of high quality music" in the early 1930s.

242   PAUL ROBESON'S VOICES

This was realized on April 27, 1933 when the Philadelphia Orchestra, onstage in the Academy of Music in Philadelphia, performed for an audience gathered in Constitution Hall in Washington, DC, transmitted by specially designed telephone line. Tellingly, the conductor chose not to direct his orchestra (the duty of which fell to his associate Alexander Smallens) but rather to control the sound signals at the output end in Washington.[135] It was Stokowski's view that in scenarios of microphone-mediated sound the control engineer was the real conductor, a role that Stokowski readily took on.[136] One feature of the system developed for the concert transmission, and which bore the conductor's influence, was its expanded volume range. Stokowski had corresponded with the Bell Labs technicians about lifting "the top edge of the volume range far above what it is in the concert hall," and to this end the system could increase the orchestra's volume tenfold.[137] It seems the same desire for sound intensity animated Bell Labs and Stokowski's "enhanced" music demonstrations of 1940 in which Robeson took part. While the demonstration was an unqualified technical success, Rachmaninoff, who was in the audience, thought it was "sometimes unmusical because of its loudness," and in general the "intensity and volcanic nature of [Stokowski's] 'enhancements' offended the sensibilities of part of the audience."[138] Much the same, as we've seen, would be said of Robeson's use of amplification in conventional recital venues. It is not improbable that Robeson's collaboration with the technologically minded Stokowski permitted the singer to think anew his relationship with sound reinforcement, and to consider presenting an enhanced voice in concert.

We should also consider how Robeson's voice was enhanced on record, and how his and his listeners' familiarity with his recorded voice informed the singer's use of sound reinforcement in concert. From the mid-1930s through the 1940s and into the 1950s, recording technology continued to improve. One outcome was the sound of high fidelity: more sensitive microphones, new approaches to reverberation and the creation of sonic space, and the introduction of tape combined to capture greater frequency and dynamic range and to achieve sonic presence.[139] And from the late 1930s, modernized home phonographs permitted, for example, "bass boosting" and greater volume control such that consumers were more "musically and technically sophisticated."[140] Robeson's voice had always been heard, on record and in concert, as rich, resonant, and deep. These were the essential characteristics of his voice's identity. Critic Alfred Frankenstein waxed that the "great Negro bass has a voice like the title of the late James Weldon Johnson's book, 'God's

A MICROPHONE VOICE   243

Trombone.' It is a voice as sonorous and full and deep as a prophetic brass choir, but it is capable of the utmost intimacy and sympathetic expression as well."[141] If one listens to a selection of synchronic snapshots for each decade Robeson recorded from the mid-1920s to the mid-1950s, it is in the high-fidelity records of the 1950s that critical descriptions of Robeson's voice receive their most complete sonic correlation. Here, Robeson's voice, especially from the independent recordings on, is remarkably—viscerally—"present," all the more magnetic for the sonic magnification that was the aim of high-fidelity recording. As Robeson's recorded voice became a product of high-fidelity engineering, so the singer, through recourse to sound reinforcement technologies, presented a concert voice that aimed to approximate the hi-fi voice his public had become accustomed to hearing on record.

Tim Anderson argues that fundamental to understanding high-fidelity sound technologies of the postwar years is a focus on the listener, but that an analysis of listening is also relevant to understanding musical production. The "relaxed listener" of high-fidelity records at mid-century, he writes, was one who "sought a moment, a space, and a technology in which the act of 'easy listening'" could be fostered.[142] Conversely we might conceive of the technologically informed performer as a relaxed singer. The technologies of performance that Robeson's microphone voice permitted and the acoustic spaces in which he performed allowed him, in the end, to sing more easily. At the very close of his career, the singer was still trying out a new technology for these ends. Embarked on an extended seven-week tour of Australia and New Zealand in 1960, Robeson revealed, to the New Zealand magazine *The Listener*, another device of self-listening:

> I've got now my own little gadget. I put this in my ear and it's like I'm standing in a very wonderful bathroom. Now all I have to do is be very quiet, and I hear my voice about five times as loud. Put it in your ear, not that ear, the other one, now say something. . . . You see it's just like built-in acoustics. Well that noise to me is as if I'm standing in a bathroom. I can talk like this the rest of the day without strain.[143]

It is not clear what the precise nature of the "little gadget" was: a crude, early type of an in-ear performance monitor (which were commercially produced only in the 1970s when they began to be used in popular music performance), a modified hearing aid, or a combination thereof. Nor is it clear all of what the device could do: simply reduce stage noise and/or provide a

244 PAUL ROBESON'S VOICES

vocal mix of sorts, as Synthea had done. It was undoubtedly a further aid to Robeson in controlling his singer's acoustic space, and as with all his uses of sound technologies on the stage it aided him in the very practical task of easy singing.

Sound Check

Throughout this chapter lies a distinction, one which, even as it has surfaced frequently, I have not pursued in any detail: the *sounds* of Robeson's concert and gramophone voices. Whether the "presence" of his transatlantic telephone voice, the missing "warmth" of his amplified voice in the Albert Hall, or the visceralness of his hi-fi recordings, Robeson's microphone voice affected the sound of his voice.[144] And different technologies effected different sounds at different moments of his career. If the Vanguard records Robeson made in the late 1950s were advertised as "the first and only discs in which full justice is done to Mr. Robeson's voice," what, we might ask, did recording do to his voice since the mid-1920s when he first recorded?

It is not known that before Robeson signed for the Victor Talking Machine Company he was courted by several other recording outfits. Already in early 1924, before he was an established concert singer, before even he had had sung a solo recital, the Chicago Music Publishing Company approached Robeson, as did Brunswick Records. Nothing came of these overtures. And just days after Robeson's unexpected recital success at the Greenwich Village Theater on April 19, 1925, he was making test records for Victor. The Victor ledger books provide the details of Robeson's first recording dates.[145] For the trial, which took place in Victor's lab in New York City on April 21, Robeson and his accompanist performed "Bye and Bye," "Ever' Time I Hear the Spirit," and "The Water Boy." The tests were good enough for the duo to proceed to Victor's Camden studios across the Hudson, and where on July 16 they recorded five songs. All but one of the five songs recorded at the session were destroyed. The first take of "Bye and Bye" was held, and the second was chosen as the master for what is thus the first extant Robeson recording. It was released in October that year on a 10-inch 78 as the B-side of Victor 19743, partnered with "Joshua Fit de Battle ob Jericho" (see Figure 6.5). The trips to Camden would continue at regular intervals until Robeson's departure for England in 1928 where he would record for HMV.

Figure 6.5. "Bye and Bye" (Victor 19743-B, 1925).

As Robeson's recording catalog grew his records began to attract attention. In early 1926 the Pittsburgh music store Goldman and Wolf, "headquarters for race artists' records," held a "Robeson week" to coincide with the singer's appearance in concert in the city.[146] The event is pregnant with meaning. First, it signaled the beginning of the relationship between concert singer and recording artist that would characterize Robeson's career. In Robeson's case his recording and concert debuts were cotemporaneous, and the articulations between these different modes and media through which he sang, some of which I have explored in this chapter, would shape his vocal practice and voice's sound. Robeson appeared on Victor's black label. Reserved for the "pop stars" of the era, the black-label discs were the lowest-priced in the catalog intended for a mass market. But whereas the majority of the black-label artists were primarily studio performers, appearing

246 PAUL ROBESON'S VOICES

in concert to sell their records, Robeson was foremost a recitalist with a significant recording output. Indeed, much of his commercial recording work (particularly for HVM) was in conflict with the artistic intentions of his concert singing.[147] Second, and as the *Pittsburgh Courier* reported, Robeson's records were used by Victor to demonstrate the company's new Orthophonic Victrola.[148] The promotion of the new sound machine by the rising star is an indication of his status as a performer even at the outset of his concert and recording career, and also of the moment of his emergence as a recording artist, and of the recordability of his voice.

Victor had released the Orthophonic playback machine in late 1925 on the back of its conversion to electric recording earlier that year. Because the new electric discs played poorly on older machines designed for acoustic records a new playback machine was needed. The Orthophonic was a "revelation to listeners accustomed to acoustic reproduction: the dramatic increase in volume, the clear sibilants, and most of all, the amazing reproduction of bass notes."[149] Robeson's first entry into the recording studio coincided precisely with the beginning of electric recording: Victor's first electric discs were released in mid-1925, and Robeson's first record was in stores a few months later.[150] His recorded voice was literally a microphone voice; it was not, what we might call, a horn voice after the mechanical device used in acoustic recording. And this meant that his recorded voice was heard in a certain way, differently from if it had been captured by horn just half a year earlier. The effects of electrical recording for Robeson's voice were several. In reviewing the singer's recording of "Water Boy," released in early 1926, the Philadelphia *Record* noted specifically that the disc was "another triumph of recording the bass voice."[151] I want then to dwell on how electrical recording captured lower voices, and I do so through the ears of the critics of *Gramophone* magazine, who reviewed Robeson records throughout his career.

One of the world's premier critics of the voice in the early twentieth century was Herman Klein, who listened to vocal records as a matter of his profession; and the relationship of critic to technology is captured in the book *Herman Klein and the Gramophone*. He reviewed Robeson records on several occasions: "a pure, rich, natural voice, and commanding a style of unsurpassable breadth and nobility."[152] I am interested in what Klein's listening tells us about the reception of developments in recording technology. In June 1924, during the terminal stages of the acoustic recording era, he reported that "I regard the gramophone of to-day as a wonderfully truthful and accurate reflection of the voice and art of the singer."[153] Two years later, and as industry and listeners became accustomed to the new technologies of electrical recording, Klein enthused that "1926 has been a year of such remarkable progress as to make it outstanding in the history of the gramophone."[154] Another two years hence and the critic's enthusiasm for recording technology had begun to waver:

> The tendency henceforward . . . will be to *flatter* the human voice instead of failing to do it justice. The gramophone will not only increase its volume by many degrees but improve its timbre and cover up many of its blemishes. In these respects I think it is going to approximate more closely than it ever has done to the art of photography, with its modern facilities for enlargement and touching-up.[155]

By 1930, Klein charged "that unconscious medium, the microphone," the "chief culprit" the amplifier, and the "man behind it" the engineer, as collectively guilty of converting "the gramophone from a true witness into a false one."[156] In these glimpses of one critic's hearing we might pause to consider the favored interpretive paradigm that has informed histories of recording. As Virgil Moorefield writes, in the first half of the twentieth century recording aimed to present the "illusion of reality," to capture as realistically as possible the sound of live performance.[157] But Klein and other early gramophone critics were attuned to recording's interventionist intentions long before historians of recording provided us with a "genealogy of [recording's] practices of deception."[158] For no voice type was this more acutely acknowledged than for the recording of bass voices.

In an article that appeared in *Gramophone* in 1933 titled "The Recorded Voice—and the Real Thing," Thomas O'Brien presented the bass voice as chief exhibit for his claim that many recorded voices "bear no more than a superficial resemblance to the real thing." This was a remarkable turnaround from the acoustic era during which it was acknowledged that the horn was least friendly to basses.[159] As example O'Brien offered Benvenuto Franci's recorded voice, which was "like about six baritones rolled into one," and Giovanni Inghilleri, as recorded, had "a very powerful voice, whereas in reality he is not powerful enough to fill Covent Garden."[160] What one pundit referred to as the "artifice" of recording, notably with regard to bass singers, was a hot topic in the pages of *Gramophone*, such that 1933 was the year of "the orgy of low notes" wrought by "a new race of pseudo-technical hotgospellers preaching the doctrine of lower notes."[161]

The precise technical means by which bass voices were recorded at the time are difficult to ascertain. Among other things, record companies were secretive about their technical knowledge and record-making was not standardized. General principles that informed the practice of reproduction are, however, known. *Gramophone* technical critic William D. Owen identified two matters that divided opinion: the amount of bass cut-off to be tolerated, and the "extent and nature of the coloration" permitted. Both had consequences for Robeson's recorded voice. It is well known that electric recording increased the frequency range that could be captured, at both ends of the spectrum; at the lower end from between 150 and 200 Hz at best in acoustic recording, although more typically 300 Hz, that is just above middle C, to 50 Hz in electric records (see Figure 6.6).[162] A fuller spectrum profile of basses, and low notes, was thus captured; and bass singers recorded by microphone sounded different—fuller and louder—from those who had sung into horns. Owen's reference to bass cut-off refers to what is called the recording characteristic, that is the method used for cutting a phonograph record defined by the relationship of frequency to amplitude and velocity, and which was not standardized until 1956 by the Recording Industry Association of America (RIAA).[163] HMV used a bass turnover frequency of 250 Hz from 1925 to 1938, and Victor's was 300 Hz (whereas for the RIAA curve it is 500

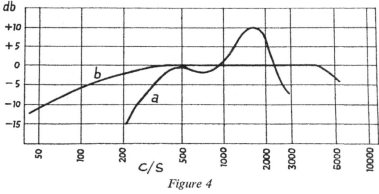

Figure 4
Recording Characteristics.
(*a*) Acoustic Recording.
(*b*) Early Electric Recording.

Figure 6.6. Response curves in acoustic and early electric recording. Percy Wilson, *The Gramophone Handbook* (London: Methuen, 1957), 39.

Hz).[164] The cut-off indicates that sounds below that frequency were recorded with a constant amplitude (known as a constant-amplitude recording characteristic) and for pitches above it the volume decreased as the pitch increased (known as a constant-velocity recording characteristic). In other words, the bulk of the register of Robeson's voice was recorded louder than was the case for the recording of basses in the acoustic era.

A further consideration, and one which tends to be neglected in discussions of recorded sound, is the effect of playback. The introduction of electrical phonographs with magnetic cartridges resulted in playback equalization becoming a feature of record listening. Magnetic cartridges exhibit the following behavior: in playing a constant-amplitude recording, the region of bass recording, its output increases as the frequency rises; whereas because they are velocity-sensitive devices, their output is flat for velocity-constant recordings. In order to achieve a flat response through the entire frequency range, playback equalization boosted the bass below the turnover frequency. Critics' complaints about bass-boosting in early electrical recordings must be seen as a function of both recording and playback practices. Finally, the move from condenser microphones to ribbon mics in the early 1930s also affected recorded sound. Ribbon mics of that era had a flatter high-frequency response, and in order to increase a record's level of brightness engineers added a high-frequency boost to the mic's preamplifiers. This enriched bass notes too because of course it is the higher partials of a fundamental that contribute to the richness of the overall timbre. Owen noted that the introduction of "missing" frequencies, and the control of their levels, "upset the balance" of frequencies such that a "lower-toned effect" was a common result. "This 'colouring' of the tone scale," he concluded, "is not necessarily an undesirable proceeding but it must be recognised as an artifice."[165] Even for Klein, recording's deceptions were not all bad: "The new Frankenstein, which ... we will call the Microphone, is invested with powers than can make it either a great friend or a great enemy."[166]

By all accounts, the microphone was a good friend to Robeson, an amity fostered in his own concert practice and first forged in the sound of his recorded voice. Although the practices of recording bass voices in the early electrical era are audible in the capturing of Robeson's voice on disc, they were applied with some restraint, and none of the hundreds of reviews of his recorded voice call it out for the transgressions attributed to other bass voices. Robeson's rerecording of "Steal Away" and "Water Boy" for HMV (both first recorded for Victor) was the "finest record" on Klein's list to review in February 1934, "beautifully sung

250   PAUL ROBESON'S VOICES

and recorded.[167] One effect of electrical recording on Robeson's singing was that it allowed him to sing low. From the outset, Victor identified Robeson as a bass: internally, in the company's recording ledgers, and publicly on disc labels. But from the first records he cut for Victor in mid-1925, just as electrical recording was introduced, one might easily hear the singer as a higher voice. His upper register is "sweet," the mid-register dominates (and we hear it lower only because it is counterpoised with his accompanist's high tenor in the duets), with nary a glimpse of a true bass sound. Robeson's higher, lighter voice in the 1920s must in part be attributed to the particular microphone that captured his voice on record. In the early years of electrical recording, until the early 1930s, condenser microphones were favored by the recording industry, and one of their characteristics was their reproduction of higher frequencies such that listeners could better hear a voice's upper register. The perceived higher and lighter sound of crooners at this time, argues Allison McCracken, was a function of microphone technology.[168]

By the time Robeson started recording for HMV in London, in mid-1928, swift advances in electrical recording afforded the production of a voice more readily identifiable as the bass the records professed to reproduce. The HMV catalog for January 1929 proclaimed to its consumers that Robeson's "deep magnificent bass voice is excellently reproduced." In "Scandalize My Name" (recorded in Studio B, in HMV's Hayes facility on June 19, 1928), Robeson sings more consistently low (listen to 1:25–1:41, e.g.). At the lowest points in several songs spanning the late 1920s and early 1930s we catch a first hearing of Robeson's much-vaunted bass voice. The spectral information for these sounds reveals how electrical recording made it possible to capture Robeson's voice in a way that acoustic records could not, and the range of frequencies inscribed in the grooves bears this out. When Robeson sings, "No! No!" roughly to the pitches $E^{\flat}_3$, C_3, $B^{\flat}_3$ in "Scandalize My Name," the range of the fundamental frequencies is around 100–170 Hz; and that for "nigh" (C_3) in "Weepin' Mary," also recorded in 1928, between 120 and 130 Hz. The horn would not have recorded these pitches at the amplitude the microphone did. By 1930, when Robeson recorded "Hail de Crown" (in the Queen's Hall in London), the lowest fundamental frequency for the singing of "Lord" drops below 100 Hz; and the same is true of the phrase "My Lord," the lowest point in "Mary Had a Baby" (recorded in late 1931 in Abbey Road Studio No. 3) (see Figures 6.7a–d; and listen to Sound Recordings 6.7a–d ⏵). In the latter work, Robeson crescendos into and through the lowest note of the song, a mark of his increasing comfort singing low and of the record's ability

A MICROPHONE VOICE 251

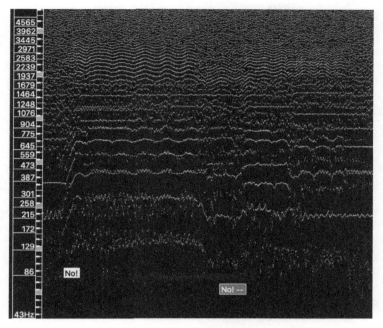

Figure 6.7a. Spectrum for "No! No!" in "Scandalize My Name" (1928).

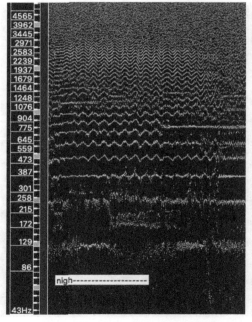

Figure 6.7b. Spectrum of "nigh" in "Weepin' Mary" (1928).

252   PAUL ROBESON'S VOICES

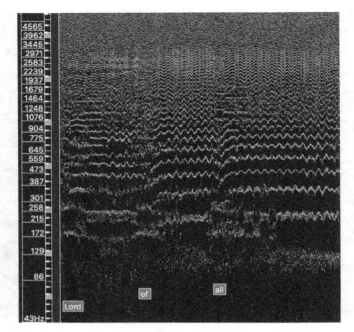

Figure 6.7c. Spectrum for "Lord of all" in "Hail de Crown" (1930).

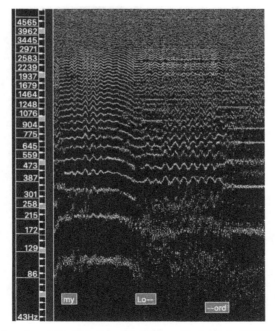

Figure 6.7d. Spectrum for "My Lord" in "Mary Had a Baby" (1931).

A MICROPHONE VOICE   253

to capture and produce his bass voice more convincingly.[169] A contemporary sound specialist explained that each octave recorded affects the quality of the resultant recorded sound differently: in the third octave, that is in the frequency range of 64–128 cycles per second, most bass notes are found which "give body to the music," whereas frequencies in the range of 128–256 cps "add what one may describe as richness to the quality."[170]

Recall that throughout the mid-1920s and into the early 1930s, Robeson received frequent if occasional voice training. This must in part account for the resonance and weight of the voice in its lowest reach we hear in the recordings of the late 1920s and early 1930s in comparison to the first records he cut in in the mid-1920s. Specifically, as he first studied the art song repertoire in late 1929 he would have focused on bass tone production in learning Sarastro's aria "O Isis und Osiris" from *Die Zauberflöte* and "Die Ehre Gottes aus der Natur" from Beethoven's song cycle *Sechs Lieder nach Gedichten von Gellert*, Op. 48, which appeared on his concert programs of the early 1930s. Robeson's voice and Mozart's bass aria shared such an affinity of tessitura that slightly later the singer confessed to preparing his voice for gramophone recording and broadcasting by singing "O Isis and Osiris": "This, he says, so fits his rich voice that no help is needed from the recording engineers."[171] Recall also that Robeson experienced classical voice training with ambivalence. He resisted, for instance, the attempt to mold him into a baritone at which his early training aimed. As the young singer developed his vocal craft as a bass, he did so in parallel to developments in electrical recording that produced bass sounds in ways hitherto unsurpassed. By 1930, one of the few negative reviews of a Robeson record thus complained that "Robeson's singing tends to become monotonous through his choice of an invariably low pitch. . . . His magnificent voice seems to have been inadequately trained, and so he is safe and comfortable only on the ground floor."[172] It would perhaps place too much weight on the phonographic effect to suggest that Robeson's bass voice was created in the recording studio, but we should acknowledge that recording was a helpmate to the singer in settling on a voice type, and that it shaped the sound of his bass voice and singing practice too.

Critics of early electrical recording not only uncovered its deceptive practices such as bass-boosting and over-amplification, which made "the organ of the singer appear bigger, more resonant, more imposing and impressive." They also observed the advantages of modern records. Klein identified the "clarifying effect" and "reinforcing of timbre" as two of the boons of the microphone's presentation of "a closer-sounding voice."[173] The gap between

254   PAUL ROBESON'S VOICES

listener and performer that the microphone closed was particularly productive for Robeson's vocal articulations. Routinely praised throughout his career and across art forms—theater, film, and song, in concert, and on record—for his enunciatory prowess, his miked voice emphasized the singer's facility with words. The London weekly *Saturday Review* considered him second only to Sir George Henschel, tellingly one of Robeson's voice coaches, in "compelling the microphone not only to reproduce the extremely personal quality of a voice but to catch and give forth again the curiosities of an unusual diction."[174] Indeed, the microphone caught and gave forth more than impeccable phonemic articulation, revealing even the vocal mechanisms of the singing body in action. The clarity of Robeson's 1930 recording of "Go Down, Moses" was notable for "the vibrations of the breath against the vocal chords often being heard."[175] (It is not clear what precisely the reviewer meant, nor do I hear the breath thus mentioned, but later records frequently bear audible traces of the mechanics of Robeson's singing.)[176] Robeson's voice on record is also characterized by a marked and progressive enriching of its timbre—the reinforcement to which Klein referred—as successive developments in high-fidelity technologies shaped his sound over time. To hear this it is instructive to listen to the records of the early and mid-1930s against those recorded later.

It is a feature of Robeson's recorded output that the singer often recorded the same song on several occasions; sometimes, and mundanely, because the master disc had worn out or he was contracted to another label, other times because both the sound of his voice and recording technology had moved on, requiring that a new take was preferred over keeping an old sound before the public. Thus the first record he made for Victor, "Bye and Bye," was "re-recorded" for HMV in 1933 (on B4480), even though, as a *Gramophone* reviewer noted, the Victor disc was "apparently, electrically recorded" and the British company was licensed to produce Robeson's Victor masters.[177] Another take of the spiritual was laid down in 1945, this time for Columbia Masterworks as part of an album set of four ten-inch 78s released in 1945 (M-610). The recording date is significant for it was just before the adoption of full frequency range recording, introduced by Decca in 1945, and followed not long thereafter by other technological markers of high-fidelity audio: magnetic tape, microgroove vinyl, and stereo. (A few years later "By an' By" was released on a long-playing microgroove *Spirituals* [Columbia ML 4015].) Robeson's voice in "By an' By" of 1945 then did not benefit from the full range of audio production techniques that characterized high-fidelity records at mid-century, and its frequency range is little different from that of the 1933 record.[178] Recorded a tone

A MICROPHONE VOICE 255

lower than in 1933, thereby perceptually emphasizing heaviness, the richness of the 1945 recording is attributable to at least two features.

First, spectral data indicate that while the frequency range is almost identical, the frequency levels in the 1945 recording are louder. Focusing on the lowest pitch, sung to the word "down" in the phrase "I'm gwine," which Robeson sings as "gonna" in the later version, "lay down my heavy load," there is minimal variation in volume of the fundamental pitch for both recordings.[179] But the sound level for the other partials is louder in the later version: for the 1945 record the first overtone's level is loudest at −18 dB and averages between −21 and −22 dB, where the average for the 1933 disc is −24 to −25 dB; and the second overtone, in 1945, is recorded at its loudest −17 dB with an average of between −18 and −19 dB, whereas the same data for 1933 are −19 dB and between −21 and −23 dB. Equally important, the higher bands of frequency in the later record are louder, visible from the spectrograms; in color graphs (▶) in the greater prominence of red waves that indicate the increased volume of the frequencies (see Figures 6.8a and 6.8b; and listen to Sound Recordings 6.8a and 6.8b ▶).[180] As I discussed in

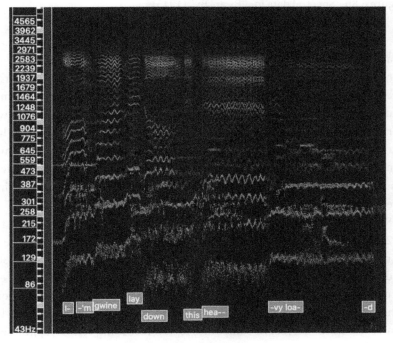

Figure 6.8a. Spectral data for "By an' By" (1933).

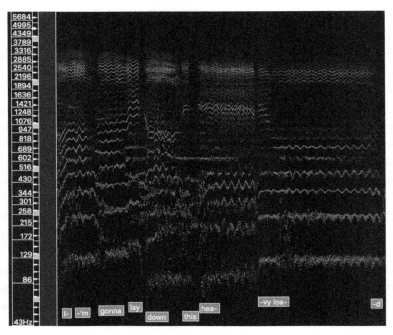

Figure 6.8b. Spectral data for "By an' By" (1945).

chapter 3, the greater intensity of the spectral information in the later recording is in part what allows us to hear Robeson's voice as richer. (In the recollection of William Schatzkamer, Robeson's supporting artist's accompanist and sometime operator of Synthea, there is the suggestion that the singer was particularly interested in hearing "the highs" from Synthea's speakers in live performance. A specialist speaker technician, identified only as Soundman Sam, and whose sound systems were used extensively in Broadway theaters, was bought on board to tweak the speakers Robeson used by building in a tweeter.)[181]

Second, the richness is enhanced by the resonance of the recording. In the 1920s, "uncontrollable reverberations and echoes posed repeated problems in recordings" such that "dead" spaces were favored. But during the 1930s, and following the lead of broadcast's turn to a more "lively" acoustic environment, reverberation became an important asset in recording. Among other enhancements, it made records sound louder.[182] The search for big "natural" sounds led record companies to new recording venues, epitomized by Columbia's acquisition of the Liederkranz Hall on East Fifty-eighth

Figure 6.9. Robeson and Lawrence Brown recording in Columbia's Liederkranz Hall, c. early to mid-1945. The Frederick and Rose Plaut Papers, Irving S. Gilmore Music Library, Yale University.

Street in New York. Because of the room's spaciousness and abundance of wood, it lent the recordings made there "more presence and seemingly more volume." It was "the most desirable recording room throughout the 1940s," where Robeson recorded for Columbia, and where he re-recorded "By an' By" (see Figure 6.9).[183] The presence of Robeson's voice in the 1945 version, and which so differentiates it from the sound of the 1933 "By an' By," is in part an effect of the acoustics of the space in which the spiritual was recorded.

These cumulative boons for the sound of Robeson's recorded voice in the early 1940s, the result of successive developments in recording technologies and practices, impacted in turn his concert practice. For instance, as his recorded voice moved toward a *profundo* bass, Robeson utilized sound technologies in an attempt to sing deep on the concert stage. Burris-Meyer reported on the singer's use of Synthea in a Carnegie Hall recital of October 6, 1940, that "Mr. Robeson was able to sing 'Water Boy' in a lower key than he had ever used before for that number in concert."[184] And by the time Robeson had begun to use a public address system regularly in concert, his voice, in amplification, could be heard in its lowest possible reaches. The

258 PAUL ROBESON'S VOICES

rumbling low D_2, on which he ushers in the refrain of "Ol' Man River" sung at a later Carnegie Hall recital in 1958, would have been barely audible to the audience if not for amplification.[185] Indeed, the 1958 Carnegie Hall recitals represent a culmination of Robeson's technologically informed singing practice: Synthea, a public address system, and the apparatus for a high-fidelity stereophonic live recording of the performance all accompanied Robeson, a trio of sound technologies that was typically present for his performances on his return to the world's concert stages in 1958.[186] The dialectical movement of sung and mediatized modes that had characterized Robeson's practice since the outset of his concert career and through which his voice was formed—as a microphone voice—was, however, not always heard as a successful synthesis, as we saw from the reception of his microphone voice in concert. An awareness of the different methods of singing and vocal production for the microphone and acoustic singing, for the gramophone and concert, was much discussed already in the 1920s and 1930s.

In response to these debates, the little-known singer, and "an expert in recording technique," John Thorne penned an article for *Gramophone*: "The Fallacy of the 'Recording Voice.'" It was a rebuttal to the pace of technological advance, the frenzy of recording activity, and the rise of the idea of a recording voice: "the past six years the whole of the gramophone world has been engaged in ceaseless effort to obtain the ideal in recording and reproduction," Thorne began, immediately countering that "there was no such thing as a 'recording voice,' but that the whole matter was a question of sound vocal technique." Thorne's purpose was to return the burden of a successful performance to the singer, to limit the interventions of the recordist and controller (early designations for the sound engineer). "Now, an enormous lot depends on the singer. . . . It is the singer whose voice is badly produced, harsh, white, and open at the top of the compass, muddy and woolly at the bottom, and whose diction is bad (an unusually common failing), that causes the recorder endless trouble and whitens the hair of the controlling engineer." At some length Thorne proceeded to itemize the "essential qualities" for an "ideal recording vocalist":

First—the voice must be sufficiently well produced to be equally forward throughout the whole of its range. If not, it will sound harsh and squeezed at the top and thin and muddy at the bottom of its compass. The voice must flow in one long, continuous line, no matter whether it be a slow, sustained aria, or in a quick diction song. The words must be superimposed on the voice without breaking the flow of sound. . . . These matters are, after all, nothing more than straightforward vocal technique.

Perhaps Thorne's complaint strikes us now as peculiar, certainly a little elitist, and a product of the art of the trained singer; he was an acolyte of Harry Plunket Greene. But it bears reminding ourselves of the sheer number of often amateur singers recorded in the field and enticed into studios, almost all long forgotten and seldom heard since, and also of professional singers flummoxed by the new technologies—a veritable legion of bad singing in the age of early electrical recording. The "majority of singers have no idea just how badly they sing, or how terribly poor is their diction." But "when they can be brought face to face with their technical deficiencies (and are prepared to correct them), and only then, shall we have intelligibility, coupled with smooth, flowing, well phrased and nuanced voices—in a word, 'Recording Voices.'"[187]

I'd like to imagine that Robeson took up the mantle of Thorpe's Recording Voice. The voice training he undertook, some of it even before his first recording sessions in mid-1925, most of it during the first half decade of his recording career, undoubtedly made him a better singer. Alongside the effusive commentary on his voice's sound, reviews of his records often noted his artistry for both the singer's interpretive sensibility and his vocal craft (even if at times, as in reviews of concert performances, shortcomings of technique were occasionally noted). Thus when in 1932 *Gramophone* divided the "singers of popular songs of the day" into "two classes"—"those who have really good voices and use their art on these trifles, and those whose chief claim to popularity is their talent in putting these songs over without the same vocal abilities"—Robeson was admitted to the first class.[188] Because Robeson had both learnt to sing and learnt to sing for the microphone—he "never turns out a bad, or even indifferent, record . . . partly due to the particularly fine microphone quality of his voice," remarked *Gramophone*—he was spared much of the criticism of other bass singers who appeared on disc.[189]

Thorpe's musings and Robeson's practice suggest that despite "a hierarchical way of thinking that treats one side of the equation between live performance and recording as the original, the real thing, and the other as a copy or substitute," that is, as "separate culture systems," we might rather "encompass them within an enlarged concept of performance," as Nicholas Cook has proposed.[190] In Robeson's case, the technologies of reproduction, which in conventional wisdom are resolutely bound to the practices and discourse of recording alone, were productive of his voice and singing on record as much as in concert. It makes, then, little sense to analytically disentangle his concert and gramophone voices, or to pursue one without documenting the other's relationship to it. This formulation of the one and the other is itself limiting. Thus I have summoned the conceit of the "microphone voice" in order to assert that Robeson's vocal gestures were technologically mediated from almost the outset of his singing career. Recognizing that the performance practice of early twentieth-century classical singers, and popular classical singers like Robeson, was also a technology-informed performance practice reveals that singers consumed sound technologies in a more "modern" way than is often acknowledged.

Afterword

In-between and Against: A Voice for the Times

When I tell people who don't know much, or anything, about Robeson that I'm writing a book on him, their responses at first typically turn on the question of what type of music he sang. The framing of our everyday musical knowledge by typology is of course ubiquitous.

"Was he a jazz singer?" I'm asked. (As if, because, he was Black and American, he'd be a jazz singer.)

"Definitely not."

"An opera singer?"

"No, but he did perform a few opera arias."

"So he was a classical singer?"

"Not really, although he did have some classical voice training." Depending on my interlocutor (and their age), I might proffer a common point of reference: "Do you know the musical *Show Boat*? Robeson made the song 'Ol' Man River' famous." (My partner's nonagenarian grandmother, who lived on the southern tip of the South Island in New Zealand, produced an LP of Robeson's *Show Boat* when I first mentioned my interest in him to her.)

"Ah, so he sang in musical theater."

"A little. But he wasn't a musical theater artist; at least not for most of his career."

If the questions haven't stopped before this they surely do now, and I'm left to explain the sound of Robeson's voice as best as words can.

Paul Robeson's Voices has pointed to the difficulty of placing Robeson's voice. Already in 1939 a British newspaper declared that Robeson "is not a classifiable singer."[1] His voice, one might conclude, sounds and operates from a place of in-betweenness. In this it exceeds philosophy's musings on the in-betweenness of the generalized voice or the voice's inherent multiplicity, two thoughts about the voice that I introduced at the outset of the book. Because Robeson's voice was formed through its interactions with several, sometimes

262   AFTERWORD: IN-BETWEEN AND AGAINST

competing, traditions, genres, and styles, it could not be anything but hybrid, sounding from being between. It was as such a voice of its time, when sonic practice and knowledge were less rigidly policed by the increasingly institutionalized disciplines and the music industrial complex, and by cultural discourse as the twentieth century wore on, when "light classics" and middlebrow culture, to use old-fashioned terms, held sway. Robeson's singing voice was formed in betweenness, mediated by the practices of schooling and the desires of sounding natural; in the interstices of accents and dialects; and modalities of song and speech; by emergent sound technologies that transformed the acoustic voice. The voice-thinking that I have advocated in this book has allowed us to encounter, sometimes in granular detail, the sonic forms of Robeson's voice; the haecceity of his voice. But in-betweenness is more than a hybrid, "a 'single mix' in which boundaries are blurred." As Min Jeong Song observes, in-betweenness "possesses the idea of 'inter-' or 'multi-' that denotes reciprocal relationships, relativity and the co-existence of multiple entities." And importantly, it implies a sense of direction.[2]

The in-betweenness of Robeson's voice proceeded from a desire for direction. At first, in the search to find his vocal self as a performer, the singer trialed and (partly) rejected a number of traditions while being shaped by his interactions with their practices. Robeson approached a tradition and then retreated from it; his voice operated *against*: gaining from the contact with a practice as it opposed it. That in-betweenness originated from a position of sounding against as much as it allowed for a stance of being against. As one of the first theorists of cultural hybridity Homi Bhabha put it, "in-between spaces provide the terrain for elaborating strategies of selfhood—singular or communal—that initiate new signs of identity, and innovative sites of collaboration, and contestation."[3] It is precisely Robeson's in-between voice that permitted his much lauded (and, in his life, also reviled) political contestation and action, and it has been my contention in this book that if we practice voice-thinking we are able to hear more clearly the directions in which Robeson's singing and politics moved. In many ways Robeson's was a countervoice. Permit me to riff on "contra."

William Dwight Whitney's *The Century Dictionary and Cyclopedia*, the preeminent American lexicographical work produced during Robeson's early life, commenced its entry on "contra" with the commonplace: "contra" means "against," but also "opposite." More than this, *The Century Dictionary* noted, contra articulates a position of being "in front of."[4] Through his oppositional voice Robeson was a leader, he stood at the forefront. The editors

AFTERWORD: IN-BETWEEN AND AGAINST   263

of *Freedomways* thus christened him "The Great Forerunner," gesturing that he was ahead of the times while thoroughly of his time. A "Freedom Fighter of the first magnitude," his "personal Odyssey" was both "inseparable from the life and struggles of the Afro-American community and the monumental changes which have taken place in the *world* over the last half-century."[5] Robeson's early career coincided with the increased essentializing and policing of racial identities in the 1920s and 1930s, when a "clearer Black/white binary" emerged;[6] and the singer's Depression-era engagement with class and labor politics—and with "the people"—in the 1930s and 1940s was expanded into an internationalist and cosmopolitan outlook in the 1940s and 1950s in service against myopic nationalisms accelerated by the rise of fascism and the Cold War world. It is unsurprising then that C. L. R. James yoked together the histories of Robeson and the world:

> A man whose history is not to be understood unless seen in the context of the most profound historical movements of our century. And, at the same time, the most profound historical movements of the twentieth century cannot be understood without taking into consideration Paul Robeson.[7]

We can add, as *Paul Robeson's Voices* has argued, that Robeson's voice and singing cannot be understood without being heard in the contexts—plural—of the many performance and song traditions he encountered, and that it is through these sonic encounters, accessed by the historian through voice-thinking, that allows us to comprehend the artist's relationship to "the most profound historical movements" of the times.

We return, then, to the idea of the resistance of Robeson's performance, to his manifold countervoicings. The singer turned away from certain repertories of song; a creator of contrafacta, he revised song lyrics; he rejected some of the vocal techniques and singing styles of several song traditions. Robeson's voice, to revisit Fred Moten, was an exemplary object of resistance, which for Moten is the essential condition of Blackness and Black performance, "an ongoing irruption that anarranges every line."[8] The phonic irruptions and interruptions of the Black voice/object disrupt and resist "certain formations of identity and interpretation by challenging the reducibility of phonic matter to verbal meaning or conventional musical form"; they function as a critique of the sign.[9] At every turn we have witnessed how Robeson's countervoice provided an interpretive challenge, contesting identity and meaning. And it did so because it sounded as in-betweenness.

264 AFTERWORD: IN-BETWEEN AND AGAINST

The in-betweenness of Robeson's voice has perhaps resisted in another way, rejected to some extent by musicological interpretation—an abject object— even as scholars have noted that, early in his career, Robeson replaced "the visual focus on his body . . . with a focus on the aural possibilities of his voice."[10] This brings to mind Moten's observations on writings about performance and sound which "are too easily subordinated to the visual/spatial and the pervasive occularcentrism": the "de-scription of sound." What voice-thinking aims at, rather, is what Moten advocates in the following injunction: "remembrance of the aural *gives*."[11] It reveals by making audible what has remained unheard, "unremembered." But, as Moten notes, the "mark of invisibility is a visible, racial mark; invisibility has visibility at its heart. To be invisible is to be seen, instantly and fascinatingly recognized as the unrecognizable, as the abject."[12] Voice-thinking exposes the not hearing of Robeson as a mark of disciplinary deafness, music studies' occlusion. But more than this, through voice-thinking we recognize that what is un/ heard in Robeson's voice and performance is always racial: it exposes the racialization of hearing—of audiences, critics, scholars, and my own. The remembrance of the aural, and specifically of Black aurality, is also, Moten proposes in a critique of the logocentric traditions, a site of "augmentation, of a beneficent and song-producing prosthesis—the augmentation of vision with the sound that it has excluded, the augmentation of reason with the ecstasy it has dismissed."[13] Through the many acts of voice-thinking we have been able to discern some of Robeson's sonic augmentations, to hear his generous additions (as prosthetic) to the voice, singing, concert practice, and sound technologies.

The beneficence of Robeson's singing is located first, and foremost, in his voice. Ecstasy and sound are correlates, and the pleasure of the voice is the ground from which Robeson's generosity—his gift, as I proposed earlier in the book—is heard. In thinking about the acousmatic voice Nina Sun Eidsheim reminds us that the acousmatic question—whose voice is this?— often tells us as much about the listener as it does about the singer's identity.[14] Many of Robeson's listeners heard authority in his voice, which issued from his very deep voice; from, if you will, his *contra*bass—the prefix "contra-" here indicating an instrument of very low register. Robeson's deep bass voices several male authorities. In *Paul Robeson's Voices* we have encountered Robeson voicing the hero and father/Father, the preacher and God. My discussion of moments in which Robeson voices God, in reciting-singing *God's Trombones* or singing the spiritual "Go Down Moses," highlights that his

AFTERWORD: IN-BETWEEN AND AGAINST 265

God-voice is uttered in his lowest range. If Robeson's contrabass presents as a God-like authority, it is also, as I argued in my discussion of the protesting voice, a countervoice that sings against authority; anti-boss, if you like. And this voice—the "bad voice" I termed it after Steven Connor—was not always "nice." It sounded against the tonal ideals of classical singing, transformed recital practices, and performed outside the institutions of the music industries, all to make a point, a counterpoint to hegemonic politics and identities. In this enterprise, of singing against, the voice had to sound in-between.

After his political turn, Robeson's singing for freedom, and against slavery (in many of its forms), came to fulfill Moten's injunction that "the freedom drive . . . animates black performances."[15] But if Robeson directed his singing toward the utopian ideal of freedom, the latter is, as Moten has shown, always "yoked" to slavery:

> the moment in which you enter into the knowledge of slavery, of yourself as a slave, is the moment you begin to think about freedom, the moment in which you know or begin to know or to produce knowledge of freedom, the moment at which you become a fugitive, the moment at which you begin to escape in ways that trouble the structures of subjection that . . . overdetermine freedom.[16]

The dialectical movement between slavery and freedom is characterized by being in-between, by an in-between being; as Moten puts it, in the "miscegenative origin of black/American identity."[17] It brings to mind Katherine Meizel's thinking about multivocality, the many ways of being in the world through voice, in terms of the border. Multivocality permits navigating "the in-betweens and border crossings" of identities and works across "the geographical and ideological borders of cultural spaces." Meizel thus conceives of the voice as borderscape, as an instrument not only of border-dwelling and border-crossing but of "de-bordering and re-bordering"; that is, voices like Robeson's "help to create, re-create, and re-shape the spaces in which they resonate." Borderland voices can also be agents of change, "erod[ing] boundaries in resistance to systems of oppression." And so again, being in-between and against are related; they are co-constitutive of Robeson's voice. Meizel has said that "the need to voice border experiences can generate singers."[18] Pursuing voice-thinking allows us to reframe this process emphasizing other voice-generative functions. Robeson's experiences of singing, of using his voice to perform within and against different traditions, practices, styles, repertoire, and aesthetics, were generative of his identity and politics. By listening to the sounds of Robeson's voices, to how the voices' sounds connect to and arise from the singer's soma, its kinaesthetic actions, and technological mediations, and by listening to the polysemic hearings/understandings of the voice and the songs it sings, we are able to discern the spiritual, affective, and ideological networks within which the voice is located, and which the voice brings into being. To hear thus is to practice voice-thinking, to hear voices as plural, collective, augmenting, revealing. That is how we must hear Paul Robeson's voice.

Notes

Prelims

1. "Paul Robeson Coming to South Africa . . . Bantu Artists Will Be Encouraged," *Bantu World*, February 2, 1935, 1.
2. Peter Abrahams, *Tell Freedom* (London: Faber & Faber, 1954), 191–192.
3. Matt Schudel, "Paul Robeson Jr., Protector of Father's Legacy, Dies at 86," *Washington Post*, April 29, 2014.

Introduction

1. Pablo Neruda, "Ode to Paul Robeson," trans. Jill Booty, in *Paul Robeson: The Great Forerunner* (New York: International Publishers, 1998), 244.
2. Gwendolyn Brooks, "Paul Robeson," *Freedomways: A Quarterly Review of the Freedom Movement* 11, no. 1 (1971): 104. Naming Robeson "Voice" was not uncommon. More prosaically, in the first book-length biography of the singer, by his wife Eslanda Robeson, the man is interpellated thus: "I've married the most beautiful Voice"; Eslanda Goode Robeson, *Paul Robeson, Negro* (New York: Harper & Brothers, 1930), 130.
3. C. L. R. James, "Paul Robeson: Black Star," in *Spheres of Existence: The Selected Writings of C. L. R. James* (London: Allison & Busby, 1980), 257–258. First published in *Black World* in 1970.
4. Shirley Graham du Bois, "Tributes," *Freedomways: A Quarterly Review of the Freedom Movement* 11, no. 1 (1971): 6.
5. Katherine Meizel, "A Powerful Voice: Investigating Vocality and Identity," *Voice and Speech Review* 7, no. 1 (2011): 267.
6. Katherine Meizel, *Multivocality: Singing on the Borders of Identity* (New York: Oxford University Press, 2020), 215, 3.
7. Paul von Blum, *Paul Robeson for Beginners* (Danbury, CT: For Beginners, 2013).
8. Henry Foner, "Foreword: Keynote Address from the 1998 Long Island University Paul Robeson Conference," in *Paul Robeson: Essays on His Life and Legacy*, ed. Joseph Dorinson and William Pencak (Jefferson, NC: McFarland, 2002), 3.
9. For the story of Robeson's Hollywood Walk of Fame star, see Shana L. Redmond, *Everything Man: The Form and Function of Paul Robeson* (Durham, NC: Duke University Press, 2020), 102–105.

268 NOTES

10. Letter from Irl G. Whitchurch to Paul Robeson, Los Angeles, March 19, 1947, Paul Robeson Papers-Series B; hereafter PRP-Series B.

11. *Yorkshire Observer*, October 2, 1938. See the note about newspaper sources in Works Cited.

12. "Robeson, the Red," *News-Sentinel* (Fort Wayne, Indiana), December 10, 1945.

13. Pete Seeger letter to Paul Robeson, n.d. [c. 1965], PRP-Series B.

14. Tony Perucci observes that scholarly focus on Robeson's film work has positioned him as "primarily a visual icon and reestablished him mainly as a film star." The consequence of this is a double erasure: of "the radical potential to be realized both in the voice and in political activism"; *Paul Robeson and the Cold War Performance Complex: Race, Madness, Activism* (Ann Arbor: University of Michigan Press, 2012), 7.

15. Peter Applebome, cited in Kate A. Baldwin, *Beyond the Color Line and the Iron Curtain: Reading Encounters between Black and Red, 1922–1963* (Durham, NC: Duke University Press, 2002), 206.

16. Ibid.; emphasis in the original. One of Robeson's chief biographers, Martin Duberman, worried that Robeson's "story is likely to be smoothed out and polished up for mainstream consumption"; cited in ibid.

17. Shana L. Redmond, "Songs of Free Men: The Sound Migrations of 'Ol' Man River,'" in *Anthem: Social Movements and the Sound of Solidarity in the African Diaspora* (New York: New York University Press, 2014), 119.

18. Simon Frith, "What Is Bad Music?," in *Bad Music: The Music We Love to Hate*, ed. Christopher J. Washburne and Maiken Derno (New York: Routledge, 2004), 15–36.

19. Chion compares vococentricity to verbocentricity, the linguistic carrier of meaning in a film's dialogue track; Michel Chion, *Audio-Vision: Sound on Screen*, trans. Claudia Gorbman (New York: Columbia University Press, 1994), 5–6.

20. Hazel V. Carby, *Race Men* (Cambridge, MA: Harvard University Press, 1998), 99.

21. Richard Dyer, "Paul Robeson: Crossing Over," in *Heavenly Bodies: Film Stars and Society* (London: Routledge, 2004 [1986]), 64–136.

22. For book-length studies on Robeson's film and theater work, see respectively Scott Allen Nollen, *Paul Robeson: Film Pioneer* (Jefferson, NC: McFarland, 2010); and Lindsey R. Swindall, *The Politics of Paul Robeson's Othello* (Jackson: University Press of Mississippi, 2011).

23. Fred Moten, *Black and Blur: Consent Not to Be a Single Being* (Durham, NC: Duke University Press, 2017), 118.

24. Nicholas Cook, *Beyond the Score: Music as Performance* (Oxford: Oxford University Press, 2013), 2–4.

25. Matthew D. Morrison, "Race, Blacksound, and the (Re)Making of Musicological Discourse," *Journal of the American Musicological Society* 72, no. 3 (2019): 782.

26. Ibid., 2.

27. Thus the work of two of the scholars with musicological backgrounds who have written on Robeson more recently intersects with race and gender studies. See Lisa Barg, "Paul Robeson's *Ballad for Americans*: Race and the Cultural Politics of

NOTES   269

'People's Music,'" *Journal of the Society for American Music* 2, no. 1 (2008): 27–70; and Redmond, "Songs of Free Men."

28. Morrison, "Race, Blacksound," 782.

29. *Cambridge Daily News*, March 31, 1934; see also *Sheffield Independent*, January 15, 1934.

30. Richard Middleton, *Voicing the Popular: On the Subjects of Popular Music* (New York: Routledge, 2006), 11.

31. Ibid., 31.

32. *Perth Advertiser* (Scotland), January 20, 1934.

33. *Perth Constitutional*, January 29, 1934.

34. Kate Guthrie, "Review-Article: Soundtracks to the 'People's War,'" *Music & Letters* 94, no. (2013): 331. See also Meizel for a discussion of middlebrow culture; *Multivocality*, 54–55.

35. Michael Denning, *The Cultural Front: the Laboring of American Culture in the Twentieth Century* (London: Verso, 1997), 115–117. Meizel notes that classical cross-over singers have often been marginalized; *Multivocality*, 50.

36. Counterpoint, *Newcastle Journal*, February 25, 1935.

37. Redmond, *Everything Man*, xiii.

38. George E. Lewis, "Americanist Musicology and Nomadic Noise," *Journal of the American Musicological Society* 64, no. 3 (2011): 691, 695; my emphasis. Lewis's contribution was part of a roundtable on "Studying U.S. Music in the Twenty-First Century."

39. Ibid., 695, 693.

40. Middleton, *Voicing the Popular*, 75. He offers this insight in a brief discussion of Robeson's, and other singers', performances in *Show Boat*; 74–75.

41. Philip S. Foner, ed., *Paul Robeson Speaks: Writings, Speeches, Interviews, 1918–1974* (New York: Citadel Press, 1978), vi. The United Nations tribute event resulted in John Henrik Clarke, ed., *Dimensions of the Struggle against Apartheid: A Tribute to Paul Robeson* (New York: African Heritage Studies Association, 1979).

42. Lenwood Davis, *A Paul Robeson Research Guide: A Selected Annotated Bibliography* (Westport, CT: Greenwood, 1982).

43. Martin Bauml Duberman, *Paul Robeson: A Biography* (New York: Ballantine Books, 1989); Sheila Tully Boyle and Andrew Bunie, *Paul Robeson: The Years of Promise and Achievement* (Amherst: University of Massachusetts Press, 2001); Paul Robeson Jr., *The Undiscovered Paul Robeson: An Artist's Journey, 1898–1939* (New York: John Wiley, 2001); and Paul Robeson Jr., *The Undiscovered Paul Robeson: An Artist's Journey, 1939–1976* (New York: John Wiley, 2010).

44. Foner, *Paul Robeson Speaks*, vi.

45. For an account of Robeson as bibliophile and book collector, see Charles L. Blockson, "Paul Robeson: A Bibliophile in Spite of Himself," in *Paul Robeson: Artist and Citizen*, ed. Jeffrey C. Stewart (New Brunswick, NJ: Rutgers University Press, 1998), 235–250.

46. Elizabeth Le Guin, *Boccherini's Body: An Essay in Carnal Musicology* (Berkeley: University of California Press, 2006), 14, 17.

270 NOTES

47. Bonnie Gordon makes a similar point about knowing, now, what it felt like to sing in the early modern world; see *Monteverdi's Unruly Women: The Power of Song in Early Modern Italy* (Cambridge: Cambridge University Press, 2004), 8.

48. Ibid., 17–18. I am indebted to Gordon's thinking about the embodied voice. "Considering music as sung," she writes, and "not just as heard or in relation to text, illuminates the inextricable intertwining of song and body. . . . Such an engagement also reinserts the corporeality of the performer's body into musicological inquiry"; 11.

49. Nina Sun Eidsheim, *The Race of Sound: Listening, Timbre and Vocality in African American Music* (Durham, NC: Duke University Press, 2019), 27–29.

50. Meizel, "A Powerful Voice," 267.

51. Meizel, *Multivocality*, 11. For an overview of scholarship on vocality see ibid., 7–11.

52. Ibid., 23.

53. Redmond, *Everything Man*, 11, 9, 8. Redmond notes that "the impact and meaning of Paul's life was in the music; it was that which represented his beliefs, his communities, and his deep solidarities with them. The form of the songs was the form of his mind"; 68. That said, there's not too much sonic information on Robeson's songs, singing, and voice in *Everything Man*.

54. Meizel, *Multivocality*, 19.

55. Mladen Dolar, *A Voice and Nothing More* (Cambridge, MA: MIT Press, 2006).

56. Ibid., 106. Dolar represents the extimacy of the object-voice by adapting "Lacan's pet scheme of the intersection of two circles," which represent the pair of opposed categories, placing the voice in the intersection of the circles; 73. See also Meizel, *Multivocality*, 15; and Martha Feldman, "The Interstitial Voice: An Opening," *Journal of the American Musicological Society* 68, no. 3 (2015): 658–659.

57. Meizel, *Multivocality*, 15.

58. Eidsheim, *The Race of Sound*, 2–3, and 10.

Chapter 1

1. Nat Low, "This Is Paul Robeson," *Pacific Tribune* (Vancouver), May 16, 1952; and "Paul Robeson's Approach to His Language Studies." Typescript of undated interview [c. 1943–1945] with Mrs Bradley, Greenboro, NC, PRP-Box 19. Robeson considered his father as his "first teacher in public speaking." For "a state-wide oratorical contest" Robeson entered in high school, for which he declaimed Wendell Phillips's "famous oration" on Toussaint L'Ouverture, he recalled having "no real appreciation of its meaning. . . . But there I was, voicing, with all the fervour and forensic skill I could muster." See Paul Robeson, *Here I Stand* (London: Denis Dobson, 1958), 27, 33; and also Duberman, *Paul Robeson*, 10; and Robeson Jr., *The Undiscovered Paul Robeson*, 17.

2. Eidsheim, *The Race of Sound*, 34; my emphasis.

3. Duberman, *Paul Robeson*, 278.

4. Frank Gill, *Billboard*, October 1943. For the *Los Angeles Examiner*, Robeson's lines in *Othello* had "the sonority and the immensity of a Bach prelude played on a cathedral

NOTES 271

organ"; January 23, 1945. See also Melanie Shaffer, "Paul Robeson's Iconic Timbre and the Negotiation of Signification," *American Music Research Center Journal* 43 (2014): 45.

5. See letter from Eslanda Robeson to Glen Byam Shaw, February 6, 1959, PRP-Series B.

6. Robeson, *Here I Stand*, 18, 23. Elsewhere, Robeson wondered if his father was one of the slaves, who "lifted their voices in song," led by "the Moses of her people" Harriet Tubman on the underground railway to freedom; "Foreword," in *Lift Every Voice! The Second People's Song Book*, ed. Irwin Silber (New York: Oak Publications, 1953), 3. See also Eslanda's account: "He led the singing in church with his big, unmanageable, but beautifully moving bass voice, and was often carried away by the religious emotion which swept the congregation with the music. He became an essential part of the church, and, in turn, the church, the music, and the people became an essential part of him"; *Paul Robeson, Negro*, 23.

7. Robeson, *Paul Robeson, Negro*, 23.

8. Programme, 34th Quadrennial Conference of the African Methodist Episcopal Zion Church, Syracuse, May 16, 1952, Paul Robeson Collection, microfilm 4; hereafter PRC-4.

9. Irving Kolodin, "Paul Robeson in Carnegie Hall," *Saturday Review*, May 24, 1958; Harriett Johnson, "Words and Music: Robeson Returns to Carnegie Hall," *New York Post*, May 11, 1958.

10. W. S. Meadmore, "Paul Robeson," *The Gramophone*, September 1928, 147.

11. Robeson, *Here I Stand*, 17, 15.

12. Lawrence D. Hogan, *The Forgotten History of African American Baseball* (Santa Barbara, CA: Praeger, 2014), 84. For more on the value of oration within the world of Black preaching, see Boyle and Bunie, *Paul Robeson*, 33; and Swindall, *The Politics of Paul Robeson's Othello*, 23–24.

13. For Robeson's thinking on "melodic speech" see Gerald Horne, *Paul Robeson: The Artist as Revolutionary* (London: Pluto Press, 2016), 12.

14. Roland Hayes, *My Songs: Aframerican Religious Folk Songs Arranged and Interpreted by Roland Hayes* (Boston: Little, Brown, 1948), 3. On the modes of voice used in recorded sermons in the 1920s and 1930s, see Paul Oliver, *Songsters and Saints: Vocal Traditions on Race Records* (Cambridge: Cambridge University Press, 1984), chs. 5–7.

15. For Robeson's childhood and school-time involvement in these vocal pastimes, see Boyle and Bunie, *Paul Robeson*, 33–35.

16. Robeson Jr., *The Undiscovered Paul Robeson*, 48, 56, 58, 64. Letter by Paul to Eslanda Robeson, August 2, 1922, PRP-Robeson Family Correspondence.

17. Incomplete, undated typescript [c. 1960], hereafter titled "Robeson Songbook" as it appears to be an introduction for a collection of songs that did not see publication, PRP-21.

18. Duberman, *Paul Robeson*, 55. The conductor and longtime director of the Yale Glee Club Marshall Bartholomew's abiding memory of Robeson's performance in *Jones* was "naturally . . . the vocal side of your work." Letter from Bartholomew, December 24, 1924, PRP-Series B.

19. Letter from Hallie Cobb, February 26, 1947, PRP-Series B.

272 NOTES

20. Press release for the 1952 Peace Arch concert, PRC-4. In exploring Robeson's "iconic voice," Shaffer employed spectrogram analysis in an attempt to demonstrate that Robeson's voice is "quantifiably unique, distinct from his contemporaries in consistently characteristic ways"; "Paul Robeson's Iconic Timbre," 30. There are several methodological problems with Shaffer's work, and my own use of spectrograms in chapters 3 and 6 endeavors to address these failings. But Shaffer's broader point is well made: Robeson's voice functioned iconically.

21. Eidsheim, *The Race of Sound*, 29, 30.

22. Meizel, *Multivocality*, 47.

23. Swindall, *The Politics of Paul Robeson's Othello*, 25.

24. See Robeson Jr., *The Undiscovered Paul Robeson*, ch. 2.

25. Scott McMillin, "Paul Robeson, Will Vodery's 'Jubilee Singers,' and the Earliest Script of the Kern-Hammerstein *Show Boat*," *Theatre Survey: The Journal of the American Society for Theatre Research* 41, no. 2 (2000): 51–70. For an extended discussion of *Show Boat*, race, and Robeson's involvement in the musical, see Todd Decker, *Show Boat: Performing Race in an American Musical* (Oxford: Oxford University Press, 2013), ch. 2.

26. Robeson Jr., *The Undiscovered Paul Robeson*, 45, 74, 83.

27. See correspondence from J. Mayo Williams to Robeson, February 7, 1924, PRP-Series B.

28. Robeson Jr., *The Undiscovered Paul Robeson*, 88.

29. Nat Hentoff, "Paul Robeson Makes a New Album," *The Reporter* (April 1958): 35.

30. See, for example, the unpublished manuscript, "Paul Robeson: Thoughts about His Music," December 1956, section 3, 10–11, and section 4, 3–4, PRP-21.

31. Shaffer shows how Robeson's speaking timbre had a similar spectral identity to that of his singing voice, and concludes that the two modes of voice mutually reinforced each other semiotically; "Paul Robeson's Iconic Timbre," 34–37.

32. One might argue that the solo recital provided greater artistic freedom than the opera stage too. Eidsheim notes that African American singers, certainly up to the mid-twentieth century and before, were racially typecast in opera, performing roles associated with the other; *The Race of Sound*, 83–84.

33. Robeson Jr., *The Undiscovered Paul Robeson*, 72–73, 91–92. Robeson Jr. writes of his father's "vow not to stoop to appearing in musicals," 137.

34. Paul Robeson, "Songs for Freedom," *Foreign Literature*, c. 1955.

35. See Meizel, *Multivocality*, 5–6.

36. HMV catalog, July 1929. The HMV catalogs were consulted at the British Library, London.

37. Letter to Lawrence Brown, April 19, 1928, PRP-Series B. Robeson gratefully cut short his work in New York on DuBose and Dorothy Heyward's play *Porgy* in 1927 to accept the London *Show Boat* offer: he battled with the demands on his voice in *Porgy* struggling to sing above the orchestral arrangements of spirituals; see Robeson Jr., *The Undiscovered Paul Robeson*, 149.

38. Reprinted in a promotional booklet published by Robeson's management company, the Metropolitan Musical Bureau, c. 1930, PRC-2. Henderson was author of several books on singing, and at the time writing for *The Sun* of New York.

NOTES 273

39. "Robeson Songbook," PRP-21.

40. Paul Anderson dates the vogue for spirituals to Hayes's introduction of spirituals to his recitals in 1923; see *Deep River: Music and Memory in Harlem Renaissance Thought* (Durham, NC: Duke University Press, 2001), 86.

41. *The Gramophone*, November 1928, 244.

42. "Robeson's History," *British Musician and Musical News* 9, no. 7 (July 1933): 157–158.

43. A *Gramophone* critic suggested that if Robeson "has recorded all the negro spirituals worth while, we should like to hear him in other types, Schubert, for instance, unless he can find really good, sincere attempts by composers of his own race to cultivate their folk idiom. . . . No one can expect to indulge much in inferior classes of songs (whether sincere or not) without getting stale"; January 1931, 404.

44. Robeson was offered the role of Amonasro in *Aida* by the Chicago Opera in 1934; letter from F[red] C. Schang, secretary of the Metropolitan Musical Bureau, to Robeson, August 24, 1934, PRP-Series B.

45. Meizel, *Multivocality*, 25 and 26; emphasis in original.

46. Sterling Stuckey, "On Being African: Paul Robeson and the Ends of Nationalist Theory and Practice," in *Slave Culture: Nationalist Theory and the Foundations of Black America* (New York: Oxford University Press, 1987), 314.

47. Information on Robeson's Carnegie Hall recital programs was obtained from the Carnegie Hall Archives database.

48. The *Cambridge Daily News* reported that "the great negro singer has decided that classical music shall play no further part in his programmes. . . . 'This is a permanent departure,' said Mr. Robeson in an interview'"; March 31, 1934. See also *Sheffield Independent*, January 15, 1934.

49. For Stuckey, Robeson's "voice was of a tradition that placed the highest premium on natural delivery"; "On Being African," 314–315.

50. Robeson Jr., *The Undiscovered Paul Robeson*, 74. There is no consolidated account of Robeson's voice training. Brief mention is made in Doris Evans McGinty and Wayne Shirley, "Paul Robeson, Musician," in *Paul Robeson: Artist and Citizen*, ed. Jeffrey C. Stewart (New Brunswick, NJ: Rutgers University Press, 1998), 111.

51. Robeson Jr., *The Undiscovered Paul Robeson*, 83. Burleigh made a single recording as a singer of "Deep River" in 1919. The classical training is obvious in his singing, but it is a halting performance, and in several ways less convincing as classical singing than Robeson's performances of the song. See Tim Brooks, *Lost Sounds: Blacks and the Birth of the Recording Industry, 1890–1919* (Urbana: University of Illinois Press, 2004), 481.

52. Robeson Jr., *The Undiscovered Paul Robeson*, 83.

53. Nicholas Lane, "History," Music at 19a Edith Grove, 2012. http://www.musicat19a. co.uk/?page_id=11. Brown's relationship with von zur-Mühlen, for whom he appears to have performed accompanying duties for the famed teacher's pupils (such as John Coates), is documented in a small collection of intimate correspondences in late 1923 and early 1924; see Lawrence Brown Papers, microfilm 2; hereafter LBP-2.

54. *Milwaukee Journal*, February 13, 1926.

55. Letter from Ira Aldridge to Eslanda Robeson, Wednesday 11pm [1925], ERP-Series C. See also Robeson Jr., *The Undiscovered Paul Robeson*, 95–96.

274 NOTES

56. See Joyce Andrews, "Amanda Aldridge, Teacher and Composer: A Life in Music," *Journal of Singing* 66, no. 3 (2010): 256, 260. Robeson received lessons in diction from Aldridge during rehearsals for *Othello* in 1930. For Aldridge's obituaries see LBP-1.

57. Quoted in Andrews, "Amanda Aldridge," 260.

58. Quoted in a four-page flyer advertisement, LBP-1.

59. "Robeson, Brown Heard in Folk Song Program," *New York-Herald Tribune*, November 15, 1925. See also Boyle and Bunie, *Paul Robeson*, 173–174.

60. Robeson, *Paul Robeson, Negro*, 126–128.

61. Ibid., 130–131.

62. D. McC., "Old Music in New Voice," *Transcript*, March 15, 1926.

63. Duberman, *Paul Robeson*, 100–101; and Robeson Jr., *The Undiscovered Paul Robeson*, 99.

64. *The Musical Leader*, April 29, 1926; *The Musical Courier*, April 29, 1926.

65. Eslanda Robeson, diary, April 20, 1926, ERP-16.

66. Robeson, *Paul Robeson, Negro*, 131–132.

67. Andrea Olmstead, *Juilliard: A History* (Champaign: University of Illinois Press, 1999), 78.

68. Letter from Walter White to the Juilliard Musical Foundation, January 6, 1927, PRP-Series B. A would-be biographer of the soprano Florence Easton reported that he had been informed that Robeson was "at the Juilliard Music Foundation around 1924 studying with Madame Anna Schoen-René"; letter from John W. MacLennan to Robeson, November 1, 1973, PRP-Series B. The date is incorrect, as Robeson would have studied with Schoen-René in 1926 and or 1927. Schoen-René does not mention Robeson in her autobiography; *America's Musical Inheritance: Memories and Reminiscences* (New York: G. P. Putnam's Sons, 1941). But she only devotes three pages to Juilliard and doesn't discuss specific pupils, with the exception of Risë Stevens and, in passing, Karin Branzell.

69. *Kansas City Times*, February 9, 1931.

70. Robeson, *Paul Robeson, Negro*, 131. Armitage was an influential member of the (American) Music Educators National Conference, and an advocate for music education in schools; see Peter W. Dykema, "Theresa Armitage Birchard," *Music Educators Journal* 30, no. 3 (January 1944): 60.

71. Robeson, *Paul Robeson, Negro*, 132–134.

72. I was not given permission to quote from the two draft typescripts of Robeson's preface, one dated July 20, 1962, London, the other undated. I was given permission to refer to Robeson's notes from the early draft of Cunelli's book that Robeson quoted; PRP-21. The material cited in this paragraph appears on the following pages in Cunelli's manuscript: 60, 135, 20, 113, 59.

73. This is suggested by Andrews, whose evidence was Aldridge's correspondence; "Amanda Aldridge," 258.

74. Letters from George Henschel to Eslanda Robeson, October 7, 1929, and May 5, 1930, ERP-Series C.

75. George Henschel, *Fifty Songs by George Henschel* (London: John Church, 1905). Robeson's copy of Henschel's book is preserved in PRP-Series Q.

NOTES 275

76. Robeson, *Paul Robeson, Negro*, 129.

77. W. J. Henderson, *New York Sun*, December 2, 1929. Another critic noted that "His diction, always good, now is the equal of any to be heard"; R. A. S., *New Yorker*, November 16, 1929.

78. Quoted in Duberman, *Paul Robeson*, 125. See also critics' praise of Robeson's tonal palette in the late 1920s: "a control of color effects that was entirely satisfying," "the employment of the greatest variety of tone color," "mastery of . . . tone-coloring," "a voice attuned in color and quality to proclaim many moods." *Wall Street Journal*, November 7, 1929; Samuel Chotzinoff, *New York World*, November 6, 1929; *New York Times*, December 2, 1929; A. J. Warner, *Times Union* (Rochester), March 23, 1927.

79. Daniel Leech-Wilkinson, *The Changing Sound of Music: Approaches to Studying Recorded Musical Performance* (London: CHARM, 2009), ch. 4, paras 19–21, http://www.charm.rhul.ac.uk/studies/chapters/intro.html.

80. Stephen West, "The Traditions of Fine Singing: An Interview with Mme. Anna E. Schoen-René," *The Etude* (November 1941): 745–746, 778.

81. Charles D. Isaacson, *New York Telegram*, November 7, 1929.

82. The *Brooklyn Daily Eagle* made mention of "his recent and intensive hours of study along serious musical lines"; November 11, 1929. "Nor has his training been permitted to spoil what the Lord so generously bestowed," noted another critic; R. L. F. McCombs, *Columbus Citizen*, December 13, 1929.

83. Eidsheim, *The Race of Sound*, 54.

84. Robeson's co-star in *Othello* Ute Hagen said that Robeson worked intermittently with her own singing coach Jerry Swinford for three years. This would have been in the early to mid-1940s; see Duberman, *Paul Robeson*, 660 n. 20.

85. Letters from Brown to Ethel Dingle, June 26 and July 14, 1931, LBP-1.

86. *New Yorker*, November 16, 1929; *New York American*, December 2, 1929.

87. The review appeared in the Hungarian newspaper *Pesti Napló*; quoted in Davis, *A Paul Robeson Research Guide*, 336. Duberman, *Paul Robeson*, 126.

88. Robeson's refined and "straight" (for which we might read awkward) renditions of popular Black genres, including jazz, received much comment. Listen to the uneasy fit between Robeson's affected vocal line and the improvising trumpet in the final strain (from 2:55) of W. C. Handy's "St. Louis Blues," about which *Gramophone's* reviewer was left speechless, registering only that Robeson's flirtation with jazz was a "shock"; Paul Robeson with orchestra, Ray Noble (conductor), "St. Louis Blues," 1934, track 10, disc 4, on *Paul Robeson: The Complete EMI Sessions, 1928–1939*, EMI Records 2 15594 2, 2008, CD; and "Three Shocks," *The Gramophone*, November 1934, 46. His singing of two Duke Ellington pieces was considered an "outrage" by the magazine; December 1937, 297. Richard Middleton calls Robeson's one attempt at the blues form, in "King Joe," "an embarrassment"; *Voicing the Popular*, 86. More recently Lisa Barg has noted "the sonic and stylistic gap between his voice and black vernacular sound"; "Paul Robeson's *Ballad for Americans*," 64.

89. Laura Tunbridge, *Singing in the Age of Anxiety: Lieder Performance in New York and London between the World Wars* (Chicago: University of Chicago Press, 2018),

276 NOTES

29; and Allison McCracken, *Real Men Don't Sing: Crooning in American Culture* (Durham, NC: Duke University Press, 2015), 82 and 8.

90. Michael Smith and Frank Andrews, *The Gramophone Company Ltd "His Master's Voice" Recordings: Plum Label "C" Series* (Lingfield, Surrey: Oakwood Press, 1974), ii.

91. Leech-Wilkinson, *The Changing Sound of Music*, ch. 3, para. 52.

92. The August 1928 catalog recognized that "Down de Lover's Lane" was "in another style [to the spirituals . . .] more in the category of a plantation song," while still being listed under the serious Vocal Records category. Thus too, for example, Peter Dawson's recordings of popular song and light classics are listed under Vocal Records not Light Vocal; see HMV catalog May 1929.

93. HMV catalog November 1931.

94. *The Gramophone*, February 1932, 388–389.

95. For the program, see PRC-2.

96. *Chicago Herald and Examiner*, December 10, 1929; and program, Royal Albert Hall concert, April 28, 1929, PRP-Series J. This continued well into Robeson's career. For example, the pianist Sylvia Ward appeared at a concert in New Orleans in 1942, and a violinist at a Jefferson City recital in 1947; see PRC-2 for the programs. It was also common practice in the structuring of song recital programs at this time. Two recitals Robeson attended in London—by Frieda Hempel at the Albert Hall on September 30, 1928, and by Feodor Chaliapin at the Queen's Hall on June 7, 1934— saw the top-billed singers share the program with guest instrumentalists; see the programs in PRP-Series A, Box 1.

97. Counterpoint, *Newcastle Journal*, February 25, 1935. The *Aberdeen Press and Journal* reviewed the concert under the title "Divided Programme and House," which the *Birmingham Post* elaborated on: "There are not many admirers of Mr. Paul Robeson, one fancies, who would go out of their way to hear chamber music, and still fewer lovers of the latter who would descend from their aesthetic high horse to the popular art of Mr. Robeson. Thus one had the impression that the Town Hall was filled—and very well filled—by two separate audiences, one of considerably greater cultural sophistication, the other, no doubt, very much larger in bulk"; see respectively G. R. Harvey, March 26, 1935; and March 21, 1935.

98. *Cambridge Daily News*, March 31, 1934; *Perth Advertiser*, January 20, 1934. "Highbrow concertgoers may complain that Robeson is not of the high and mighty school of singing, where every recital must contain operatic arias galore and songs that give indication of trickiness. Not for Roberson are these shills." Robeson shared the concert, however, with an orchestra that played Mozart and Richard Strauss; see Philip Klein, *Philadelphia Daily News*, August 2, 1940. Traditions of national taste also contributed to how Robeson was heard. The singer thus complained that "People in the United States have me classified in the 'heavy music' bracket. In London they know me as a singer of lighter songs. . . . I hope I can break down that feeling Americans have that I'm a 'heavy singer' "; Chester Brouwer, Fort Wayne *Journal-Gazette*, March 29, 1943.

99. W. L., *Manchester Guardian*, January 20, 1936.

100. *Dublin Evening Mail*, March 24, 1939.

NOTES 277

101. Elizabeth Shepley Sergeant, "The Man with His Home in a Rock: Paul Robeson," *New Republic* (March 3, 1926), 40, 44. The heading for this section comes from P. P., "Dusky Chaliapin," *Evening Standard*, July 4, 1928. Throughout I use the English spelling of Chaliapin that was prevalent in the early part of the twentieth century.

102. *Chicago Herald-Examiner*, December 10 and 8, 1929.

103. See letter by Charlotte Kett to Mrs. Paul Robeson, June 27, 1939, regarding Kett's article "Paul Robeson—World Citizen," PRP-Series B. Chaliapin's daughter Marfa Hudson Davies wrote to Robeson to thank him for the "kind words" Robeson had often offered about her father throughout his life, and to let him know that "my father in turn admired you"; October 8, 1960, PRP-Series B.

104. Boyle and Bunie, *Paul Robeson*, 303.

105. "Inside Paul Robeson," *The Listener* (New Zealand), November 11, 1960.

106. Robeson would even characterize himself as Russian: in describing his "esoteric" outlook he concluded that he was "very Russian I guess"; letter to Eslanda, August 2, 1932, PRP-Robeson Family Correspondence.

107. "Paul Robeson's testimony, House Un-American Activities Committee, June 12, 1956," accessed June 14, 2108, https://www.youtube.com/watch?v=kmFjjaFN HKo: from 8:18.

108. Chaliapin's internationalism must also have appealed to Robeson; and I discuss Robeson's internationalist politics in chapter 4. Asked by *The Star* (London) to write on "Internationalism in Music," the Russian defined it as "an effort to remove the barriers, political and others, between nations, and to promote a community of interest"; "A Message to 'The Star' from Chaliapin," November 16, 1937.

109. This was only exceptionally noted during Robeson's time. The *Daily Telegraph* critic dismissed "the comparisons that are in the air just now between Robeson and Chaliapin [as] ridiculous"; R. H. L., *Daily Telegraph*, February 17, 1930.

110. Richard Taruskin, *Defining Russia Musically* (Princeton, NJ: Princeton University Press, 1997), 39.

111. *Evening Standard*, July 4, 1928. In similar vein the *Edinburgh Evening News* explained that the "Russian language enhances the power of a natural bass voice, and Mr Paul Robeson's notes, especially in the lower register, responds duly with telling effect"; January 22, 1935.

112. *Detroit News*, January 29, 1926. For the notice of radio broadcasts, see *New York World*, with June 12, 1927; and for the programs, LBP-4.

113. The 1926 recording is Victor 19824-A, the 1933 HMV B.8103, and the 1945 recording appears on *Paul Robeson: Songs of Free Men-Spirituals*, Columbia 32 16 0268.

114. Edward Moore, "Mellowest Voice of Year Is Revealed by Colored Singer," *Chicago Daily Tribune*, February 11, 1926.

115. See, for example, Eslanda's accounts of Robeson's bass singing in the church choir and impromptu harmonizations at parties and street corners in Harlem; *Paul Robeson, Negro*, 23, 70–71.

116. Robeson's annotation to the early version of Cunelli's "Sing or Not to Sing," 20, PRP-21.

278   NOTES

117. *New York Herald-Tribune*, November 15, 1926; *Bulletin*, January 23, 1926; *New York Sun*, January 2, 1926; *Milwaukee Journal*, February 13, 1926.

118. *Daily Mail*, July 4, 1928; *New Yorker*, November 16, 1929.

119. Richard Miller notes that most of the opera and art song literatures for low male voices are for the lyric baritone; *Securing Baritone, Bass-Baritone, and Bass Voices* (Oxford: Oxford University Press, 2008), 9.

120. "Robeson—World Citizen," *The Easterner* 1, no. 3 (May 1946): 15.

121. Hackett, *Chicago Evening Post*, February 11, 1926.

122. Miller, *Securing Baritone, Bass-Baritone, and Bass Voices*, 4.

123. Hackett, *Chicago Evening Post*, February 11, 1926. Compare Richard Davis in the *Milwaukee Journal*: "It is a low voice—more bass than baritone," but the "singer knows how to bring it into focus in the higher register"; February 13, 1926.

124. *Wichita Beacon*, January 25, 1927.

125. Robeson sang "Water Boy" as one of three songs for the test recordings he did for Victor in April 1925. He then recorded the song several times in the space of half a year, starting in July 1925, but it was only the later recording, of January 1926, that was released as Victor 19824, with "Li'l Gal" on the reverse side, in April 1926; see "Paul Robeson," Discography of American Historical Recordings, accessed October 30, 2018, https://adp.library.ucsb.edu/index.php/mastertalent/detail/102809/Robeson_Paul.

126. While Robeson's early recorded voice was not always sonically reproduced as a categorical bass, the recording industry ironically identified him as a bass more readily than the institutions of concert singing. He appears as a bass in the Victor ledgers, with the "Water Boy" disc label specifying "bass with piano" (Victor 19824-A). If anything, the recording of Robeson's voice, even in the late 1920s, was offered as evidence for technological progress in the recording of lower voices. HMV's own catalog advertised Robeson's "deep magnificent bass voice" as being "excellently reproduced"; January 1929. Likewise the Philadelphia *Record* claimed that a new Robeson disc was "another triumph of recording the bass voice"; March 3, 1926.

127. Miller, *Securing Baritone, Bass-Baritone, and Bass Voices*, 9.

128. Hackett, *Chicago Evening Post*, February 11, 1926.

129. *Morning Advertiser*, July 4, 1928; *Daily Sketch*, July 4, 1928.

130. *New Yorker*, November 16, 1929.

131. *Capitol Times* (Madison, Wisconsin), December 11, 1929.

132. Robeson, *Paul Robeson, Negro*, 153–155.

133. Ibid., 156, 164–165.

134. Meizel, *Multivocality*, 25–26.

135. Jacques Attali, *Noise: The Political Economy of Music* (Manchester: Manchester University Press, 1985).

136. Fred Moten, *In the Break: The Aesthetics of the Black Radical Tradition* (Minneapolis: University of Minnesota Press, 2003), 16.

137. Eidsheim, *The Race of Sound*, 32.

138. Meizel, *Multivocality*, 6, 27–28.

NOTES 279

Chapter 2

1. Sergeant, "The Man with His Home in a Rock," 40.
2. Salemme, quoted in Boyle and Bunie, *Paul Robeson*, 156, 154. The Salemme reference later in this paragraph is from the same source. For a fuller account of the sculpture, see Michelle Ann Stephens, *Skin Acts: Race, Psychoanalysis, and the Black Male Performer* (Durham, NC: Duke University Press, 2014), 72–74.
3. Specifically, Robeson performed the "concert spiritual," "an art song genre distinct from the large body of songs emerging from the experiences of enslaved Africans in the U.S."; see Marti K. Newland, "Sounding 'Black': An Ethnography of Racialized Vocality at Fisk University" (PhD diss., Columbia University, 2014), 43.
4. For more on the "pure beauty ideology" that informed Salemme's sculpting, and on the classicism of other visual representations of Robeson in the 1920s, see Dyer, "Paul Robeson," 118–120.
5. Carby, *Race Men*, 48, 50, 77, 83. Dyer concludes similarly in focusing on the media's methods of "containing" Robeson; "Paul Robeson," *passim*. And Tony Perucci describes the popularization of the spiritual in the early twentieth century as a shift in its status from "testimony to artefact" that detached the spiritual from the politics of slavery; *Paul Robeson*, 123–124.
6. This is particularly the case for reviews of the concert performances. With the practice of record reviewing then still in its infancy, writings on the recordings are by and large more of the order of notices and brief notes.
7. *The World*, April 20, 1925.
8. Eidsheim, *The Race of Sound*, 9 and 11–12.
9. For a short contemporary biographical profile of Hayes, see Helen L. Kaufmann and Eva E. Vom Baur Hansl, *Artists in Music of Today* (New York: Grosset & Dunlap, 1933), 45.
10. Boyle and Bunie, *Paul Robeson*, 156.
11. Quoted in Lloyd L. Brown, *The Young Paul Robeson: "On My Journey Now"* (Boulder, CO: Westview Press, 1997), 124. It was during the time of sitting for *Negro Spiritual* and just after his first professional recital in Boston in November 1924 that Robeson penned a little-known "Appreciation" of Hayes, which I was not given permission to cite. See "A few words of appreciation and thanks to Roland Hayes," November 8, 1924, the Morgan Library and Museum, New York. As far as I know, the "Appreciation" has not featured in any of the extensive biographical literature on Robeson. It was addressed to Herbert J. Seligmann, author of the (then) recent *The Negro Faces America* (New York: Harper & Brothers, 1920), which concluded with a discussion of the New Negro. Seligmann was publicity director for the National Association for the Advancement of Colored People (NAACP). It was probably in the latter capacity that Seligmann requested the eulogy from Robeson, as the NAACP awarded Hayes the Spingarn Medal "for outstanding achievement by a black American" in 1924.

280 NOTES

12. Samuel A. Floyd Jr., "Music in the Harlem Renaissance: An Overview," in *Black Music in the Harlem Renaissance: A Collection of Essays*, vol. 1, ed. Samuel A. Floyd Jr. (New York: Greenwood Press, 1990), 1–27.

13. For an account of the place of the spirituals in Harlem Renaissance thought, see Paul Allen Anderson, *Deep River: Music and Memory in Harlem Renaissance Thought* (Durham, NC: Duke University Press, 2001), ch. 2.

14. Alain Locke, "The Negro Spirituals," in *The New Negro* (New York: Albert and Charles Boni, 1925), 199; Carl Van Vechten, "Paul Robeson and Lawrence Brown," in *Keep A-inchin' Along: Selected Writings of Carl Van Vechten about Black Art and Letters*, ed. Bruce Kellner (Westport, CT: Greenwood Press, 1979 [1925]), 158.

15. MacKinley Helm, *Angel Mo' and Her Son, Roland Hayes* (Boston: Little, Brown, 1942), 189.

16. Sterling Brown, "Roland Hayes: An Essay," *Opportunity: A Journal of Negro Life* 3, no. 30 (June 1925): 174.

17. "Ambassador of the Negro People," *The Register*, January 19, 1926.

18. "Racial Harmony Goal of Negro Spiritual Singer," *Detroit Evening Times*, November 20, 1926.

19. Langston Hughes, "The Negro Artist and the Racial Mountain," *The Nation* 122 (June 23, 1926): 692–694.

20. Newland, "Sounding 'Black,' " 44.

21. Morrison, "Race, Blacksound," 796.

22. Eidsheim, *The Race of Sound*, 50; emphasis in original.

23. Walter White's letter of recommendation for Robeson for the Juilliard Musical Foundation presented the singer as the preeminent interpreter of spirituals: "Mr. Robeson's greatest distinction and his greatest success, however, has been as a concert artist in programs of Negro Spirituals. Having been born in the South and knowing through personal contact of the way in which these Spirituals are and should be sung, I am convinced that Mr. Robeson interprets this music as no other person of our time has done." Letter from Walter White to the Juilliard Musical Foundation, January 6, 1927, PRP-Series B.

24. Alain Locke, "Roland Hayes: An Appreciation," in *The Opportunity Reader: Stories, Poetry, and Essays from the Urban League's* Opportunity *Magazine*, ed. Sondra Kathryn Wilson (New York: The Modern Library, 1999 [1923]), 347.

25. Ibid.

26. Literature on Hayes has glossed over this point. Jennifer Hildebrand, for instance, makes no mention of the all-Black music programs Hayes performed in her "'Two Souls, Two Thoughts, Two Unreconciled Strivings': The Sound of Double Consciousness in Roland Hayes's Early Career," *Black Music Research Journal* 30, no. 2 (2010): 273–302. Compare Brooks's documentation of Hayes's singing of arranged spirituals from at least 1916 through the remainder of the 1910s and into the early 1920s; *Lost Sounds*, 440–449. Laura Tunbridge offers a brief account of Hayes's reception in England (and Europe) in the early to mid-1920s, which was "shaped by both his race and his eventual mastery of German song"; *Singing in the*

NOTES   281

Age of Anxiety, 30. Tunbridge's account of Hayes's successes singing *Lieder*, even in Vienna, suggests we should take Eidsheim's statement that the tenor "experienced considerable resistance to his performance of lieder" with a grain of salt; *The Race of Sound*, 81.

27. Helm, *Angel Mo'*, 132. For the Chapel Royal program the songs were all arrangements of spirituals and were presented again in contrasting groups: Sorrow Songs were followed by Songs of Anticipation and Songs of Hope and Joy. For the programs for these concerts see LBP-4.

28. Writing of Robeson's concert of April 1925 in the Greenwich Village Theatre, Martin Duberman states: "The concert marked the first time a black soloist—rather than a choral group . . .—had devoted an entire program to spiritual and secular songs"; *Paul Robeson*, 80.

29. Anderson dates the vogue for recitals of spirituals to Hayes's introduction of spirituals into his programs of the Western art songs on a 1923 tour of Europe; *Deep River*, 86. Floyd gives this claim a Renaissance spin: "it seems that music officially and une-quivocally became a part of the Renaissance no later than 1923, when Roland Hayes presented his Town Hall concert"; "Music in the Harlem Renaissance," 14–15. But Hayes, as I have noted, had been singing spirituals before this. J. Rosamond Johnson and Taylor Gordon were also giving programs of all spirituals in 1925; see PRP-Series J, Box 37.

30. For Van Vechten's "racialist primitivism," see Anderson, *Deep River*, 95–96.

31. Robeson Jr., *The Undiscovered Paul Robeson*, 45, 83.

32. Two of the five songs, "repeated by special request" in the second concert, were by Burleigh. Concert program of May 3, 1925, LBP-4.

33. Van Vechten, "Paul Robeson and Lawrence Brown," 158, 156; *The World* (New York), April 20, 1925.

34. The spelling of song titles is from the program, PRC-2; the quoted descriptions are from Van Vechten, "Paul Robeson and Lawrence Brown," 156.

35. Zora Neale Hurston, "Spirituals and Neo-Spirituals," in *Negro: Anthology*, ed. Nancy Cunard (London: Wishart & Co., 1934), 359.

36. Brown, "Roland Hayes," 174.

37. Boyle and Bunie, *Paul Robeson*, 111–112, 444 n. 36.

38. "My own people—many of them," remarked Robeson, "have felt that the old Spirituals were not in keeping with the aspirations of the modern Negro"; "Racial Harmony."

39. Van Vechten, "Paul Robeson and Lawrence Brown," 156.

40. Paul Robeson, "Songs for Freedom," *Foreign Literature* (ca. 1955), PRP-Box 21.

41. For an overview of these critiques, see Anderson, *Deep River*, 82–84. A detailed ac-count of the middle-class ideology of racial uplift is written in Kevin Gaines, *Uplifting the Race: Black Leadership, Politics, and Culture in the Twentieth Century* (Chapel Hill: University of North Carolina Press, 1996). We should dismiss outright an ar-gument that would propose Robeson's all-Black programs as an artistic instance of Garveyan separatism, for reasons of both the overwhelmingly white audiences

282 NOTES

who listened to Robeson and Robeson's integrationist aims for his concertizing. For Robeson's rejection of Marcus Garvey's radical politics, see Robeson Jr., *The Undiscovered Paul Robeson*, 44, 142; and Murali Balaji, *The Professor and the Pupil: The Politics and Friendship of W. E. B. Du Bois and Paul Robeson* (New York: Nation Books, 2007), 25.

42. Ronald Radano, *Lying Up a Nation: Race and Black Music* (Chicago: University of Chicago Press, 2003), 278–279.

43. W. E. B. Du Bois, *The Souls of Black Folk: Essays and Sketches* (Chicago: A. C. McClurg, 1904), vii, 251. Carby has persuasively shown how the spirituals and their performance practices structure *The Souls of Black Folk*, so that each chapter "is a composition of improvised lyrics upon the musical fragments [of spirituals] that precede them"; *Race Men*, 88. See also Eric J. Sundquist, *To Wake the Nations: Race in the Making of American Literature* (Cambridge, MA: Harvard University Press, 1993), especially ch. 5.

44. Radano, *Lying Up a Nation*, 279–281. The sorrow songs, Anderson writes, provided for Du Bois a passage into an elite "kingdom of culture," where spirituals would find expression in European art forms; *Deep River*, 6, 16.

45. See, for example, Vanessa D. Dickerson, *Dark Victorians* (Champaign: University of Illinois Press, 2008), especially ch. 4.

46. Radano, *Lying Up a Nation*, 281.

47. Du Bois, *The Souls of Black Folk*, 4, 109. For discussions of Du Bois as "an ambivalently Europeanized 'black man of culture,'" for whom aesthetic contemplation and self-culture were also political matters, see Anderson, *Deep River*, 39, 42, and ch. 1; and Dickerson, *Dark Victorians*, ch. 4.

48. Du Bois outlines another scenario, in which white-authored music draws on the spiritual, and includes the "debasements and imitations" represented by coon minstrel songs; *The Souls of Black Folk*, 256–257.

49. Ibid., 189. For a brief parallel reading of Sharp's poem and the lyrics of "Steal Away," see Dickerson, *Dark Victorians*, 121.

50. Locke, "The Negro Spirituals," 199. Locke proffered a similar argument for African art, in opposition to the dominant primitivist discourse; Anderson, *Deep River*, 107–109.

51. Sergeant, "The Man with His Home in a Rock," 43–44.

52. Herman Devries, *Chicago American*, February 11, 1926. The *Detroit Times* commented on the "true musical importance of the Negro songs" in recital, distinguishing them from their alter ego on the vaudeville stage; January 29, 1926.

53. Roland Hayes, *My Songs*. For accounts of Robeson's cosmopolitan programs, see Jonathan Karp, "Performing Black-Jewish Symbiosis: The 'Hassidic Chant' of Paul Robeson," *American Jewish History* 91, no. 1 (2003): 53–81; and my "'The World Is His Song': Paul Robeson's 1958 Carnegie Hall Concerts and the Cosmopolitan Imagination," *Journal of the Society for American Music* 7, no. 2 (2013): 165–195.

54. *Detroit News*, December 7, 1929.

NOTES 283

55. December 7, 1929. Another Detroit critic contrasting the two singers noted that as Robeson's "interests are so diversified . . . he has not acquired [Hayes's] perfection in the matter of detail and so he wisely keeps to the field in which he is at his best"; *Saturday Night*, December 14, 1929.

56. "Robeson Songbook," PRP-Box 21.

57. Carby, *Race Men*, 93–94. Carby's unconvincing interpretation of Robeson's and Brown's 1925 recording of "Steal Away" exemplifies her will to hear resistance in Brown's piano playing. Recent scholarship has also argued that Robeson's singing of spirituals was an act of resistance, enacted through what Perucci terms lyrical and sonic "reversioning." But this claim can only convincingly be made for a later time, from the mid-1930s at the earliest and more consistently from the 1940s onward (as I argue in chapter 4). See Perucci, *Paul Robeson*, 124, 126–129.

58. Van Vechten, "Paul Robeson and Lawrence Brown," 157–158; and "Folksongs of the American Negro," in *Keep A-inchin' Along: Selected Writings of Carl Van Vechten about Black Art and Letters*, ed. Bruce Kellner (Westport, CT: Greenwood Press, 1979), 38.

59. Anderson, *Deep River*, 93–95. Van Vechten summoned Yvette Guilbert and Chaliapin as models for Robeson, whom he presented as the sonic embodiments of Frenchness and Russianness with roots in the culture of the common man. Van Vechten, "Paul Robeson and Lawrence Brown," 157. Similarly, he lauded Caruso for his "authentic interpretation" of Neapolitan folk song; "Folksongs of the American Negro," 38.

60. Van Vechten, "Paul Robeson and Lawrence Brown," 157–158.

61. Van Vechten, "Folksongs of the American Negro," 35.

62. Van Vechten, "Paul Robeson and Lawrence Brown," 156–157.

63. Ibid., 157–158. On this point Locke agreed with Van Vechten, lamenting the "loss of the vital sustained background of accompanying voices" and pronouncing that "the proper idiom of Negro folk song calls for choral treatment"; Locke, "The Negro Spirituals," 208. Locke's point was different from Van Vechten's, though: "With its harmonic versatility and interchangeable voice parts, Negro music is only conventionally in the four-part style, and with its kipped measures and interpolations it is at the very least potentially polyphonic. It can therefore undergo without breaking its own boundaries, intricate and original development in directions already the line of advance in modernistic music"; ibid., 208–209. Zora Neale Hurston limited her definition of the spirituals to their expression by the group: "The nearest thing to a description one can reach is that they are Negro religious songs, sung by a group"; Hurston, "Spirituals and Neo-Spirituals," 359. See also James Weldon Johnson, "Preface," in *The Book of American Negro Spirituals* (New York: Viking, 1925), 21.

64. Van Vechten, "Paul Robeson and Lawrence Brown," 157, 155.

65. Robeson and Brown first recorded "Ezekiel Saw de Wheel" in 1927 for Victor, recording it again in 1936 for HMV (which is the version I discuss); Paul Robeson and Lawrence Brown (piano), "Ezekiel Saw de Wheel," recorded 1936, track 24, disc 4 on *Paul Robeson: The Complete EMI Sessions, 1928–1939*, EMI Records 2 15586 2, 2008, CD. To my knowledge the only recording of the song made by Hayes dates from 1954. By this time, he was in his late sixties and not, as many reviewers have noted, in best

284 NOTES

voice; Roland Hayes and Reginald Boardman (piano), "Ezekiel Saw de Wheel," recorded 1954, track 21, disc 1 on *The Art of Roland Hayes: Six Centuries of Song*, Preiser Records 93462, 2009, CD.

66. Roland Hayes, *My Songs*, 26.

67. Ibid.

68. Robeson, Hayes, Marian Anderson, and others recorded Brown's "Every Time I Feel the Spirit" rather than Burleigh's arrangement of the spiritual.

69. Van Vechten, "Paul Robeson and Lawrence Brown," 158.

70. Although Robeson and Brown used "Ev'ry Time I Feel de Spirit" in the test recordings for Victor in April 1925, it seems that the first commercially released recording, the one I reference here, was done for HMV only in 1938; Paul Robeson and Lawrence Brown (piano), "Ev'ry Time I Feel de Spirit," recorded 1938, track 19, disc 6, on *Paul Robeson: The Complete EMI Sessions, 1928–1939*, EMI Records 2 15598 2, 2008, CD. See "Paul Robeson," Discography of American Historical Recordings. The dialect spellings for the quoted lyrics are from Lawrence Brown, "Ev'ry Time I Feel de Spirit" (London: Schott and Co., 1923).

71. Van Vechten, "Paul Robeson and Lawrence Brown," 158.

72. *Ohio State Journal*, March 13, 1927.

73. Johnson, "Preface," 30.

74. Radano, *Lying Up a Nation*, 213–214, 187–188.

75. "Racial Harmony."

76. Boyle and Bunie, *Paul Robeson*, 138.

77. Hurston, "Spirituals and Neo-Spirituals," 360. See also Johnson, "Preface," 37.

78. Paul Robeson and Lawrence Brown (piano), "Every Time I Feel the Spirit," recorded 1952, track 4 on *Paul Robeson: The Peace Arch Concerts*, Folk Era FE1442CD, 1998, CD. Instances where Brown's evangelical arrangements are not repeated note-for-note can be explained for other reasons. For example, where the lead voice in the 1925 Victor recording of "Joshua Fit de Battle ob Jericho" is unusually taken by Brown it is ceded to Robeson in the HMV 1936 recording of the spiritual, a change dictated by Robeson's status by this time as a major international star, whereas in July 1925 Brown was the senior creative partner; Paul Robeson and Lawrence Brown (piano), "Joshua Fit de Battle ob Jericho," recorded 1925, track 12 on *Good News: Vintage Negro Spirituals*, Living Era CD AJA 5622, 2006, CD; and "Joshua Fit de Battle ob Jericho," recorded 1936, track 25, disc 4 on *Paul Robeson: The Complete EMI Sessions*, EMI Records 2 15586 2, 2008, CD.

79. Johnson, "Preface," 37–38. Van Vechten made the same observation: "the piano, to a certain extent, fills in the harmony properly supplied by the other singers"; Van Vechten, "Folksongs of the American Negro," 38.

80. These dialoguing gestures of the piano-as-voice are in fact clearer in Robeson's performances in which Brown's voice is absent, for example in Robeson's 1958 Vanguard recording of "Ev'ry Time" with another accompanist (at 0:46–0:53); Paul Robeson and Alan Booth (piano), "Every Time I Feel the Spirit," recorded 1958, track 1 on *Paul Robeson at Carnegie Hall*, Vanguard VMD 72020, 2005, CD.

81. Van Vechten, "Paul Robeson and Lawrence Brown," 157–158, my emphasis.

NOTES   285

82. For Robeson's involvement with the Kings, see Boyle and Bunie, *Paul Robeson*, 98–101.
83. Brooks, *Lost Sounds*, 456; and for more on the Four Harmony Kings, see 452–462.
84. Quoted in Wayne D. Shirley, "The Coming of 'Deep River,'" *American Music* 14, no. 5 (1997): 520.
85. Robeson, *Paul Robeson, Negro*, 109. He also resumed his acquaintance with John Payne, another Black American in London, and singer of popular song, whom he had met a few years earlier, and who had also performed spirituals with Brown accompanying him.
86. Layton and Johnstone, "Spiritual Medley" ("I Got a Robe—Steal Away—Ev'ry Time I Feel the Spirit—Nobody Knows de Trouble I've Seen"), recorded 1932, track 15 on *Good News: Vintage Negro Spirituals*, Living Era CD AJA 5622, 2006, CD.
87. Johnson, "Preface," 26–27.
88. Ibid., 35–36.
89. R.A.S., *New Yorker*, November 16, 1929.
90. McCracken, *Real Men Don't Sing*, 8–9 and 77.
91. Meizel, *Multivocality*, 69.
92. Karl Hagstrom Miller, quoted in McCracken, *Real Men Don't Sing*, 77.
93. Van Vechten, "Paul Robeson and Lawrence Brown," 157–158.
94. See Radano, *Lying Up a Nation*, 223, 247, 272. The space that rhythm occupies in Johnson's explanatory essay on the spirituals exemplifies this turn to rhythm. See Johnson, "Preface."
95. Anderson, *Deep River*, 89.
96. See "Paul Robeson," Discography of American Historical Recordings. In this elementary statistic I have not considered the examples of arranged secular folk songs, nor original compositions Robeson recorded for this period. Brown's evangelically performed arrangements decreased as Robeson established himself as a concert singer.
97. Hurston, "Spirituals and Neo-Spirituals," 360.
98. Ibid., and Hurston, "Characteristics of Negro Expression," in *Negro: Anthology*, ed. Nancy Cunard (London: Wishart & Co., 1934), 39–49.
99. "The two artists give us nearly as is humanly possible a correct replica of the singing of the Negro as it was in the past"; *Musical Courier*, November 16, 1929.
100. Burton Davis, *Morning Telegraph*, November 15, 1926. Others were less enchanted by Brown's voice. The critic for the *New York Evening Post* noted his "very modest tenor" on November 6, 1929; and the reviewer in *Lewiston Sun*, while acknowledging that his accompanying work was "priceless," opined that "when he raised his voice in song with Mr. Robeson's it was not so good"; November 11, 1929.
101. *New York Sun*, January 2, 1926.
102. W. J. Henderson, one of America's finest music critics, noted this of a New York Town Hall recital of 1929. Brown added "some vocal decorations to one or two numbers" only, and even then, "though not quite with the amount of elaboration provided by Rosamund [*sic*] Johnson when associated with Taylor Gordon"; *New York Sun*, December 2, 1929. The Victor recordings, made between 1925 and 1927,

286 NOTES

included seven duets with Brown, whereas no duets were recorded during the first few years of recording for HMV from 1928 to the latter part of 1933, even when Brown accompanied Robeson in fast spirituals. See "Paul Robeson," Discography of American Historical Recordings; and *Paul Robeson: The Complete EMI Sessions*.

103. Hayes recalled an instance of this from a childhood hearing of the forester-preacher Will Garlington "felling a tree and chanting a monotony of syllables, transforming the felling of the tree, and himself, into an entity"; Hayes, *My Songs*, 24.

104. In the song, wrote one critic, the singer "exhibited the fullest richness and profundity of his voice"; *Capitol Times* (Madison, WI), December 11, 1929. See also *Journal of Commerce* (New York), November 7, 1929.

105. Noel Straus, *New York Evening World*, November 6, 1929; and Charles D. Isaacson, *New York Telegram*, November 7, 1929. Robeson first recorded "Deep River" in 1927 for Victor. The next known recording of the spiritual was for the film *Proud Valley* (1939), and the increasing bassness of his voice is plainly audible in the later recording.

106. Van Vechten, "Paul Robeson and Lawrence Brown," 158; and "Folksongs of the American Negro," 38. In a similar vein, Carl Sandburg contrasted Hayes's "methods from the white man's conservatories" with the "real thing" of Robeson, who had "not allowed the schools to take it away from him"; *Chicago News*, September 29, 1926.

107. Johnson, "Negro Folk Songs and Spirituals," *The Mentor*, February 1929, 52; and "Preface," 28–29. Van Vechten proclaimed authoritatively, "I do not think white singers can sing Spirituals" (neither could, he claimed, women); "Folksongs of the American Negro," 38. But as Eidsheim demonstrates in Martina Arroyo's learning to sing spirituals "through careful coaching in vocal and musical style," "style is learnt"; it is not innate; *The Race of Sound*, 87–88.

108. Locke, "The Negro Spirituals," 206–207.

109. Van Vechten, "Paul Robeson and Lawrence Brown," 157.

110. Locke, "The Negro Spirituals," 208.

111. Hayes's recording of "Ev'ry Time" dates from 1954, and I am not aware of an earlier recording of this spiritual; Roland Hayes and Reginald Boardman (piano), "Every Time I Feel the Spirit," recorded 1954, track 24, disc 1 on *The Art of Roland Hayes: Six Centuries of Song*, Preiser Records 93462, 2009, CD.

112. Du Bois, *The Souls of Black Folk*, 190–191.

113. Robeson and Booth, "Every Time I Feel the Spirit," *Paul Robeson at Carnegie Hall*.

114. *Philadelphia Bulletin*, January 23, 1926.

115. *Indianapolis News*, January 21, 1926. For the *London Daily Mail*, "Were You There?" was "a lyric drama" in Robeson's voice; October 31, 1927.

116. Jason King, "The Sound of Velvet Melting: The Power of 'Vibe' in the Music of Roberta Flack," in *Listen Again: A Momentary History of Pop Music*, ed. Eric Weisbard (Durham, NC: Duke University Press, 2007), 184–185, 189.

117. Even Van Vechten acknowledged "the poignant simplicity of [Robeson's] art," and that Robeson's voice was "under such complete control and such studied discipline that he always suggests the possession of a great reserve force"; "Paul Robeson and Lawrence Brown," 157. According to Richard Dyer, Robeson's "containment," both

NOTES 287

in the singer's own performance practice and in his representations in a variety of media, is precisely what enabled him to be a successful crossover artist in the 1920s and 1930s; "Paul Robeson: Crossing Over," 64–136.

118. Paul Robeson and Lawrence Brown (piano), "Were You There? (When They Crucified My Lord)," recorded 1925, track 16 on *Ol' Man River: Paul Robeson*, Mastersong, 1999/2000, CD; and Roland Hayes and Reginald Boardman (piano), "Were You There?" recorded 1954, track 29, disc 2 on *The Art of Roland Hayes: Six Centuries of Song*, Preiser Records 93462, 2009, CD.

119. Du Bois had included "silent rapt countenance" as constitutive of the aesthetics of what he called the "frenzy" (or shouting) that informed Black religious culture; *The Souls of Black Folk*, 191.

120. Hurston, "Characteristics of Negro Expression," 36; and Van Vechten, "Paul Robeson and Lawrence Brown," 157.

121. Newland, "Sounding 'Black,'" 72.

122. Eidsheim, *The Race of Sound*, 51.

123. Robeson Jr., *The Undiscovered Paul Robeson*, 83, 45; Anderson, *Deep River*, 93; Van Vechten, "Paul Robeson and Lawrence Brown," 157. Anderson makes claim for "an aspiration that Robeson and Van Vechten shared: to legitimate the concert performances of black folksong through vocal techniques distinguishable from formal European styles"; *Deep River*, 93. The initial proposition concerning the concert performance of Black folk song was indeed a shared ideal, commonly held by mainstream ideologues of the Harlem Renaissance and other performers, notably Hayes. But the claim that the performance of Black song was affected by non-European vocal practice does not hold true for Robeson as clearly as Van Vechten wished or Andersen suggests.

124. *Chicago Defender*, May 19, 1934. Anderson cites this statement by Robeson to support his claim that Van Vechten and Robeson shared an aesthetic outlook; *Deep River*, 97. Robeson's own statements made from time to time against the art music repertoire and its style of performance need to be considered in the specific contexts of their utterance.

125. Boyle and Bunie, *Paul Robeson*, 238.

126. Interviews with English author Rebecca West and Reginald Boardman; cited in Boyle and Bunie, *Paul Robeson*, 236. "Once he found out how hard [singing] lieder was," recalled a friend Glenway Westcott, "he lost his enthusiasm"; ibid., 237.

127. Robeson was not, however, entirely estranged from the art song repertoire. As I discuss in chapter 4, a small selection of the English songbook, a few of the more popular European vocal classics, and some Eastern European, especially Russian, art music became part of his core repertoire. See also William Pencak, "Paul Robeson and Classical Music," in *Paul Robeson: Essays on His Life and Legacy*, ed. Joseph Dorinson and William Pencak (Jefferson, NC: McFarland, 2002), 152–159. Pencak surely overstates the case in suggesting that Robeson "brought to whatever he sang . . . perfectly refined classical singing technique"; 153.

128. Robeson, *Paul Robeson, Negro*, 129–30.

129. Johnson, "Preface," 50.

288   NOTES

130. See Meizel, *Multivocality*, 29 and 27–28.

131. Robeson, *Paul Robeson, Negro*, 130.

132. Helm, *Angel Mo'*, 124, 118. For more on Hayes's career in terms of Du Bois's "double consciousness," see Hildebrand, "'Two Souls, Two Thoughts.'"

133. Meizel, *Multivocality*, 25.

134. Two pieces of this kind are Sergeant's "The Man with His Home in a Rock," and Douglas's "James Douglas Is Captivated by a Negro Genius in London," *Daily Express*, July 5, 1928.

135. Du Bois, *The Souls of Black Folks*, 193.

136. (London) *Evening Standard*, June 20, 1928.

137. *Detroit News*, January 21, 1926; my emphasis.

138. Jon Cruz, *Culture on the Margins: The Black Spiritual and the Rise of American Cultural Interpretation* (Princeton, NJ: Princeton University Press, 1999), 121, 22, 193. See also Radano, *Lying Up a Nation*, 181–182.

139. Carby, *Race Men*, 98–99, 48–50. Carby's otherwise compelling account of what she terms the "modernist invention" of Robeson falls short on several counts: she denies Robeson agency, and makes use of evidence anachronistically from the 1930s, from the moment that is that a more politically engaged Robeson begins to emerge. The singer's relative political disinterest in the 1920s, and his sometime opportunistic involvement in politically questionable projects, has at times proved uncomfortable for scholars.

140. (Boston) *Transcript*, March 15, 1926; Sergeant, "The Man with His Home in a Rock," 43.

141. Carby, *Race Men*, 98.

142. Ibid., 95. On this point we should recognize also that central to Du Bois's critique is his celebration of the difference of African American identities; Radano, *Lying Up a Nation*, 279.

143. Radano, *Lying Up a Nation*, 181. More generally, Radano argues that the spiritual "marked the outer limits of a racialized unknown existing beyond its makers' own access. Eventually, the inaccessibility of the spiritual would become in itself a fetish object that generated desperate attempts at recovery and control"; 184; also 169 and 177–178.

144. *Courant* (Hartford, CT), November 17, 1929. And see also *Chicago Herald and Examiner*, February 11, 1926; and *Detroit Times*, January 29, 1926. Ernest Newman attributed the vogue for the spirituals to the "sentimental background of emotion derived from [British] nineteenth century religiosity"; *Sunday Times*, May 5, 1929, and "Newman on Spirituals," *Musical Courier*, June 15, 1929.

145. Sergeant, "The Man with His Home in a Rock," 41. Sergeant cast Robeson as a vessel: "It is true that Paul Robeson, even on the concert stage, seems sometimes to have the gift of possession. He himself does not know just how certain forces take control of his being."

146. *Wichita Beacon*, January 25, 1927; *Daily Express*, July 5, 1928; and see also *Musical Courier*, December 7, 1929. Another iteration of Robeson's spiritual voice presented it as the voice of God, a not uncommon move by critics. When Robeson sings "Go

Down, Moses," for example, we can imagine hearing the voice of God, the spiritual's lyrical voice manifest sonically in Robeson's acoustic voice (in a way that it is not possible to hear, say, Hayes's voice in the same song). Robeson's God-voice, as it utters the imperative to Moses to "Tell ole Pharaoh, to let my people go," gains the authority of command *in the sounding of* his acoustically thundering voice (listen to Robeson sing the final lines from 1:35); Paul Robeson and Alan Booth (piano), "Go Down, Moses," recorded 1958, track 3 on *Paul Robeson: The Original Recording of Ballad for Americans and Great Songs of Faith, Love and Patriotism*, Vanguard VCD 117/18, 1989, CD. The Wikipedia entry for "Go Down Moses" is a gauge of popular sentiment: Robeson's "voice, deep and resonant as it was, was said by some to have attained the status of the voice of God"; accessed July 11, 2013, http://en.wikipedia.org/wiki/Go_Down_Moses. Lawrence Kramer reminds us that (at least in the Western tradition) "the voice of male authority . . . is low"; "Beyond Words and Music," 304.

147. Carby, *Race Men*, 93.

148. *Bath Chronicle*, March 6, 1933.

149. Robeson viewed the efforts of "our modern American Negro musicians" in terms of this modernist narrative: "they are copying the French modern school. But the French moderns are going to Africa for their inspiration"; *Chicago Tribune*, January 30, 1931.

150. Adriana Cavarero, *For More Than One Voice: Toward a Philosophy of Vocal Expression*, trans. Paul A. Kottman (Stanford, CA: Stanford University Press, 2005), ch. 1.3, 12–13. In this habit of thinking, the voice, "receiving a metaphysical vote of no confidence" as Mladen Dolar puts it, is prejudiced: the voice's destination is speech, and the voice not headed for speech is deemed a lack; *A Voice and Nothing More*, 43.

151. Lawrence Kramer, "Beyond Words and Music: An Essay on Songfulness," in *Word and Music Studies: Defining the Field. Proceedings of the First International Conference on Word and Music Studies*, ed. Walter Bernhart, Steven Paul Scher, and Werner Wolf (Amsterdam: Rodopi, 1999), 305.

152. Cavarero, *For More than One Voice*, 83, 88–89; my emphasis. Elsewhere Cavarero reminds us that for the early Greeks, strange as it may now seem, "thinking was done with the lungs, not the brain"; see the chapter "When Thinking Was Done with the Lungs. . . ."

153. Glenn Dillard Gunn, *Chicago Herald and Examiner*, February 11, 1926.

154. Karleton Hackett, *Chicago Evening Post*, February 11, 1926; and *Columbus State Journal*, December 9, 1929.

155. *Sunday Times*, May 5, 1929, and see also "Tuning In with Europe: Newman on Spirituals," *Musical Courier*, June 15, 1929. At the same time, New York critic John Powell enthused: "So rich and mellow, so manfully beautiful is this voice that it often takes the attention even more than his satisfying way of singing negro spirituals"; *New York Evening Post*, December 2, 1929.

156. Kramer, "Beyond Words and Music," 305–306.

290 NOTES

Chapter 3

1. Robeson Jr., *The Undiscovered Paul Robeson*, 157.
2. Duberman, *Paul Robeson*, 125 and 608.
3. The other test recordings, of "Bye and Bye" and "Every Time I Hear the Spirit," were duets with Lawrence Brown.
4. For the chronology of the "Water Boy" recordings, see "Paul Robeson," Discography of American Historical Recordings.
5. Middleton, *Voicing the Popular*, 69.
6. Eidsheim, *The Race of Sound*, 27.
7. Gordon, *Monteverdi's Unruly Women*, 12.
8. *Glasgow Evening News*, March 4, 1930; *Daily Mail*, October 31, 1927.
9. *Manchester Evening News*, September 2, 1930.
10. Ronald Radano, *Lying Up a Nation*, 181.
11. Quoted in ibid., 260–261.
12. Ibid., 261.
13. Redmond, *Everything Man*, 20–21. See Eidsheim for a discussion, and critique, of what she calls the "acousmatic question," which posits that in listening to a human voice we assume we can learn something about an individual: "We assume that when we ask the acousmatic question we inquire about the essential nature of a person"; *The Race of Sound*, 2–3, and *passim*. "Introduction."
14. *Musical Courier*, November 16, 1929.
15. "Singing by Nature More than by Art," (Manchester) *Daily Express*, March 17, 1930.
16. In exploring Vera Lynn's "natural" singing, Christina Baade has noted how the attribution of simplicity and sincerity to Lynn's singing and personality were markers also of class and gender, "the terrain of naïve girls and simpler classes"; "'Sincerely Yours, Vera Lynn': Performing Class, Sentiment, and Femininity in the 'People's War,'" *Atlantis: Critical Studies in Gender, Culture and Social Justice* 30, no. 2 (2006): 41.
17. Morrison, "Race, Blacksound," 816; emphasis in the original.
18. *The Register*, January 19, 1926; *Morning Post*, September 26, 1928.
19. Carl Van Vechten, "Paul Robeson and Lawrence Brown," 158. See also "Paris under Spell of Paul Robeson," *Musical Courier*, April 5, 1930; and Belfast *Irish News*, January 21, 1932.
20. "Paul Robeson's Songs," *Sheffield Independent*, January 29, 1937.
21. See, e.g., "Robeson's Return," *Time*, November 18, 1929.
22. *Chicago Evening Post*, February 11, 1926. For critic Noel Straus, Robeson kept his "readings simple and racial"; *New York Evening World*, November 6, 1929.
23. *New York World*, November 6, 1929.
24. *Sunday Times*, May 5, 1929.
25. *Glasgow Herald*, March 4, 1930.
26. See McCracken, *Real Men Don't Sing*, 77 and 88.
27. *Magyarság*, April 13, 1929, my emphasis; "Singing by Nature More than by Art," Manchester *Daily Express*, March 17, 1930. There was no "theatricality" in Robeson's

NOTES 291

performance, observed the *Dundee Advertiser*, for "the most striking feature of [his] performance was its sincerity"; March 5, 1930.

28. R. L. F. McCombs, *Columbus Citizen*, December 13, 1929. For Sergeant, "perhaps nobody has done anything for Paul Robeson but God Almighty, who gave him . . . his voice"; "The Man with His Home in a Rock," 43.

29. See Dyer's analysis of the discourse on Robeson's early acting career, which presented Robeson as a natural, "born" actor; "Paul Robeson: Crossing Over," 122–123.

30. *Columbus Citizen*, December 13, 1929; *Boston Globe*, January 27, 1932.

31. Robeson, *Paul Robeson, Negro*, 129.

32. *Boston Globe*, January 27, 1932.

33. "Robeson, the Negro Baritone," *Pesti Hirlap*, April 15, 1929.

34. *Columbus Citizen*, December 13, 1929; *Daily Chronicle*, April 29, 1929.

35. *Boston Herald*, January 27, 1932, my emphasis.

36. Dyer, "Paul Robeson: Crossing Over," 111, 132, 135; and Carby, *Race Men*, 99. Middleton speaks of Robeson's "classicizing" performance of "Ol' Man River," which he reads as possibly subversive against the song's "projection of exotic otherness"; *Voicing the Popular*, 74. For a later moment in Robeson's career, the 1940s, Lisa Barg notes that Robeson was not able to perform the "criteria of black folk authenticity." As a mass-mediated crossover star his voice was "hopelessly compromised"; "Paul Robeson's *Ballad for Americans*," 57 and 63. Compare Sterling Stuckey's Africanist reading which privileges natural performance: "Thus, the very music of slaves . . . was the music he sang. . . . That the voice was of a tradition that placed the highest premium on *natural delivery* meant that . . . [w]hen he sang, the slave community expressing itself in song was as much in evidence as its expression in the folktale or in dance"; "On Being African: Paul Robeson and the Ends of Nationalist Theory and Practice," in *Slave Culture: Nationalist Theory and the Foundations of Black America* (New York: Oxford University Press, 1987), 314–315.

37. The London *Evening News* is an example of the power-checked interpretation of restraint: Robeson sang "simply, with apparently as much restraint of power. At certain moments he reminds you of what Chaliapin used to be, when that genius did what he liked with his voice and affected an audience by simplicity and restraint as much as by tempestuousness"; July 4, 1928.

38. *Indianapolis News*, January 21, 1926. For a fuller discussion of "Were you there?" see chapter 2.

39. *Chicago American*, February 11, 1926.

40. *The Observer* (London), February 23, 1930.

41. *Evening Standard* (London), April 29, 1929. And if we pursue voice-thinking into the recording studio, then we should note that singing for recording at this time had its own set of practices, one of which eschewed high decibel singing; see, e.g., Mark Katz, *Capturing Sound: How Technology Changed Music* (Berkeley: University of California Press, 2004), 37–39.

42. *The Race of Sound*, 66 and 88.

43. The test recording was made on April 21, 1925, in New York, just days after the success of the Greenwich Village Theater concert; and the first (destroyed) recordings were

292 NOTES

made in July at Victor's Camden, New Jersey, studio; see "Paul Robeson," Discography of American Historical Recordings.

44. Moten, *Black and Blur*, x. Contrary to claims in the biographical literature, Robeson did not sing many work songs, at least not until the later 1930s. And some of the songs that at first appear to be work songs are not: the mistitled "Hammer Song" is a blues number "O Honey Baby Feelin' Mighty Low" (which, like "Water Boy," has an *a cappella* intro and conclusion and upbeat middle section), and Robeson's version of "John Henry," on the subject of the African American railway worker, is the ballad rather than the hammer song. Robeson recorded at least two work songs for HMV in 1937 and 1938, "Work All de Summer" and "Lay Down Late," which had appeared in Lawrence Gellert's *Negro Songs of Protest* (1936) and coincided with Robeson's association with left labor at the time.

45. Deane L. Root, "Wolfe, Jacques," in *Grove Music Online*, ed. Deane Root (Oxford University Press), accessed April 16, 2014.

46. Avery Robinson, arr., "Water Boy, A Negro Convict Song" (London: Winthrop Rogers, 1922).

47. For an account of Robeson's informal singing of "Water Boy" with friends in the early 1920s, see Boyle and Bunie, *Paul Robeson*, 142–143.

48. Payne was described as the "unofficial ambassador to the court of St. James's" for visiting American Blacks. For more on Payne, see Boyle and Bunie, *Paul Robeson*, 105–106. Robinson wrote of Robeson's recording of "Water Boy" that it was "perfect": "I have never heard a better record and shall never hear WATER BOY better sung. . . . It has the real flavor of the South and reminds me of my boy-hood days in Kentucky"; letter from Avery Robinson to Mrs. Robeson, London, February 10, 1926, ERP–Series C.

49. I am not aware of any recordings of "Water Boy" that predate the publication of Robinson's arrangement of Wolfe's song. See Craig Martin Gibbs, *Black Recording Artists, 1877–1926: An Annotated Discography* (Jefferson, NC: McFarland, 2013), 187.

50. Johnson, "Preface," 32.

51. Roland Hayes, *My Songs*, 103. That "Water Boy" was from Georgia perhaps attracted the Georgian-born Hayes to the song.

52. While speech might be considered more natural than song, speech does not occupy the same position vis-à-vis the voice. For a discussion of the denaturalizing operations of speech with regard to the voice, see Dolar, *A Voice and Nothing More*, 186–187 and 26.

53. The meanings of dialect in song are dependent on its authorship and reception at different historical moments of its production, and we are reminded that dialect in minstrelsy, for example, was "an invented stage lingua franca"; see William J. Mahar, *Behind the Burnt Cork Mask: Early Blackface Minstrelsy and Antebellum American Popular Culture* (Urbana: University of Illinois Press, 1999), 100. I return to a discussion of the place of dialect in Robeson's performance in chapter 5.

54. Newland, "Sounding 'Black,'" 42–43. I draw on Newland's research extensively in chapter 5 in my discussion of Robeson's ambivalent performance of dialect.

NOTES 293

55. Marcyliena Morgan argues that linguistic insecurity is a feature of African American culture because of the ambiguity speakers experience in navigating the systems of what is called African American English and General English; see *Language, Discourse and Power in African American Culture* (Cambridge: Cambridge University Press, 2002), 68.

56. *Chicago American*, February 11, 1926. By the end of the decade the *New Yorker* reported that his diction was "the equal of any to be heard"; November 16, 1929.

57. Richard Miller, *The Art of Singing* (Oxford: Oxford University Press, 1996), 19.

58. Robeson's maximizing of tone is notable in his rejection of the performance instructions in the score at the song's conclusion. The vocal part in the final measures, after the return of the call, is headed "*with closed lips*." Payne follows the instruction to hum (at 2:07), where Robeson uses an open mouthed "hah" (from 2:30). And where the very last iteration of "Water Boy" carries the instruction "*(Sung) sospirante*," Robeson sings the phrase in full throat, or at least as far as he is able to in the very depths of his register (at 2:45).

59. The opening four measures of Payne's recording is around 19 seconds, and in Robeson's it is half a minute, although Robeson's recording begins with a six-second rolled chord in the piano, presumably a means to give the singer his first note.

60. *Boston Globe*, January 27, 1932.

61. Anna Julia Cooper, "The Negro's Dialect," in *The Voice of Anna Julia Copper*, ed. Charles Lemert and Esme Bhan (Lanham, MD: Rowman & Littlefield, 1988), 244.

62. Montague Smith, *Glasgow Evening Citizen*, March 4, 1930.

63. Roger Freitas, "The Art of Artlessness, or, Adelina Patti Teaches Us How to Be Natural" (paper presented at the 19th Congress of the International Musicological Society, Rome, Italy, July 3, 2012).

64. P. P., *Evening Standard*, August 26, 1930.

65. A. J. S., *Birmingham Post*, March 9, 1930.

66. R. H. L., *Daily Telegraph*, February 17, 1930.

67. *Birmingham Post*, March 21, 1935.

68. Samuel Chotzinoff, *New York World*, November 6, 1929.

69. *Wall Street Journal*, November 7, 1929.

70. *Daily Telegraph*, October 5, 1931.

71. April 4, 1938. Similarly, for the Glasgow *Evening Times* the Russian songs "gave him opportunities of displaying his great gift of drama"; September 2, 1938.

72. Owen Jander and Ellen T. Harris, "Singing: 19th Century," in *Grove Music Online*, ed. Deane Root (Oxford University Press, 2001), accessed June 23, 2014.

73. Paul Robeson and Lawrence Brown (piano), "Exhortation," recorded 1930, track 2, disc 2 on *Paul Robeson: The Complete EMI Sessions, 1928–1939*, EMI Records 2 15590 2, 2008, CD.

74. Joyce Marie Jackson, "Quartets: Jubilee to Gospel," in *African American Music: An Introduction*, ed. Mellonee V. Burnim and Portia K. Maultsby (New York: Routledge, 2015), 79, 82. Brooks states that the Harmony Kings performed "in a style that was in some ways more appropriate to a period twenty years earlier . . . to a gentler era"; *Lost Sounds*, 456

294 NOTES

75. Jander and Harris, "Singing: 19th Century." See also Leech-Wilkinson, *The Changing Sound of Music*, ch. 4, para. 17.

76. Paul Robeson and Lawrence Brown (piano), "Steal Away," recorded 1925, track 14 on *Paul Robeson: A Lonesome Road*, ASV Living Era CD AJA 5027, 1984, CD; Roland Hayes and Lawrence Brown (piano), "Steal Away," recorded 1922, track 2 on *Good News: Vintage Negro Spirituals*, Living Era CD AJA 5622, 2006, CD.

77. Brooks, *Lost Sounds*, 456, 459.

78. McCracken, *Real Men Don't Sing*, 10.

79. Paul Robeson and Lawrence Brown (piano), "Swing Low, Sweet Chariot," Gramophone B-2339, 1926, shellac record; straight transfer from disc, British Library Sound Archive.

80. Paul Robeson and G. Ruthland Clapham (piano), "Swing Low, Sweet Chariot," HMV B-8372, 1933, shellac record; straight transfer from disc, British Library Sound Archive. Not all Robeson's early recordings of his young voice exhibit a reluctance to tackle the upper register without a change in voice. We hear this in the 1927 Victor recording of "Deep River" at the octave jump between "is" and "over" in the phrase my "my home is over Jordan" (although in doing so Robeson's tone is far from desirable); Paul Robeson and Lawrence Brown (piano), "Deep River," recorded 1927, track 13 on *Good News: Vintage Negro Spirituals*, Living Era CD AJA 5622, 2006, CD.

81. Paul Robeson and G. Ruthland Clapham (piano), "Steal Away," HMV B-8103, 1933, shellac record; straight transfer from disc, British Library Sound Archive.

82. McCracken, *Real Men Don't Sing*, 8–11, 3, and 6. McCracken points to the significance of technological developments in this process: new microphones in the early 1930s enhanced midrange male voices, producing more warmth and fullness, making "sound recorded before this period seem high, tinny, distant, and less warm to our ears"; 8 and 280.

83. Olga Samaroff, *New York Evening Post*, May 12, 1927; Grena Bennett, *New York American*, May 12, 1927.

84. *New York Times*, December 2, 1929; *Daily Telegraph*, October 5, 1931.

85. Brooks, *Lost Sounds*, 457. For the African American quartet tradition, see Jackson, "Quartets: Jubilee to Gospel," 75–96.

86. *Boston Herald*, January 27, 1932.

87. Freitas, "The Art of Artlessness," 1.

88. H. T., *Yorkshire Post*, January 24, 1934.

89. Freitas, "The Art of Artlessness," 4 and 5; emphasis in the original.

90. Ibid., 9.

91. Milton Metfessel, "The Vibrato in Artistic Voices," in *Studies in the Psychology of Music*, ed. C. E. Seashore (Iowa City: University of Iowa Press, 1932), 18. Around the same time, Carl Seashore's investigations found that "*All recognized professional singers sing with a pitch vibrato in about 95% or more of their tones*"; *Psychology of the Vibrato in Voice and Instrument* (Iowa City: University of Iowa Press, 1936), 48, emphasis in original. See also Douglas Stanley and J. P. Maxfield, *The Voice, Its Production and Reproduction* (New York: Pitman, 1933), 99–100.

NOTES 295

92. See Jander and Harris, "Singing: 19th Century"; Leech-Wilkinson, *The Changing Sound of Music*, ch. 7, para. 18.

93. Isidoro Ferrante, "Vibrato Rate and Extent in Soprano Voice: A Survey on One Century of Singing," *Journal of the Acoustical Society of America* 130, no. 3 (2011): 1688.

94. In the following analysis I used the audio analysis software Sonic Visualiser. The data used was taken from only the first refrain of the song (until 0:42 in the 1925 recording and 0:36 in the 1933 record), and for vibrato rate I typically only considered notes with at least eight vibrato cycles. For more on the musicological uses of Sonic Visualiser, see Nicholas Cook and Daniel Leech-Wilkinson, "A Musicologist's Guide to Sonic Visualiser" (2009), http://www.charm.rhul.ac.uk/analysing/p9_1.html.

95. This accords with Stanley and Maxfield's contemporaneous recommendation for the "ideal vibrato": a frequency of 6.2–6.6 pulses per second; *The Voice*, 100.

96. Seashore's findings, based on data from recordings of both concert and operatic singers for the period of Robeson's young voice, were that an artistic vibrato oscillates on average at around a semitone and at a rate of 6.3 cycles per second, considering a "pitch extent greater than .55 [of a semitone] as wide"; *Psychology of the Vibrato*, 61, 68.

97. Paul Robeson and Alan Booth (piano), "Swing Low, Sweet Chariot," recorded 1956/1957, track 9 on *On My Journey: Paul Robeson's Independent Recordings*, Smithsonian Folkways Recordings SFW CD 40178, 2007, CD.

98. Jander and Harris remark on this commonplace: "One of the distinct changes resulting from the cultivation of the heavier voice was the increase in vibrato"; "Singing: 19th Century."

99. *New York Evening Post*, November 6, 1929.

100. Stanley and Maxfield noted that an increase in vibrato results in an increase in "intensity," a "*sense* of increase in loudness or emotion may be conveyed by means of a greater swing of the vibrato"; *The Voice*, 96; my emphasis. Seashore attributed the "nature of beauty in the vibrato" to its "enrichment of tone," which it achieved, he concluded, through its "periodic series of changes in timbre, loudness, and pitch"; *Psychology of the Vibrato*, 108–109.

101. Robeson spoke about his delicate voice in an interview with the London *Evening Post*, April 12, 1937; see also Robeson Jr., *The Undiscovered Paul Robeson*, 328.

102. *New York Evening Post*, May 7, 1924.

103. Dyer, "Paul Robeson: Crossing Over," 132; my emphases.

104. *Indianapolis News*, January 21, 1926. A Hungarian critic described Robeson's "organ" as such: "a voice, bass, free and brilliant, not overly big or strong, but warm and appealing"; *Pesti Hirlap*, April 15, 1929.

105. Sanborn also commented on the "excessive reserve about Mr. Robeson's performance"; *New York Telegram*, November 6, 1929.

106. Boyle and Bunie, *Paul Robeson*, 210. Robeson's valet Joe Andrews recalled that the singer didn't like the Albert Hall and was probably not too ill to appear as publicized: "It was too big and the acoustic inadequate. He had his usual worries about his voice and whether it would carry"; ibid., 250–251. Letter from Eslanda Robeson to Lawrence Brown, December 24, 1932, LBP-3.

296 NOTES

107. Edward Moore, *Chicago Daily Tribune*, February 11, 1926; *[London] Daily Mail*, July 4, 1928.
108. London *Evening Post*, April 13, 1937.
109. "Paul Robeson in Songs"; newspaper clipping of unknown source, May 20, 1925, PRP-Box 27: Concerts 1925.
110. *Chicago American*, February 11, 1926. A few years later Detroit critic Russell McLaughlin also called Robeson a basso-cantante; *Detroit News*, December 7, 1929. For definitions of bass voices, see Scott L. Balthazar, *Historical Dictionary of Opera* (Lanham, MD: Scarecrow, 2013), 46.
111. Montague Smith, *Glasgow Evening Citizen*, March 4, 1930.
112. *Ohio State Journal*, March 13, 1927.
113. *Chicago Herald Examiner*, December 8, 1929.
114. R. L. F. McCombs, *Columbus Citizen*, December 13, 1929. The *Musical Times* found Robeson's singing tended toward the "monotonous through his choice of an invariably low pitch," conjecturing from this that he was "apparently . . . unable to manage top notes comfortably"; August 1, 1930.
115. *Springfield Daily Republican*, October 2, 1945; Willard M. Clark, *Springfield Union*, October 2, 1945. A little earlier the *Sheffield Independent* thought his performance of the English folk song " 'No John' was just a bit heavy, but at least it was not made a foolish burlesque"; January 29, 1937. The earliest reference to Robeson as a *profundo* bass I have come across is from late 1929. But here the Pittsburgh critic Harvey Gaul summons the term to describe one aspect of the singer's voice, which he identifies primarily as a baritone: "the Robeson voice it is a baritone splendidly timbred. In fact he is the only baritone we know who at one and the same time is a basso-profundo"; *Pittsburgh Post-Gazette*, December 4, 1929.
116. Paul Robeson and Alexander Yeroklin (piano), "Over the Mountains," recorded 1949, track 1 on *Paul Robeson: The Legendary Moscow Concert*. Revelation Records RV70004, 1997, CD.
117. The three recordings of "Swing Low, Sweet Chariot" appear on: Gramophone B-2339, 1926; HMV B-8372, 1933; and the 1956/1967 recording on *On My Journey*.
118. William Vennard, *Singing: The Mechanism and the Technique*, 5th ed. (New York: Carl Fischer, 1968), 66, 77.
119. Mark Mynett, "Achieving Intelligibility Whilst Maintaining Heaviness When Producing Contemporary Metal Music," *Journal on the Art of Record Production* 6 (2012), http://arpjournal.com.
120. Harris M. Berger and Cornelia Fales, "'Heaviness' in the Perception of Heavy Metal Guitar Timbres: The Match of Perceptual and Acoustic Features Over Times," in *Wired for Sound: Engineering and Technologies in Sonic Cultures*, ed. Paul D. Greene and Thomas Porcello (Middletown, CT: Wesleyan University Press, 2005), 193–195. In what follows, my methodology is closely aligned to that used by Berger and Fales; see ibid., 183.
121. We hear bands of frequencies rather than individual frequencies for the upper partials; Leech-Wilkinson, *The Changing Sound of Music*, ch. 8, para. 63.
122. The parameter settings used in Sonic Visualiser, including a gain boost of 5 dB, are the same for both recordings. The graphs are best viewed in color and on screen. The

NOTES 297

software does not permit the export of high resolution, print-ready image formats. See the companion website for color graphs [▶].

123. While there is no acoustic information beyond 2.8 kHz (except for sibilance and non-musical noise) in the refrain of the 1926 recording, this is not so for the entire recording. For example, in the first verse beginning "I look'd over Jordan . . .," which is recorded louder than the refrain, the "ca-" of "carry" exhibits a frequency band in the 4–5 kHz range trailing off into the 6 kHz region (0:41).

124. A decibel (dB) is a relative unit of measurement, and because the software Sonic Visualiser uses zero as the reference level, which is the strongest or loudest a signal can be, all values are negative, that is weaker or quieter than the reference level. A −25 dB reading means the sound is 25 dB weaker than the reference level.

125. Leech-Wilkinson, *The Changing Sound of Music*, ch. 8, para. 62. The shape of vowel sounds of course also colors the spectral information, so I have chosen instances of vowel equivalence: Robeson pronounces "low" and "home" the same.

126. Ibid.

127. *Yorkshire Evening Post*, November 18, 1925; and *Wall Street Journal*, November 7, 1929. See also *Detroit News*, January 29, 1928; Madison *Capitol Times*, December 11, 1929.

128. Charles D. Isaacson, *New York Telegram*, November 7, 1929; Manchester *Guardian*, March 17, 1930. Significantly, the critical discourse of vocal effortlessness eases after the start of the new decade after, that is, Robeson's half decade of vocal training and his first learning of the art song repertoire.

129. Evidence is legion of Robeson's struggles with his voice as a professional singer. For his difficulties in the early 1930s, and anecdotes from fellow professional musicians and friends attesting to this, see Boyle and Bunie, *Paul Robeson*, 236–237.

130. Robeson Jr., *The Undiscovered Paul Robeson*, 158.

131. Dolar, *A Voice and Nothing More*, 186–187.

132. Ibid., 13 and 26.

133. Hurston, "Spirituals and Neo-Spirituals," 359.

134. Dolar, *A Voice and Nothing More*, 14, and 15, 23.

135. Ibid., 23–24, and 71. And see Cavarero similarly on Levinas, and her critique of Plato's dematerialization of the soul's voice; *For More than One Voice*, 32 and chs. 1.4 and 1.7.

136. Robeson, *Paul Robeson, Negro*, 129–130.

137. Dolar, *A Voice and Nothing More*, 22 and 26.

138. Ibid., 135–136.

139. Ibid., 28.

Chapter 4

1. See, respectively, Columbia Concerts Corporation, artist management promotion leaflet, c. 1941; and *Negro Digest* 8, no. 5 (March 1950), cover, PRC-3.

298 NOTES

2. Perucci, *Paul Robeson*, 100. Perucci gives the year as 1949 but Susan Robeson contends it was in 1948 as part of the Progressive Party campaign tour; pers. comm., January 13, 2023. Robeson "gave himself over entirely to electing the Progressive Party ticket and prepared to appear at rallies ranging from the anonymity of high-school gyms to the hoopla of Madison Square Garden—and in every section of the country"; Duberman, *Paul Robeson*, 324 and ch. 16 *passim*.

3. The full poem is reproduced in *Paul Robeson: The Great Forerunner* (New York: International Publishers, 1998), 239.

4. Ian Shaw, "Paul Robeson: The Peace Arch Concerts." Liner notes for *Paul Robeson: The Peace Arch Concerts* (Folk Era FE1442CD, 1998), 10, and 6–13.

5. M. Nazvanov, "An Open Letter to Paul Robeson," March 8, 1952, PRP-Series B.

6. Kate Baldwin argues that "racist imagery pervaded popular consciousness" in the Soviet Union at this time, from which not even Robeson was immune; *Beyond the Color Line*, 245, 242–249.

7. See, e.g., Perucci, *Paul Robeson*, 11.

8. Redmond, "Songs of Free Men," 104, and 100; Perucci, *Paul Robeson, passim*.

9. "Actors Are Citizens: The Great Negro Artist Discusses the Social Background to the Modern American Theatre, in an Interview with Alexander Baron," *New Theatre* 5, no. 10 (April 1949): 3.

10. For more on Robeson's involvement in the Spanish Civil War, see my "The Spanish War as Dress Rehearsal for Paul Robeson's Political Song," *Journal of War and Culture Studies*, 14, no. 4 (2021): 390–407.

11. Robeson, *Here I Stand*, 59–61.

12. Ibid. For more on Robeson's involvement in, and the geopolitical context of, the Spanish Civil War, see Boyle and Bunie, *Paul Robeson*, chs. 16 and 17.

13. Boyle and Bunie, *Paul Robeson*, 377–378.

14. There is no evidence that Robeson routinely programmed "The Internationale" for formal concerts and there is no known recording of it, but it is likely he continued to sing it occasionally for receptive audiences. Duberman mentions its being sung for Communist organizations during a 1949 tour of Scandinavian and Eastern Bloc countries, whereas when Robeson sang an unnamed "Soviet song" for a general audience in Stockholm he was booed; *Paul Robeson*, 349–350.

15. Jesús Cano Reyes, "Un melómano en la guerra: Alejo Carpentier, corresponsal de la Guerra Civil Española," *Estudios filológicos* 62 (2018): 129.

16. Katia Chornik, "Politics, Music, and Irony in Alejo Carpentier's Novel *La consagración de la primavera (The Rite of Spring)*," in *Performativity in Word and Music Studies*. ed. Walter Bernhart (Amsterdam: Rodopi, 2011), 59.

17. Ibid., 64. Javier Pérez López's doctoral research on the music of the International Brigades includes a brief discussion of Robeson's involvement in the war and with the Brigades; "La música en las Brigadas Internacionales: Las canciones como estrategia de guerra" (PhD thesis, Universidad de Castilla-La Mancha, 2014), 190–192.

18. Robeson and "The Internationale" feature in another fictional account of wartime Europe. Literary scholars have argued that the singer's presence "hovers" throughout Ralph Ellison's "In a Strange Country" (1944); see Daniel G. Williams, *Black Skin,*

NOTES 299

Blue Books: African Americans and Wales, 1845–1945 (Cardiff: University of Wales Press, 2012), 245–246. Ellison's short story is a meditation on the experience of Blacks in Britain and the protagonist Parker's increasing self-identification as an (African) American. This plays out in Wales in the context of a choir rehearsal. Among other music, the choir sings the Welsh anthem with gusto, "followed by a less stirring rendition of 'God Save the King,'" proceeds to "The Internationale" before concluding with "The Star Spangled Banner." Williams points out that the anthem of international socialism connects those of Wales and the United States. And those familiar with Robeson's own Welsh connection will spot the parallels. For example, Robeson performed at the Welsh National Memorial Meeting in December 1938 in South Wales to welcome back the Welsh members of the International Brigades and to honor those killed in the Spanish War. Of the many such gatherings it was, according to one account, "the largest, and perhaps most revealing of the support for internationalism which the Spanish struggle had represented," and one can imagine Robeson singing "The Internationale" with the Rhondda Unity Choir, which participated at the meeting, much as the anthem appeared in Ellison's Welsh story; Boyle and Bunie, *Paul Robeson*, 396–397. (Robeson and the Rhondda choir shared the stage again, during the weeklong peace festival, Music for the People, held at the Royal Festival Hall in April 1939; ibid., 398.) For a detailed account of Robeson's and Wales's places in mutually shaping their political and cultural imaginaries in the 1930s and 1940s, see Williams, *Black Skin, Blue Books*, ch. 3: "'They feel me a part of that land': Paul Robeson, Race, and the Making of Modern Wales"; and Robeson, *Here I Stand*, 61–62.
19. Carby, *Race Men*, 83.
20. Denning, *The Cultural Front*, xviii, and 4.
21. Ibid., 130, and 129–135.
22. Robeson makes brief appearances in, e.g., Nico Slate, *Colored Cosmopolitanism: The Shared Struggle for Freedom in the United States and India* (Cambridge, MA: Harvard University Press, 2012).
23. Barg, "Paul Robeson's *Ballad for Americans*," 53–54, 65.
24. Alys Eve Weinbaum, "Reproducing Racial Globality: W. E. B. Du Bois and the Sexual Politics of Black Internationalism," *Social Text* 19, no. 2 (2001): 18. It is significant that Weinbaum's subject is Du Bois's broadening conceptualization of racial politics. Du Bois was of course Robeson's close friend and mentor.
25. See Ashley Dawson, "The Rise of the Black Internationale: Anti-imperialist Activism and Aesthetics in Britain during the 1930s," *Atlantic Studies* 6, no. 2 (2009): 159–174. Dawson focuses on Robeson's film and theater work in Britain in the late 1930s. See also Redmond, "Songs of Free Men," 110–116.
26. For more on the Lincoln Battalion, see Peter N. Carroll, *The Odyssey of the Abraham Lincoln Brigade: Americans in the Spanish Civil War* (Stanford, CA: Stanford University Press, 1994). Lincoln veterans would "pay back" Robeson's favor of singing to them in Spain. In 1949, during what become known as the Peekskill riots, when Robeson's performances in New York State were disrupted by violent mobs, Lincoln veterans served as bodyguards for the singer; ibid., 305.
27. Duberman, *Paul Robeson*, ch. 9 "The Discovery of Africa."

300   NOTES

28. The Letters include "Robeson Speaks about Art and the Negro" (1930), "Paul Robeson and Negro Music" (1931), "Thoughts on the Colour Bar" (1931), "Robeson Spurns Music He 'Doesn't Understand'" (1933), "The Culture of the Negro" (1934), "I Want to Be African" (1934), "Negroes—Don't Ape the Whites" (1935), and others, all collected in Foner, *Paul Robeson Speaks*. Due to the accessibility of the African Letters, and because Foner's selection presents them as representative of Robeson's main (even sole) concern at the time, they have perhaps received undue prominence.

29. See, e.g., Sterling Stuckey, "'I Want to Be African': Paul Robeson and the Ends of Nationalist Theory and Practice, 1914–1945,'" in *Going through the Storm: The Influence of African American Art in History* (New York: Oxford University Press, 1994), 187–227.

30. See Stuckey "'I Want to Be African,'" 215.

31. Stuckey claims, but provides no evidence, that Robeson was "the first major artist outside Africa to sing in various African languages, presenting African songs in concerts in America, Europe, and in the West Indies"; "'I Want to Be African,'" 219. Similarly, see Redmond's conclusion that Robeson's study of African languages and cultures was incorporated into "his artistic repertoire"; "Songs of Free Men," 111. For a rare instance of Robeson's stated intention to perform African song, see "The Culture of the Negro," 87.

32. "The Culture of the Negro," 86–87. See also Duberman, *Paul Robeson*, 170, 623 n. 34; and Boyle and Bunie, *Paul Robeson*, 417 n. 54, 288.

33. Robeson's personal library included at least 120 books on language; see PRP-Series Q.

34. *Edinburg Evening Dispatch*, March 16, 1935.

35. Robeson, "I Want to Be African," in *What I Want From Life*, ed. E. G. Cousins (London: George Allen & Unwin, 1934), 71–77. See also "Negroes—Don't Ape the Whites," 93.

36. Robeson had been pondering the different types of influence on artistic production already in the late 1920s. In response to an interviewer's question on the future of the Black artist in America, the singer suggested African American art could proceed from two directions: the anthropological, for example by studying African arts and incorporating it, after the manner of European modernism; and the "psychological," taking the "interior source of inspiration"; E. B. and H. K., "The Negro and His Arts by Paul Robeson," *Wisconsin Literary Magazine*, November 1, 1929.

37. "Robeson Spurns Music He 'Doesn't Understand,'" 85.

38. Ibid.; and "Negroes—Don't Ape the Whites."

39. Robeson's performance of Russian song was part of his learning of the Western art song repertoire, and at first seems to have consisted of standard Russian art song; for example, music by Borodin, Gretchaninov, Cui, and Mussorgsky featured regularly on the singer's recital programs in 1931 and 1932. Thereafter he started to include Russian folk material too.

40. "'I Am at Home,' Says Robeson at Reception in Soviet Union" (January 1935), in Foner, *Paul Robeson Speaks*, 95.

NOTES 301

41. Baldwin, *Beyond the Color Line*, 2, 4, and 7. Despite Soviet internationalism's foundations in national culture, Robeson would also counter US anticommunism by deploying an international imaginary to challenge boundaries of nation and race; ibid., 208.

42. Ibid., 208, 210–211.

43. See Denning, *The Cultural Front*, 132.

44. "I Breathe Freely" (July 1935), in Foner, *Paul Robeson Speaks*, 101–102; my emphasis.

45. Baldwin, *Beyond the Color Line*, 211.

46. *Cambridge Daily News*, March 31, 1934; *Sheffield Independent*, January 15, 1934; *Mona's Herald*, August 10, 1933; *Liverpool Express*, January 18, 1934.

47. "Ambassador of the Negro People," *Register*, January 19, 1926.

48. Robeson, *Paul Robeson, Negro*; and Shirley Graham, *Paul Robeson: Citizen of the World* (New York: J. Messner, 1946).

49. *Cambridge Daily News*, March 31, 1934. Elsewhere he explained: "I would rather sing . . . a song expressing the heart of a people, their feeling, if you like to put it so, about themselves and their relationship to God, than to try to interpret the music of one man, a Bach, say, or a Brahms"; *Liverpool Express*, January 18, 1934.

50. "The Songs of the People," *Liverpool Echo*, November 22, 1937.

51. Neruda, "Ode to Paul Robeson," 247.

52. "I Breathe Freely," 102. This list is taken from British news reports, reviews, and interviews of 1933 and 1934.

53. Baldwin, *Beyond the Color Line*, 217.

54. See Mark D. Naison, "'Americans through Their Labor': Paul Robeson's Vision of Cultural and Economic Democracy," in *Paul Robeson: Essays on His Life and Legacy*, ed. Joseph Dorinson and William Pancak (Jefferson, NC: McFarland, 2002), 192; and Jeffrey C. Stewart, "I Sing the Black Body Electric: Transnationalism and the Black Body in Walt Whitman, Alain Locke, and Paul Robeson," in *Recharting the Black Atlantic: Modern Cultures, Local Communities, Global Connections*, ed. Annalisa Oboe and Anna Scacchi (New York: Routledge, 2008), 276.

55. For the Popular Front, "the people" was "the central trope . . . the imagined ground of political and cultural activity. . . . The cultural front imagined itself as a 'people's culture'"; Denning, *The Cultural Front*, 124. One of the earliest references to Robeson as a "people's artist" was in relation to the Spanish Civil War. The New York *Daily Worker* correspondent described the singer such in its account of a radio broadcast Robeson gave on WQXR promoting the US release of Ernst Busch's *Six Songs for Democracy* recorded by the Thaelmann Battalion during "the war for Spanish democracy"; Keynote Records, K101, 1940; see *Daily Worker*, September 20, 1940.

56. On the workers' theater group Unity Theatre and Robeson's involvement in *Planet in the Sun*, see Boyle and Bunie, *Paul Robeson*, 389–395. By contrast, Robeson's political naïveté and/or indifference early in the decade is striking: Boyle and Bunie argue that for Robeson's performance in another labor-themed play—Eugene O'Neill's *Hairy Ape* of 1931, in which Robeson played a stoker aboard a transatlantic line—"he almost completely missed the political and social implications of the play," 245.

302 NOTES

57. The earliest occasion on which Robeson performed "Joe Hill" that I have come across is from late 1938 or early 1939; see "'Organise!' said Joe Hill," *Daily Worker*, January 18, 1939. Redmond gives a slightly later date; see "Songs of Free Men," 116.

58. The imperial Russian composer's song "The Laborer's Plaint" no doubt dates from Robeson's learning of the Russian art song repertoire in the early 1930s. One review noted that the singer's range of vocal color in the song succeeded in suggesting the requisite "hunger, need and cold"; *Huddersfield Express*, April 13, 1934.

59. Redmond, "Songs of Free Men," 116.

60. P. P., *Evening Standard*, August 26, 1930. See also the *Eastbourne Gazette*: "The fact is, Mr. Robeson is not a lieder singer"; September 2, 1931. Not all critics agreed, however, and some praised Robeson's singing of German music, or select songs, or aspects thereof. See, e.g., the *Daily Telegraph*'s review of a Crystal Palace concert; October 5, 1931. Of the early 1932 American concert tour, the *New York Evening Post* reminisced about the "Russian music he sings so well"; Charles Pike Sawyer, July 30, 1932. Not all reviews were uniformly complimentary about Robeson's singing of Russian and English art song.

61. Robeson's German-language songs for the tour included works by Beethoven, Mozart, and Schumann.

62. Robeson's preference for English and Russian song continued into the mid-1930s, such that a review of an Albert Hall concert in early 1936 was titled "Robeson in Russian and English Songs"; W. Mc. N., *Evening News*, January 20, 1936.

63. Boyle and Bunie, *Paul Robeson*, 303.

64. Brown's and Quilter's correspondence forms part of the Lawrence Brown Papers in the Schomburg Center. In the early 1920s, Quilter offered Brown artistic guidance, friendship, and material help. "Dear Larry," wrote Quilter from Frankfurt in 1922, "I have been thinking about you and I felt I must write to you." "Music is such an elusive mistress. She needs the most assiduous courting, and one has to take many rebuffs before she will give herself to you with any good will! Dear Larry, I do want so much for you to get on in the life that you like; and how happy I shall be if I can help you at all. I look forward to many happy times with you. One must always strive forward and upward—and what an encouragement it is when those we care for are doing the same"; September 4, 1922, LBP-3. Their wartime correspondence reveals a decline in Quilter's living conditions in Britain, during which time Brown sent Quilter food parcels over several years.

65. Boyle and Bunie, *Paul Robeson*, 139–140, 236. Brown also performed Quilter's songs with other singers. He accompanied Mark Raphael, one of Quilter's foremost interpreters; Gillian Thornhill, *The Life, Times, and Music of Mark Raphael* (Bloomington, IN: AuthorHouse, 2012), 28. And see, e.g., the Quilter songs on the programs of Brown's US tour of late 1932 and early 1933 with the Black American singer William Lawrence; LBP-5. Brown's work with other singers also exposed him to different song traditions. He accompanied, for example, the soprano Maria Sandra, or Mrs. Phyllis Beardmore, "better known" as a "singer of songs of many lands in many languages"; *Gramophone*, January 1930. Robeson recalled that Brown initially "carried the burden of our concert years": "he brought along some beautiful songs he always has stored away, songs of every land and of every nation . . he

NOTES 303

had played much of the folk music of other peoples, had played the great classics of Western song literature (and, yes, many of these are based upon folk themes and dances)"; undated [c. 1950s] typescript on language, PRP-Box 20.

66. *Times* (Kansas City), February 9, 1931.

67. *Mercury* (New Bedford, MA), June 16, 1932. At the time, Robeson was starring in the Broadway revival of *Show Boat*. He first performed in the musical in London in 1928.

68. "Negroes—Don't Ape the Whites," 92. Similarly, Robeson informed the press that he had a "fortunate" advantage in learning the English accent, because, he claimed, the "negro accent is nearer the English than the ordinary American is"; *Daily Herald*, May 7, 1930.

69. Ibid., 93.

70. *Times* (Kansas City), February 9, 1931. For a British paper Robeson spoke about the "difficulty of my American accent," explaining how he had "bought Shakespeare's plays with their original spelling," and that he read back beyond Shakespeare, "Wyatt and Spenser and other Elizabethans." "And then I understood why you put in all those vowels Americans leave out. . . . So I learnt my part from a facsimile of Shakespeare's original 'Othello,' and that helped me to remember the way to pronounce your words"; *Evening Standard* (London), May 20, 1930.

71. Stephen Banfield, *Sensibility and English Song* (Cambridge: Cambridge University Press, 1985), 126.

72. "Sea Fever" was programmed for tours of late 1931 and early 1932; see *Eastbourne Gazette*, September 2, 1931; and Henry Beckett, *New York Post*, January 28, 1932. Robeson recorded the song on September 29, 1939, at the Abbey Road studios, probably at the request of HMV's artists' and recording manager Walter Legge who, on hearing of the singer's departure for the United States, suggested making "a good and substantial batch of records to keep your name and voice constantly fresh before the British public"; letter from Walter Legge to Robeson, August 19, 1939, PRP-Box 17.

73. Paul Robeson and Lawrence Brown (piano), "Sea Fever," recorded 1939, track 22, disc 7 on *Paul Robeson: The Complete EMI Sessions, 1928–1939*, EMI Records 2 15600 2, 2008, CD.

74. Terry was a noted scholar also of Tudor music, which points to the dual interests pursued by influential segments of English musical life in the early twentieth century: early modern English music and folk music. The revival of these traditions within the ambit of the modern English musical renaissance corresponded with—and perhaps informed?—Robeson's own historical schema in which the West's spiritual and aesthetic decline was dated to the Renaissance. In Robeson's words, the "art standards of the West have steadily declined" since the Renaissance, Reformation, or Elizabethan England; "Negroes—Don't Ape the Whites," 93; and "I Want Negro Culture," 97.

75. *Music Trade Review*, June 1936. Robeson's concert singing of "Shenandoah," and other English folk songs, such as "Oh, No, John," that appeared on his programs at the same time, was not always well received by critics. He was inclined to "oversentamentalise," was "out of his element," and sounded "ludicrously inappropriate"; see respectively, "Paul Robeson's Songs," *Sheffield Independent*, January 29,

304   NOTES

1937; W. Mc. N., "Robeson in Russian and English Songs," *Evening News*, January 20, 1936; and W. L., *Manchester Guardian*, January 20, 1936.

76. *Sheffield Independent*, January 15, 1934. Robeson would sing other shanties or shanty-inspired songs, e.g., "The Skye Boat Song" "founded on an old 'CHANTY' . . . Four bars taken down from Hebridean boatmen four bars added by A.C. Macleod"; arranged by A. C. Macleod (London: Lowe and Brydone, n.d.); LBS-Box 5. Another was "Roll the Old Chariot Along," which has a complex genealogy with claims to being both a spiritual and shanty; see Stan Hugill, *Shanties from the Seven Seas* (London: Routledge and Kegan Paul, 1961), 121–122.

77. Marjory Kennedy-Fraser and Kenneth Macleod, *Songs of the Hebrides. Collected and Arranged for Voice and Pianoforte with Gaelic and English Words*, vol. 3 (London: Boosey & Co., 1921), ix and x. Robeson's annotated copy is located in PRP-Series Q. Robeson must have felt vindicated in reading *Songs*. Five years earlier he had contested an American professor's claim that African American folk song was influenced by Scottish folksong through the agency of Scottish settlers to the United States. Robeson disagreed with the direction of the influence, while acknowledging "some point of contact between negro and Scottish folksongs"; *Glasgow Citizen*, March 3, 1930. Robeson quoted Kennedy-Fraser also in *Here I Stand*, 58.

78. "Paul Robeson and Folk Songs. Hebridean and African Music the Same. World Wide Melodies," *Edinburg Evening Dispatch*, March 16, 1935. In addition to his singing demonstration at the press conference, Robeson drew on his studies of languages, and on other evidence, playing "gramophone records" from his "magnificent lingual library," which included twenty-five Gaelic records, to prove his point about the connectedness of human culture. For another instance of Robeson demonstrating at the piano "how much akin were the folk songs of the different countries," see the *Evening Herald* (Dublin), February 16, 1935.

79. "Folk Tune Master," *Yorkshire Telegraph*, February 23, 1935; "Paul Robeson's New Songs," *Manchester Guardian*, January 31, 1935.

80. *Lancashire Daily Post*, February 26, 1930; *Evening Herald* (Dublin), February 16, 1935. Robeson must have misremembered Morgan's singing as occurring when they worked on *The Emperor Jones* because the actors worked together on another O'Neill play *The Hairy Ape* in 1931. "Negroes—Don't Ape the Whites," 92. For an early comparison of the spirituals with "Jewish synagogue music," see "The Source of the Negro Spirituals" (1927), in Foner, *Paul Robeson Speaks*, 74.

81. "The Related Sounds of Music" (September 1957), in Foner, *Paul Robeson Speaks*, 443–444. See also the highly abbreviated, two-page statement in the appendix to his autobiography, on the "universal" pentatonic scale; "A Universal Body of Folk Music—A Technical Argument by the Author," in *Here I Stand*, 123–125.

82. *Here I Stand*, 56–57. The journalist Nat Low reported that "it was through the folk song and the Negro spiritual that Robeson first began to develop a social consciousness"; "This Is Paul Robeson", *Pacific Tribune* (Vancouver), May 16, 1952.

83. As far as I have been able to establish, Robeson did not sing "No More Auction Block for Me" in the mid-1920s as Redmond suggests; "Songs of Free Men," 132. He sang "Auction Block" at the Empire Exhibition Concert Hall, Scotland, in 1938;

NOTES 305

and recorded it as simply "No More" for HMV in October 1937, along with "Work all de Summer," advertised as a "Negro song of protest" for a gala performance at the Society for Cultural Relations with the USSR in the same month; see "Programmes," LBP-5, and Paul Robeson and Lawrence Brown (piano), "No More" and "Work All de Summer," recorded 1937, tracks 2 and 3, disc 6 on *Paul Robeson: The Complete EMI Sessions, 1928–1939*, EMI Records 2 15598 2, 2008, CD.

84. *Daily Worker* (New York), September 20, 1940.

85. Liner notes for *Paul Robeson: Songs of Free Men-Spirituals* (CBS Classics MP 39512, 1968, LP reissue). For more on the origins and international performance history of the concentration camp song "Peat Bog Soldiers" see Guido Fackler, "Moorsoldatenlied," in Music and the Holocaust, accessed February 28, 2017, http://holocaustmusic.ort.org/places/camps/music-early-camps/moorsoldatenlied/.

86. *The Chronicle*, October 12, 1940. See also *Daily Worker*, October 9, 1940. Others were less generous, calling his concerts a "soap-box"; Russell McLaughlin, *Detroit Times*, December 7, 1940. Robeson's revising of songs, especially their lyrical texts, to agree with his developing protest politics dates from this period in the late 1930s. For example, Redmond has documented in detail Robeson's revisions of "Ol' Man River"; "Songs of Free Men."

87. *Saint Paul Pioneer Press*, October 24, 1940; *Sunday Oregonian*, November 3, 1940; and *Seattle Times*, November 7, 1940. Lisa Barg has concluded about his work on *Ballad for Americans*, which Robeson performed at the same time, often as part of the concerts here reviewed, that it symbolized "the unfinished business of universal democracy"; "Paul Robeson's *Ballad for Americans*," 65.

88. See, e.g., Redmond, "Songs of Free Men." For an overview of Robeson's changing repertoire over the course of this career, see McGinty and Shirley, "Paul Robeson, Musician," 105–121.

89. *Perth Advertiser* (Scotland), January 20, 1934; and *Cambridge Daily News*, March 31, 1934.

90. *Times* (London), October 25, 1932.

91. *Perth Constitutional* (Scotland), January 29, 1934.

92. W. L., *Manchester Guardian*, January 20, 1936; and Philip Klein, *Philadelphia Daily News*, August 2, 1940. If, for the Irish *News and Belfast Morning News*, the "idea of dividing people into highbrows and lowbrows is a little silly," Robeson's audience was "all very lowbrow." Although the critic conceded that Robeson's repertoire— "Trees," "Ol' Man River," and "Loch Lomond" were mentioned—was "an almost classical product by comparison with the popular songs of to-day"; March 28, 1939.

93. For the late 1930s see, e.g., Boyle and Bunie, *Paul Robeson*, 387–389; and also Redmond, "Songs of Free Men," 133 and 131. Boyle and Bunie note that Robeson upped his appearances at London's music hall venues, working in the Trocadero, the Elephant and Castle, and the Hammersmith, in the late 1930s, and that, at three performances a day with admission a sixpence, it was hard work for little pay. Eighteen music hall performances brought him the same pay for one Queen's Hall recital; *Paul Robeson*, 389.

306 NOTES

94. *Chicago Sun*, January 20, 1947.

95. The correspondence located in the Paul Robeson Papers, which largely excludes legal and financial matters, as well as hate mail, all of which are catalogued separately, is not numerated, but consists, in my very rough estimate, of at least 5,000 items. My reading is selective because of the volume of the correspondence, but also because I focus on English-language writing, issuing primarily from the United States and the British Commonwealth.

96. Unless otherwise stated, all the letters referred to in this section are from the Paul Robeson Papers, Series B-Correspondence, which is arranged alphabetically by surname.

97. John Dickens letter, Auckland, New Zealand, n.d. (c. early 1960s). The title for this section is taken from a letter by Charles A. Petioni, April 15, 1944.

98. Mark Duffett, "Fan Words," in *Popular Music Fandom: Identities, Roles and Practices*, ed. Mark Duffett (New York: Routledge, 2014), 160.

99. Jo Love letter, Nathrop, CO, November 12, 1964. For an overview of the dominant account of fandom as pathological, until the early 1990s, see Tony Whyton, "Song of Praise: Musicians, Myths and the 'Cult' of John Coltrane," in *Popular Music Fandom: Identities, Roles and Practices*, ed. Mark Duffett (New York: Routledge, 2014), 102.

100. Mona Frame letter, Huntsville, Australia, March 27, 1963. Jean Campbell commenced her letter as follows: "I suppose this is what cynics would call a 'fan letter,' but I don't think all the inspiration and emotion that fills the hearts of the thousands of people who hear you sing can be labelled quite so easily"; Los Angeles, August 6, 1934.

101. David Miller letter, Saskatoon, Canada, January 18, 1975. Many other writers accepted the nomenclature of the fan letter while noting it was the first such letter they'd written, a confession indicative perhaps of an attempt to locate their correspondence outside their own routine practice.

102. Don Johns letter, Victoria, Australia, November 21, 1960; Sylvia J. Lamond letter, Cammeray, Australia, November 10, 1960. See also the following letters for informal address accompanied by an apology: Mrs. Norma Han, April 1, 1963, Sydney; John Mills, September 29, 1959, Epsom, Surrey, England; Joe Coffey[?], n.d. (after c. 1948); Zena Duckman, March 10, 1958, San Francisco; Mrs. Enid Ho(s?)kin, March 28, 1963, Australia; Frederick R. Kattenburg, April 16, 1973.

103. As Mark Duffett has said, we need to discuss "the difference that music genre can make to fandom"; "Introduction," in *Popular Music Fandom: Identities, Roles and Practices*, ed. Mark Duffett (New York: Routledge, 2014), 10.

104. Jess Andrews letter, Belfast, Ireland, April 12, 1959. Similarly for Edith M. Baskett[?]: "Whenever I have heard your voice it has seemed like the voice of a friend"; Lymington, England, October 9, 1959. See also Mrs. L. Fisher letter, Edinburgh, Scotland, October 21, 1959.

105. Aspects of friendship expressed in fan letters that I do not consider here include the importance of shared memories (of the sound of Robeson's voice, specific songs associated with him, and particular events); and the various forms of psychological support his singing offered.

NOTES 307

106. Letter from Robert Blomquist, San Francisco, April 20, 1963.
107. R. Copeland letter, Southall, Middlesex, November 25, 1959; and Peter Fielding letter, Nottingham, England, November 5, 1959. William Penn from Newcastle upon Tyne wrote: "I feel I must write and congratulate you on the first broadcast today, it was a real work of art . . . but also a work of sincerity and love. On the subject of art in any form you always give me an impression of intense love and sincerity and knowledge"; August 8, 1959.
108. Elizabeth Perkins letter, Victoria, Australia, undated.
109. See Timothy D. Taylor, "Music and the Rise of Radio in Twenties America: Technological Imperialism, Socialization, and the Transformation of Intimacy," in *Wired for Sound: Engineering and Technologies in Sonic Cultures*, ed. Paul D. Greene and Thomas Porcello (Middletown, CT: Wesleyan University Press, 2005), 245–268.
110. Mrs. W. Smith letter, September 2, 1959.
111. U. Sunny Nwogu letter, August 28, 1960.
112. McCracken documents the rise of the romantic crooner as popular singers exploited the potential of the microphone's audio intimacy; *Real Men Don't Sing*.
113. John Mills letter, Epsom, Surrey, September 29, 1959. In the account of a young fan, William Penn from Newcastle upon Tyne, Robeson's vocal warmth entered the boy's body and soul: "As I lay in bed on Sunday, with the wireless slightly on the loud side, your voice seemed to fill the room and enter my bloodstream carrying warmth and satisfaction all through my body. It was as though I had been given an injection of spiritual satisfaction. A wonderful experience for which I am very grateful!!"; letter of August 8, 1959.
114. "Paul Comes Home," *National Guardian*, May 19, 1958.
115. Ernő Mihályfi, "Letter of Invitation to Paul Robeson," c. 1958.
116. Harry Fomison letter, Sheffield, September 13, 1959.
117. Miguel A. Fonseka, London, October 22, 1959. Because some fans listened to Robeson throughout their lives he was considered a "lifelong friend"; see, e.g., letter from Terese Leitch, St. Kilda, Australia, November 19, 1960.
118. Mona Frame, March 27, 1963, Huntsville, Australia.
119. Mrs. Fisher from Edinburgh wrote to thank Robeson for his radio broadcasts, recount her experiences of hearing the singer in concert the previous year—"like welcoming back an old friend"—reminisced about first seeing him when eight years old in 1938, and invited him to the family's "small tenement flat" where he was "very welcome at our home." A postscript noted that she and her five-year-old daughter had been singing "Jacob's Ladder" for several weeks non-stop. "I don't think the neighbours think we're much good at it!" she concluded; letter from Mrs. L. Fisher, October 21, 1959.
120. Cornel Sandvoss, *Fans: The Mirror of Consumption* (Cambridge: Polity, 2005), 64.
121. Mrs. Charles L. Peard, June 19, 1964, New Jersey; Florence H. Luscomb, January 6, 1964, Cambridge, MA.
122. For cosmopolitanism theory on the home as "plurilocal" see Marsha Meskimmon, *Contemporary Art and the Cosmopolitan Imagination* (London: Routledge, 2011), 15 and ch. 1.

308 NOTES

123. Martin Popper letter, April 16, 1965.

124. Boyle and Bunie, *Paul Robeson*, 386.

125. Cards, notes, telegrams, and even gifts were routine expressions of fans' well wishes. Less common, although not exceptional, were instances of fans gathering to celebrate the singer's birthday. "The celebration of your birthday," explained Maura Cram, "has always been an occasion when friends gathered to listen to your records and learn more about Robeson the artist . . . the giant man who stands firmly on the side of all oppressed people." Cram informed Robeson that her son was named for the singer, also not a unique occurrence and a common enough expression of fandom; letter, November 17, 1969, Newcastle, Australia.

126. Jo Love letter, January 19, 1966; emphasis in the original. The quoted lyrics are from a Robeson standard, the "Kaddish" or "Hassidic Chant" attributed to Levi Yitzhak Berditchev and arranged by Joel Engel.

127. To welcome Robeson back to Britain after the restoration of his passport in 1958, British composer Alan Bush wrote "The World Is His Song" for mezzo solo, mixed choir, and small orchestra; letter, September 18, 1958.

128. J. B. Neumann letter, September 3, 1942, New York.

129. An English teacher in Japan, who had never met the singer, addressed Robeson as "My most respected friend and brother." "Dear brother," he wrote, "please imagine how great was the impression on me, and how I felt sincere friendship toward you. From the bottom of my heart I look up to you as our hero, and I love you as our greatest brother"; Kenzo Nishikawa letter, July 23, 1959.

130. Letter from Robeson to Lionel Kenner, October 21, 1951.

131. William L. Patterson, open letters, November 4 and 14, 1955, PRC-6.

132. Paul Ricoeur, *The Hermeneutics of Action*, ed. Richard Kearney (London: Sage, 1996), 10, and 32–33. Ricoeur's thoughts on the gift occur in a discussion on forgiveness. The gift, he writes, belongs to the "'poetics' of the moral life" if one considers poetics in terms of "the sense of creativity at the level of the dynamics of acting and the sense of song and hymn at the level of verbal expression"; 10. For Jacques Derrida, the "gift is that which gives friendship; it is needed for there to be friendship, beyond all comradeship"; *The Politics of Friendship*, trans. George Collins (London: Verso, 1997), 284.

133. Meskimmon, *Contemporary Art*, 44–46. Ricoeur, *The Hermeneutics of Action*, 33.

134. Redmond, *Everything Man*, 1–2. In part, Redmond draws on Eidsheim's model of singing as "vibrational practice," which emphasizes, among other things, transmission, interconnectedness, and relationships of self and other enacted through sound; see *Sensing Sound: Singing and Listening as Vibrational Practice* (Durham, NC: Duke University Press, 2015), 19–20, and 25.

135. See, e.g., Agnew Bidwell letter, March 11, 1971, North Battleford, Canada; and Dorothy Haven: "It is an honor to greet you, and join in the efforts of your friends, to send you out into the world, as our finest ambassador. We salute your wonderful gift of voice and of languages—a gift that has grown through the years, upheld by you constant study and thought"; letter from Dorothy Haven, Conn., May 20, 1954, PRC-6.

NOTES 309

136. See letters from Helen Herrick, "Your gift to people everywhere is priceless and I think you have a right to know that"; May 6, 1973, Philadelphia; and James Hendron: we "will always keep alive the precious gift you have made to the world"; August 16, 1969, San Francisco.

137. Susan Bell letter, November 19, 1960, Bannockburn, Australia. Canadian Myrtle Bergen, the wife of a logger, played Robeson's Peace Arch record "countless times, lent it out to the neighbours, and had many people in to hear it. And how many tears of sympathy and comradeship it has stirred! It is impossible for me to describe the strength of that record and the bond of solidarity with which it reaches out to encompass all its listeners!" Bergen was fortunate enough to attend a Robeson concert, the telling of which she framed as an instance of surrogacy politics: "Sometimes we feel our own little corner of the world is pretty placid and insignificant, but when I saw you yesterday, I can only say I felt drawn so close to the international struggle of which you are playing such a great part"; July 24, 1955.

138. Thanking Robeson for his "actions, voice, and courage," a fan confessed: "Because of the views you hold, I have always tried to make friends with all races, so now in New Zealand my best friends are Maoris, Samoans, and Fijian Indians. Were it not for you, I probably would have cared little and thought nothing about them or any other people in this world"; John Dickens letter, Auckland, New Zealand, n.d. (c. early 1960s). See also the letters from Jean M. Okey, April 29, 1973, Canada; and Alison Barton, November 14, 1960, Australia.

139. Mary Donnell letter, October 28, 1960, Christchurch, New Zealand.

140. Eileen Clare Gibson, September 26, 1959, Kent, England. For Australian "housewife, mother and office secretary" Sylvia J. Lamond, it was "important" to hear Robeson, "a real lover of humanity," while on his 1960s concert tour of the antipodes because she drew courage from him: "when our Government is trying to force an iniquitous Crimes Act Amendment on the people, and we need to gather the courage to fight it with all our strength. You gave me that courage, because you seemed to have some to spare and I took it without hesitation"; November 10, 1960, Cammeray, Australia.

141. Meskimmon, *Contemporary Art*, 6. The cosmopolitan effects of this type of fan-as-friend distinguish it from the typical operations of *Heimat*, which like fandom is based on "acts of textual and social discrimination," dividing communities through the construction of imagined others, although Sandvoss notes that there are "many possibilities for reconciling a sense of *Heimat* with the endorsement of difference"; *Fans*, 65.

142. The stranger is a persistent topos in recent writings on cosmopolitanism: Derrida's meditation on the obligation of hospitality to strangers and Appiah's essay on the ethics of living in a world of strangers are two such enterprises. See Jacques Derrida, *On Cosmopolitanism and Forgiveness*, trans. Mark Dooley and Michael Hughes (London: Routledge: 2001); and Kwame Anthony Appiah, *Cosmopolitanism: Ethics in a World of Strangers* (London: Penguin, 2006).

143. Letter from Brenda Laing, December 12, 1966, London.

144. Seyla Benhabib, *Situating the Self: Gender, Community and Postmodernism in Contemporary Ethics* (Cambridge: Polity, 1992), 10, and 11–12.

310 NOTES

145. Redmond, *Everything Man*, 4.
146. In thinking about Robeson's concert practice as an instance of everyday cosmopolitanism I signal my debt to the body of writing that has issued from the new or critical cosmopolitanism that gained currency in the early 2000s. Examples of work that theorize the concept can be found in Steven Vertovec and Robin Cohen, eds., *Conceiving Cosmopolitanism: Theory, Context, and Practice* (Oxford: Oxford University Press, 2002). The idea of "colored cosmopolitanism," which bears similarities with Black internationalism, would be another line of inquiry by which one might productively pursue Robeson's thought and practice; see, e.g., Slate, *Colored Cosmopolitanism*.
147. David A. Hollinger, "Not Universalists, Not Pluralists: The New Cosmopolitans Find Their Own Way," in *Conceiving Cosmopolitanism: Theory, Context, and Practice*, ed. Steven Vertovec and Robin Cohen (Oxford: Oxford University Press, 2002), 227–239.
148. Robeson, *Here I Stand*, 56–57.
149. For more on the cosmopolitan themes presented in a typical late-career Robeson concert, see Olwage, " 'The World Is His Song.'" For a discussion of Alain Locke's cosmopolitanism, see Anderson, *Deep River*, ch. 3.
150. Robeson, *Here I Stand*, 115.
151. Samuel Haynes, "Robeson Had 'Whole World in His Hands,'" *Afro-American*, May 17, 1958.
152. Dorothy Dandridge, "Coast Critics Praise Robeson's New Program," *Washington Afro-American*, March 18, 1958. Robeson discoursed extensively on these topics, for example in *Here I Stand*. In an article for *Jewish Life* he wrote about the "the interweaving of people's cultures," and the "wonder-woven fabric of human culture which unites us"; Paul Robeson, "Bonds of Brotherhood," *Jewish Life*, November 1954. In concert, it became the singer's habit to prefix his performance of a given work with a short introductory talk in which he explored the genealogical connections of the music he performed. See, e.g., Paul Robeson, "Patterns of Folk Song," recorded 1958, side 1, track 4 on *Paul Robeson: Ballad for Americans and Carnegie Hall Concert*, vol. 2, Vanguard VSD 79193, 1965, LP; and also Karp, "Performing Black-Jewish Symbiosis," 70–71.
153. Daniel Hiebert, "Cosmopolitanism at the Local Level: The Development of Transnational Neighbourhoods," in *Conceiving Cosmopolitanism: Theory, Context, and Practice*, ed. Steven Vertovec and Robin Cohen (Oxford: Oxford University Press, 2002), 212.
154. Edward Goring, "Robeson's Answer Is a Brothering Song," *London Mail*, July 12, 1958.
155. *Sunday Times* (London), May 5, 1929. Around the same year the *Musical Courier* pronounced that the "cult of the negro spiritual is overdone"; "Tuning In with Europe," June 15, 1929.
156. *Edinburg Evening Dispatch*, March 16, 1935; and *Northern Whig* (Belfast, Ireland), March 27, 1939.
157. On a related point: Contrary to Robeson's practice, recitalists who shared his mass appeal, such as McCormack and Tauber, "begin their concerts at 3 p.m. with 'the

NOTES 311

classics,' and wend their ways down to the common denominator of popular taste by half-past four"; W. L., *Manchester Guardian*, January 20, 1936.

158. "Robeson Songbook," PRP-21. On song groups in recital practice, see Shirlee Emmons and Stanley Sonntag, *The Art of the Song Recital* (New York: Schirmer, 1979), 6, 23, and ch. 2.

159. The "English" songs for the Purdue concert were the Mendelssohn aria "Lord God of Abraham" from *Elijah*, Parry's "Jerusalem," Quilter's "Now Sleeps the Crimson Petal," and "Oh, No, John!" arranged by Cecil Sharp. The "Russian" items sung at Columbia University were Dargomischky's "Eastern Romance," Mussorgsky's "Evening Song" and "Silent Room," and "Prayer" [the "Hassidic Chant"] arranged by Engel. For the programs see PRC-3. Robeson Jr. remembered that a "typical" program of the late 1940s was still structured by groups, and included "a group by Mussorgsky, a group of folk songs from several lands, a set of Negro spirituals" and a group of art songs; Robeson Jr., *The Undiscovered Paul Robeson*, 136, and 20.

160. For the programs, see LBP-5.

161. For the typescript program, see PRC-5; for more on the Peace Arch concerts, read Shaw, "Paul Robeson: The Peace Arch Concerts."

162. Robeson Jr., *The Undiscovered Paul Robeson*, 238.

163. *Sacramento Bee*, October 26, 1957; my emphasis.

164. Perhaps the presentation of cosmopolitanism in song grouping distinguishes it from the "performative black internationalism" that Lisa Barg has argued embodied the singer's concert programs at the time of his Popular Front work in the early 1940s. Barg explains this as Robeson's "intertwined commitments to the universalism of folk expression and to black cultural and political nationalism through carefully planned programs that typically combined a core group of spirituals within an international repertoire that emphasized folk and protest songs"; "Paul Robeson's *Ballad for Americans*," 54.

165. John Tomlinson, "Interests and Identities in Cosmopolitan Politics," in *Conceiving Cosmopolitanism: Theory, Context, and Practice*, ed. Steven Vertovec and Robin Cohen (Oxford: Oxford University Press, 2002), 253.

166. Harriett Johnson, "Words and Music: Robeson Returns to Carnegie Hall," *New York Post*, May 11, 1958; and Haynes, "Robeson Had 'Whole World in His Hands.'"

167. Irving Kolodin, "Paul Robeson in Carnegie Hall," *Saturday Review*, May 24, 1958. Harold Schonberg noted that Robeson "illustrated" his "lecture on the relationships between African and Chinese music" by "singing brief excerpts without the assistance of his pianist"; "Paul Robeson Sings, Lectures in First City Recital in 11 Years," *New York Times*, May 11, 1958. In doing so Robeson drew on a practice he had used in interviews and press conferences since the mid-1930s.

168. Johnson, "Words and Music."

169. Thomas Albright, "Robeson Makes Triumphal Return," *San Francisco Chronicle*, February 19, 1958; and Theodore C. Stone, "Paul Robeson Wins Great Ovation at Mandel Hall," *Chicago Defender*, April 19, 1958.

170. "The Magic of Robeson," *Dundee Evening Telegraph & Post*, November 10, 1958.

171. Wien[?], "A New Paul Robeson Wows N.Y.," *Variety*, May 14, 1958.

312 NOTES

172. "Paul Comes Home," *National Guardian*, May 19, 1958.

173. See, e.g., *Times Union* (Rochester, NY), March 23, 1927; *Ithaca Journal*, October 13, 1945; *Chicago Daily News*, May 5, 1946; and Haynes, "Robeson Had 'Whole World in His Hands.'"

174. Carl E. Lindstrom, *Hartford Times*, October 29, 1945.

175. "Jacob's Ladder" is not listed on the program of either recital, though it appears as the final item on the LP live recording of the May 9 recital, hence my designation of it as an encore. Robeson changes "Soldiers of the cross" to "Soldiers in this fight" for the first two verses, then reverts to the standard "Soldiers of the cross" for the penultimate verse; Paul Robeson and Alan Booth (piano), "Jacob's Ladder," recorded 1958, side 2, track 8 on *Paul Robeson at Carnegie Hall*, Vanguard LP VRS-9051, 1960, LP.

176. Nira Yuval-Davis et al., eds., *The Situated Politics of Belonging* (London: Sage, 2006), 2.

177. Letter from Jo Love, Nathrop, CO, November 12, 1964. A correspondent identified only as Bill wrote to Robeson that "Your handling of the 'singing audience' was kindly and effective"; letter May 10, 1958.

178. Redmond, *Everything Man*, 38 and 2. "Black antiphonal life arrives as a vibrational practice shared openly and freely, across space and time. It's a will to question, to shapeshift, to rescue; to seek out radical intimacy; and, if necessary, to wait. Deterrents and violence are expected, for we know we aren't meant to feel and act together. Some will be taken too soon, but they never truly leave. We sing, think, and live differently because of them, and when summoned, they return. Dal segno. And this Paul does"; ibid., 140.

179. Robeson, *Paul Robeson, Negro*, 23.

180. Baldwin, *Beyond the Color Line*, 240–241.

181. The communal singing of Robeson's brothering song ideal is an instance of what Matt Hills, writing about digital fandom, calls multisocial interaction or fan-fan sharing. Hills presents this as a critique of a dominant concept in fan studies, that is para-social or imagined interactions between fan and celebrity, which has been conceptualized as different from "real," co-present social relationships; Matt Hills, "From Para-Social to Multisocial Interaction: Theorizing Material/Digital Fandom and Celebrity," in *A Companion to Celebrity*, ed. P. David Marshall and Sean Redmond (Oxford: John Wiley and Sons, 2016), 463–482.

182. As late as 1958, Paul Endicott, who served as a local concert promoter for the Midwest, wrote to Robeson that in Detroit the two main concert halls wouldn't rent their venues to the singer, but that he could secure a large union hall and Negro churches, with one large white church also showing interest; and in Ohio two campus clubs were available; letter of March 24, 1958, PRP-Series B.

183. Paul Robeson, "Speech," recorded 1953, track 25 on *Paul Robeson: The Peace Arch Concerts*, Folk Era FE1442CD, 1998, CD, 2:35–3:10.

184. Woodard noted further: "These three forms of musical expression—hymns, spirituals, and gospel—may be seen as mirrors reflecting divisions within the African American community of the era: socioeconomic, generational, and geographic"; Patricia Woodard, "Singing Up to Freedom Land: Hymns, Spirituals, and Gospel Songs in the Civil Rights Movement," *The Hymn* 67, no. 2 (2016): 8.

NOTES   313

185. Paul Robeson, *Solid Rock: Favorite Hymns of My People*, Othello Records, L-201, 1954. See also chapter 6.

186. Paul Robeson and Allan Booth (accompanist), "We Are Climbing Jacob's Ladder," recorded 1958, side 2, track 7 on *Paul Robeson in Live Performance*, Columbia Masterworks M30424, 1970, LP.

187. Bernice Johnson Reagon, "Let the Church Sing 'Freedom,'" *Black Music Research Journal* 7 (1987): 106, 109; and Bernice Johnson Reagon, "The Civil Rights Period: Music as an Agent of Social Change," in *Issues in African American Music: Power, Gender, Race, Representation*, ed. Portia K. Maultsby and Mellonee V. Burnim (New York: Routledge, 2017), 344. There are also differences between Robeson's recital performance in a church and the songleader's work at mass meetings, as Reagon's research makes clear. Notably, Robeson's son claimed that Robeson did not change a hymn's words when sung in church, as was his habit when singing in other contexts; see Robert H. Cataliotti, "On My Journey: Paul Robeson's Independent Recordings." Liner notes for *On My Journey: Paul Robeson's Independent Recordings* (Smithsonian Folkways Recordings FW CD 40178, 2007): 25.

188. See speech after Paul Robeson and Allan Booth (accompanist), "Sometimes I Feel Like a Motherless Child," recorded 1958, side 2, track 6 on *Paul Robeson in Live Performance*, Columbia Masterworks M30424, 1970, LP.

189. "I Breathe Freely" (July 1935), in Foner, *Paul Robeson Speaks*, 102.

190. Robert Cantwell, *When We Were Good: The Folk Revival* (Cambridge, MA: Harvard University Press, 1996). For the social bonds created by collective singing at hootenannies, see also Stephen Petrus and Ronald D. Cohen, *Folk City: New York and the American Folk Music Revival* (Oxford: Oxford University Press, 2015), 103.

191. Letter from Pete Seeger to Robeson, June 22, 1964, PRP-Series B. One of Robeson's influences on the folk song movement was its commitment to an international repertory. See David Evans's chronology of the folk song revival; in Cantwell, *When We Were Good*, 34–35.

192. Redmond, "Songs of Free Men," 129, 132, 136. Although not grounded in empirical historical scholarship, Stewart offers a similar theoretical conclusion: Robeson forged transnational connections with the international worker, and enabled diverse audiences to connect with each other beyond themselves in creating a new corporate body; "I Sing the Black Body Electric," 276–280.

193. Boyle and Bunie, *Paul Robeson*, 381.

194. Daniel Gray, *Homage to Caledonia: Scotland and the Spanish Civil War* (Edinburgh: Luath Press, 2008), 73.

195. López, "La música en las Brigadas Internacionales," 373–374.

196. Alejo Carpentier, *La consagración de la primavera* (Coyoacán, Mexico: Siglo Veintiuno Editores, 1978), 146–147.

197. *Springfield Republican*, May 20, 1946. Robeson claimed to know around twenty-five languages; see the *Radio Times*, September 4, 1959.

198. López, "La música en las Brigadas Internacionales," 29–40, and 535.

199. Oscar Thompson, *New York Sun*, October 7, 1940. See also Harriett Johnson, "Words and Music."

314 NOTES

200. For the 1958 Carnegie Hall concerts the Mussorgsky numbers were the only foreign-language works on the program not to receive this treatment, perhaps because they are through-composed, although Robeson prefaced them with a spoken introduction in English.

201. Meskimmon, *Contemporary Arts*, 80, 85.

202. Morris Browda, "The World and Music," *California Jewish Voice*, June 6, 1952, PRC-4. Elsewhere Robeson told a reporter that "'Learning other people's languages is a wonderful thing. . . . It brings people all over the world closer together'"; "Mr. Robeson Minds His P's and Queues," *Liverpool Daily Post*, November 20, 1958.

203. Letter from John Gray, Robeson's secretary, to Ted Ward, of the British Columbia District Union, International Union of Mine, Mill and Smelter Workers, July 23, 1952, PRC-4.

204. Irwin Silber, "Pete Seeger, Paul Robeson on New Long-Play Discs," *Sing Out! A People's Artists Publication* 4, no. 4 (March 1954): 15–16. Because folk music was "functional and designed for direct, personal communication," Silber deemed it an oversight that folk song recordings tended to lack the presence of a live audience; ibid.

205. Philip Auslander, "Live and Technologically Mediated Performance," in *The Cambridge Companion to Performance Studies*, ed. Tracy Davis (Cambridge: Cambridge University Press, 2008), 108. And for how community functions in live and recorded performance, see Philip Auslander, *Liveness: Performance in a Mediatized Culture* (London: Routledge, 1999), 55–57.

206. Paul Sanden, *Liveness in Modern Music: Musicians, Technology, and the Perception of Performance* (New York: Routledge, 2013), 11.

207. Cook, *Beyond the Score*, 372.

208. Letter from Myrtle Bergen, July 24, 1955, PRP-Series B.

209. Letter from Moses Smith to Robeson, October 8, 1940, PRP-Series B.

210. Harold Schonberg, "Paul Robeson Sings, Lectures in First City Recital in 11 Years," *New York Times*, May 11, 1958.

Chapter 5

1. "Sonny Boy" was written by Ray Henderson, Buddy DeSylva, and Lew Brown for Al Jolson in *The Singing Fool* of 1928. It was the first song from a film to sell over a million recordings. With reference to the release of a selection of songs from *The Singing Fool*, Robeson's British recording company HMV noted that "Now that the 'Talkie' is taking its place as a popular form of musical entertainment, it is but natural that gems from the most up-to-date of them should be recorded"; HMV catalog, May 1929, 8, BLSA.

2. Alan Dent, *The Queen*, April 3, 1929. Raymond Garnett was no doubt spot-on in noting that "Robeson is undeniably a fine artiste, but it is doubtful whether 'Sonny Boy' is quite in his line"; *Everybody's Weekly*, March 1, 1929. See also *Variety*, March 20, 1929; and *Britannia* [possibly *Britannia and Eve*], May 1929.

NOTES 315

3. The *Sussex Daily News* wrote of the singer's "Incursions into the White World" in reference to Robeson's performance of Russian and English song; March 9, 1936.

4. See Allan Moore, *Rock: The Primary Text* (Aldershot: Ashgate, 2001), 45; also Alexander G. Weheliye, *Phonographies: Grooves in Sonic Afro-Modernity* (Durham, NC: Duke University Press, 2005), 37.

5. Dolar, *A Voice and Nothing More*, 20.

6. Paul Robeson with orchestra, Carroll Gibbons (conductor), "Sonny Boy," recorded 1929, track 18, disc 1, on *Paul Robeson: The Complete EMI Sessions, 1928–1939*, EMI Records 2 15588 2, 2008, CD. For a discussion of the /r/-lessness in the competing varieties of American speech in the early twentieth century, see Jonathan Ross Greenberg, "Singing Up Close: Voice, Language, and Race in American Popular Music, 1925–1935" (PhD diss., University of California, Los Angeles, 2008), 215–219.

7. For a British audience it was probably no coincidence that the *Britannia* review of Robeson's "Sonny Boy" mentioned also John McCormack's disc of 1928, yet another release of the song (rather than Austin's or Etting's), because the Irish tenor's art-trained voice approximates Robeson's more closely in several aspects, including his use of the trilled r.

8. Daniel Jones, *An English Pronouncing Dictionary* (London: Dent, 1917): xx; in *Daniel Jones: Selected Works*, vol. 3, ed. Beverley Collins and Inger M. Mees (London: Routledge, 2003). Jones' observations about the fricative <r> remained the same in the fourth edition of 1937. For foreigners, Jones had the following advice: "To those foreigners whose object is to be able to converse on terms of social equality with the persons referred to [that is, RP speakers] the pronunciation here recorded will probably commend itself as a suitable one for them to acquire"; x. Collins and Mees claim that Jones's *Dictionary* "established itself rapidly as the only reliable guide to the pronunciation of British English," a status unchallenged until the 1990s; "Introduction," n.p.

9. Robeson, *Here I Stand*, 32. Eslanda Robeson wrote that they were "invited to select Mayfair drawing rooms"; letter to Carl Van Vechten, July 8, 1928, quoted in Boyle and Bunie, *Paul Robeson*, 198.

10. Greenberg, "Singing Up Close," 221–223. Greenberg's analysis of Ethel Waters's singing is illuminating, and focuses on her usage of three English phonemes, including the rolled r, with "particularly strong racial and geographic associations"; 202.

11. A blogger on English dialect points out the use of tapped r's in older types of RP was often a deliberate theatrical choice that was not present in actors' everyday speech; Ben T. Smith, "Was There Ever a 'Veddy British' R?" (2012), http://dialectblog.com/2012/01/10/was-there-a-veddy-british-r/.

12. Robeson owned parts 1, 2, and 5 of the series, preserved in PRP-Series Q.

13. *Daily Telegraph and Morning Post*, November 10, 1937. The *Edinburg Evening Dispatch* reported that he possessed a "magnificent lingual library, not merely of actual tongues, but of dialect shades and styles"; March 16, 1935.

14. Eslanda's opinion of Gielgud's performance was such: "Think he gives a fine, intelligent, sensitive performance. He is ideally cast. Only fault I found was a very slight mannerism, partly Oxfordian, partly raving"; diary, May 7, 1930; ERP-Box 16. Just days earlier, Robeson had sung at the aristocrat Sir Phillip Sassoon's House in Park Lane for a charity event; ibid.

316 NOTES

15. Around the same time Robeson was also involved with the sometime actress and upper class Yolande Jackson, so the pillow talk was also in elite accents.

16. In the 1944 studio recording of the Broadway production of *Othello*, made for an American audience and half a decade after Robeson had left Britain, the actor had lost much of his earlier articulation of r's, though the odd "veddy British" r remains, and Robeson's performance is devoid of an explicitly broad American pronunciation unlike some of his American co-actors, most notably Jack Manning.

17. C. B. Purdom, "Paul Robeson as 'Othello,'" *Everyman*, May 29, 1930.

18. For more on Robeson's 1930 Othello and the politics of race, see Swindall, *The Politics of Paul Robeson's Othello*, ch. 2.

19. *Daily Herald* (London), May 7, 1930.

20. On the influence of the voice coach Margaret Carrington in remaking John Barrymore's actor's voice, see Michael A. Morrison, "The Voice Teacher as Shakespearean Collaborator: Margaret Carrington and John Barrymore," *Theatre Survey* 38, no. 2 (1997): 129–158.

21. London *Daily Herald*, May 7, 1930. See also Johnson, *The Book of American Negro Spirituals*, 45.

22. *Evening Standard*, May 20, 1930. See also Swindall, *The Politics of Paul Robeson's Othello*, 27.

23. *Evening Standard*, May 20, 1930.

24. *Daily Herald*, May 7, 1930. I came across only two instances of criticism of his accent: "The slight American accent is a trouble at first, but one soon gets used to this"; *Morning Post*, May 20, 1930; and "He spoke his lines in perfect English except for a slight American turn of his 'r's,' which is rarely got over"; *Liverpool Post*, May 20, 1930. From this time Robeson frequently included recitations—a monologue from *Othello*, a recitation of a poem, a scene from a play in which he had acted—in his concerts. A favorite item was William Blake's "The Little Black Boy," often performed as an encore. The *Hastings Observer* (no month, 1930) thought the "Little Black Boy" was "beautifully recited in the richest of speaking voices and delivered with perfect English diction"; and the *Huddersfield Express* concurred: "his direct delivery, his feeling for the beauty of the English tongue . . . put so many English elocutionists to shame"; April 13, 1934.

25. See "Paul Robeson Discusses Othello," accessed 30 May 2017, https://www.youtube.com/watch?v=-DF7YQrC7HM: 0:38–1:47.

26. Ruth Reese, *My Way: A Life in Music* (London: Akira, 1987), 105, 110–111.

27. Received pronunciation in song was one focus of Harry Plunket Greene's manual *Interpretation in Song* (1912). Concerned primarily with the singing of English, the "treatment of the letter *r*," as he phrased it, received the most extensive consideration of all the consonants. "There is no question that the *r*, wherever it comes in the word, ought by rights to be sounded," he pronounced. Plunket Greene categorized the rules and practices of the rolled r in singing, including its "misuses"—"as a cloak to cover a multitude of sins"—and Robeson's uses thereof follow Plunket Greene's guidelines almost to the letter. See Harry Plunket Greene, *Interpretation in Song* (New York: Macmillan, 1912), 115–116, 120. We might consider Plunket Greene's

NOTES   317

own singing practice: his restrained use of "r" in an English version of Schubert's "*Der Leiermann*," admittedly recorded in 1934, perhaps as r's received more moderated attention in RP, is in contrast to his more explicitly "Irish" pronunciation and exaggerated r's in "The Garden Where the Praties Grow" recorded in the same session; "The Hurdy-Gurdy Man" (Columbia DB 1377, 1934) and "The Garden Where the Praties Grow (Columbia, DB 1321, 1934).

28. Valerie Langfield, *Roger Quilter: His Life and Music* (Woodbridge, Suffolk: Boydell, 2002), 22–23. Gervase Elwes, "Now Sleeps the Crimson Petal," Columbia L 1055, 1916; John McCormack, "Now Sleeps the Crimson Petal," Victor 1307-B, 1927; Paul Robeson and Lawrence Brown (piano), "Now Sleeps the Crimson Petal," H.M.V. B 9281, 1939, shellac record; straight transfer from disc, British Library Sound Archive.

29. *Gramophone*, February 1940, 324.

30. Ben Short, "Paul Robeson Record for Basque Children," *Daily Worker*, August 12, 1937; and Paul Robeson, "Minstrel Man," recorded 1937, track 25, disc 5, on *Paul Robeson: The Complete EMI Sessions, 1928–1939*, EMI Records 2 15596 2, 2008, CD.

31. See Steven C. Tracy, "Langston Hughes and Afro-American Vernacular Music," in *A Historical Guide to Langston Hughes*, ed. Steven C. Tracy (Oxford: Oxford University Press, 2004), 85–118.

32. For the mid-Atlantic dialect, see Kathryn LaBouff, *Singing and Communicating in English: A Singer's Guide to English Diction* (Oxford: Oxford University Press, 2008), ch. 15. Robeson's singer's English accent was thus modified and aspects of rhoticity moderated, a move that also correlated with the decline in rolled r's in received pronunciation as the century progressed, and with his move back to the United States toward the end of 1939. Thus in later recordings of "Now Sleeps," made in the 1950s, the singer trills only when r's are terminal, not when they are part of a consonant cluster or occur elsewhere. For the decrease in rolled r's in RP, see Smith, "Was There Ever a 'Veddy British' R?"

33. Henry Louis Gates, Jr., *The Signifying Monkey: A Theory of African American Literary Criticism* (Oxford: Oxford University Press, 1988), 119. For more on minstrelsy as a framework through which whites "understood" African Americans, and which in part characterized slaves as childlike, docile, and happy, and of minstrelsy thus as a mechanism of social control and representation of racial hierarchy, see Cruz, *Culture on the Margins*, 28.

34. *Northern Whig*, March 27, 1939. Despite his best efforts, and well into his career, the singer would continue to be heard in terms of the minstrel figure. One critic compared Robeson's "simpler basso minstrelsy" to the "season of valiant opera singing" heard in the city's Memorial Opera House; Alexander Fried, *San Francisco Examiner*, November 13, 1940. For Redmond, the dialect in *Show Boat* "demonstrates a particular version of blackness out of sync with the 'fine intelligence' of Robeson"; "Songs of Free Men," 105.

35. See Newland, "Sounding 'Black,'" 51. Greenberg concludes that Ethel Waters's phonological choices, which included a penchant for the rolled r, may be thought of as "a kind of protest against visions of American identity that did not allow dynamic space for African Americans"; "Singing Up Close," 202 and 225.

318 NOTES

36. Gates, *The Signifying Monkey*, 188.
37. E. B. and H. K., "The Negro and His Arts by Paul Robeson," *Wisconsin Literary Magazine*, November 1, 1929.
38. Ibid.
39. Gates, *The Signifying Monkey*, 193.
40. See also the discussion on Robeson's performance of dialect in "Water Boy" in chapter 3.
41. Newland, "Sounding 'Black,'" 40. In her own research, on the singing practices at Fisk University, she explores how "an entire ideology of black experience and identity, and a particular, related history of performing blackness, are embedded in the seemingly narrow area of vocality, and the even more precise domain of vocal diction"; 45.
42. Ibid., 190 and 192.
43. The *Manchester Guardian* deemed Robeson's recitation of *God's Trombones* "profoundly moving": "The lovely details of the Creation, the spirituals, the fine inflection of Mr. Robeson's voice—all would bear many hearings for us to grasp and remember their full beauty"; October 24, 1931. I have been unable to locate any extant recordings of Robeson performing from *God's Trombones*. He received the book as a gift from Johnson in 1927 and performed it until at least 1959, for radio broadcasts in the United Kingdom; letter from James Weldon Johnson to Robeson, May 17, 1927, PRP-Series B.
44. James Weldon Johnson, *God's Trombones: Seven Negro Sermons in Verse* (New York: Penguin, 2008 [1927]), 5–7. Roland Hayes would reaffirm the importance of the preacher and the folk sermon for his own musical practice in *My Songs*. Noelle Morrissette distinguishes between Johnson's avoidance of dialect in his own modernist creations and his promotion thereof in the "sound-orientated prefaces" of, e.g., *The Book of American Negro Spirituals* (1925); Noelle Morrissette, *James Weldon Johnson's Modern Soundscapes* (Iowa City: University of Iowa Press, 2013), 138–140.
45. Ralph Holms, *Detroit Evening Times*, December 7, 1929. The recording of the work received the following comment: Robeson's "fervent singing of the naïve sentiments forms a marked contrast to the shop balladry of the accompaniments"; *Musical Mirror*, September, 1930.
46. Hayes, *My Songs*, 8.
47. Will Marion Cook, *Three Negro Songs* (New York: Schirmer, 1912); Paul Robeson and Lawrence Brown (piano), "Exhortation."
48. Newland, "Sounding 'Black,'" 75–80. She reminds us that "bridging the past and the present, concert spiritual singing vocalizes the traditions of the U.S. black middle class"; 77–78.
49. Gates, *The Signifying Monkey*, 188.
50. Paul Robeson and Ruthland Clapham (piano), "Li'l Gal," recorded 1931, track 16, disc 2, on *Paul Robeson: The Complete EMI Sessions, 1928–1939*, EMI Records 2 15590 2, 2008, CD; and Paul Robeson and Alan Booth (piano), "Li'l Gal," recorded 1956, track 26 on *On My Journey: Paul Robeson's Independent Recordings, 1928–1939*, Smithsonian Folkways Records SFW CD 440178, 2007, CD. Redmond notes how in

NOTES   319

Robeson's late career singing of "Ol' Man River" he "extinguished its exaggerated dialect"; "Songs of Free Men," 120.

51. Johnson, *The Book of American Negro Spirituals*, 43. Johnson catalogued the "rules" of the "dialect-speaking Negro" extensively; ibid., 43–45.

52. Johnson, *God's Trombones*, 5, 7, and 2. See Morrissette for Johnson's celebration of the rhythm and tonality of the Black preaching arts in *God's Trombones*; *James Weldon Johnson's Modern Soundscapes*, ch. 6. For the influence of the African American "sermonic tradition" on Black authors' writing, see Dolan Hubbard, *The Sermon and the African American Literary Imagination* (Columbia: University of Missouri Press, 1994). See also Jon Michael Spencer, *Sacred Symphony: The Chanted Sermon of the Black Preacher* (Westport, CT: Greenwood Press, 1987), which essays a "musical" analysis of transcriptions of sermons.

53. Typescript drafts of the script titled "God' Trombones"—A Recital by Paul Robeson, and other documents related to the broadcast, are located in PRP-Series H: Scripts.

54. Alfred Frankenstein, *San Francisco Chronicle*, November 13, 1940.

55. For a brief discussion of accent in popular song, see Simon Frith, *Performing Rites: Evaluating Popular Music* (Oxford: Oxford University Press, 1996), 166–168.

56. Dolar, *A Voice and Nothing More*, 20 and 191 n. 8.

57. "The New Urge That Is in Paul Roberson," *Evening Express*, January 18, 1939.

58. Neruda, "Ode to Paul Robeson," 244–245.

59. Baldwin, *Beyond the Color Line*, 214–218.

60. Locke, "The Negro Spirituals," 206; Natalie Curtis-Burlin, *Negro Folk-Songs*, Book II (New York: G. Schirmer, 1918), 9. For an overview of the scholarship on African American stylistic features of performance practice, see Barbara Steinhaus-Jordan, "An Analysis of Marian Anderson's Interpretation of Black Spiritual Art Songs in Selected Recordings" (DMA diss., University of Georgia, 1997), 11–12.

61. Milton Metfessel, *Phonophotography in Folk Music: American Negro Songs in New Notation* (Chapel Hill: University of North Carolina Press, 1928), 18, 29, 33, 44, 127–129.

62. Paul Robeson and Lawrence Brown (piano), "On Ma Journey," Gramophone B-2326, 1926; straight transfer from disc, British Library Sound Archive; Paul Robeson and Alan Booth (piano), "On My Journey: Mount Zion," recorded 1957, track 1 on *On My Journey: Paul Robeson's Independent Recordings*, Smithsonian Folkways Recordings SFW CD 40178, 2007, CD.

63. Paul Robeson and Alan Booth (piano), "Amazing Grace," recorded 1956, track 15 on *On My Journey: Paul Robeson's Independent Recordings*, Smithsonian Folkways Recordings SFW CD 40178, 2007, CD. I draw on Steinhaus-Jordan's terminology in her analysis of Marian Anderson's use of African American stylistic features in her singing of spirituals; see "An Analysis of Marian Anderson." She has also documented William Warfield's approach to the performance of "black spiritual art song." Warfield, who "idolized" Robeson, also made extensive use of melodic embellishment; "Black Spiritual Art Song: Interpretive Guidelines for Studio Teachers," *Journal of Singing* 61, no. 5 (2005): 477–485.

64. Locke, "The Negro Spirituals," 207.

320   NOTES

65. Steinhaus-Jordan, "An Analysis of Marian Anderson," 108.

66. For an account of some of the variety of uses of portamento and other pitch sliding in early twentieth-century art singing, see Leech-Wilkinson, *The Changing Sound of Music*, ch. 4, and n. 11.

67. "Paul Robeson: Thoughts about His Music," section 3, 10-11, PRP-21.

68. For connections between Black and Jewish vocality, see Meizel, *Multivocality*, 135–136; and Karp, "Performing Black-Jewish Symbiosis."

69. Barg, "Paul Robeson's *Ballad for Americans*," 64, and 33.

70. Dolar, *A Voice and Nothing More*, 22; Cavarero, *For More than One Voice*, 173, and ch. 3.2 *passim*.

71. Dolar, *A Voice and Nothing More*, 22. See also Barthes's discussion on evaluating the grain of the voice; Roland Barthes, "The Grain of the Voice," in *Image, Music, Text*, trans. Stephen Heath (New York: Hill & Wang, 1977), 188–189.

72. Cavarero, *For More than One Voice*, 178, 180.

73. Ibid., 182. See also my discussion of Dolar at the end of chapter 3, and Eidsheim's concept of vibrational practice.

74. Carl Van Doren, "Introduction," in Graham, *Paul Robeson*.

75. Lawrence Kramer, *Interpreting Music* (Berkeley: University of California Press, 2011), 123.

76. Letter from Kenzo Nishikawa to Robeson, Japan, July 23, 1959, PRP-Series B; "By Pete Seeger," in *Paul Robeson: The Great Forerunner* (New York: International Publishers, 1998), 311.

77. Roark Bradford, "Paul Robeson IS John Henry," *Collier's*, January 13, 1940; "'Organise!' said Joe Hill," *Daily Worker*, January 18, 1939. For Robeson the "cultural hero" in Soviet Russia, see Baldwin, *Beyond the Color Line*, 231.

78. Stewart, "I Sing the Black Body Electric," 276–278.

79. Unidentified newsclipping, c. 1931, PRP-Series G: Newsclippings; Isadora Smith, *Pittsburgh Courier*, October 19, 1940.

80. John Chapman, *Sunday News*, October 24, 1943.

81. In the Aristotelian tradition the "heroic [meter] is the stateliest and most massive," making it suitable for the form of the epic which "conduces to grandeur of effect," and less pleasingly "divert[s] the mind of the hearer" from the plot. See Aristotle, *The Poetics of Aristotle*, 3rd ed., trans. S. H. Butcher (London: Macmillan, 1902), section 24, 93.

82. Edwin H. Schloss, *Philadelphia Record*, October 5, 1943; L. M., *Philadelphia Inquirer*, October 5, 1943. *Billboard* critic Frank Gill commented at length on Robeson's musically booming voice and its effects on the production; October 1943.

83. "Black Majesty," *New Yorker*, October 30, 1943; *Time*, November 1, 1943. Several reviews of the out-of-town, pre-Broadway, run in 1942 noted Robeson's performance in the "Grand Manner," perhaps a hangover from the older, histrionic style that dominated the English stage when he first learned Othello; see, e.g., Louis Kronenberger, *PM*, August 13, 1942; and *Time*, August 24, 1942.

84. Alisha Lola Jones, "Singing High: Black Countertenors and Gendered Sound in Gospel Performance," in *The Oxford Handbook of Voice Studies*, ed. Nina Sun Eidsheim and Katherine Meizel (New York: Oxford University Press, 2019), 39.

NOTES   321

85. In Graham, *Paul Robeson*, 245.
86. Dolar, *A Voice and Nothing More*, 21.
87. Dolan Hubbard makes the link between the Black preacher and the heroic mode explicit. Tracing the Black preacher's oral modes of expression in African American writings, he calls "the black sermon" the "heroic voice of black America"; *The Sermon*, 25.
88. "Our Music Critic," *Dundee Evening Telegraph & Post*, November 10, 1958.
89. Given Robeson's well-known revisions to song texts, and his appropriation thereof for his own oppositional politics, this is a more likely reading than the conventional meaning attributed to the spiritual, in which the slave's restless desire is for the hereafter; see Cataliotti, "On My Journey," 30; and Paul Robeson and Alan Booth (piano), "Stand Still, Jordan," recorded 1955/1956, track 20 on *On My Journey: Paul Robeson's Independent Recordings*, Smithsonian Folkways Recordings SFW CD 40178, 2007, CD.
90. Stewart, "I Sing the Black Body Electric," 276.
91. In an article on "Robeson, Citizen of the World," a Chicago newspaper concluded that "more than any other American . . . he typifies the individual whose world outlook contains a sympathetic understanding of the common men of every nation, race and clime"; John Robert Badger, *Chicago Defender*, April 14, 1945.
92. For this reason, among others, it differs from the operatic tenor as vocal hero. For the rise of the tenor see, e.g., John Rosselli, *Singers of Italian Opera: The History of a Profession* (Cambridge: Cambridge University Press, 1992), ch. 8.
93. Stewart, "I Sing the Black Body Electric," 263, 278.
94. The title for this section is the English translation of German lyrics to a song Robeson recorded for Joris Ivens's documentary film *The Song of the Rivers* (1954), "a song of peace and freedom, a song of brotherhood for working people of all lands"; Paul Robeson, "A Song to Sing," *Masses and Mainstream* 8, no. 10 (1954): 12–13, PRP-Series E-Box 21.
95. James, "Paul Robeson: Black Star," 262.
96. "Editorial: Paul Robeson: The Great Forerunner," *Freedomways: A Quarterly Review of the Freedom Movement* 11, no. 1 (1971): 5.
97. "Robeson Songbook" [c. 1960], PRP-Box 21.
98. Dolar, *A Voice and Nothing More*, 105–107.
99. Ibid., 113–114.
100. Fred Moten, *In the Break*, 1, 6, and 16; and Fred Moten, *Stolen Life: Consent Not to Be a Single Being* (Durham, NC: Duke University Press, 2018), 131.
101. Steven Connor, *Dumbstruck: A Cultural History of Ventriloquism* (Oxford: Oxford University Press, 2000), 30–31. In classic psychoanalytic theory the lack is the infant's cry uttered for the missing breast.
102. Ibid., 37.
103. Moten, *In the Break*, 14. Moten explains that if "subjectivity is defined by the subject's possession of itself and its objects," such as the voice, "it is troubled by a dispossessive force objects exert such that the subject seems to be possessed—infused, deformed—by the object it possesses." The fugitive/bad voice functions through what Moten calls "the phonic materiality of such propriative exertion"; ibid., 1.

322 NOTES

104. Connor, *Dumbstruck*, 37.
105. Moten, *In the Break*, 22. Moten is interested in the manifestations of the scream in free jazz.
106. Connor, *Dumbstruck*, 37.
107. Ibid., 35 and 37.
108. Moten, *In the Break*, 5–6.
109. Perucci, *Paul Robeson*, 14 and chs. 3 and 4.
110. Paul Robeson, "My Answer," *Negro Weekly*, September 17, 1949.
111. Perucci, *Paul Robeson*, 71–73.
112. *Globe Democrat* (St. Louis), January 25, 1947.
113. Carl E. Lindstrom, *Hartford Times*, October 29, 1945.
114. "Paul Robeson Sings Engel's Kaddish. An Interpreter of All Peoples," *Jewish Chronicle*, April 8, 1938; *Daily Mail*, April 4, 1938.
115. J.W., "Cheers Greet Paul Robeson," *Daily Telegraph*, August 11, 1958. Thomas Albright noted the duality: Robeson's voice was "rough" sometimes, but "smooth" elsewhere; "Robeson Makes Triumphal Return," *San Francisco Chronicle*, February 19, 1958.
116. Nat Low began his profile of the singer "This is the story of an angry man"; "This Is Paul Robeson," *Pacific Tribune* (Vancouver), May 16, 1952.
117. Partially unidentified newsclipping, "Albany Audience Acclaims Robeson's Victory Concert," May 9, 1949, PRC-3: Post-Peekskill clippings.
118. Paul Robeson and Lawrence Brown (piano), "The Four Insurgent Generals," recorded 1942, track 9 on *Paul Robeson: Songs of Free Men*, Sony Classical MHK 63223, 1997, CD; and Paul Robeson and Alexander Yeroklin (piano), "The Four Insurgent Generals," recorded 1949, track 7 on *Paul Robeson: The Legendary Moscow Concert*, Revelation RV 70004, 1997, CD.
119. Lee Goodman, "Music Review: Paul Robeson Knocks Throng for Loop in Concert at Wrigley," *Daily News* (Los Angeles), October 1, 1949; Carl E. Lindstrom, *Hartford Times*, October 29, 1945.
120. Drawing on political acts of African American nonviolence, from the late nineteenth century to "Civil Rights Movement philosophies for peaceful demonstrations of dissent against institutional racism," Newland proposes a parallel: "non-violence marks the Fisk Jubilee Singers' performance of a Western classical singing principle through which 'healthy' vocal technique keeps singers from 'hurting' their voices by avoiding perceptions and practices of vocal excess and fatigue" such as stridence, loudness, rasp, uneven registers; "Sounding 'Black,'" 42.
121. Moten, *In the Break*, 6.
122. Paul Robeson and Lawrence Brown (piano), "Theme from Beethoven's 9th Symphony," recorded 1953, track 17 on *Paul Robeson: The Peace Arch Concerts*, Folk Era FE1442CD, 1998, CD.
123. It is another instance of what in Kleinian analysis is called the "part-object": a part of the body that provokes desire or repulsion and is split off from the body, like the infant's cry for the mother's breast; Connor, *Dumbstruck*, 30.

NOTES 323

124. Paul Robeson with Chinese Chorus, *Chee Lai: Songs of New China*, Keynote Recordings, Album 109 K 520-522, 1941, shellac records. In Liangmo's account Robeson learned the song from listening to Liangmo sing it twice when they first met, with Robeson first singing it in public several weeks later at a Lewisohn Stadium concert in New York as an encore, and "in perfect Mandarin"; Liu Liangmo, "Paul Robeson: The People's Singer," in *Chinese American Voices: From the Gold Rush to the Present*, ed. Judy Yung, Gordon H. Chang, and Him Mark Lai (Berkeley: University of California Press, 2006), 204–208; originally published in 1950 in the *China Daily News* (New York).

125. Paul Robeson and Lawrence Brown (piano), "Chin Chin (Chinese Marching Song)," recorded 1953, track 24 on *Paul Robeson: The Peace Arch Concerts*, Folk Era FE1442CD, 1998, CD.

Chapter 6

1. Robeson's secretary, lawyer, and civil rights activist William Patterson invoked the idea of "national arrest" to describe Robeson's confinement to the United States in the wake of the state's revocation of his passport which denied the singer the ability to travel. Open letter from William L. Patterson, November 14, 1955, PRC-6.

2. Letter from Boris Polevoy to Paul Robeson, December 21, 1954, PRC-1. For a detailed account of Polevoy's Russian writings on Robeson, see Baldwin, *Beyond the Color Line*, 232–236.

3. Polevoy letter.

4. Baldwin, *Beyond the Color Line*, 234.

5. Polevoy letter.

6. Redmond, *Everything Man*, 16. Redmond considers three such "scenes" but doesn't consider in detail the specific sound technologies, nor their histories, in the mediation of Robeson's voice, as I do in this chapter. There are similarities between my brief introductory description of Robeson's hologram in Moscow and Redmond's account of his appearance at the 1955 Asian-African Conference of Non-Aligned States in Bandung, Indonesia.

7. Baldwin, *Beyond the Color Line*, 218. Redmond's account of Robeson's taped performance for the Bandung conference, also from 1955, makes a similar point: "how recording technologies attend the deconstruction of borders and subversion of institutions of power": Robeson's "singing voice betrayed his physically situated body through its flight; as he (in body) struggled against his imposed national detention in the United States, his voice was located where he believed it ought to be: in the Third World"; "Songs of Free Men," 134–138. Charles Musser has written similarly about Robeson's use of film as a "utopian medium in its ability to transcend space and time—to outwit state oppression"; "Utopian Visions in Cold War Documentary: Joris Ivens, Paul Robeson and *Song of the Rivers*," *Cinémas: Revue d'études cinématographiques* 12, no. 3 (2002/2003): 109–153.

324 NOTES

8. Redmond, "Songs of Free Men," 138.

9. Schedule for the Paul Robeson Concert, St. Pancras Town Hall, London, 1957, Papers of Clive Jenkins. It was released on LP as *Paul Robeson's Transatlantic Concert*, Topic 10 T 17, 1957.

10. Correspondence between Cedric Belfrage and Eslanda Robeson, May 1, 13, 20, 27, and June 5, 1957, PRP-Series B. The following paragraph draws from this correspondence. Redmond documents another slightly later telephone concert, to Wales on October 5, 1957; see *Everything Man*, 28–33.

11. Telephone diffusion services, some of which carried live concerts, began to appear toward the end of the nineteenth century in Europe and the United States, with their heyday occurring in the first two decades of the next. Historians consider them as precursors to radio broadcast services. See Thomas H. White, "News and Entertainment by Telephone," United States Early Radio History, accessed June 28, 2016, http://earlyradiohistory.us/sec003.htm#part080; and Carolyn Marvin, *When Old Technologies Were New: Thinking about Electric Communication in the Late Nineteenth Century* (New York: Oxford University Press, 1988), 231.

12. "Robeson Concert Heard in Britain," *Afro-American*, June 1, 1957, 11.

13. Belfrage-Robeson correspondence, May 27 and June 5, 1957.

14. "TAT-1," *Hidden Histories of the Information Age*, episode 2, BBC Radio 4, October 21, 2014, http://www.bbc.co.uk/programmes/b04m3bcc: 12:40–12:48. The radio documentary suggests that transmission quality was so good that the members of the audience believed they were listening to recordings of Robeson; 10:49–11:40. There were other telephone concerts, both transatlantic—from New York Robeson sang at a miners' eisteddfod in Porthcawl, Wales, in October 1957—and intracontinental: he performed a fifteen-minute program for the Convention of the International Union of Mine, Mill, and Smelter Workers of Canada by telephone into a loudspeaker (c. 1952); see Silber, "Peter Seeger, Paul Robeson," 16. On at least one occasion a Robeson concert was "wired into" a nearby convention hall from the Embassy Auditorium in Los Angeles in which he was performing so as to accommodate the overflow audience; Browda, "The World and Music."

15. "Our London Correspondence," *Manchester Guardian*, May 28, 1957, 6.

16. Belfrage-Robeson correspondence, June 5, 1957.

17. The promotional video accompanying the Science Museum exhibition concludes with the following moral: the "message" of Robeson's transatlantic concert was heard "well beyond the Town Hall" by, it suggests, the US Supreme Court, which the following year declared it unconstitutional for Robeson to be barred a passport. Robeson was free, the video concludes, due in part to the information age, "giving us all a voice"; "Information Age: Paul Robeson, McCarthy and the submarine repeater," *The Guardian*, October 23, 2014, http://www.theguardian.com/science/blog/2014/oct/23/information-age-paul-robeson-mccarthy-science-museum: 2:48–3:06. See also "TAT-1," 10:24–10:48. But as the 1950s progressed the intensity of the domestic (American) red scare abated, and the US Supreme Court held that the State Department could not withhold passports for ideological reasons, as had been the case with Robeson; see Perucci, *Paul Robeson*, 15–16.

NOTES 325

18. Perucci, *Paul Robeson*, 1.
19. Pete Seeger letter to Paul Robeson, n.d. [c. 1965], PRP-Series B.
20. Perucci, *Paul Robeson*, 15. Listed as one of the top ten highest-paid concert artists in the early 1940s, his income plummeted from over $100,000 in 1947 to about $6,000 in 1952; Foner, *Paul Robeson Speaks*, 40.
21. Cataliotti, "On My Journey," 17–18.
22. Letter from Robeson's lawyers to the Secretary, Department of State, August 1, 1950, PRP-Series D-Box 17.
23. Letters from Charles Ringrose, London, to Robeson, April 17, 1950; and A. Wasserman, general manager of Collet's Holdings, London, to the Othello Record Corporation, New York, January 12, 1953, PRP-Series D-Box 17. The extent of the British state's collaboration with the United States in acting against Robeson has been recently exposed; see, e.g., Jordan Goodman, *Paul Robeson: A Watched Man* (London: Verso, 2013). Collet's felt the effect of British trade sanctions against Robeson. Due to "our Government's" "complete embargo" on the transfer of dollars to Robeson, Collet's could not recompense Robeson for the Othello records they wished to buy; letter from Wasserman.
24. Alexis Petridis, "Topic Records—70 Years of Giving Voice to the People," *The Guardian*, August 23, 2009, http://www.theguardian.com/music/2009/aug/23/topic-records-70th-anniversary.
25. For more on Othello Records see Robeson Jr., *The Undiscovered Paul Robeson*, 222.
26. Perucci, *Paul Robeson*, 2.
27. Liner notes for *Robeson Sings* (Othello Recording Corporation L-101, 1953).
28. Othello Recording Corp., Memorandum, undated c. 1954–1955, PRP-Series D-Box 17.
29. Letter from Secretariat of the World Council of Peace, Vienna, to Robeson, February 3, 1955, PRP-Series D-Box 17.
30. See PRP-Series D-Box 17.
31. Robeson, "A Song to Sing," 12–14, PRP-Box 21.
32. Cataliotti, "On My Journey," 18. Robeson's accompanist for the transatlantic telephone concert did not want her name in print, choosing to appear under the alias Winifred Harrison; letter from Eslanda Robeson to Cedric Belfrage, June 5, 1957, PRP-Series B.
33. Robeson Jr., *The Undiscovered Paul Robeson*, 222.
34. Cataliotti, "On My Journey," 17. There is only passing reference to the engineers Robeson worked with in Cataliotti, and Robeson Jr., *The Undiscovered Paul Robeson*.
35. Robeson Jr., *The Undiscovered Paul Robeson*, 222.
36. Cataliotti, "On My Journey," 21.
37. Undated notice, c. 1955, Othello Recording Corp., PRP-Series D-Box 17. Underscoring in the original.
38. Letter from Paul Robeson Jr. to Desmond Buckle, London, February 11, 1955, PRP-Series D-Box 17.
39. Paul Robeson Jr., "Technical Notes on the Recordings," December 1, 1954, PRP-Series D-Box 17. In this instance the notes were for recordings for Mezhdunarodnaya Kniga, an imprint of the Soviet record company Melodiya.

326 NOTES

40. Michael Fremer, "Sonic Spectacular Twice as Good at 45rpm," AnalogPlanet, July 1, 2010, accessed March 24, 2016, http://www.analogplanet.com/content/sonic-spec tacular-twice-good-45rpm-0#sEBzLX7TaQpLzaW2.97.

41. Liner notes for Art Blakey, *A Midnight Session with the Jazz Messengers* (Elektra EKL-120, 1957). The celebrated engineer and producer Richard Alderson, who regarded Hancock as a mentor, recalled that Hancock was "the kind of engineer who recorded everything with only two ribbon microphones; more than that was a sin to him." For Alderson, it was a technique "more appropriate for classical music"; Jason Weiss, *An Oral History of ESP-DISK', The Most Outrageous Record Label in America* (Middletown, CT: Wesleyan University Press, 2012), 150.

42. See Susan Schmidt Horning, *Chasing Sound: Technology, Culture & the Art of Studio Recording from Edison to the LP* (Baltimore: Johns Hopkins University Press, 2013), 111–112; and Charles L. Granata, *Sessions with Sinatra: Frank Sinatra and the Art of Recording* (Chicago: Chicago Review Press, 2004), 22–23.

43. David B. Hancock, "A New Ribbon Microphone," *db: The Sound Engineering Magazine* 2, no. 8 (September 1968): 21–22.

44. Cataliotti, "On My Journey," 17.

45. Weiss, *An Oral History of ESP-DISK'*, 62.

46. John Marks, post on the "RIP David Nadien" thread, AudioAsylum, June 11, 2014, accessed March 24, 2016, http://www.audioasylum.com/cgi/t.mpl?f=music&m=207277.

47. *Paul Robeson Favorite Songs*, Monitor Records MPS 580, 1959, LP; and *Encore, Robeson! Paul Robeson: Favorite Songs, Vol. 2*, Monitor Records MPS 581, 1960, LP.

48. Quoted in Cataliotti, "On My Journey," 23.

49. "Monitor Records," Smithsonian Folkways, accessed November 15, 2016, http://www. folkways.si.edu/monitor-records/smithsonian.

50. *Robeson*, Vanguard VSD-2015, 1958, LP. The album was released under other imprints and labels in other parts of the world.

51. While Robeson was undoubtedly embraced by the mainstream recording industry at this time, he continued to work with independent labels too, promoting more explicitly political music. *Gramophone* gave notice of two EPs released on Topic, "the label mostly concerned with raw folk material": "*Freedom Songs* [TOP62] and *Songs of Liberty* [TOP63] (notice the nice differentiation!) . . . It doesn't need great powers of perception to determine the political colours of these performances, which seem to me to be rather out-of-date in the Affluent Society and the Welfare State; I prefer my Robeson, too, when he is not singing about workers marching for freedom and that sort of thing"; June 1961. For the complete list of Robeson's Topic records, see Mainly Norfolk: English Folk and Other Good Music, accessed November 15, 2016, https:// mainlynorfolk.info/folk/records/paulrobeson.html.

52. Letter from Sherwin Cody to Robeson, January 17, 1944, New York, PRP-Series B. The other two great voices were those of Roosevelt and Orson Wells.

53. Letters from Stanley H. Silverman to Robeson, April 12 and 23, 1944, PRP-Series B. Robeson was invited to serve on a committee to identify "Negro composers" whose music could be used to promote war bonds by the War Finance Division of the

NOTES 327

Treasury Department; see Letter from Robert J. Smith to Robeson, August 27, 1944, PRP-Series B.

54. For Robeson's recitations of the monologue, see Swindall, *The Politics of Paul Robeson's Othello*, 128, 160–165.

55. Letter from Eslanda Robeson to Glen Byam Shaw, November 15, 1957, PRP-Series B. Underscore in the original.

56. Letter from Lawrence Brown to Eslanda Robeson, Seattle, October 13, 1946, ERP-Series C.

57. Swindall, *The Politics of Paul Robeson's Othello*, 166.

58. For instance, of Robeson's recorded output for this time Redmond speaks of the "limited number of recordings for fans around the world"; "Songs of Free Men," 136.

59. Mail-order subscription notice for *Solid Rock* c. 1954, PRC-4. Of course Robeson's recording of hymns on *Solid Rock*, as opposed to the spirituals with which he had long been associated, was also a calculated political move. As much as the hymns represented another repertoire of Black music, and on which he had been raised in his father's churches, they presented an opportunity for the singer to (re)connect with the broader Black community, some constituencies of which Robeson had become alienated from. In an interview on the release of *Solid Rock*, Robeson confessed that "in our political activities and our struggles for peace and a better world, we have managed to get so doctrinaire among ourselves that we have failed to reach out and draw the people into the struggle." He acknowledged the importance of the Black church, and its music, in this endeavor, regarding the album as a "major breakthrough" in "communicating with my people." See Elihu S. Hicks, "Robeson on Records," *Daily People's World*, June 5, 1953, PRC-4.

60. "Robeson on Records Again!" Typescript dated December 1952, PRC-4. A memorandum for the nationwide concert tour of June to October 1953, the main purpose of which was to "reaffirm Mr. Robeson's right to function as a concert artist" and to "defeat reactions [*sic*] efforts to isolate him from the masses of people," outlined the importance of recordings as one of the three major "organizational objectives" of the tour: "In each city, a major feature of the tour will be the popularization and sale of the new recordings which Mr. Robeson is making for the Othello Recording Corporation"; "The Paul Robeson 1953 Tour," undated typescript, PRC- 4.

61. Hicks, "Robeson on Records"; and Victor royalty statements for 1927 and 1928, PRP-Series B-Box 17.

62. Baldwin, *Beyond the Color Line*, 242.

63. Liner notes for *Paul Robeson at Carnegie Hall* (Vanguard LP VRS-9051, 1960).

64. Cook, *Beyond the Score*, 345.

65. To use Mark Katz's phrase, I explore the "phonograph effects," that is, the influence of sound recording technologies broadly conceived, on Robeson's concert singing; see *Capturing Sound*, 9.

66. Schmidt Horning, *Chasing Sound*, 7.

67. For instance, the technologically enabled singing style of crooning, which Timothy Taylor has called the first modern style of singing because of its use of the microphone

328 NOTES

and origins in radio broadcasting, has been much written about. See "Music and the Rise of Radio in Twenties America," 260. McCracken's research on crooning, however, is sensitive to the interrelationships between live performance and technologically mediated singing; see *Real Men Don't Sing*.

68. Schmidt Horning, *Chasing Sound*, 8–9.

69. Sarah Benzuly, "McCune Sound: 74 Years and Still Going Strong," *Mix*, January 10, 2006, accessed July 4, 2016, http://www.mixonline.com/news/live-gear/local-crew-mccune-sound/368480.

70. Percy Cater, "It's Belafonte versus Robeson," *Daily Mail*, August 11, 1958. The heading for this section is from a sub-heading from this article.

71. Ibid.; Noël Goodwin, "Paul Robeson Uses a Mike," *Daily Mail*, August 1958.

72. Cater, "It's Belafonte versus Robeson."

73. Thomas Albright, "Robeson Makes Triumphal Return," *San Francisco Chronicle*, February 19, 1958. For Arthur Bloomfield, Robeson "did not need the mic he insisted upon using"; "Ovation for Paul Robeson," *San Francisco Call-Bulletin*, February 10, 1958.

74. Leslie Mallory, "Robeson Hides Behind Mike," *News Chronicle*, August 11, 1958.

75. "Warm Welcome for Mr. Paul Robeson," *Times*, August 11, 1958.

76. "Sincerity and Artistry. Mr. Paul Robeson at Albert Hall," *Times*, December 1, 1958.

77. "Warm Welcome."

78. Mallory, "Robeson Hides Behind Mike."

79. One critic noted of the Albert Hall concert that Robeson "kept signalling to the control engineer to turn it up louder"; Goodwin, "Paul Robeson Uses a Mike."

80. For more on the discourse of fidelity in the history of sound reproduction see Jonathan Sterne, *Audible Past: The Cultural Origins of Sound Reproduction* (Durham, NC: Duke University Press, 2003), ch. 5. See also Tim Anderson on the prioritization of live performance experience even in the domain of high-fidelity stereo recordings in the 1950s and 1960s; *Making Easy Listening: Material Culture and Postwar American Recording* (Minneapolis: University of Minnesota Press, 2006), 149–150.

81. Cook, *Beyond the Score*, 355. For more on the "eschewal of technological mediation within classical recordings" see Donald Greig, "Performing for (and against) the Microphone," in *The Cambridge Companion to Recorded Music*, ed. Nicholas Cook, Eric Clarke, Daniel Leech-Wilkinson, and John Rink (Cambridge: Cambridge University Press, 2009), 20.

82. Sanden, *Liveness in Modern Music*, 13. For an overview, and critique, of the argument that "recorded music is essentially *disembodied* sound," see Sanden, 51–53.

83. Irving Kolodin, "Paul Robeson in Carnegie Hall," *Saturday Review*, May 24, 1958.

84. See Sterne, *Audible Past*, 285, and 392.

85. Ernest Bradbury, *Yorkshire Post and Leeds Mercury*, November 3, 1958.

86. Desmond Wilcox, "No Politics—I'm Here To Sing, says Robeson," London *Daily Mirror*, July 12, 1958. That the music critics reviewing the Albert Hall concert seemed not to be aware of Robeson's long use of the mic suggests the extent of their surprise on hearing his microphone voice in person and or their remove from the society and news reportage that covered Robeson's airport press conference.

NOTES 329

87. *Daily Express*, November 19, 1931; quoted in Boyle and Bunie, *Paul Robeson*, 250.

88. Andrews interviews, November 13–20, 1974; quoted in Boyle and Bunie, *Paul Robeson*, 251.

89. Andrews, quoted in Boyle and Bunie, *Paul Robeson*, 377. For more on the event and Robeson's involvement in the Spanish Civil War, see Boyle and Bunie, *Paul Robeson*, 374–378. For the photograph of Robeson singing at the Spanish War Relief Concert, see PRP-Photographs-Concerts; I was not given permission to reproduce this photograph. I found no earlier photographic evidence of Robeson using a mic in concert in the extensive collection of photographs in the Robeson archival material in the Schomburg Center and Moorland-Spingarn Research Center. A photograph of an earlier Albert Hall concert, on December 13, 1931, shows Robeson singing without technological aid; Paul Robeson Portrait Collection, Schomburg Center, Box 2, SC-CN-98-0033. HMV released a 78 of material sung at the Spanish War Relief Concert (HMV B8604) recorded afterward at the Abbey Road studios. It included the spiritual "Sometimes I Feel Like a Motherless Child" and a poem "Minstrel Man" by Langston Hughes on one side, and on the other side Palmgren's arrangement of "The Wanderer"; see *Daily Worker*, August 2, 1937.

90. Eslanda's diaries record that Robeson "radioed," as she put it, on at least four occasions in 1925 alone: on January 1, for station WOR; April 1, for WGBS; October 18 and 30, in London, the latter date for a half-hour show; ERP-Box 16. William Barlow thus claims incorrectly that prior to 1939 Robeson had made only two cameo radio appearances in the United States; *Voice Over: The Making of Black Radio* (Philadelphia: Temple University Press, 1999), 61. Robeson also gave a recital on the Edison Hour for WRNY in June 1927, with a second Edison Hour broadcast on July 19, and appeared in the summer concert series sponsored by Maxwell House Coffee in mid-September 1927 broadcast throughout the Northeast and Midwest. See *New York World*, June 12, 1927; and *New York Telegram*, July 20, 1927.

91. *New York American*, December 18, 1924.

92. *Gramophone*, June 1934, 21.

93. London *Daily News*, March 28, 1929.

94. By the late 1930s, Robeson was performing with a public address system regularly, if a *New York Times* report is to be believed. The article made mention of "the discovery two years ago by Mr. Robeson": "he stood in front of the microphone of a public address system which was being used in a concert"; "'Acoustic Envelope' Lets Singer Hear Self," *New York Times*, November 16, 1940.

95. Barlow, *Voice Over*, 59.

96. Robeson Jr., *The Undiscovered Paul Robeson*, 19. The first documented occasion of the singer using a public address system for outdoor performance was when he performed on the battlefields somewhere near Barcelona during the Spanish Civil War in early 1938. *Time* reported on Robeson's visit to "the front lines, where a huge loudspeaker will throw his voice, during a lull in fighting to Leftist and Rightist alike"; January 31, 1938. Songs of the International Brigades, associated with the *La guerra*, would occupy an important place in Robeson's repertory.

330 NOTES

97. Emily Thompson, *The Soundscape of Modernity: Architectural Acoustics and the Culture of Listening in America, 1900-1933* (Cambridge, MA: MIT Press, 2002), 241. The Hollywood Bowl was amplified c. 1936.

98. Stanley and Maxfield, *The Voice*, 16–17.

99. Thompson, *The Soundscape of Modernity*, 248–256, and 234–246. The gist of Thompson's work is to describe how the architectural acoustics of recording venues, talking picture palaces and soundstages, broadcasting studios, and concert halls, and the cultures of listening they fostered, produced a "modern sound."

100. For a brief discussion of the Bowl's acoustics, see ibid., 254–256.

101. "Little Cynthia Has a Big Voice Just Like Paul Robeson's," *Evening Bulletin*, December 13, 1940. A photograph of a 1942 recording session with the Count Basie Orchestra shows Robeson standing apart from the band singing into an acoustic screen or shell; see Susan Robeson, *The Whole World in His Hands: A Pictorial Biography of Paul Robeson* (Secaucus, NJ: Citadel Press, 1981), 123.

102. The same biographer also claims Stokowski as the "first electronically knowledgeable conductor"; William Andre Smith, *The Mystery of Leopold Stokowski* (London: Associated University Presses, 1990), 103.

103. "Little Cynthia." For an account of the Stokowski–Bell Labs experiment, which resulted in concert presentations on April 9 and 10, 1940, see Greg Milner, *Perfecting Sound Forever: The Story of Recorded Music* (New York: Faber & Faber, 2010), 50–51; and Robert E. McGinn, "Stokowski and the Bell Telephone Laboratories: Collaboration in the Development of High-Fidelity Sound Reproduction," *Technology and Culture* 24, no. 1 (1983): 62–68. The concerts have been described as the first demonstration of a "practical true stereophonic recording"; see Tim J. Anderson, "Training the Listener: Stereo Demonstration Discs in an Emerging Consumer Market," in *Living Stereo: Histories and Cultures of Multichannel Sound*, ed. Paul Théberge, Kyle Devine, and Tom Everrett (New York: Bloomsbury, 2015), 111.

104. Anderson, *Making Easy Listening* 118–119, and 147.

105. "Little Cynthia."

106. Harold Burris-Meyer, "The Control of Acoustic Conditions on the Concert Stage," *Journal of the Acoustic Society of America* 12, no. 3 (January 1941): 335.

107. Robeson's rights in the system were spelled out clearly by Burris-Meyer: "I feel I cannot enter into any commitments with respect to the system without consultation with you for the protection of your rights therein." Letter from Harold Burris-Meyer, February 25, 1941, PRP-Series B. The arrival of Synthea was widely reported by, among others, motion picture trade magazines, acoustics research journals, popular science publications, general music magazines, and the news press. Robeson's supporting artist, thereminist Clara Rockmore, explained that it was called Synthea "because it's synthetic sound"; see William Schatzkamer, "Travels with Paul," *African American Review* 45, nos. 1–2 (Spring/Summer 2012): 218.

108. "Little Cynthia."

109. Schatzkamer, "Travels with Paul," 219.

NOTES 331

110. In a brief history of monitors Johannes Mulder claims that Synthea was "possibly the first attempt at a 'fold back' system"; "Making Things Louder: Amplified Music and Multimodality" (PhD thesis, University of Technology Sydney, 2013), 157. The stage monitor is one of the many sound technologies yet to attract any significant scholarly historical attention, and much of the historical knowledge on monitors comes from soundmen's recollections. See, e.g., the forum posts on the matter at "A Little Wedge History..??," Gearslutz, January 10, 2008 to March 6, 2009, accessed July 4, 2016, https://www.gearslutz.com/board/live-sound/168565-little-wedge-hist ory.html. For Garland's use of side monitors in concert at the San Francisco Civic Auditorium concert of September 13, 1961, see Benzuly, "McCune Sound." And for the challenges of doing archival research on sound technologies, and the reliance on engineers' knowledge, see Schmidt Horning, *Chasing Sound*, 7.

Burris-Meyer's primary interest, however, was in sound effects design and not in live sound for musical performance. For more on Burris-Meyer's varied contributions to sound technologies, see James Tobias, "Composing for the Media: Hanns Eisler and Rockefeller Foundation Projects in Film Music, Radio Listening, and Theatrical Sound Design," Rockefeller Archive Center Research Reports Online (2009), 8, http://www.rockarch.org/publications/resrep/tobias.pdf. There is some indication that Synthea had application in theater sound design and performance; for instance, for offstage choruses and upstage singers to better hear themselves and the orchestra at the Metropolitan Opera. See "Robeson Technique of Acoustics Control," *Radio-Craft*, March 1941, 561.

111. "Robeson Technique of Acoustics Control," 561–562.

112. "Little Cynthia."

113. Ibid.

114. "Robeson Technique of Acoustics Control," 562.

115. "Little Cynthia." Burris-Meyer also applied the directional use of sound to the theater, sending a "disembodied chorus marching up the center aisle" of the Metropolitan Opera House; ibid.

116. Harold Burris-Meyer and Vincent Mallory, *Sound in the Theatre* (Mineola, NY: Radio Magazines, 1959), 40.

117. "Robeson Technique of Acoustics Control," 562.

118. Burris-Meyer, "The Control of Acoustic Conditions on the Concert Stage," 337.

119. Schmidt Horning, *Chasing Sound*, 86–93; and Thompson, *The Soundscape of Modernity*, 234–236.

120. See Letters from Harold Burris-Meyer to Robeson, February 25, 1941, PRP-Series B; and to Eslanda Robeson, December 4, 1940, ERP.

121. "Little Cynthia." Photographic evidence suggests Robeson was using the hand-cupping technique in non-public performances already in the late 1930s, such as during the radio broadcast of the patriotic cantata *Ballad for Americans* in 1939; see Susan Robeson, *The Whole World in His Hands*, 120.

122. The unidentified photograph, which I was not given permission to reproduce, is in PRP-Photographs-Concerts-PR227. For other photographic evidence, see Susan Robeson, *The Whole World in His Hands*. The different microphone types were

332   NOTES

probably used for different purposes: the public address, Synthea, broadcasting, and live recording.

123. *The Ogden*, March 14, 1947.

124. Certainly, when Robeson found himself in situations at which Synthea wasn't available the singer took to cupping his hand to his ear in performance; see Robeson Jr., *The Undiscovered Paul Robeson*, 19. A live performance of Robeson, singing for construction workers at the Sydney Opera House in 1960, shows him using the hand-to-ear technique; https://www.youtube.com/watch?v=Eg7bPgrosAE, accessed November 5, 2015.

125. Irving Kolodin, "Paul Robeson in Carnegie Hall," *Saturday Review*, May 24, 1958. See also Harriett Johnson, "Words and Music: Robeson Returns to Carnegie Hall," *New York Post*, May 11, 1958. Reviewing the Albert Hall recital of later that year, Noël Goodwin was less generous: he "kept cupping his right hand to his ear—a classroom dodge to check how the voice is sounding, hardly customary in public." Goodwin also reported that Robeson "kept signalling to the control engineer to turn it up louder," one assumes in reference to Synthea's volume rather than that of the house speakers; see "Paul Robeson uses a mike."

126. "Little Cynthia."

127. "Manual for Local Sponsoring Groups," 1952, PRC-3.

128. Correspondence between Bob Stein and John Gray, March 4, 11, 13, 1954, PRC-5.

129. From the evidence available, Synthea did not require an engineer for its operation. The exception was when Robeson performed with an orchestra. See letter from Harold Burris-Meyer to Eslanda Robeson, December 4, 1940, ERP.

130. See also my discussion of the size of Robeson's voice in chapter 3.

131. London *Evening Post*, April 13, 1937. More perceptive critics had long noted that the size of Robeson's voice was not directly proportional to his large body. It was a "voice of great beauty, small perhaps, but unfailingly pleasing to the ear," commented one critic; *Indianapolis News*, January 21, 1926. Others distinguished between the affective power of Robeson's singing and vocal volume. Carl E. Lindstrom thus enthused over Robeson's "wonderfully smooth textured voice which created a sense of power rather than actual volume and one that had a certain mesmeric persuasion on the gentler levels"; *Hartford Times*, October 29, 1945. Two further instances, from the theater, of Robeson's vocal limitations may be cited. Of the 1932 Broadway revival of *Show Boat* the singer told a reporter: "Mr. Ziegfeld was afraid my interpretation wouldn't be liked here as it would be too quiet for Broadway audiences"; quoted in Boyle and Bunie, *Paul Robeson*, 466 n. 3. And of a proposed production of *The Emperor Jones* Eslanda cautioned her husband to consider "the size of the theatre," and "how you stand the wear and tear of the voice work." Although she conceded that the theatre size should be less a problem in the United States as "most of the theatres are modern and well built and not too spread out"; Eslanda to Robeson, June 25, 1939, PRP-Robeson Family Correspondence.

132. Shaw, "Paul Robeson: The Peace Arch Concerts," 10. For more on Robeson's first Peace Arch concert, including brief mention of his use of sound technologies, see Redmond, "Songs of Free Men," 131–134. Redmond concludes that the Peace Arch

NOTES   333

performance was "an experiment in accessibility" in part because it was amplified. Commentary on Robeson's less than typical recital practice dates to the mid-1930s. One critic noted that "Robeson has done a great deal to dissolve the genteel torpor that identifies the concert hall and its substantial devotees"; New York *Daily Worker*, October 9, 1940. For an extended discussion of Robeson's innovations to the song recital, see the section "Brothering Song" in chapter 4.

133. For a discussion of how the technologies of sound amplification and radio mediated the political rhetoric of four early twentieth-century politicians, see Huub Wijfjes, "Spellbinding and Crooning: Sound Amplification, Radio, and Political Rhetoric in International Comparative Perspective, 1900–1945," *Technology and Culture* 55 no. 1 (2014): 148–185. See also Melissa Dinsman, *Modernism at the Microphone: Radio, Propaganda, and Literary Aesthetics during World War II* (London: Bloomsburg, 2015).

134. C. E. L., *Hartford Times*, June 24, 1946.

135. McGinn, "Stokowski and the Bell Telephone Laboratories," 55.

136. Schmidt Horning, *Chasing Sound*, 97.

137. McGinn, "Stokowski and the Bell Telephone Laboratories," 55.

138. Ibid., 65–66.

139. For an overview of these developments see Schmidt Horning, *Chasing Sound*, chs. 4 and 5.

140. Ibid., 79–80.

141. Alfred Frankenstein, *San Francisco Chronicle*, November 13, 1940.

142. Anderson, *Making Easy Listening*, 107, and ch. 5.

143. "Inside Paul Robeson," *The Listener*, November 11, 1960, 6–7.

144. For the lack of warmth in Robeson's 1958 Albert Hall performance, see Cater, "It's Belafonte versus Robeson."

145. The information in the paragraph that follows comes from "Paul Robeson," Discography of American Historical Recordings.

146. "Local Music Dealer to Observe 'Robeson' Week," *Pittsburgh Courier*, January 23, 1926.

147. For more on Victor's black label, see John R. Bolig, *The Victor Black Label Discography: 16000–17000 Series* (Denver: Mainspring, 2007), xii and xvi.

148. Ibid.

149. Andre Millard, *America on Record: A History of Recorded Sound*, 2nd ed. (Cambridge: Cambridge University Press, 2005), 143.

150. For an account of the conversion to electric recording, see Allan Sutton, *Recording the 'Twenties: The Evolution of the American Recording Industry, 1920–29* (Denver, CO: Mainspring, 2008), chs. 15 and 16. For Victor's early electrical recording, see John R. Bolig, *The Victor Black Label Discography: 18000–19000 Series* (Denver: Mainspring, 2008), xii–xiv.

151. *Record*, March 3, 1926.

152. William R. Moran, ed., *Herman Klein and the Gramophone* (Portland, OR: Amadeus, 1990), 568.

153. "The Gramophone and the Singer," *The Gramophone*, June 1924, in ibid., 65.

334 NOTES

154. "The Year's Best Opera Records," *The Gramophone*, December 1926, in ibid., 167.

155. "The New HMV Opera Records—I," *The Gramophone*, February 1928, in ibid., 215.

156. "The Distortions of Over-Amplification," *The Gramophone*, December 1930, in ibid., 309–310.

157. Virgil Moorefield, *The Producer as Composer: Shaping the Sounds of Popular Music* (Cambridge, MA: MIT Press, 2015), xiv.

158. For one of many accounts of "the idea of phonographic verisimilitude" as "an acoustic construct," see Colin Symes, *Setting the Record Straight: A Material History of Classical Recording* (Middletown, CT: Wesleyan University Press, 2004), 62.

159. Boris Semeonoff recalled that voices in the acoustic era recorded from best to worst in "the following order: tenors, sopranos, mezzos, baritones, contraltos, basses"; *Record Collecting: A Guide for Beginners* (Chislehurst, Kent: Oakwood Press, 1949), 10.

160. Thomas O'Brien, "The Recorded Voice—and the Real Thing," *The Gramophone*, November 1933, 252. See also P. Wilson, "Reproduction and the Real Thing," *The Gramophone*, July 1934. The only indication that recording may have "enlarged" Robeson's voice comes from a review of a HMV disc (B3381), of "Peter, Go Ring Dem Bells" and "Go Down Moses": Robeson's "voice is rather big for the average room . . . such power needs the theatre's room"; *Yorkshire Observer*, May 22, 1930.

161. William D. Owen, "Standards of Reproduction [part 1]," *The Gramophone*, December 1933, 295.

162. Percy Wilson, *The Gramophone Handbook* (London: Methuen, 1957), 39. *Gramophone*'s longtime technical editor, Wilson had started writing for the magazine in 1924, just prior to the conversion to electrical recording.

163. For the information in this paragraph and the next I draw on Gary A. Galo, "Disc Recording Equalization Demystified," in *The LP Is Back!* (Peterborough, NH: Audio Amateur Publications, 1999), 44–54. Galo provides a useful glossary of terms.

164. James R. Powell Jr., "The Audiophile's Guide to Phonorecord Playback Equalizer Settings," *ARSC Journal* 20, no. 1 (1989): 14–23.

165. William D. Owen, "Standards of Reproduction [part 2]," *The Gramophone*, January 1934, 337. For the production of Rudy Vallée's and Bing Crosby's voices as lower and deeper in the early 1930s due to the introduction of ribbon microphones, see McCracken, *Real Men Don't Sing*, 260, 278–280.

166. "The Singer and the Microphone," *The Gramophone*, May 1933, in *Herman Klein and the Gramophone*, 372.

167. *The Gramophone*, February 1924, 361; my emphasis.

168. McCracken, *Real Men Don't Sing*, 91–92.

169. The recordings discussed in this paragraph are digital transfers, remastered from the original 78s, and appear on *Paul Robeson: The Complete EMI Sessions, 1928–1939*, EMI Classics 2 15586 2, 2008, CD. See the notes in chapter 3 for information on the spectral analysis and the resultant graphs.

170. Wilson, *The Gramophone Handbook*, 50.

171. *Edinburgh Evening News*, January 20, 1934.

172. *Musical Times*, August 1, 1930.

NOTES 335

173. "The Distortions of Over-Amplification," 310; and "The Gramophone as a Vocal Instructor," May 1932, in *Herman Klein and the Gramophone*, 372.

174. "Broadcasting," *Saturday Review*, September 28, 1929.

175. *Musical Mirror* (London), September 1930.

176. The vocal presence that was a hallmark of high-fidelity recording was a feature of hi-fi's production of the material conditions of the sound source. Its aim was to reveal "'sound signatures' that betray . . . performers through 'non-musical' means," such that "listeners engage these material sources through once inaudible acoustic inscriptions"; Anderson, *Making Easy Listening*, xliii.

177. *Gramophone*, September 1933, 142. HMV advertised the Victor-made recording of "Bye and Bye" in its catalog of February 1931. For the association between Victor and HMV, or the Gramophone Company, see Bolig, *The Victor Black Label Discography: 18000–19000 Series*, xviii.

178. For an overview of high-fidelity recording, see Millard, *America on Record*, ch. 10. The term "high-fidelity" was first used in radio broadcasting in the late 1920s, and was in common usage in *Gramophone*'s pages in the mid-1930s. Its early use referred, in general, to "the faithfulness of the machines' reproduction of the original music," and variously to "wide frequency response, flat frequency response (in that all sounds are reproduced at equal levels), wide dynamic levels, and low distortion and noise"; Millard, *America on Record*, 208.

179. The audio data come from "straight" transfers from the original recordings, undertaken, that is, without equalization and changes to the volume, by the Sound Archive of the British Library.

180. Shaffer's spectral analysis too reveals that Robeson's voice is characterized by both strong low frequencies and strong high frequencies; "Paul Robeson's Iconic Timbre," 33.

181. Schatzkamer, "Travels with Paul," 219.

182. Schmidt Horning, *Chasing Sound*, 78–79.

183. Ibid., 87–88. Schmidt Horning discusses the increasing importance of a studio's sound, and hence of acoustic design, from the mid-1940s on for record production; see ch. 4.

184. Burris-Meyer, "The Control of Acoustic Conditions," 337.

185. Paul Robeson and Alan Booth (piano), "Old Man River," recorded 1958, side 1, track 8, on *Paul Robeson at Carnegie Hall*, Vanguard LP VRS-9051, 1960, LP. The earliest (live) recording of Robeson performing the song in G Major, descending to the low D, is of the Peace Arch concert of 1952; Paul Robeson and Lawrence Brown (piano), "Ol' Man River," recorded 1952, track 12 on *Paul Robeson: The Peace Arch Concerts*, Folk Era FE1442CD, 1998, CD. Redmond has noted how Robeson's Peace Arch performance of "Ol' Man River"—slow, low, and bluesy—would "not have been legible [*sic*] without the assistance provided by the mic"; "Songs of Free Men," 133.

186. A similar set up was in use for Robeson's performances in London, at the Royal Albert Hall, and Moscow of that year, the latter including a broadcast.

187. John Thorne, "The Fallacy of the 'Recording Voice,'" *Gramophone*, January 1929, 351.

188. *Gramophone*, February 1932, 388–389.

336 NOTES

189. *Gramophone,* June 1934, 21.
190. Cook, *Beyond the Score,* 356–358.

Afterword

1. *Dublin Evening Mail,* March 24, 1939.
2. Min Jeong Song, "Mechanisms of In-Betweenness: Through Visual Experiences of Glass" (PhD thesis, Royal College of Art, 2014), 23.
3. Homi K. Bhabha, *The Location of Culture* (London: Routledge, 1994), 2.
4. William Dwight Whitney, *The Century Dictionary and Cyclopedia: A Work of Universal Reference in All Departments of Knowledge,* vol. 2 (New York: The Century Co., 1906), 1230.
5. "Editorial: Paul Robeson: The Great Forerunner," 5; emphasis in the original.
6. McCracken, *Real Men Don't Sing,* 8 and 14.
7. James, "Paul Robeson: Black Star," 261.
8. Moten, *In the Break,* 1, 14.
9. Ibid., 6, 12.
10. Baldwin, *Beyond the Color Line,* 238.
11. Moten, *In the Break,* 47, 180; my emphasis.
12. Ibid., 68.
13. Ibid., 179–180.
14. Eidsheim, *The Race of Sound,* 24.
15. Moten, *In the Break,* 12.
16. Moten, *Black and Blur,* xii and 76.
17. Moten, *In the Break,* 71.
18. Meizel, *Multivocality,* 7, 14–15. For more on the voice as borderscape, see ibid., 15–17.

Works Cited

Major Archival Sources

British Library Sound Archive.

Clive Jenkins Papers, MSS.79/6/CJ/3/110, Modern Records Centre, University of Warwick.

Eslanda G. Robeson Papers, Moorland-Spingarn Research Center, Howard University, Washington, DC. Abbreviated in the notes as ERP.

Lawrence Brown Papers, Schomburg Center, New York Public Library. Abbreviated in the notes as LBP.

Lawrence Brown Scores, New York Public Library for the Performing Arts. Abbreviated in the notes as LBS.

Paul Robeson Collection, Schomburg Center, New York Public Library. Abbreviated in the notes as PRC.

Paul Robeson Papers, Moorland-Spingarn Research Center, Howard University, Washington, DC. Abbreviated in the notes as PRP.

Paul Robeson Portrait Collection, Schomburg Center, New York Public Library.

Newspapers

Most of the newspaper articles cited in the book were obtained from the extensive collection of clippings in the Paul Robeson Papers, Moorland-Spingarn Research Center: Series G: Newspaper clippings, Boxes 27–34. Many of these have incomplete bibliographic information. In the notes I have included the available information from the clippings.

Secondary Sources

Abrahams, Peter. *Tell Freedom*. London: Faber & Faber, 1954.

"Actors Are Citizens: The Great Negro Artist Discusses the Social Background to the Modern American Theatre, in an Interview with Alexander Baron." *New Theatre* 5, no. 10 (April 1949): 3.

Anderson, Paul. *Deep River: Music and Memory in Harlem Renaissance Thought*. Durham, NC: Duke University Press, 2001.

Anderson, Tim J. *Making Easy Listening: Material Culture and Postwar American Recording*. Minneapolis: University of Minnesota Press, 2006.

Anderson, Tim J. "Training the Listener: Stereo Demonstration Discs in an Emerging Consumer Market." In *Living Stereo: Histories and Cultures of Multichannel Sound*, edited by Paul Théberge, Kyle Devine, and Tom Everrett, 107–124. New York: Bloomsbury, 2015.

338   WORKS CITED

Andrews, Joyce. "Amanda Aldridge, Teacher and Composer: A Life in Music." *Journal of Singing* 66, no. 3 (2010): 253–268.

Appiah, Kwame Anthony. *Cosmopolitanism: Ethics in a World of Strangers*. London: Penguin, 2006.

Aristotle. *The Poetics of Aristotle*. 3rd ed. Translated by S. H. Butcher. London: Macmillan, 1902.

Attali, Jacques. *Noise: The Political Economy of Music*. Translated by Brian Massumi. Manchester: Manchester University Press, 1985.

Auslander, Philip. "Live and Technologically Mediated Performance." In *The Cambridge Companion to Performance Studies*, edited by Tracy C. Davis, 107–119. Cambridge: Cambridge University Press, 2008.

Auslander, Philip. *Liveness: Performance in a Mediatized Culture*. London: Routledge, 1999.

Baade, Christina. "'Sincerely Yours, Vera Lynn': Performing Class, Sentiment, and Femininity in the 'People's War.'" *Atlantis: Critical Studies in Gender, Culture and Social Justice* 30, no. 2 (2006): 36–49.

Balaji, Murali. *The Professor and the Pupil: The Politics and Friendship of W. E. B. Du Bois and Paul Robeson*. New York: Nation Books, 2007.

Baldwin, Kate A. *Beyond the Color Line and the Iron Curtain: Reading Encounters between Black and Red, 1922–1963*. Durham, NC: Duke University Press, 2002.

Balthazar, Scott L. *Historical Dictionary of Opera*. Lanham, MD: Scarecrow, 2013.

Banfield, Stephen. *Sensibility and English Song*. Cambridge: Cambridge University Press, 1985.

Barg, Lisa. "Paul Robeson's *Ballad for Americans*: Race and the Cultural Politics of 'People's Music.'" *Journal of the Society for American Music* 2, no. 1 (2008): 27–70.

Barlow, William. *Voice Over: The Making of Black Radio*. Philadelphia: Temple University Press, 1999.

Barthes, Roland. "The Grain of the Voice." In *Image, Music, Text*. Translated by Stephen Heath, 179–189. New York: Hill & Wang, 1977.

Benhabib, Seyla. *Situating the Self: Gender, Community and Postmodernism in Contemporary Ethics*. Cambridge: Polity, 1992.

Benzuly, Sarah. "McCune Sound: 74 Years and Still Going Strong." *Mix*, January 10, 2006. http://www.mixonline.com/news/live-gear/local-crew-mccune-sound/368480.

Berger, Harris M., and Cornelia Fales. "'Heaviness' in the Perception of Heavy Metal Guitar Timbres: The Match of Perceptual and Acoustic Features Over Times." In *Wired for Sound: Engineering and Technologies in Sonic Cultures*, edited by Paul D. Greene and Thomas Porcello, 181–197. Middletown, CT: Wesleyan University Press, 2005.

Bhabha, Homi K. *The Location of Culture*. London: Routledge, 1994.

Blockson, Charles L. "Paul Robeson: A Bibliophile in Spite of Himself." In *Paul Robeson: Artist and Citizen*, edited by Jeffrey C. Stewart, 235–250. New Brunswick, NJ: Rutgers University Press, 1998.

Bolig, John R. *The Victor Black Label Discography: 16000–17000 Series*. Denver: Mainspring, 2007.

Bolig, John R. *The Victor Black Label Discography: 18000–19000 Series*. Denver: Mainspring, 2008.

Boyle, Sheila Tully, and Andrew Bunie. *Paul Robeson: The Years of Promise and Achievement*. Amherst: University of Massachusetts Press, 2001.

Brooks, Gwendolyn. "Paul Robeson." *Freedomways: A Quarterly Review of the Freedom Movement* 11, no. 1 (1971): 104.

Brooks, Tim. *Lost Sounds: Blacks and the Birth of the Recording Industry, 1890–1919*. Urbana: University of Illinois Press, 2004.

WORKS CITED 339

Brown, Lloyd L. *The Young Paul Robeson: "On My Journey Now."* Boulder, CO: Westview Press, 1977.

Brown, Sterling. "Roland Hayes: An Essay." *Opportunity: A Journal of Negro Life* 3, no. 6 (June 1925): 173–174.

Burris-Meyer, Harold. "The Control of Acoustic Conditions on the Concert Stage." *Journal of the Acoustic Society of America* 12, no. 3 (January 1941): 335–337.

Burris-Meyer, Harold, and Vincent Mallory. *Sound in the Theatre.* Mineola, NY: Radio Magazines, 1959.

Cantwell, Robert. *When We Were Good: The Folk Revival.* Cambridge, MA: Harvard University Press, 1996.

Carby, Hazel V. *Race Men.* Cambridge, MA: Harvard University Press, 1998.

Carpentier, Alejo. *La consagración de la primavera.* Coyoacán, Mexico: Siglo Veintiuno Editores, 1978.

Carroll, Peter N. *The Odyssey of the Abraham Lincoln Brigade: Americans in the Spanish Civil War.* Stanford, CA: Stanford University Press, 1994.

Cataliotti, Robert H. "On My Journey: Paul Robeson's Independent Recordings." Liner notes for *On My Journey: Paul Robeson's Independent Recordings.* Smithsonian Folkways Recordings FW CD 40178, 2007, compact disc.

Cavarero, Adriana. *For More than One Voice: Toward a Philosophy of Vocal Expression.* Translated by Paul A. Kottman. Stanford, CA: Stanford University Press, 2005.

Cheah, Pheng, and Bruce Robbins, eds. *Cosmopolitics: Thinking and Feeling beyond the Nation.* Minneapolis: University of Minnesota Press, 1998.

Chion, Michel. *Audio-Vision: Sound on Screen.* Translated by Claudia Gorbman. New York: Columbia University Press, 1994.

Chornik, Katia. "Politics, Music, and Irony in Alejo Carpentier's Novel *La consagración de la primavera (The Rite of Spring)*." In *Performativity in Word and Music Studies*, edited by Walter Bernhart, 53–70. Amsterdam: Rodopi, 2011.

Clarke, John Henrik, ed. *Dimensions of the Struggle against Apartheid: A Tribute to Paul Robeson.* New York: African Heritage Studies Association, 1979.

Connor, Steven. *Dumbstruck: A Cultural History of Ventriloquism.* Oxford: Oxford University Press, 2000.

Cook, Nicholas. *Beyond the Score: Music as Performance.* Oxford: Oxford University Press, 2013.

Cook, Nicholas, and Daniel Leech-Wilkinson. "A Musicologist's Guide to Sonic Visualiser." Centre for the History and Analysis of Recorded Music, 2009. http://www.charm.rhul.ac.uk/analysing/p9_1.html.

Cook, Will Marion. *Three Negro Songs.* New York: Schirmer, 1912.

Cooper, Anna Julia. "The Negro's Dialect." In *The Voice of Anna Julia Cooper*, edited by Charles Lemert and Esme Bhan, 238–247. Lanham, MD: Rowman & Littlefield, 1988.

Corbin, Alain. *Village Bells: The Culture of the Senses in the Nineteenth-Century French Countryside.* New York: Columbia University Press, 1998.

Cruz, Jon. *Culture on the Margins: The Black Spiritual and the Rise of American Cultural Interpretation.* Princeton, NJ: Princeton University Press, 1999.

Curtis-Burlin, Natalie. *Negro Folk-Songs*, Book II. New York: G. Schirmer, 1918.

Davis, Lenwood. *A Paul Robeson Research Guide: A Selected Annotated Bibliography.* Westport, CT: Greenwood, 1982.

Dawson, Ashley. "The Rise of the Black Internationale: Anti-imperialist Activism and Aesthetics in Britain during the 1930s." *Atlantic Studies* 6, no. 2 (2009): 159–174.

340 WORKS CITED

Decker, Todd. *Show Boat: Performing Race in an American Musical*. Oxford: Oxford University Press, 2013.

Denning, Michael. *The Cultural Front: The Laboring of American Culture in the Twentieth Century*. London: Verso, 1997.

Derrida, Jacques. *On Cosmopolitanism and Forgiveness*. Translated by Mark Dooley and Michael Hughes. London: Routledge, 2001.

Derrida, Jacques. *The Politics of Friendship*. Translated by George Collins. London: Verso, 1997.

Dickerson, Vanessa D. *Dark Victorians*. Champaign: University of Illinois Press, 2008.

Dinsman, Melissa. *Modernism at the Microphone: Radio, Propaganda, and Literary Aesthetics during World War II*. London: Bloomsbury, 2015.

Dolar, Mladen. *A Voice and Nothing More*. Cambridge, MA: MIT Press, 2006.

Duberman, Martin Bauml. *Paul Robeson: A Biography*. New York: Ballantine, 1989.

Du Bois, Shirley Graham. "Tributes." *Freedomways: A Quarterly Review of the Freedom Movement* 11, no. 1 (1971): 6–7.

Du Bois, W. E. B. *The Souls of Black Folk: Essays and Sketches*. 5th ed. Chicago: A. C. McClurg, 1904.

Duffett, Mark. "Fan Words." In *Popular Music Fandom: Identities, Roles and Practices*, edited by Mark Duffett, 146–164. New York: Routledge, 2014.

Duffett, Mark. "Introduction." In *Popular Music Fandom: Identities, Roles and Practices*, edited by Mark Duffett, 1–15. New York: Routledge, 2014.

Dyer, Richard. "Paul Robeson: Crossing Over." In *Heavenly Bodies: Film Stars and Society*, 64–136. London: Routledge, 2004 [1986].

Dykema, Peter W. "Theresa Armitage Birchard." *Music Educators Journal* 30, no. 3 (1944): 60.

"Editorial: Paul Robeson: The Great Forerunner." *Freedomways: A Quarterly Review of the Freedom Movement* 11, no. 1 (1971): 5.

Eidsheim, Nina Sun. *The Race of Sound: Listening, Timbre and Vocality in African American Music*. Durham, NC: Duke University Press, 2019.

Eidsheim, Nina Sun. *Sensing Sound: Singing and Listening as Vibrational Practice*. Durham, NC: Duke University Press, 2015.

Emmons, Shirlee, and Stanley Sonntag. *The Art of the Song Recital*. New York: Schirmer, 1979.

Fackler, Guido. "Moorsoldatenlied." Music and the Holocaust. Accessed February 28, 2017. http://holocaustmusic.ort.org/places/camps/music-early-camps/moorsoldatenlied/.

Feldman, Martha. "The Interstitial Voice: An Opening." *Journal of the American Musicological Society* 68, no. 3 (2015): 653–659.

Ferrante, Isidoro. "Vibrato Rate and Extent in Soprano Voice: A Survey on One Century of Singing." *Journal of the Acoustical Society of America* 130, no. 3 (2011): 1683–1688.

Fishzon, Anna. *Fandom, Authenticity, and Opera: Mad Acts and Letter Scenes in Fin-de-Siècle Russia*. New York: Palgrave, 2013.

Floyd, Samuel A., Jr. "Music in the Harlem Renaissance: An Overview." In *Black Music in the Harlem Renaissance: A Collection of Essays*, vol. 1, edited by Samuel A. Floyd Jr., 1–27. New York: Greenwood Press, 1999.

Foner, Henry. "Foreword: Keynote Address from the 1998 Long Island University Paul Robeson Conference." In *Paul Robeson: Essays on His Life and Legacy*, edited by Joseph Dorinson and William Pencak, 1–4. Jefferson, NC: McFarland, 2002.

WORKS CITED   341

Foner, Philip S., ed. *Paul Robeson Speaks: Writings, Speeches, Interviews, 1918–1974*. New York: Citadel Press, 1978.

Freitas, Roger. "The Art of Artlessness, or, Adelina Patti Teaches Us How to Be Natural." Paper presented at the 19th Congress of the International Musicological Society, Rome, Italy, July 3, 2012.

Fremer, Michael. "Sonic Spectacular Twice as Good at 45rpm." AnalogPlanet, July 1, 2012. http://www.analogplanet.com/content/sonic-spectacular-twice-good-45rpm-0#sEBzLX7TaQpLzaW2.97.

Frith, Simon. *Performing Rites: Evaluating Popular Music*. Oxford: Oxford University Press, 1996.

Frith, Simon. "What Is Bad Music?" In *Bad Music: The Music We Love to Hate*, edited by Christopher J. Washburne and Maiken Derno, 15–36. New York: Routledge, 2004.

Gaines, Kevin. *Uplifting the Race: Black Leadership, Politics, and Culture in the Twentieth Century*. Chapel Hill: University of North Carolina Press, 1996.

Galo, Gary A. "Disc Recording Equalization Demystified." In *The LP Is Back!*, 44–54. Peterborough, NH: Audio Amateur Publications, 1999.

Gates, Henry Louis, Jr. *The Signifying Monkey: A Theory of African American Literary Criticism*. Oxford: Oxford University Press, 1988.

Gibbs, Craig Martin. *Black Recording Artists, 1877–1926: An Annotated Discography*. Jefferson, NC: McFarland, 2013.

Goodman, Jordan. *Paul Robeson: A Watched Man*. London: Verso, 2013.

Gordon, Bonnie. *Monteverdi's Unruly Women: The Power of Song in Early Modern Italy*. Cambridge: Cambridge University Press, 2004.

Graham, Shirley. *Paul Robeson: Citizen of the World*. New York: J. Messner, 1946.

Granata, Charles L. *Sessions with Sinatra: Frank Sinatra and the Art of Recording*. Chicago: Chicago Review Press, 2004.

Gray, Daniel. *Homage to Caledonia: Scotland and the Spanish Civil War*. Edinburgh: Luath Press, 2008.

Greenberg, Jonathan Ross. "Singing Up Close: Voice, Language, and Race in American Popular Music, 1925–1935." PhD diss., University of California, Los Angeles, 2008.

Greig, Donald. "Performing for (and against) the microphone." In *The Cambridge Companion to Recorded Music*, edited by Nicholas Cook, Eric Clarke, Daniel Leech-Wilkinson, and John Rink, 16–29. Cambridge: Cambridge University Press, 2009.

Guthrie, Kate. "Review-Article: Soundtracks to the 'People's War.'" *Music & Letters* 94, no. 2 (2013): 324–333.

Hancock, David B. "A New Ribbon Microphone." *db: The Sound Engineering Magazine* 2, no. 8 (September 1968): 21–22.

Hayes, Roland. *My Songs: Aframerican Religious Folk Songs Arranged and Interpreted by Roland Hayes*. Boston: Little, Brown, 1948.

Helm, MacKinley. *Angel Mo' and Her Son Roland Hayes*. Boston: Little, Brown, 1942.

Henschel, George. *Fifty Songs by George Henschel*. London: John Church, 1905.

Hentoff, Nat. "Paul Robeson Makes a New Album." *The Reporter*, April 1958, 34–35.

Hiebert, Daniel. "Cosmopolitanism at the Local Level: The Development of Transnational Neighbourhoods." In *Conceiving Cosmopolitanism: Theory, Context, and Practice*, edited by Steven Vertovec and Robin Cohen, 209–223. Oxford: Oxford University Press, 2002.

Hildebrand, Jennifer. "'Two Souls, Two Thoughts, Two Unreconciled Strivings': The Sound of Double Consciousness in Roland Hayes's Early Career." *Black Music Research Journal* 30, no. 2 (2010): 273–302.

342 WORKS CITED

Hills, Matt. "From Para-Social to Multisocial Interaction: Theorizing Material/Digital Fandom and Celebrity." In *A Companion to Celebrity*, edited by P. David Marshall and Sean Redmond, 463–482. Oxford: John Wiley and Sons, 2016.

Hogan, Lawrence D. *The Forgotten History of African American Baseball*. Santa Barbara, CA: Praeger, 2014.

Hollinger, David A. "Not Universalists, Not Pluralists: The New Cosmopolitans Find Their Own Way." In *Conceiving Cosmopolitanism: Theory, Context, and Practice*, edited by Steven Vertovec and Robin Cohen, 227–239. Oxford: Oxford University Press, 2002.

Horne, Gerald. *Paul Robeson: The Artist as Revolutionary*. London: Pluto Press, 2016.

Hubbard, Dolan. *The Sermon and the African American Literary Imagination*. Columbia: University of Missouri Press, 1994.

Hughes, Langston. "The Negro Artist and the Racial Mountain." *The Nation* 122 (June 23, 1926), 692–694.

Hugill, Stan. *Shanties from the Seven Seas*. London: Routledge and Kegan Paul, 1961.

Hurston, Zora Neale. "Characteristics of Negro Expression." In *Negro: Anthology*, edited by Nancy Cunard, 39–49. London: Wishart & Co., 1934.

Hurston, Zora Neale. "Spirituals and Neo-Spirituals." In *Negro: Anthology*, edited by Nancy Cunard, 359–361. London: Wishart & Co., 1934.

Ihde, Don. *Listening and Voice: Phenomenologies of Voice*. Albany: State University of New York Press, 2007.

"Information Age: Paul Robeson, McCarthy and the Submarine Repeater." *The Guardian*, October 23, 2014. http://www.theguardian.com/science/blog/2014/oct/23/informat ion-age-paul-robeson-mccarthy-science-museum.

Jackson, Joyce Marie. "Quartets: Jubilee to Gospel." In *African American Music: An Introduction*, edited by Mellonee V. Burnim and Portia K. Maultsby, 75–96. New York: Routledge, 2015.

James, C. L. R. "Paul Robeson: Black Star." In *Spheres of Existence: The Selected Writings of C. L. R. James*, 256–264. London: Allison & Busby, 1980.

Jander, Owen, and Ellen T. Harris. "Singing: 19th Century." In *Grove Music Online*, edited by Deane Root. Oxford University Press, 2001. Accessed June 23, 2014. https://0-doi-org.innopac.wits.ac.za/10.1093/gmo/9781561592630.article.25869.

Johnson, James Weldon. *God's Trombones: Seven Negro Sermons in Verse*. New York: Penguin, 2008 [1927].

Johnson, James Weldon. "Negro Folk Songs and Spirituals." *The Mentor*, February 1929, 50–52.

Johnson, James Weldon. "Preface." In *The Book of American Negro Spirituals*, 11–50. New York: Viking, 1925.

Jones, Alisha Lola. "Singing High: Black Countertenors and Gendered Sound in Gospel Performance." In *The Oxford Handbook of Voice Studies*, edited by Nina Sun Eidsheim and Katherine Meizel, 35–51. New York: Oxford University Press, 2019.

Jones, Daniel. *Daniel Jones: Selected Works*. Vol. 3, edited by Beverley Collins and Inger M. Mees. London: Routledge, 2003.

Karp, Jonathan. "Performing Black-Jewish Symbiosis: The 'Hassidic Chant' of Paul Robeson." *American Jewish History* 91, no. 1 (2003): 53–81.

Katz, Mark. *Capturing Sound: How Technology Changed Music*. Berkeley: University of California Press, 2004.

Kaufmann, Helen, and Eva E. Vom Baur Hansl. *Artists in Music of Today*. New York: Grosset & Dunlap, 1933.

WORKS CITED 343

Kennedy-Fraser, Marjory, and Kenneth Macleod. *Songs of the Hebrides. Collected and Arranged for Voice and Pianoforte with Gaelic and English Words*. Vol. 3. London: Boosey & Co., 1921.

King, Jason. "The Sound of Velvet Melting: The Power of 'Vibe' in the Music of Roberta Flack." In *Listen Again: A Momentary History of Pop Music*, edited by Eric Weisbard, 172–199. Durham, NC: Duke University Press, 2007.

Kramer, Lawrence. "Beyond Words and Music: An Essay on Songfulness." In *Word and Music Studies: Defining the Field. Proceedings of the First International Conference on Word and Music Studies*, edited by Walter Bernhart, Steven Paul Scher, and Werner Wolf, 303–319. Amsterdam: Rodopi, 1999.

Kramer, Lawrence. *Interpreting Music*. Berkeley: University of California Press, 2011.

LaBouff, Kathryn. *Singing and Communicating in English: A Singer's Guide to English Diction*. Oxford: Oxford University Press, 2008.

Lane, Nicholas. "History." Music at 19a Edith Grove. 2012. http://www.musicat19a.co.uk/ ?page_id=11.

Langfield, Valerie. *Roger Quilter: His Life and Music*. Woodbridge, Suffolk: Boydell, 2002.

Leech-Wilkinson, Daniel. *The Changing Sound of Music: Approaches to Studying Recorded Musical Performance*. London: Centre for the History and Analysis of Recorded Music, 2009. http://www.charm.rhul.ac.uk/studies/chapters/intro.html.

Le Guin, Elizabeth. *Boccherini's Body: An Essay in Carnal Musicology*. Berkeley: University of California Press, 2006.

Lewis, George E. "Americanist Musicology and Nomadic Noise." *Journal of the American Musicological Society* 64, no. 3 (2011): 691–695.

Liangmo, Liu. "Paul Robeson: The People's Singer." In *Chinese American Voices: From the Gold Rush to the Present*, edited by Judy Yung, Gordon H. Chang, and Him Mark Lai, 204–208. Berkeley: University of California Press, 2006.

Locke, Alain. "The Negro Spirituals." In *The New Negro*, 199–213. New York: Albert and Charles Boni, 1925.

Locke, Alain. "Roland Hayes: An Appreciation." In *The Opportunity Reader: Stories, Poetry, and Essays from the Urban League's "Opportunity" Magazine*, edited by Sondra Kathryn Wilson, 343–348. New York: The Modern Library, 1999 [1923].

López, Javier Pérez. "La música en las Brigadas Internacionales: Las canciones como estrategia de guerra." PhD thesis, Universidad de Castilla–La Mancha, 2014.

Low, Nat. "This Is Paul Robeson." *Pacific Tribune*, May 16, 1952.

Mahar, William J. *Behind the Burnt Cork Mask: Early Blackface Minstrelsy and Antebellum American Popular Culture*. Urbana: University of Illinois Press, 1999.

Marvin, Carolyn. *When Old Technologies Were New: Thinking about Electric Communication in the Late Nineteenth Century*. New York: Oxford University Press, 1998.

McCracken, Allison. *Real Men Don't Sing: Crooning in American Culture*. Durham, NC: Duke University Press, 2015.

Meadmore, W. S. "Paul Robeson." *The Gramophone*, September 1928, 147–149.

Metfessel, Milton. *Phonophotography in Folk Music: American Negro Songs in New Notation*. Chapel Hill: University of North Carolina Press, 1928.

Metfessel, Milton. "The Vibrato in Artistic Voices." In *Studies in the Psychology of Music*, edited by C. E. Seashore, 14–117. Iowa City: University of Iowa Press, 1932.

McGinn, Robert E. "Stokowski and the Bell Telephone Laboratories: Collaboration in the Development of High-Fidelity Sound Reproduction." *Technology and Culture* 24, no. 1 (1983): 62–68.

344 WORKS CITED

McGinty, Doris Evans, and Wayne Shirley. "Paul Robeson, Musician." In *Paul Robeson: Artist and Citizen*, edited by Jeffrey C. Stewart, 104–121. New Brunswick, NJ: Rutgers University Press, 1998.

McMillin, Scott. "Paul Robeson, Will Vodery's 'Jubilee Singers,' and the Earliest Script of the Kern-Hammerstein *Show Boat*." *Theatre Survey: The Journal of the American Society for Theatre Research* 41, no. 2 (2000): 51–70.

Meizel, Katherine. *Multivocality: Singing on the Borders of Identity*. New York: Oxford University Press, 2020.

Meizel, Katherine. "A Powerful Voice: Investigating Vocality and Identity." *Voice and Speech Review* 7, no. 1 (2011): 267–274.

Meskimmon, Marsha. *Contemporary Art and the Cosmopolitan Imagination*. London: Routledge, 2011.

Middleton, Richard. *Voicing the Popular: On the Subjects of Popular Music*. New York: Routledge, 2006.

Millard, Andre. *America on Record: A History of Recorded Sound*. 2nd ed. Cambridge: Cambridge University Press, 2005.

Miller, Richard. *The Art of Singing*. Oxford: Oxford University Press, 1996.

Miller, Richard. *Securing Baritone, Bass-Baritone, and Bass Voices*. Oxford: Oxford University Press, 2008.

Milner, Greg. *Perfecting Sound Forever: The Story of Recorded Music*. New York: Faber & Faber, 2010.

Moore, Allan. *Rock: The Primary Text*. Aldershot: Ashgate, 2001.

Moorefield, Virgil. *The Producer as Composer: Shaping the Sounds of Popular Music*. Cambridge, MA: MIT Press, 2015.

Moran, William R., ed. *Herman Klein and the Gramophone*. Portland, OR: Amadeus, 1990.

Morgan, Marcyliena. *Language, Discourse and Power in African American Culture*. Cambridge: Cambridge University Press, 2002.

Morrison, Matthew D. "Race, Blacksound, and the (Re)Making of Musicological Discourse." *Journal of the American Musicological Society* 72, no. 3 (2019): 781–823.

Morrison, Michael A. "The Voice Teacher as Shakespearean Collaborator: Margaret Carrington and John Barrymore." *Theatre Survey* 38, no. 2 (1997): 129–158.

Morrissette, Noelle. *James Weldon Johnson's Modern Soundscapes*. Iowa City: University of Iowa Press, 2013.

Moten, Fred. *Black and Blur: Consent Not to Be a Single Being*. Durham, NC: Duke University Press, 2017.

Moten, Fred. *In the Break: The Aesthetics of the Black Radical Tradition*. Minneapolis: University of Minnesota Press, 2003.

Moten, Fred. *Stolen Life: Consent Not to Be a Single Being*. Durham, NC: Duke University Press, 2018.

Mulder, Johannes. "Making Things Louder: Amplified Music and Multimodality." PhD thesis, University of Technology Sydney, 2013.

Musser, Charles. "Utopian Visions in Cold War Documentary: Joris Ivens, Paul Robeson and *Song of the Rivers*." *Cinémas: Revue d'études cinématographiques* 12, no. 3 (2002–2003): 109–153.

Mynett, Mark. "Achieving Intelligibility Whilst Maintaining Heaviness When Producing Contemporary Metal Music." *Journal on the Art of Record Production* 6 (2012). http://arpjournal.com.

WORKS CITED

Naison, Mark D. "'Americans through Their Labor': Paul Robeson's Vision of Cultural and Economic Democracy." In *Paul Robeson: Essays on His Life and Legacy*, edited by Joseph Dorinson and William Pancak, 187–193. Jefferson, NC: McFarland, 2002.

Neruda, Pablo. "Ode to Paul Robeson." Translated by Jill Booty. In *Paul Robeson: The Great Forerunner*, 244–250. New York: International Publishers, 1998.

Newland, Marti K. "Sounding 'Black': An Ethnography of Racialized Vocality at Fisk University." PhD diss., Columbia University, 2014.

Nollen, Scott Allen. *Paul Robeson: Film Pioneer*. Jefferson, NC: MacFarland, 2010.

Oliver, Paul. *Songsters and Saints: Vocal Traditions on Race Records*. Cambridge: Cambridge University Press, 1984.

Olmstead, Andrea. *Juilliard: A History*. Champaign: University of Illinois Press, 1999.

Olwage, Grant. "The Spanish War as Dress Rehearsal for Paul Robeson's Political Song." *Journal of War and Culture Studies* 14, no. 4 (2021): 390–407.

Olwage, Grant. "'The World Is His Song': Paul Robeson's 1958 Carnegie Hall Concerts and the Cosmopolitan Imagination." *Journal of the Society for American Music* 7, no. 2 (2013): 165–195.

"Paul Robeson." Discography of American Historical Recordings. Accessed October 30, 2018. https://adp.library.ucsb.edu/index.php/mastertalent/detail/102809/Robeson_Paul.

Pencak, William. "Paul Robeson and Classical Music." In *Paul Robeson: Essays on His Life and Legacy*, edited by Joseph Dorinson and William Pencak, 152–159. Jefferson, NC: McFarland, 2002.

Perucci, Tony. *Paul Robeson and the Cold War Performance Complex: Race, Madness, Activism*. Ann Arbor: University of Michigan Press, 2012.

Petridis, Alexis. "Topic Records—70 Years of Giving Voice to the People." *The Guardian*, August 23, 2009. http://www.theguardian.com/music/2009/aug/23/topic-records-70th-anniversary.

Petrus, Stephen, and Ronald D. Cohen. *Folk City: New York and the American Folk Music Revival*. Oxford: Oxford University Press, 2015.

Plunket Greene, Harry. *Interpretation in Song*. New York: Macmillan, 1912.

Powell, James R., Jr. "The Audiophile's Guide to Phonorecord Playback Equalizer Settings." *ARSC Journal* 20, no. 1 (1989): 14–23.

Radano, Ronald. *Lying Up a Nation: Race and Black Music*. Chicago: University of Chicago Press, 2003.

Reagon, Bernice Johnson. "The Civil Rights Period: Music as an Agent of Social Change." In *Issues in African American Music: Power, Gender, Race, Representation*, edited by Portia K. Maultsby and Mellonee V. Burnim, 343–367. New York: Routledge, 2017.

Reagon, Bernice Johnson. "Let the Church Sing 'Freedom.'" *Black Music Research Journal* 7 (1987): 105–118.

Redmond, Shana L. *Everything Man: The Form and Function of Paul Robeson*. Durham, NC: Duke University Press, 2020.

Redmond, Shana L. "Songs of Free Men: The Sound Migrations of 'Ol' Man River.'" In *Anthem: Social Movements and the Sound of Solidarity in the African Diaspora*, 99–140. New York: New York University Press, 2014.

Reese, Ruth. *My Way: A Life in Music*. London: Akira, 1987.

Reyes, Jesús Cano. "Un melómano en la guerra: Alejo Carpentier, corresponsal de la Guerra Civil Española." *Estudios filológicos* 62 (2018): 129–150.

Ricoeur, Paul. *The Hermeneutics of Action*, edited by Richard Kearney. London: Sage, 1996.

Robeson, Eslanda Goode. *Paul Robeson, Negro*. London: Victor Gollancz, 1930.

346 WORKS CITED

Robeson, Paul. "Foreword." In *Lift Every Voice! The Second People's Song Book*, edited by Irwin Silber, 3. New York: Oak Publications, 1953.

Robeson, Paul. "I Want to Be African." In *What I Want from Life*, edited by E. G. Cousins, 71–77. London: Allen & Unwin, 1934.

Robeson, Paul. *Here I Stand*. London: Denis Dobson, 1958.

Robeson, Paul. "A Song to Sing." *Masses and Mainstream* 8, no. 10 (1954): 12–14.

Robeson, Paul, Jr. *The Undiscovered Paul Robeson: An Artist's Journey, 1898–1939*. New York: John Wiley, 2001.

Robeson, Paul, Jr. *The Undiscovered Paul Robeson: An Artist's Journey, 1939–1976*. New York: John Wiley, 2010.

Robeson, Susan. *The Whole World in His Hands: A Pictorial Biography of Paul Robeson*. Secaucus, NJ: Citadel Press, 1981.

"Robeson Technique of Acoustics Control." *Radio-Craft*, March 1941, 561–562.

Robinson, Avery, arr. "Water Boy, a Negro Convict Song." London: Winthrop Rogers, 1922.

Root, Deane L. "Wolfe, Jacques." In *Grove Music Online*, edited by Deane Root. Oxford University Press, 2001. Accessed April 16, 2014. https://0-doi-org.innopac.wits.ac.za/10.1093/gmo/9781561592630.article.47063.

Rosselli, John. *Singers of Italian Opera: The History of a Profession*. Cambridge: Cambridge University Press, 1992.

Sanden, Paul. *Liveness in Modern Music: Musicians, Technology, and the Perception of Performance*. New York: Routledge, 2013.

Sandvoss, Cornel. *Fans: The Mirror of Consumption*. Cambridge: Polity, 2005.

Schatzkamer, William. "Travels with Paul." *African American Review* 45, nos. 1 and 2 (2012): 217–223.

Schmidt Horning, Susan. *Chasing Sound: Technology, Culture & the Art of Studio Recording from Edison to the LP*. Baltimore: Johns Hopkins University Press, 2013.

Schoen-René, Anna. *America's Musical Inheritance: Memories and Reminiscences*. New York: G. P. Putnam's Sons, 1941.

Schudel, Matt. "Paul Robeson Jr., Protector of Father's Legacy, Dies at 86." *Washington Post*, April 29, 2014.

Seashore, Carl E. *Psychology of the Vibrato in Voice and Instrument*. Iowa City: University of Iowa Press, 1936.

Seashore, Carl E., ed. *The Vibrato*. Iowa City: University of Iowa Press, 1932.

Semeonoff, Boris. *Record Collecting: A Guide for Beginners*. Chislehurst, Kent: Oakwood Press, 1949.

Sergeant, Elizabeth Shepley. "The Man with His Home in a Rock: Paul Robeson." *New Republic* March 3, 1926, 40–44.

Shaffer, Melanie. "Paul Robeson's Iconic Timbre and the Negotiation of Signification." *American Music Research Center Journal* 43 (2014): 29–48.

Shaw, Ian. "Paul Robeson: The Peace Arch Concerts." Liner notes for *Paul Robeson: The Peace Arch Concerts*. Folk Era FE1442CD, 1998, compact disc.

Shirley, Wayne D. "The Coming of 'Deep River.'" *American Music* 14, no. 5 (1997): 493–534.

Silber, Irwin. "Pete Seeger, Paul Robeson on New Long-Play Discs." *Sing Out! A People's Artists Publication* 4, no. 4 (March 1954): 15–16.

Slate, Nico. *Colored Cosmopolitanism: The Shared Struggle for Freedom in the United States and India*. Cambridge, MA: Harvard University Press, 2012.

Smith, Ben T. "Was There Ever a 'Veddy British' R?" 2012. http://dialectblog.com/2012/01/10/was-there-a-veddy-british-r/.

WORKS CITED   347

Smith, Michael, and Frank Andrews. *The Gramophone Company Ltd "His Master's Voice" Recordings: Plum Label "C" Series*. Lingfield, Surrey: Oakwood Press, 1974.

Smith, William Andre. *The Mystery of Leopold Stokowski*. London: Associated University Presses, 1990.

Song, Min Jeong. "Mechanisms of In-Betweenness: Through Visual Experiences of Glass." PhD thesis, Royal College of Art, London, 2014.

Spencer, Jon Michael. *Sacred Symphony: The Chanted Sermon of the Black Preacher*. Westport, CT: Greenwood Press, 1987.

Stanley, Douglas, and J. P. Maxfield. *The Voice, Its Production and Reproduction*. New York: Pitman, 1933.

Steinhaus-Jordan, Barbara. "An Analysis of Marian Anderson's Interpretation of Black Spiritual Art Songs in Selected Recordings." DMA diss., University of Georgia, 1997.

Steinhaus-Jordan, Barbara. "Black Spiritual Art Song: Interpretive Guidelines for Studio Teachers." *Journal of Singing* 61, no. 5 (2005): 477–485.

Stephens, Michelle Ann. *Skin Acts: Race, Psychoanalysis, and the Black Male Performer*. Durham, NC: Duke University Press, 2014.

Sterne, Jonathan. *Audible Past: The Cultural Origins of Sound Reproduction*. Durham, NC: Duke University Press, 2003.

Stewart, Jeffrey C. "The Black Body: Paul Robeson as a Work of Art and Politics." In *Paul Robeson: Artist and Citizen*, edited by Jeffrey Stewart, 135–163. New Brunswick, NJ: Rutgers University Press, 1998.

Stewart, Jeffrey C. "I Sing the Black Body Electric: Transnationalism and the Black Body in Walt Whitman, Alain Locke, and Paul Robeson." In *Recharting the Black Atlantic: Modern Cultures, Local Communities, Global Connections*, edited by Annalisa Oboe and Anna Scacchi, 259–281. New York: Routledge, 2008.

Stuckey, Sterling. "'I Want to Be African': Paul Robeson and the Ends of Nationalist Theory and Practice, 1914–1945.'" In *Going Through the Storm: The Influence of African American Art in History*, 187–227. New York: Oxford University Press, 1994.

Stuckey, Sterling. "On Being African: Paul Robeson and the Ends of Nationalist Theory and Practice." In *Slave Culture: Nationalist Theory and the Foundations of Black America*, 303–358. New York: Oxford University Press, 1987.

Sundquist, Eric J. *To Wake the Nations: Race in the Making of American Literature*. Cambridge, MA: Harvard University Press, 1993.

Sutton, Allan. *Recording the 'Twenties: The Evolution of the American Recording Industry, 1920–29*. Denver, CO: Mainspring, 2008.

Swindall, Lindsey R. *The Politics of Paul Robeson's Othello*. Jackson: University Press of Mississippi, 2011.

Symes, Colin. *Setting the Record Straight: A Material History of Classical Recording*. Middletown, CT: Wesleyan University Press, 2004.

Taruskin, Richard. *Defining Russia Musically*. Princeton, NJ: Princeton University Press, 1997.

"TAT-1." *Hidden Histories of the Information Age*, episode 2, BBC Radio 4, October 21, 2014. http://www.bbc.co.uk/programmes/b04m3bcc.

Taylor, Timothy D. "Music and the Rise of Radio in Twenties America: Technological Imperialism, Socialization, and the Transformation of Intimacy." In *Wired for Sound: Engineering and Technologies in Sonic Cultures*, edited by Paul D. Greene and Thomas Porcello, 245–268. Middletown, CT: Wesleyan University Press, 2005.

348 WORKS CITED

Thompson, Emily. *The Soundscape of Modernity: Architectural Acoustics and the Culture of Listening in America, 1900–1933*. Cambridge, MA: MIT Press, 2002.

Thornhill, Gillian. *The Life, Times, and Music of Mark Raphael*. Bloomington, IN: AuthorHouse, 2012.

Tobias, James. "Composing for the Media: Hanns Eisler and Rockefeller Foundation Projects in Film Music, Radio Listening, and Theatrical Sound Design." Rockefeller Archive Center Research Reports Online, 2009. http://www.rockarch.org/publications/resrep/tobias.pdf.

Tomlinson, John. "Interests and Identities in Cosmopolitan Politics." In *Conceiving Cosmopolitanism: Theory, Context, and Practice*, edited by Steven Vertovec and Robin Cohen, 240–253. Oxford: Oxford University Press, 2002.

Tracy, Steven C. "Langston Hughes and Afro-American Vernacular Music." In *A Historical Guide to Langston Hughes*, edited by Steven C. Tracy, 85–118. Oxford: Oxford University Press, 2004.

Tunbridge, Laura. *Singing in the Age of Anxiety: Lieder Performance in New York and London between the World Wars*. Chicago: University of Chicago Press, 2018.

Van Vechten, Carl. "Folksongs of the American Negro." In *Keep A-inchin' Along: Selected Writings of Carl Van Vechten about Black Art and Letters*, edited by Bruce Kellner, 34–39. Westport, CT: Greenwood Press, 1979 [1925].

Van Vechten, Carl. "Paul Robeson and Lawrence Brown." In *Keep A-inchin' Along: Selected Writings of Carl Van Vechten about Black Art and Letters*, edited by Bruce Kellner, 154–158. Westport, CT: Greenwood Press, 1979 [1925].

Vennard, William. *Singing: The Mechanism and the Technique*. 5th ed. New York: Carl Fischer, 1968 [1949].

Vertovec, Steven, and Robin Cohen, eds. *Conceiving Cosmopolitanism: Theory, Context, and Practice*. Oxford: Oxford University Press, 2002.

Von Blum, Paul. *Paul Robeson for Beginners*. Danbury, CT: For Beginners, 2013.

Weheliye, Alexander G. *Phonographies: Grooves in Sonic Afro-Modernity*. Durham, NC: Duke University Press, 2005.

Weinbaum, Alys Eve. "Reproducing Racial Globality: W. E. B. Du Bois and the Sexual Politics of Black Internationalism." *Social Text* 19, no. 2 (2011): 15–41.

Weiss, Jason. *An Oral History of ESP-DISK', The Most Outrageous Record Label in America*. Middletown, CT: Wesleyan University Press, 2012.

West, Stephen. "The Traditions of Fine Singing: An Interview with Mme. Anna E. Schoen-René." *The Etude*, November 1941, 745–746, 778.

White, Thomas H. "News and Entertainment by Telephone (1876–1930)." United States Early Radio History. Accessed June 28, 2016. http://earlyradiohistory.us/sec003.htm#part080.

Whitney, William Dwight. *The Century Dictionary and Cyclopedia; A Work of Universal Reference in All Departments of Knowledge*, vol. 2. New York: The Century Co., 1906.

Whyton, Tony. "Song of Praise: Musicians, Myths and the 'Cult' of John Coltrane." In *Popular Music Fandom: Identities, Roles and Practices*, edited by Mark Duffett, 97–114. New York: Routledge, 2014.

Wijfjes, Huub. "Spellbinding and Crooning: Sound Amplification, Radio, and Political Rhetoric in International Comparative Perspective, 1900–1945." *Technology and Culture* 55, no. 1 (2014): 148–185.

Williams, Daniel G. *Black Skin, Blue Books: African Americans and Wales, 1845–1945*. Cardiff: University of Wales Press, 2012.

Wilson, Percy. *The Gramophone Handbook*. London: Methuen, 1957.

WORKS CITED 349

Woodard, Patricia. "Singing Up to Freedom Land: Hymns, Spirituals, and Gospel Songs in the Civil Rights Movement." *The Hymn* 67, no. 2 (2016): 7–15.

Yuval-Davis, Nira, Kalpana Kannabirān, and Ulrike M. Vieten, eds. *The Situated Politics of Belonging*. London: Sage, 2006.

Discography

Ernst Busch. *Six Songs for Democracy*. Keynote Records, K101, 1940.

Gervase Elwes. "Now Sleeps the Crimson Petal." Columbia L 1055, 1916.

Harry Plunket Greene. "The Garden Where the Praties Grow." Columbia DB 1321, 1934.

Harry Plunket Greene. "The Hurdy-Gurdy Man." Columbia DB 1377, 1934.

John McCormack. "Now Sleeps the Crimson Petal." Victor 1307-B, 1927.

Layton and Johnstone. "Spiritual Medley" ("I Got A Robe—Steal Away—Ev'ry Time I Feel the Spirit—Nobody Knows de Trouble I've Seen"). Recorded 1932. Track 15 on *Good News: Vintage Negro Spirituals*. Living Era CD AJA 5622, 2006, CD.

Paul Robeson and Lawrence Brown (piano). "Joshua Fit de Battle ob Jericho." Recorded 1925. Track 12 on *Good News: Vintage Negro Spirituals*. Living Era CD AJA 5622, 2006, CD.

Paul Robeson and Lawrence Brown (piano). "Steal Away." Recorded 1925. Track 14 on *Paul Robeson: A Lonesome Road*. ASV Living Era CD AJA 5027, 1984, CD.

Paul Robeson and Lawrence Brown (piano). "Were You There? (When They Crucified My Lord)." Recorded 1925. Track 16 on *Ol' Man River: Paul Robeson*. Mastersong, 1999/2000, CD.

Paul Robeson and Lawrence Brown (piano). "On Ma Journey." Gramophone B-2326, 1926, shellac record.

Paul Robeson and Lawrence Brown (piano). "Swing Low, Sweet Chariot." Gramophone B-2339, 1926, shellac record.

Paul Robeson and Lawrence Brown (piano). "Water Boy." Victor 19824-A, 1926, shellac record.

Paul Robeson and Lawrence Brown (piano). "Deep River." Recorded 1927. Track 13 on *Good News: Vintage Negro Spirituals*, Living Era CD AJA 5622, 2006, CD.

Paul Robeson with orchestra, Carroll Gibbons (conductor). "Sonny Boy." Recorded 1929. Track 18, disc 1 on *Paul Robeson: The Complete EMI Sessions, 1928–1939*. EMI Records 2 15588 2, 2008, CD.

Paul Robeson and Lawrence Brown (piano). "Exhortation." Recorded 1930. Track 2, disc 2 on *Paul Robeson: The Complete EMI Sessions, 1928–1939*. EMI Records 2 15590 2, 2008, CD.

Paul Robeson and Ruthland Clapham (piano). "Li'l Gal." Recorded 1931. Track 16, disc 2 on *Paul Robeson: The Complete EMI Sessions, 1928–1939*. EMI Records 2 15590 2, 2008, CD

Paul Robeson and G. Ruthland Clapham (piano). "Steal Away." HMV B-8103, 1933, shellac record.

Paul Robeson and G. Ruthland Clapham (piano). "Swing Low, Sweet Chariot." HMV B-8372, 1933, shellac record.

Paul Robeson and G. Ruthland Clapham (piano). "Water Boy." Recorded 1933. Track 4, disc 4 on *Paul Robeson: The Complete EMI Sessions, 1928–1939*. EMI Records 2 15594 2, 2008, CD.

Paul Robeson with orchestra, Ray Noble (conductor). "St. Louis Blues." Recorded 1934. Track 10, disc 4 on *Paul Robeson: The Complete EMI Sessions, 1928–1939*. EMI Records 2 15594 2, 2008, CD.

350 WORKS CITED

Paul Robeson and Lawrence Brown (piano). "Ezekiel Saw de Wheel." Recorded 1936. Track 24, disc 4 on *Paul Robeson: The Complete EMI Sessions, 1928–1939*. EMI Records 2 15586 2, 2008, CD.

Paul Robeson and Lawrence Brown (piano). "Joshua Fit de Battle ob Jericho." Recorded 1936, track 25, disc 4 on *Paul Robeson: The Complete EMI Sessions*. EMI Records 2 15586 2, 2008, CD.

Paul Robeson. "Minstrel Man." Recorded 1937. Track 25, disc 5 on *Paul Robeson: The Complete EMI Sessions, 1928–1939*. EMI Records 2 15596 2, 2008, CD.

Paul Robeson and Lawrence Brown (piano). "No More." Recorded 1937. Track 2, disc 6 on *Paul Robeson: The Complete EMI Sessions, 1928–1939*. EMI Records 2 15598 2, 2008, CD.

Paul Robeson and Lawrence Brown (piano). "Work All de Summer." Recorded 1937. Track 3, disc 6 on *Paul Robeson: The Complete EMI Sessions, 1928–1939*. EMI Records 2 15598 2, 2008, CD.

Paul Robeson and Lawrence Brown (piano). "Ev'ry Time I Feel de Spirit." Recorded 1938. Track 19, disc 6, on *Paul Robeson: The Complete EMI Sessions, 1928–1939*. EMI Records 2 15598 2, 2008, CD.

Paul Robeson and Lawrence Brown (piano). "Now Sleeps the Crimson Petal." HMV B 9281, 1939, shellac record.

Paul Robeson and Lawrence Brown (piano). "Sea Fever." Recorded 1939. Track 22, disc 7 on *Paul Robeson: The Complete EMI Sessions, 1928–1939*. EMI Records 2 15600 2, 2008, CD.

Paul Robeson with Chinese Chorus, *Chee Lai: Songs of New China*. Keynote Recordings, Album 109 K 520-522, 1941, shellac records.

Paul Robeson and Lawrence Brown (piano). "The Four Insurgent Generals." Recorded 1942. Track 9 on *Paul Robeson: Songs of Free Men*. Sony Classical MHK 63223, 1997, CD.

Paul Robeson and Lawrence Brown (piano). "Water Boy." Recorded 1945. Track 6, side 2, on *Paul Robeson: Songs of Free Men—Spirituals*. Columbia 32 16 0268, 1945, LP.

Paul Robeson and Alexander Yeroklin (piano). "The Four Insurgent Generals." Recorded 1949. Track 7 on *Paul Robeson: The Legendary Moscow Concert*. Revelation RV 70004, 1997, CD.

Paul Robeson and Alexander Yeroklin (piano). "Over the Mountains." Recorded 1949. Track 1 on *Paul Robeson: The Legendary Moscow Concert*. Revelation Records RV70004, 1997, CD.

Paul Robeson and Lawrence Brown (piano). "Every Time I Feel the Spirit." Recorded 1952. Track 4 on *Paul Robeson: The Peace Arch Concerts*. Folk Era FE1442CD, 1998, CD.

Paul Robeson and Lawrence Brown (piano). "Ol' Man River." Recorded 1952. Track 12 on *Paul Robeson: The Peace Arch Concerts*. Folk Era FE1442CD, 1998, CD.

Paul Robeson and Lawrence Brown (piano). "Chin Chin (Chinese Marching Song)." Recorded 1953. Track 24 on *Paul Robeson: The Peace Arch Concerts*. Folk Era FE1442CD, 1998, CD.

Paul Robeson. "Speech." Recorded 1953. Track 25 on *Paul Robeson: The Peace Arch Concerts*. Folk Era FE1442CD, 1998, CD.

Paul Robeson and Lawrence Brown (piano). "Theme from Beethoven's 9th Symphony." Recorded 1953. Track 17 on *Paul Robeson: The Peace Arch Concerts*. Folk Era FE1442CD, 1998, CD.

Paul Robeson. *Solid Rock: Favorite Hymns of My People*. Othello Records, L-201, 1954, LP.

Paul Robeson and Alan Booth (piano). "Stand Still, Jordan." Recorded 1955/1956. Track 20 on *On My Journey: Paul Robeson's Independent Recordings, 1928–1939*. Smithsonian Folkways Recordings SFW CD 40178, 2007, CD.

WORKS CITED 351

Paul Robeson and Alan Booth (piano). "Amazing Grace." Recorded 1956. Track 15 on *On My Journey: Paul Robeson's Independent Recordings, 1928–1939*. Smithsonian Folkways Recordings SFW CD 40178, 2007, CD.

Paul Robeson and Alan Booth (piano). "Li'l Gal." Recorded 1956. Track 26 on *On My Journey: Paul Robeson's Independent Recordings, 1928–1939*. Smithsonian Folkways Records SFW CD 440178, 2007, CD.

Paul Robeson and Alan Booth (piano). "Swing Low, Sweet Chariot." Recorded 1956/1957. Track 9 on *On My Journey: Paul Robeson's Independent Recordings, 1928–1939*. Smithsonian Folkways Recordings SFW CD 40178, 2007, CD.

Paul Robeson and Alan Booth (piano). "On My Journey: Mount Zion." Recorded 1957. Track 1 on *On My Journey: Paul Robeson's Independent Recordings, 1928–1939*. Smithsonian Folkways Recordings SFW CD 40178, 2007, CD.

Paul Robeson. *Paul Robeson's Transatlantic Concert*. Topic 10 T 17, 1957, LP.

Paul Robeson and Alan Booth (piano). "Every Time I Feel The Spirit." Recorded 1958. Track 1 on *Paul Robeson at Carnegie Hall*. Vanguard VMD 72020, 2005, CD.

Paul Robeson and Alan Booth (piano). "Go Down, Moses." Recorded 1958. Track 3 on *Paul Robeson: The Original Recording of "Ballad for Americans" and Great Songs of Faith, Love and Patriotism*. Vanguard VCD 117/18, 1989, CD.

Paul Robeson and Alan Booth (piano). "Jacob's Ladder." Recorded 1958. Side 2, track 8 on *Paul Robeson at Carnegie Hall*. Vanguard LP VRS-9051, 1960, LP.

Paul Robeson and Alan Booth (piano). "Old Man River." Recorded 1958. Side 1, track 8 on *Paul Robeson at Carnegie Hall*. Vanguard LP VRS-9051, 1960, LP.

Paul Robeson. "Patterns of Folk Song." Recorded 1958. Side 1, track 4 on *Paul Robeson: Ballad for Americans and Carnegie Hall Concert*, vol. 2. Vanguard VSD 79193, 1965, LP.

Paul Robeson. *Robeson*. Vanguard VSD-2015, 1958, LP.

Paul Robeson and Allan Booth (accompanist). "Sometimes I Feel Like a Motherless Child." Recorded 1958. Side 2, track 6 on *Paul Robeson in Live Performance*. Columbia Masterworks M30424, 1970, LP.

Paul Robeson and Allan Booth (accompanist). "We Are Climbing Jacob's Ladder." Recorded 1958. Side 2, track 7 on *Paul Robeson in Live Performance*. Columbia Masterworks M30424, 1970, LP.

Paul Robeson. *Paul Robeson Favorite Songs*. Monitor Records MPS 580, 1959, LP.

Paul Robeson. *Encore, Robeson! Paul Robeson: Favorite Songs, Vol. 2*. Monitor Records MPS 581, 1960, LP.

Paul Robeson. *Paul Robeson: The Complete EMI Sessions, 1928–1939*. EMI Classics 2 15586 2, 2008, CD.

Roland Hayes and Lawrence Brown (piano). "Steal Away." Recorded 1922. Track 2 on *Good News: Vintage Negro Spirituals*. Living Era CD AJA 5622, 2006, CD.

Roland Hayes and Reginald Boardman (piano). "Every Time I Feel the Spirit." Recorded 1954. Track 24, disc 1 on *The Art of Roland Hayes: Six Centuries of Song*. Preiser Records 93462, 2009, CD.

Roland Hayes and Reginald Boardman (piano). "Ezekiel Saw de Wheel." Recorded 1954. Track 21, disc 1 on *The Art of Roland Hayes: Six Centuries of Song*. Preiser Records 93462, 2009, CD.

Roland Hayes and Reginald Boardman (piano). "Were You There?" Recorded 1954. Track 29, disc 2 on *The Art of Roland Hayes: Six Centuries of Song*. Preiser Records 93462, 2009, CD.

Index

For the benefit of digital users, indexed terms that span two pages (e.g., 52–53) may, on occasion, appear on only one of those pages.

The subject of all entries is Paul Robeson, unless obviously or indicated otherwise. Figures are indicated by *f* following the page number

accents. *See also* African American vernacular practices
  African American, 181–82
  English, 181–86, 190, 191
  implications, 191, 195
  international, 185–86, 189, 190–91, 199–202
acting. *See* stage acting
activism, 2, 3–6, 153, 195, 202. *See also* persecution; politicization
  anticolonial, 137–38, 140–41, 159–60
  anti-fascist, 44, 135, 137, 150–51, 202, 262–63
  civil rights, 4, 132, 172–73, 193–94, 204–5, 207
  labor, 4, 135, 143–44, 150, 151–52, 196–97
  political voice, 2–3, 12, 134, 208 (*see also* people's voice)
  politics, 134–35, 137, 138–39, 150–51, 159–60
  Spanish Civil War and, 134–37, 151, 173–77
  supporters, 132, 133, 204, 210, 214–16
African American culture. *See* Black culture
African American music traditions, 137–38. *See also* folk music; spirituals
  congregational singing, 20, 77–78, 168–70, 172–74, 193–94
  evangelical (*see* evangelical arrangements/expression)
  glee, 76–77, 81, 112
  male singing, 77–78
  performance, 20–21, 52–53, 68, 69

preaching, 20–21, 25, 69–70, 90–91, 166–68, 188, 190–91
quartets, 21, 42, 76–77, 78, 102–3, 112–14, 115, 129–30
vaudeville, 76–78
African American vernacular practices. *See also* accents
  accents and dialects, 65–66, 180, 185–91
  melodic, 20–21, 78–79, 192–95
  preaching and, 20–21, 25, 69–70, 90–91, 166–68, 188, 190–91
  vocal modalities, 83–84, 106–7
Africanism, 138–40
African Methodist Episcopal Zion Church (AME), 20–21, 172–73
Aldridge, Amanda, 31–32, 36–37, 181–82
"Amazing Grace," 192–94
American Civil War, 92–93, 97
American tours. *See* tours, North American
Armitage, Theresa, 33–36
art music/songs, 7–8, 28, 52, 65–66, 78–79, 83, 129–30, 176–77. *See also* classical tradition
  African American, 40–42, 59–61, 63–64
  attitudes to (Robeson's), 29, 48, 87–88, 140, 144, 188, 192–93
  English, 7–8, 32, 111–12, 144, 146–48, 183
  German 8, 52, 144 (see also *Lieder*)
  "natural" singing and, 54–57, 88, 99, 111–12
  programming and, 165–66

354 INDEX

art music/songs (*cont.*)
  repertoire, 32, 42, 47, 52, 58–59, 62–63,
    65–66, 87–88, 112, 140, 253
  Russian, 7–8, 43–46, 112, 140–41,
    144–46, 147–48, 209–10
  spirituals and (*see* spirituals)
  authenticity, 11–12, 74–75, 88–89,
    99–100, 107–8
  folk, 9, 65–66, 157, 195
  racial, 57–59, 65–66, 78, 83,
    92–93, 95–96
  spirituals and, 62–63, 68, 69–70, 78,
    79–84, 91

Ballad for Americans, 6, 9, 212–13,
    229–30, 239–40
biography (early), 11, 21–22. *See
    also* career
  Black church, role of, 20–22, 29, 90–91,
    170, 172–73
  childhood, 18–20
  community, 19–20, 21–22
  father, 19, 20, 21–22
  school and college, 21
Black churches, 19–21, 68–70, 90–91,
    170–73, 193–94. *See also* Black
    preaching
Black culture and cultural politics, 19, 29,
    56–57, 138
  elite (*see* elites/elitism)
  folk, 64–65
  institutional, 21–22
  political, 15–16, 26–141, 150–51
Black internationale, 137–38, 151–52. *See
    also* "The Internationale"
Black preaching, 20–21, 25, 69–70, 90–91,
    166–68, 188, 190–91. *See also* Black
    churches
Blackness, 26, 57, 86–87, 92–93, 98, 102,
    189, 203, 263
Blacksound, 8–9, 10–11, 57–58
Boston concerts, 23–25, 33–34, 59, 87
broadcasts. *See* radio broadcasts
Broadway performances, 18–19, 21,
    23–25, 221–22
Brooks, Gwendolyn, 1–2
brotherhood, 132, 155–56, 159–61,
    164–65, 169–70
  brothering song, 166–68, 177, 178

Brown, Lawrence, 11–12, 23–25, 30–31,
    59, 64–65, 144–46, 257*f*
  arrangements, 73–75, 77, 79–81
  influences, 77–78
  performance descriptions, 69–75,
    77–82, 104–5
  performance partnership, 27, 67–68,
    76–77, 95
Burleigh, Harry T., 28, 59–63, 65, 75, 77,
    86*f*, 87, 102–3
  coaching/influence, 25–26, 30, 61, 83
Burris-Meyer, Harold, 231–36, 257–58
Busch, Ernst, 151, 173–74, 175–76

career, 12–13, 22
  early, 26–27, 28–29, 33, 46, 52, 56, 66,
    81–82, 94, 112–14, 262–63
  late, 20, 35–36, 123, 164, 168–69, 173,
    177–78, 193–94, 212–13
  mid, 5–6, 42–44, 52, 102, 110–11, 134,
    140, 142, 229
  start, 21–22, 27–28, 29, 42, 59–27
  theatrical, 21–22
Carnegie Hall recitals, 36–38, 157, 169–70
  debut, 27–28
  programs, 29, 144, 145*f*, 151,
    166–68, 167*f*
  reviews, 38–39, 99, 112, 120–21, 128,
    176–78, 227
  sound technology, use of, 227, 231,
    234–35, 235*f*, 237, 257–58
Carpentier, Alejo, 39–40, 136–37, 175
Chaliapin, Feodor, 43–46
Chicago Music Publishing Company,
    23–25, 244
church concerts, 170–74
civil rights/civil rights movement, 4, 132,
    172–73, 193–94, 204–5, 207
Civil War. *See* American Civil War;
    Spanish Civil War
classical tradition, 8–9, 42–43, 87–88.
    See also art music
  attitudes to (Robeson's), 29, 48, 87–88,
    140, 144, 188, 192–93, 253
  Brown, Lawrence and, 30–31
  Burleigh, Harry T. and, 61, 62–63, 87
  Hayes, Roland and, 54–56, 58–59, 64, 83
  performance culture and, 7–8, 239–40
  spirituals and, 40–42, 58–59, 64–65

INDEX   355

vocal pedagogy, 102–3, 108–9,
  111–14, 195–96
voice training, 6–7, 21–22, 30, 31,
  35–38, 47, 111–14
Cold War, 6, 9, 132, 214–16, 262–63
colonialism/anticolonialism, 57, 97,
  137–38, 140–41, 159–60
Columbia Masterworks, 177–78, 213–14,
  254–55, 256–57
communal singing, 168–70, 173–74. *See
  also* congregational tradition
congregational tradition, 20, 77–78,
  168–70, 172–74, 193–94. *See also*
  communal singing
cosmopolitanism, 12, 57, 64, 66, 149,
  158–59, 162–63, 179–80, 191–92,
  262–63. *See also* internationalism
  concept, 164
  everyday practices and, 163–64
  ideals, 153, 163, 164–65
  programming and, 66, 164–68, 170, 178
  non-English languages and, 176–77, 191
comparativism, 62–63, 99, 138–39, 140,
  141, 144, 147–48, 149–50, 181–82
critics. *See* reviews
cultural politics, 15–16, 26–141, 150–51
Cunelli, Georges, 35–36, 47

debating, 18–19, 21
"Deep River," 54, 77, 82
dialects
  African American, 107–8
  debates around, 186, 187–88
  Robeson's use of, 108, 185–86,
    187–90, 191
  Scots Lallans, 157, 191
  transatlantic, 185–86
diction, 107–9, 183–85, 187–88,
  189, 258–59
Du Bois, W. E. B., 63–65, 84, 90–91, 92–93

ecstatic aesthetics, 73, 83–85, 86–87,
  188, 264–65. *See also* evangelical
  arrangements/expression
elites/elitism, 63, 64, 185–86, 191, 192–93,
  195–96, 259
  anti-elitism, 136–37, 153
  English, 32, 180–81, 183–85, 190
  Harlem, 23–25, 42, 57, 63

embodied/disembodied vocalities, 14–16,
  21–22, 58, 96, 189, 227
English art music, 7–8, 32, 111–12, 144,
  146–48, 183
essentialization, 21–22, 57–58, 78, 86–87,
  138, 189, 262–63
evangelical arrangements/expression,
  68–70, 73–81, 83–84. *See also* ecstatic
  aesthetics
  vs art tradition, 78–79
  exuberance/spontaneity, 69–73
  programming, 79–81
  dialoguing/vocal interpolations,
    73, 81–82
"Ev'ry Time I Hear de Spirit," 73–75, 75*f*,
  76*f*, 77–79, 84
"Ezekiel Saw de Wheel," 70–73, 84

fans, 12, 153–60, 161–63, 169–70,
  175–76, 196–97
fantasization, 94, 131, 203–4
  idealization, 92–93
  "natural" voices and, 54–56, 96–103,
    110–12, 121–22, 128, 129–30
  primitivist and racist, 57–58, 59–61, 131
fascism/anti-fascism, 44, 135, 137, 150–51,
  202, 262–63
Fisk Jubilee Singers, 59, 81, 86–87, 97
folk music/songs, 65–66, 69, 101,
  141–42, 147–48
  aesthetics, 8–9, 173–74
  African American, 59–61,
    83–84, 137–38
  authenticity and, 9, 65–66, 195
  as Black art, 63–65
  English and Russian, 45–46, 98–99,
    140–41, 144–46, 147–48
  internationalism and, 140–42, 144,
    148–50, 152–53, 164–66, 168
  politics and, 142–44, 149, 150
  praxis, 191–93
  sea music, 147–48
  universal theory of, 25, 149, 194–95
folk studies, 144, 148–49, 159–60,
  164–65, 175–76

glee, 76–77, 81, 112
"Go Down Moses," 61–62, 253–54
God's Trombones, 187–88, 190–91, 264–65

356 INDEX

Gramophone, 28, 40–42, 185, 229, 246, 247, 248–49, 254–55, 258, 259
Gramophone Company. *See* His Master's Voice (HMV)
gramophones (technology), 246–49, 258–59. *See also* recordings
gramophone voice, 227, 234–35, 236–37, 244, 259–60. *See also* recordings
Greenwich Village Theater concerts, 29–30, 46, 56, 59–63, 67–68, 74–75, 79–81

Hancock, David, 217–18, 219–20
Harlem Renaissance, 69–70, 81, 91, 164
    aesthetic agenda, 23, 40–42, 57, 63–64, 65–66, 92, 186–87, 190
    elites/elitism, 23–25, 42, 57, 63
    ideals, 56–57, 138, 139–40
    spirituals and, 56–57, 66, 73–74, 81, 88–89, 150
Hayes, Roland, 11–12, 20–21, 28, 30–31, 57–59, 67–68, 78–79, 81–82, 90–91, 187
    aesthetic-political purpose, 56–57
    arrangements/interpretations, 70–73, 82, 84, 85–87, 106–7, 115–17
    influence (on Robeson), 54–56, 58, 61–63, 65–66
    programming/repertoire, 58–61, 63, 64, 65–66
    reception/reviews, 56–57, 59–61, 78–79, 83–84, 89–90, 99
    as Renaissance man, 56–57
    spirituals, 58–59
    voice/voice history, 83, 89
Henschel, George, 32, 36–37, 253–54
hero (Robeson as), 6, 196–97, 199–202
    for activists, 202, 208
    for fans, 2, 154, 155–56, 196–97
    heroic representations, 199–202
    heroic voice, 12, 196–207, 208, 264–65
highbrow/lowbrow categories, 9, 42–43, 107–8, 110–12, 153. *See also* middlebrow culture/orientation
high-fidelity audio/records, 156–57, 212, 223, 227, 243, 254–55, 257–58

Hikmet, Nâzim, 132–34
His Master's Voice (HMV), 39–40, 45–46, 152, 185, 212–13, 220–21, 248–49, 250–53
Holt, Harold, 5, 152–53
Holt International Celebrity Concert tours, 42, 152–53
House Un-American Activities Committee, 44–45, 205, 216
Hughes, Langston, 57–58, 185–87
humanism, 150, 151–52, 159–60, 191
Hurston, Zora Neale, 61–62, 74–75, 81, 86–87, 129–30
hymns, 172–73, 193–94

identities, 10–11, 52–53, 69, 74–75, 137, 139–40, 187, 191–92, 196, 263, 264–66
    as People's Artist (*see* people's voice [Robeson as])
    politics of, 11–12, 58, 139–40, 141, 142, 195
    racial, 58, 63–64, 94, 139–40, 142, 181, 262–63
    self, 44–45, 142, 196–97, 265–66
    vocal, 3, 11, 16–17, 18, 28–29, 39–40, 45–46, 195, 242–43
imperialism/anti-imperialism, 136–37, 150–51, 191, 204
internationalism, 135–38, 140–41, 151–52, 163, 262–63. *See also* cosmopolitanism
    African influence, 138–40
    allegiances, 135, 143–44
    genealogy, 12, 134, 135, 164
    labor movement and, 4, 143–44
    programming and, 164
    Russian/Soviet influence, 140–41, 146–47
    song practice and, 137–38, 140, 146–51 (*see also* folk music)
    Spanish influence, 137–38, 175–76 (*see also* Spanish Civil War)
    "The Internationale," 136–37
    voice and, 185–86, 190–91, 199–202

James, C. L. R., 2, 202, 262–63
"Jerusalem," 164, 165–66, 185

INDEX 357

Johnson, James Weldon, 20–21, 73–74, 75, 77–78, 105, 186–88

Klein, Herman, 246–47, 249–50, 253–54

labor
  activism/politics, 144, 150, 151–52, 262–63
  movement, 4, 135, 143–44
  songs, 143–44, 174, 196–97 (*see also* "Water Boy"; "The Internationale")
La consagración de la primavera, 136–37
languages. *See* multilingualism
Layton and Johnstone (duo), 77–79
Lieder, 8–9, 47, 87–88, 111–12, 144–46, 253
Locke, Alain, 83–84, 197
  music history theory, 65
  on spirituals, 56–57, 58–59, 65, 83–84, 192–94
London School of Oriental Studies, 138–39, 149
lowbrow culture. *See* highbrow/lowbrow categories
Lulu Belle, 26

materiality. *See* voice materiality
McCarthy era, 5–6, 217–18
media reviews. *See* reviews
memorialization, 3–4, 5–6
microphones, 129–30, 156–57, 219–20, 223–25, 227–28, 242–43, 248–50, 257*f*
microphone voice, 223–26, 239–42, 243. *See also* sound technologies and vocal sound
  adoption, 229–30, 231
  disembodiment, 227
  distancing effect, 226–27
  reception/reviews, 224–28
  vs "real" voice, 225, 226, 227, 229, 259–60
  sonic quality, 224–25, 230–31, 232–33, 244
middlebrow culture/orientation, 9, 42–43, 152–53, 261–62. *See also* highbrow/middlebrow orientation
"Minstrel Man," 185–88

modernism, 54–56, 68, 69, 91, 92–93
Monitor Records, 220–21
multilingualism, 25, 51–52, 136–37, 146, 157, 175–76
  affinity with Russian, 44, 144–47
  language studies, 138–39, 175–77
  in performances, 176–77, 191, 207–8, 211
multivocality, 3, 10–11, 21–22, 78–79, 101, 265–66
musical theatre, 23, 39, 261. See also *Show Boat*
musicology
  Americanist, 10
  classical, 7–8
  exclusion of Robeson, 3, 7–9
  nomadic, 10–11
  performance culture and, 7–8
  scholarship (about Robeson), 6–8, 9–10, 12–14, 76–77, 134, 195

"natural" discourse
  analysis of, 96–97
  construction of Robeson as, 11–12, 29–30, 95–98, 100–3, 117, 128–30
  simplicity and sincerity tropes, 98–100, 110–12, 156, 225–26
  sound technology and, 226, 229
  "Water Boy" and, 103–4, 107–8, 109–10
Nazvanov, Mikhail, 133–34
Negro Spiritual (sculpture), 54–56, 55*f*, 92
Neruda, Pablo, 1, 142–43, 191–92
"Now Sleeps the Crimson Petal," 183–85, 184*f*, 194–95

"Ol' Man River," 6, 23, 103–4, 146, 174–75, 257–58, 261
opera, 28–29, 39–40, 47, 111–12, 261
oration and recitation, 18–19, 20–21
oriental studies, 138–39, 149
Othello, 18–19. *See also* Shakespeare
  English (London) performances, 18–19, 31–32, 146–47, 181–82, 221–22
  language mastery, 146–47, 182–85
  North American performances, 18, 146–47, 197–98, 221–22
  recordings, 212–13, 221–22

358 INDEX

Othello Recording Corporation, 214, 216–17, 218, 219–20, 221–22

Patti, Adelina, 117
Payne, John, 104–5, 106–9
Peace Arch concerts, 74–75, 132–33, 165–66, 170–72, 177, 207–8, 239–40
People's Songs, 199–202
people's voice (Robeson as), 12, 134
  aesthetics, 134
  audiences, 152–53, 174, 175–77
  brotherhood/brothering song, 159–61, 164–65, 166–68, 178
  communal singing, 168–70, 172–74
  emergence of, 134
  folk music and, 141–43, 148–50
  multilingualism, 175–77
performance culture, 7–8, 13–14, 209, 239–40
persecution, 5–6, 20, 44, 132, 173, 212–13. *See also* activism
  American "lynching imagination," 132, 204
  blacklisting, 5, 132–33, 157, 170, 193–94, 207, 212–13, 214, 220, 223
  responses to, 132–33, 170–72
  travel ban, 132–33, 209–10
Plantation Revue, 26
political activism. *See* activism
political voice. *See* activism; people's voice (Robeson as)
politicization, 5–7, 9–10, 11–12, 27, 47, 87–88, 134, 187, 208, 239–40. *See also* activism
Popular Front, 137–38, 140–41, 143–44
popular music, 8–9, 39, 77–78, 103–4, 111–12, 154–55
preaching. *See* Black preaching
primitivism, 59–61, 68, 70, 78
programming, 11–12, 26–27, 40–42, 58–61, 66, 148. *See also* repertoires
  aims/strategies, 58, 62–63, 65, 81–82, 137–38, 165–66, 168
  cosmopolitan and internationalist see cosmopolitanism; internationalism
  debates, 65–66, 81
  folk music (*see* folk music)
  influences, 81–82, 151

protest music, 144, 150–51
  spirituals (*see* spirituals, programming)
Proschowsky, Frantz, 33–34, 35–36
protest music/songs, 8–9, 150–52, 174–75, 206–8. *See also* voice/voices, protesting

quartets, 21, 42, 76–77, 78, 102–3, 112–14, 115
Quilter, Roger, 32, 67–68, 122–23, 144–46, 147–48, 165–66, 183–85

race, 7–8, 45–46, 52–53, 56–58, 63, 88–89, 94, 111–12, 142, 191, 197
racialization, 7–9, 11–12, 57–58, 68, 78, 95–96, 103, 195, 264
  racist tropes, 96–99, 131 (*see also* "natural" discourse)
radio broadcasts, 135, 146–47
  BBC, 156–57, 162, 187–88, 221–22, 229
  CBS, 229–30
  Soviet, 122–23
  WGBS, 229
  WRYN, 46
recording industry, 23–25, 39–40, 152, 185, 212–14, 216–19, 220–23
recordings, 39–40, 46–47, 117–20, 123, 151, 177, 185, 222, 244–60, *See also* gramophones; microphone voice categorization, 39–40
  "Steal Away," 114
  "Swing Low," 124–28
  "Water Boy," 49–51, 95, 103–4, 128–29
repertoires, 8–9, 23–25, 29, 39–40, 52, 65–66, 79–81, 129–30, 142, 150, 151–52. *See also* programming
  art song, 32, 42, 47, 52, 58–59, 62–63, 65–66, 87–88, 112, 140, 253
  cosmopolitan, 66, 164–68, 170, 178
  folk songs (*see* folk music/songs)
  internationalist, 137–38, 142–44, 151–52, 165, 179–80, 199–202 (*see also* internationalism)
  labor-themed, 143–44
  protest songs, 174–75, 206–7 (*see also* protest music)
  spirituals (*see* spirituals)
restraint. *See* vocal restraint

INDEX 359

reviews, 5, 8–9, 48–49. *See also* fans;
    reception
    of art songs, 144
    of Black music and, 54–56
    of cosmopolitan repertoire, 166–68
    of dramatic avoidance, 112
    of folk songs, 149
    on informality, 178
    on multilingualism, 176–77
    and "the natural," 96–103, 110–12, 117
    of *Othello*, 183, 197–98
    of programming, 166
    of protest music, 5, 151
    racial lenses, 56–57
    of recordings, 177, 179–80
    of sound technology use, 225, 227–28,
        249–50, 253–54
    of spirituals, 54–56, 84–85, 92–93
    of voice, 21, 45–46, 50–51, 112, 115,
        119–23, 246–47
Robeson, Eslanda, 20, 25, 30, 33–35,
    51–52, 88–89, 97–98, 100–1, 130,
    159–60, 221–22
romanticism, 93–94, 96–97, 130,
    156–57, 196–97
Royal Albert Hall, 42, 112, 120–21,
    174–75, 205, 224–25, 228
Russian music, 7–8, 43–46, 112, 140–41,
    144–46, 147–48, 209–10
Russian/Soviet influence, 140–41, 146–47

Salemme, Antonio, 54–56
Schoen-René, Anna, 34, 37
School of Oriental Studies, 138–39, 149
sculpture. See *Negro Spiritual*
"Sea Fever," 147–48, 185
sea music, 147–48
Shakespeare, 64, 122–23. *See also* Othello
    Shakespearian language (mastering),
        147–48, 181–83
Shakespeare Memorial Theatre,
    18–19, 221–22
"Shenandoah," 148
Show Boat, 23, 26, 27, 51, 95, 103–4, 261
Shuffle Along, 21, 76–77
simplicity and sincerity tropes, 98–100,
    110–12, 156, 225–26
slavery/slaves, 19–20, 54–56, 65, 69,
    96–97, 103–4, 185–86, 203, 265–66

as concert material, 26–27, 62–63, 69
lineage, 44, 76–77, 90–91, 203
slave songs, 64–65, 92–93, 105. *See also*
    "Water Boy"
socialism, 136–37, 140–41, 143–44
Solid Rock: Favorite Hymns of My People,
    172–73, 193–94, 218, 222
Songs of Free Men, 151, 206–7, 212–13
"Sonny Boy," 179–80, 185
sound technologies, 6–7, 11, 233*f*, 235*f*
    amplification, 226–27, 232, 238,
        240–42, 253–54, 257–58
    effects on voice (*see* microphone voice;
        sound technologies and vocal sound)
    electroacoustic systems (*see* "Synthea")
    gramophones, 246–49, 258–59 (*see also*
        gramophone voice)
    high-fidelity audio/recordings, 156–57,
        212, 223, 227, 243, 254–55, 257–58
    microphones, 129–30, 156–57, 219–20,
        223–25, 227–28, 242–43, 248–
        50, 257*f*
    sound engineering, 217–18, 219–20,
        230, 242–43, 258
sound technologies and vocal sound,
    46–47, 121, 124–28, 244, 246, 247,
    258–59 (*see also* microphone voice)
    bass-boosting, 247–53, 257–58
    clarifying effect, 253–54
    frequency levels and range, 255–56,
        258–59
    playback, 249
    recorded vs "real" voice, 247
    richness, 256–57
    timbre reinforcement, 253–54
Soviet Union, 44, 135, 140–41, 150–51,
    209–10, 216
Spanish Civil War, 135–37, 173–77, 206–7.
    See also Spanish influence
Spanish influence, 137–38, 175–76. *See*
    also Spanish Civil War
spirituals, 6–7, 20, 26–27, 54, 57–58,
    84–85, 192–94
    as art songs, 23, 28, 40–42, 165
    Brown, Lawrence and (*see* Brown,
        Lawrence)
    Burleigh, Harry T. and, 30, 61–62,
        77, 92–93
    dialects and (*see* accents and dialects)

360   INDEX

spirituals (*cont.*)
  Du Bois, W. E. B. and, 63–65, 84
  evangelical, 68–82, 83–84
  as expressions of Black subjectivity,
    91, 98–99
  Greenwich Village concerts and, 61–63
  Harlem Renaissance and, 56–57, 66,
    73–74, 81, 88–89, 150
  Hayes, Roland and (*see* Hayes, Roland)
  nature discourse and (*see* "natural"
    discourse)
  programming/repertoire, 29, 47, 58–63,
    66, 81–82, 130, 137–38, 150–51
  reviews of, 54–56, 84–85, 90, 92–93
  rhapsodic, 90–94, 120–21
  significance/value, 56–57, 62–
    63, 137–38
  theory of, 65
  Van Vechten, Carl and (*see* Van
    Vechten, Carl)
stage acting, 18–19, 21, 97–98, 102,
  117–18, 119–20, 197–98
"Steal Away," 64–65, 77–78, 110, 113–14,
  115–17, 118–19, 249–50
Stokowski, Leopold, 231, 234–35
subjectivities, 3, 16–17, 63–65, 91,
  130, 162–63
"Swing Low, Sweet Chariot," 79–81, 114,
  123–28, 141–42
symbolization, 2, 15–16, 45–46, 91,
  137–38, 162–63, 199–202, 203–4
"Synthea," 231–32, 256–58
  amplification, 237–39
  critical response, 231–32, 237
  effects, 233–36
  features, 233–35
  setup, 232–33, 236–37

The Book of American Negro Spirituals,
  73–74, 75
The Emperor Jones, 21, 23–25, 31, 54,
  77–78, 103–4, 105–6, 119–20,
  229, 231
The Four Harmony Kings, 76–78,
  102–3, 112–14
"The Internationale," 136–37. *See also*
  Black internationale

The Souls of Black Folk, 63–64
tours
  Australian and New Zealand, 243
  British Isles, 42, 110–11, 144,
    152–53, 224–25
  European, 23–25, 135, 149, 159–60
  North American, 18, 31, 33–34, 42,
    48–49, 144, 172–73, 221–22, 229–30
transcendence (aesthetics of), 63–64,
  92–93, 136–37, 170, 203–4
transnationalism, 133, 134, 136–37,
  140–41, 197, 199–202

universalism, 150, 153, 160–61, 164,
  178, 194–95

Van Vechten, Carl, 56–57, 59–62, 68–70,
  73, 75, 78–81, 83–84, 86–87, 98–99
vaudeville, 76–78
Victor Talking Machine Company, 23–25,
  29–30, 79–81, 185, 212–13, 244–46,
  249–50, 254–55
vocality, 3, 15–16, 18, 25, 82, 190, 205. *See
  also* multivocality
vocal restraint, 85, 102–3, 115,
  117, 120–21
voice characteristics (Robeson's)
  baritone, 33–34, 46–47, 48, 50–51,
    121–22, 253
  bass, 20, 21, 45–47, 48–49, 50–51, 82,
    120–22, 124, 179–80, 190–91,
    247–53, 257–58
  pitch/vibrato, 117–19, 121, 123–24,
    248–49, 253, 255–56
  range and register, 49–50,
    121–14, 219–20
  smoothness, 37, 51, 115–17,
    119, 206–7
  strength, 112–13, 119–21, 198–202
  weight, 115, 121–22, 123–24,
    197–99, 253
voice classification, 11, 39, 42–43,
  123, 261–62
voice formation, 2–3, 6–7, 11, 12–13,
  21–22, 82
  and Black churches, 20–21
  in childhood, 18–22

INDEX 361

father's influence, 20
mature voice, 12–13, 82, 87–88, 118–19, 122–23, 189, 194–95, 207
training (*see* voice training)
young voice, 48, 76–77, 81–82, 112–14, 115, 117–22
voice gendering, 97–98, 114, 197, 198–99
voice materiality, 12, 15–16, 92, 95–96, 136–37, 179–80
voice styles
dramatic, 82, 112–13, 114–18, 119–20, 123, 197–98
heroic, 196–202
lyrical, 50–51, 109, 112–13, 115, 121–22, 123
rhapsodic, 90–94, 120–21

voice-thinking, 10–11, 14–17, 52–53, 66, 87, 92, 93–94, 95–96, 134, 151–52, 223, 261–62, 264, 265–66
voice training, 6–7, 18, 21–22, 25–26, 30, 31, 35–38, 47, 48, 82, 88–89, 147–48
vs "natural voice," 95–96, 100–2, 103–4, 111–12, 128–29, 130

"Water Boy," 46–47, 49*f*, 49–51, 54, 95, 103–10, 112–13, 128–29, 246, 257–58
"We Are Climbing Jacob's Ladder," 165–66, 169–70, 172–73
"Were You There?" 84–87, 102–3
Wolfe, Jacques, 104
World War II, 135, 151

The manufacturer's authorised representative in the EU for product
safety is Oxford University Press España S.A. of El Parque Empresarial
San Fernando de Henares, Avenida de Castilla, 2 - 28830 Madrid
(www.oup.es/en or product.safety@oup.com). OUP España S.A. also acts
as importer into Spain of products made by the manufacturer.
Printed and bound by CPI Group (UK) Ltd, Croydon, CR0 4YY

22/07/2025

01921862-0008